Baseball's Best

To Peg
wife, editor, and friend

Baseball's Best

*Hall of Fame Pretenders
Active in the Eighties*

by
Robert E. Kelly

McFarland & Company, Inc., Publishers
Jefferson, North Carolina, and London

Library of Congress Cataloguing-in-Publication Data

Kelly, Robert E.
  Baseball's best.

  Bibliography: p. 195.
  Includes index.
  1. Baseball—United States—Records. 2. National
Baseball Hall of Fame and Museum. 3. Baseball players—
United States—Biography. I. Title.
GV877.K4 1988   796.357′092′2 [B]   88-42507

ISBN 0-89950-352-7 (sewn softcover; acid-free natural paper)

Manufactured in the United States of America.

McFarland & Company, Inc., Publishers
  Box 611, Jefferson, North Carolina 28640

Contents

Foreword

The objective of Hall of Fame (HOF) selection committees is to reward, from time to time, certain retired ballplayers by voting favorably on their lifetime records, thereby joining their names with those of the immortals of the sport in the National Baseball Hall of Fame and Museum, Cooperstown, N.Y., and assuring that their exploits on the field will be remembered.

For the purposes of this book, an active player is one that played in the 1986 season. The primary objective of the work is to appraise developing records of active players, and identify HOF candidates of the future — Of the players active today, which perform at levels of excellence equal to those established by HOF members?

All active players are potential candidates for HOF status after they have been retired for at least five years. In this book, the best are called "The Pretenders." Not all active players were selected for measurement. Screening standards were set to assure that only time-tested abilities would be analyzed. Fielders who played in 800 + games and pitchers with 1,000 + innings pitched were included. Such standards weed out Johnny-come-latelies, and result in a listing of mature players who have had time to demonstrate a fair sample of skill potential.

Screening tests were also established for HOF members. Players born after 1894 were included in the survey. This screen eliminates most "dead ball" players and produces a member list of those who spent most of their careers in the "live ball" era.

A secondary objective of this book is to audit the performance of HOF selection committees.

In making measurements required by the study, two meaningful standards were used: For fielders, *Production Per at Bat* (PAB) was used to rank all players, new or old. For pitchers, *Earned Runs Per Nine Inning Game* (ERA) was the yardstick used to rank all players, new or old.

Production per at bat is the total of runs scored (excluding home runs), runs-batted-in (excluding home runs), and home runs, per at bat. If readers agree that the offensive purpose of a team is to score runs, they will also agree that the ability of a player to produce them, directly or indirectly, is a fair test of greatness, however he manages it, whether by scoring, RBIs, or home runs.

The ERA of a pitcher equals the total of earned runs scored divided by equivalent complete games (innings pitched divided by nine). If readers agree that the defensive purpose of a team is to keep opponents from scoring, they will also agree that the ability of a pitcher to do so, through control, variety of pitches, or strikeout power, is a fair test of greatness, however he manages it.

Although there are exceptions (e.g., Brooks Robinson and Luis Aparicio), any objective analysis of selections of position players to the HOF results in the conclusion that offensive skills draw the most attention; defensive skills in players who have survived in the major leagues are presumed to be adequate. Outstanding defensive skills alone are not sufficient justification for HOF consideration.

This philosophy biases *against* highly skilled defensive players with modest offensive talents, and *for* run producers with modest defensive skills. Some great fielders have been overlooked, while some single-skilled sluggers have been chosen.

One may question the offensive bias of committees, but it isn't the purpose of this book to challenge it. The bias has been followed, although the reader will find more references to fielding skills in upcoming pages than are usually found in books of this type.

A unique characteristic of this analysis is the system of classifications employed, which, together with the sorting factors used (PAB and ERA), results in a list of players in descending order of demonstrated overall skills. Four grades or classes were developed into which players were slotted. The result is four groups of players with similar skills. This facilitates comparative analysis. Grades were established as follows, using PAB for fielders and ERA for pitchers:

1. A simple average of the factors for all players was calculated. The answer defines the average HOF or active player in PAB or ERA terms.
2. Using a statistical device (standard deviation), a factor was developed which when added or subtracted to the average provides the range within which most players fall.

Players can then be placed in one of five categories:

Class 1. A factor above the high end of the calculated range in #2 above. This is superstar territory.

Class 2. The midpoint to the high point of the range calculated in #2 above. This is the above average player who is somewhat shy of superstar quality.

Class 3. The midpoint to the low point of the range calculated in #2 above. This is the player who is or was a slightly less than average performer.

Class 4. A factor below the low point of the range calculated in #2 above. This is the resting place for men with skills well below the average of the player group being examined. From an empirical point of view, the low point in this range is the lowest PAB or ERA in the HOF.

Class 5. Not scientifically developed, and used for the active players only. Those with a factor below that of the lowest rated HOF member fall into this classification.

For all HOF players, the application of the above system resulted in the following classifications, regardless of position:

	Fielders PAB	*Pitchers* ERA
Average	.304	3.19
Class 1	.351 +	2.88 –
Class 2	.304–.350	2.89–3.19
Class 3	.258–.303	3.20–3.50
Class 4	.200–.257	3.51–3.80
Class 5 (actives only)	.199 –	3.81 +

Position plays a part in player rating. It is generally true that the higher the skill demands of a defensive position, the lower the offensive expectations from players who man the position. Thus, for example, a shortstop can survive with a PAB that isn't tolerated in an outfielder. For this reason, the above rate ranges for *all* players are but a first step in player evaluation. To get closer to the truth of relative value, ranges by position are needed. In the following pages, this is done using methods explained above.

What is a position? For the purpose of this book, a position is as follows: Outfield; Infield, excluding first base; First base; Catcher.

First base is a position to which managers attempt to assign a slugger. This has been sufficiently the case over the years to make it unwise to blend first base performance statistics into general infield statistics. Results are clearer and fairer if first basemen are separated. This may not continue to be true in future years. As you will see, there are no Gehrigs and Foxxes on the horizon to distort the numbers as they did.

Introduction
The Hall of Fame of Baseball

Two Abners, Graves and Doubleday, were from Cooperstown, New York. As youngsters, both were involved in the game that we know today as baseball. Doubleday has been given most of the credit for inventing the sport. When the idea for a museum grew, it was appropriate that the hometown of the Abners be considered. As unlikely a choice as it seems to be from a geographical standpoint, it has worked out well. About a quarter of a million people a year trek to the little town and visit the museum.

Stephen Clark was the first to exhibit baseball objects in Cooperstown. Public interest was surprisingly high, and included that of Alexander Cleland, a friend of Clark's. Apparently a dynamic individual (with lots of time on his hands), Cleland visited baseball men around the country, including Ford Frick, discussing the possibilities for establishing a museum of baseball in Cooperstown. Frick, president of the National League, picked up the ball. He embellished the general idea, and sold Commissioner Landis and American League president Harridge on the idea of a shrine in honor of the greats of the game. In 1935, plans were approved to build the museum in Cooperstown by 1939, the 100th anniversary of baseball.

As part of the preparation, the Baseball Writers Association of America (BBWAA) was asked to select the first HOF members. In January 1936, they announced the choices of 226 ballots: Ty Cobb, Babe Ruth, Honus Wagner, Christy Mathewson, and Walter Johnson.

The first museum was ready in 1939, a three-story brick building. In 1950, 1958, and 1968 it was expanded due to its enthusiastic acceptance by the public. With the nearby library and baseball field, it is now an attractive and noble complex which annually appeals to the hero worshipping, fun-loving American public.

Two committees select new members to the HOF. The first deals

1

with players active sometime during the past 20 years, but inactive for the last five years. The second deals with older players who, to over-simplify, were overlooked by the processes of the first.

The first committee is controlled by the BBWAA. At annual meet-ings, a six-man screening committee is elected, the function of which is to screen eligible candidates down to a list of not more than 30 names. The list is sent to BBWAA members, who vote for not more than ten of the listed players. To be elected, a candidate must be a selection on at least 75 percent of ballots cast.

The second committee is controlled by the board of directors of the National Baseball Hall of Fame and Museum, Inc. Its members are elected, or vacancies are filled, by the board. There are 18 committee members, made up of HOF players, baseball executives, and members of BBWAA. Generally speaking, they deal with candidates who have been retired for at least 23 years. They also deal with baseball executives, other non-players deemed worthy of consideration, and players who performed in old Negro leagues. The committee can elect not more than two men per year from these groups. To be elected, a man must appear on 75 percent of ballots cast.

To qualify as a candidate, a player must have played in ten major league seasons. The choice is based upon an appraisal of ability, integ-rity, sportsmanship, character, and contribution to his team. Given the subjective character of criteria, it is difficult to criticize choices of either committee. But, we will!

Part I
Hall of Fame Election Results by Decade

Fielders

This study includes fielders born after 1894. Babe Ruth was the first choice in 1936. Since that year, and including Ruth, 65 fielders as of 1987 have been elected to the HOF.*

1930s

	AB	HR	R	RBI	PAB	BA	SA
Ruth	7,287	.091	.179	.181	.451	.347	.708
Gehrig	8,001	.062	.174	.187	.423	.340	.632
Average	7,644	.077	.177	.184	.437	.344	.670

Ruth's statistics are Yankee statistics only. When playing with Boston in the dead-ball era, Ruth functioned mostly as a pitcher (HOF quality). With the Yankees, he functioned as an outfielder in the live-ball era.

Certainly, Lou Gehrig was an appropriate addition to the HOF group which, by the end of the decade, was made up mostly of dead-ball era players. As things turned out, Ruth and Gehrig established standards of performance no subsequent players could equal. To permit the continued growth of the HOF, lower standards had to be applied to future candidates, else the museum would have ended as a memorial to just two live-ball era players. Since the 1930s, no player has appeared to seriously challenge the awesome levels of talent demonstrated by the two Yankees.

1940s

	AB	HR	R	RBI	PAB	BA	SA
Hornsby	8,173	.037	.156	.156	.349	.358	.577
Gehringer	8,860	.021	.179	.140	.340	.320	.480
Cochrane	5,169	.023	.178	.138	.339	.320	.478
Traynor	7,559	.008	.149	.161	.317	.320	.435
Frisch	9,112	.012	.157	.125	.293	.316	.432
Average	7,775	.020	.164	.144	.328	.327	.480

*AB = at bats, HR = home runs, R = runs, RBI = runs batted in, PAB = production per at bat, BA = batting average, SA = slugging average. Home runs, runs, and RBIs are percentages of each per at bat, and their total comprises the PAB.

The odd part about the selections of the 1940s is that new members were non-sluggers, according to standards of the time. Under a modern schedule (say 550 at bats) Hornsby was good for about 20 home runs a year, and the others would produce less than 15 homers on the same basis, well under the Ruthian 50, or the Gehrig 34 rate.

Cochrane was the first modern catcher to be elected to the HOF, and no catcher after him did what he did so well. The others were offensively aggressive infielders. Standards set by this group were well below those of the first two superstars, but would nonetheless prove to be harsh but fair benchmarks to apply to future candidates.

1950s

	AB	HR	R	RBI	PAB	BA	SA
Foxx	8,134	.066	.150	.171	.386	.325	.609
Greenberg	5,193	.064	.139	.182	.384	.313	.605
DiMaggio, J.	6,821	.053	.151	.172	.376	.325	.579
Simmons	8,761	.035	.137	.173	.346	.334	.535
Ott	9,456	.054	.143	.143	.339	.304	.533
Cronin	7,577	.022	.140	.165	.328	.302	.468
Terry	6,428	.024	.150	.144	.318	.341	.506
Dickey	6,300	.032	.116	.160	.307	.313	.486
Waner, P.	9,459	.012	.160	.127	.298	.333	.473
Hartnett	6,432	.037	.098	.147	.281	.297	.489
Average	7,456	.040	.139	.158	.337	.319	.528

As a group, these new members exceeded production standards of the most previous group. They featured more power with somewhat less pure batting skill. Enough historical data was now in to proclaim that a PAB of .340 + announced the presence of a playing star of major proportions. Foxx, Greenberg, Simmons, and Joe DiMaggio fell into this category. Also, enough had been seen to declare that homers per at bat of .060 + proclaimed the existence of a major power hitter, a designation earned by Foxx and Greenberg.

Ott with durability and power, Cronin with outstanding clutch hitting, and Terry with pure batting skill were legitimate additions. Each was more productive than Frisch and Traynor, the weakest producers of the previous group. Dickey was not as talented a batsman as Cochrane, but his career was long and outstanding. Paul Waner and Hartnett joined Frisch as the only HOF players with PABs below .300, but both had other outstanding offensive characteristics and their selection did not necessarily suggest that standards were being lowered unjustifiably.

1960s

	AB	HR	R	RBI	PAB	BA	SA
Williams, T.	7,706	.068	.166	.171	.404	.344	.634
Goslin	8,654	.029	.143	.157	.329	.316	.500
Robinson, J.	4,877	.028	.166	.122	.317	.311	.474
Musial	10,972	.043	.134	.135	.312	.331	.559
Medwick	7,635	.027	.130	.154	.311	.324	.505
Cuyler	7,161	.022	.160	.127	.309	.321	.486
Manush	7,653	.014	.154	.139	.307	.330	.479
Campanella	4,205	.058	.092	.146	.295	.276	.500
Appling	8,857	.005	.144	.121	.270	.310	.398
Waner, L.	7,772	.004	.151	.073	.228	.316	.394
Average	7,549	.030	.144	.135	.309	.318	.493

The class of the 1960s was the weakest to date, but reasons for the apparent deterioration can be seen and rationalized.

Williams loomed above the others as a slugger, run producer, and batsman of superstar quality. Steady Goslin, swift Jack Robinson, balanced and durable Musial, clutch Medwick, and hawk-eyed Cuyler and Manush were of obvious HOF caliber with PABs comfortably above .300.

Campanella joined Robinson as the second black in the HOF, a slugging catcher of considerable skill during a short career.

The selection of Appling was a healthy sign that HOF committees did not intend to completely ignore talented but non-slugging infielders; the election of Lloyd Waner suggested that superior batsmen would get HOF consideration despite relatively low production performance.

The HOF class of the 1960s was a good one. The lowering of de facto HOF standards caused by these additions was legitimate, understandable, and defendable.

1970s

	AB	HR	R	RBI	PAB	BA	SA
Wilson	4,760	.051	.134	.172	.358	.307	.545
Averill	6,358	.037	.155	.146	.338	.318	.533
Mantle	8,102	.066	.141	.120	.327	.298	.557
Bottomley	7,471	.029	.128	.161	.319	.310	.500
Hafey	4,625	.035	.133	.145	.313	.317	.526
Kiner	5,205	.071	.116	.124	.311	.279	.548
Combs	5,748	.010	.196	.099	.306	.325	.462
Mays	10,881	.061	.129	.114	.304	.302	.557

	AB	HR	R	RBI	PAB	BA	SA
Sewell, J.	7,132	.007	.153	.140	.300	.312	.413
Berra	7,555	.047	.108	.142	.297	.285	.482
Youngs	4,627	.009	.166	.120	.295	.322	.441
Mathews	8,537	.060	.117	.110	.287	.271	.509
Kelly	5,993	.025	.112	.145	.287	.297	.452
Lindstrom	5,611	.018	.141	.120	.280	.311	.449
Clemente	9,454	.025	.124	.113	.262	.317	.475
Boudreau	6,030	.011	.132	.120	.262	.295	.415
Banks	9,421	.054	.084	.119	.258	.274	.500
Herman	7,707	.006	.145	.103	.254	.304	.407
Average	6,955	.035	.134	.129	.298	.302	.487

The 1970s was the fifth decade of HOF selections. Earlier choices were obvious, not too controversial, and resulted in the following profile of de facto HOF standards:

	Total	Class 1	Class 2	Class 3
Outfielders				
Number	12	4	7	1
PAB	.334	.394	.315	.228
First base				
Number	4	3	1	
PAB	.378	.398	.318	
2B, 3B, SS				
Number	7	2	4	1
PAB	.316	.345	.314	.270
Catcher				
Number	4	0	4	0
PAB	.306		.306	

The 1970 class of 18 players was the biggest to date, made up of nine outfielders, two first basemen, five infielders (2b, 3b, ss), and one catcher. Ten could be considered old-timers and eight of fairly modern vintage. As a group, they lowered all de facto HOF standards. Old timers were made up of Wilson, Averill, Hafey, Combs, and Youngs as outfielders, Bottomley and Kelly at first base, Sewell, Lindstrom, and Herman as infielders. At the time of election, their ages ranged from 66 to 79 years old.

Wilson was a superstar, Averill nearly so. The selection of them raised the HOF standard for outfielders. Hafey and Combs lowered the HOF standard for outfielders, but both were PAB men of over .300, a relatively rare accomplishment. Youngs with a PAB of .295 and a batting average of .322 was apparently selected because of pure batting skill, as was Paul Waner in the 1950s.

Why did it take so long to recognize the talent of these men? One was a superstar. Four are among the top 25 producers in the HOF. Except for Kelly and Herman, all out-performed an earlier appointee.

Mantle, Kiner, Mays, and Clemente were the outfielders of the relatively modern players; Banks the first baseman, Mathews and Boudreau the infielders, and Berra the catcher.

Mantle and other outfielders of the 1970 class lowered 1960 de facto standards (fattened by the rare and perhaps not-to-be-seen-again abilities of Ruth, Williams, and DiMag), but, at the same time, Mantle out-performed six of 12 outfielders who preceded him into the HOF, and was the sixth most prolific home run hitter in history. Kiner, the second best home run hitter in history, generated a PAB equal or superior to that of five outfielders who preceded him into the HOF. Mays, the tenth best home run hitter of all time, had a PAB of .304, better than that of the Waner brothers. Clemente, a low PAB man (.262), had a batting average of .317. He out-produced Lloyd Waner and had a slightly higher batting average — if Waner belongs, so does Clemente. This was an outstanding group of outfielders. It added three top sluggers to the HOF roster, and many feel that Mantle, Mays, and Clemente were also among the best defensive outfielders of baseball history. A good crop!

Banks was a slugger just shy of superstar quality. He had a long career and was a versatile athlete who played several positions during his career, although designated as a first baseman. These are his strong points. Banks was a good, but not superior hitter. Other than home run ability, his production statistics are not strong. His PAB is well below that of all first basemen who preceded him into the HOF. On the record, there is no apparent reason why Banks was selected for HOF recognition at 46 years of age, especially when so many other players of equal or superior ability were ignored, or overlooked, for so long.

Mathews and Boudreau lowered the 1960 HOF standard for infielders. Despite this, Mathews was a stronger PAB man than Appling, and was a slugger of near superstar ability — clearly the best home run hitter of HOF infielders. The selection of Herman justified the choice of Boudreau — weak PAB men of comparable batting skill. Their selection represented new ground for HOF committees who, heretofore, had recognized only infielders with strong offensive talent. A fair deduction seems to be that infielders with low PABs now have a chance for HOF recognition when defensive skills are regarded as superior, and when batting averages are in the vicinity of .300.

It's difficult to argue with this position since it provides opportunity for recognition to the defensive geniuses of the game. But why open up such recognition with these two? Were there none more deserving?

Berra reduced the 1960 HOF standard for catchers, which was heavily weighted by the powerful numbers of Cochrane. But Berra was a more productive player than either Hartnett or Campanella, both of whom preceded Yogi to the HOF. Except for Campanella (who didn't play nearly as long as Berra) Yogi sits on top of all HOF catchers as a home run hitter.

After the election of the 1970 class, the HOF roster and the lowered de facto standards looked like this:

	Total	Class 1	Class 2	Class 3
Outfielders				
Number	21	5	14	2
PAB	.325	.387	.314	.245
First base				
Number	7	3	3	1
PAB	.343	.398	.306	.258
2B, 3B, SS				
Number	12	2	7	3
PAB	.301	.345	.303	.262
Catcher				
Number	5	0	5	0
PAB	.304		.304	

1980s

	AB	HR	R	RBI	PAB	BA	SA
Mize	6,443	.056	.118	.152	.325	.312	.562
Klein	6,486	.046	.134	.139	.319	.320	.543
Snider	7,161	.057	.119	.129	.305	.295	.540
Robinson, F.	10,006	.059	.124	.123	.305	.294	.537
Vaughan	6,622	.014	.163	.125	.302	.318	.453
Aaron	12,364	.061	.115	.125	.301	.305	.555
Slaughter	7,946	.021	.136	.143	.300	.300	.453
Doerr	7,093	.031	.124	.144	.299	.288	.461
Kaline	10,116	.039	.121	.117	.297	.297	.480
Jackson, T.	6,086	.022	.115	.130	.291	.291	.433
Killebrew	8,147	.070	.087	.124	.282	.256	.509
McCovey	8,197	.064	.086	.126	.276	.270	.515
Williams, B.	9,350	.046	.105	.112	.263	.290	.492

	AB	HR	R	RBI	PAB	BA	SA
Reese	8,058	.016	.150	.094	.260	.269	.377
Kell	6,702	.012	.120	.118	.250	.306	.414
Lombardi	5,855	.032	.070	.137	.239	.306	.460
Ferrell, R.	6,028	.005	.109	.117	.231	.281	.363
Brock	10,332	.014	.142	.073	.229	.293	.410
Robinson, B.	10,654	.025	.090	.102	.218	.267	.401
Aparicio	10,230	.008	.122	.069	.200	.262	.343
Average	8,197	.035	.118	.120	.273	.291	.465

Continuing the 1970 trend, it appears the 1980s will feature a bumper crop of new HOF fielders. In seven years we have seen 20 appointments, which suggests that about 30 men will be selected before the decade is finished — more than were elected in the first four decades.

So far in the 1980s (through 1987), 20 players have been selected to the HOF: eight outfielders, three first basemen, seven infielders, and two catchers. Eight can be considered as old-timers; the remaining 12 as relatively modern players.

Concerning older players, Klein and Slaughter represent the outfield, Mize the first baseman, Jackson, Vaughan and Doerr the infield, Ferrell and Lombardi the catchers.

Klein was 76 when elected. His PAB is higher than 12 of the 21 outfielders in the HOF at the end of the 1970s. A well-rounded hitter with a lifetime BA of .320, Klein deserved HOF recognition long before he got it. Why was he overlooked for so long?

Slaughter was appointed to the HOF in 1985 at the age of 69. He entered with a production record superior to that of several outfielders, including Kaline and Clemente.

Mize was 68 when elected. Only Gehrig, Foxx, and Greenberg of the HOF first sackers had a higher PAB. A home run hitter just shy of superstar quality, Mize had a lifetime batting average of .312. What kind of a selection system is it that overlooks such credentials for so long?

Travis Jackson produced a PAB superior to that of Herman or Boudreau, and his batting average was similar to theirs. One could argue that Jackson was one of the first beneficiaries of the philosophy that was introduced in the 1970s with the selection of Herman and Boudreau. In short, if they deserved HOF status, so did Jackson.

Vaughan needs no comparative arguments to justify his HOF selection. The only question concerning him is why it took so long to appoint him. He's the sixth most productive player in the HOF infield group.

As the talented Vaughan was overlooked, so was Bobby Doerr until he was elected in 1986 at 68 years of age. Ridiculous! Of the few ranked above him, only Hornsby hit with more power. Aside from being one of the classiest second basemen to ever cover the position, Doerr was a better producer than many more highly touted players — for example, Mathews and Killebrew.

Ferrell was a top defensive catcher who produced a decent lifetime batting average. Other than that, his offensive credentials do not compare with those who preceded him to the HOF. To say the least, his selection was not an obvious one and it established admission standards which are too low for a HOF catcher.

Lombardi was elected in 1986. A solid hitting machine and defensive catcher, Ernie was not a great production man — only a tad better than the powerless Ferrell. It is said that he once lost a foot race with a snail.

Frank Robinson, Snider, Aaron, Kaline, Brock, and Billy Williams represent the modern outfielder in the class of the 1980s, Killebrew and McCovey the first basemen, Reese, Kell, Brooks Robinson, and Aparicio the infielders. Hall of Fame standards were lowered further as a result of these appointments.

Frank Robinson had a PAB of .305 which, though lower than the 1970 standard for outfielders, was better than the PAB of five outfielders who preceded him into the HOF. A slugger just shy of superstar standing, Frank was a balanced offensive force for a long time — one of the seven HOF players with over 10,000 at bats — class plus durability.

Snider was almost the statistical twin of Robinson, although he didn't play as long. With the same PAB as Frank, he also lowered HOF standards, yet was more productive than several who preceded him. When great defensive outfielders are discussed, Duke is mentioned.

Aaron heads the group of super-durable players which, combined with considerable talent, explains how he broke the lifetime career home run mark of Ruth. Apart from durability, Aaron is also the tenth ranking home run hitter in the HOF, and generated a PAB of .301 over a long and distinguished career, higher than that of four HOF outfielders who were elected before him.

Kaline is another of the durability group headed by Aaron with over 10,000 at bats. He had a strong defensive reputation but was not offensively outstanding when measured against HOF standards. Only Clemente and the Waner brothers were less productive outfielders. Kaline was 46 when elected. Mize was 68, and one of the best hitters in history. Why the rush to elect Kaline? Why so slow to elect Mize?

Brock is also a member of the durability club that features over 10,000 at bats. A formidable base stealer, and a good enough hitter to generate a lifetime batting average of close to .300, he squeezes into the

HOF outfield corps just above Lloyd Waner, the lowest rated outfielder of the group.

Billy Williams is the most recent outfielder to be elected. He is 49 years old, and has been retired since 1976. He was a steady contact hitter with better than average power and durability.

Killebrew is the third-ranked home run hitter in the HOF roster. Except for this considerable talent, he was not an overall producer of outstanding proportions. He ranks behind all HOF first basemen except Banks and the recently (1986) elected McCovey. With his .256 batting average, Harmon ranks as the poorest contact hitter in the HOF. Killebrew was 48 years old when elected to the HOF. His quick election demonstrates as well as anything the home run mystique that taints the HOF selection process.

The selection of McCovey in 1986 represents the continuation of the HOF power hitting romance. Willie retired in 1980 — he couldn't have been elected sooner. Why the rush? He hit over 500 home runs, the ninth ranking home run hitter in the HOF. But he is also one of its lowest scorers, a below average RBI man.

Prior to the 1980s, the lowest rated HOF infielders were Boudreau and Herman; Boudreau with a PAB of .262 and a BA of .295; Herman with a PAB of .254 and a BA of .304. Kell fits this mold.

But with the selection of Reese, Robinson, and Aparicio, HOF committees broke new ground. None of these infielders meet the new and lower standards which embraced Boudreau, Herman, and Kell. In addition to having PABs lower than any other HOF infielder, all posted lifetime batting averages well below the .300 mark. The only major attribute left to qualify these men was defensive skill. When elected, Reese was 64, Robinson 46, and Aparicio 50 years old. A number of questions are raised by the selection of these men, especially the rapid recognition of Robinson:

> 1. Granted that defensive skills were largely ignored in the past, is the pendulum now swinging too far in the other direction?
> 2. Of all retired and eligible infielders, were these three obviously the best at the time of their appointment?
> 3. As measured against HOF standards, should single-skilled players be hastily recognized when many broadly-skilled players are totally ignored, or belatedly recognized?

Notice that in this decade-by-decade analysis of HOF appointments, standards regularly dropped. In each decade, reasons were offered for selections of lower rated players, but the naked fact remains:

Under a measurement system equally and fairly applied, the quality of the HOF corps has persistently slipped, a fact that has been subtly hidden by the belated appointments of productive old-timers which draws attention away from weaknesses of more modern players.

The point is more clearly made if HOF talent is separated by age instead of election date, as follows:

Born 1927 or Before			Born 1928 or After		
Outfielders	*PAB*	*BA*	*Outfielders*	*PAB*	*BA*
Ruth	.451	.347	Mantle	.327	.298
Williams, T.	.404	.344	Robinson, F.	.305	.294
DiMaggio, J.	.376	.325	Mays	.304	.302
Wilson	.358	.307	Aaron	.301	.305
Simmons	.346	.334	Kaline	.277	.297
Ott	.339	.304	Williams, B.	.263	.290
Averill	.338	.318	Clemente	.262	.317
Goslin	.329	.316	Brock	.229	.293
Klein	.319	.320			
Hafey	.313	.317			
Musial	.312	.331			
Medwick	.311	.324			
Kiner	.311	.279			
Cuyler	.309	.321			
Manush	.307	.330			
Combs	.306	.325			
Snider	.305	.295			
Slaughter	.300	.300			
Waner, P.	.298	.333			
Youngs	.295	.322			
Waner, L.	.228	.316			
First Base			*First Base*		
Gehrig	.423	.340	Killebrew	.282	.256
Foxx	.386	.325	McCovey	.276	.270
Greenberg	.384	.313	Banks	.258	.274
Mize	.325	.312			
Bottomley	.319	.310			
Terry	.318	.341			
Kelly	.282	.297			
Infield	*PAB*	*BA*	*Infield*	*PAB*	*BA*
Hornsby	.349	.358	Mathews	.287	.271
Gehringer	.340	.320	Boudreau	.262	.295
Cronin	.328	.302	Kell	.250	.306
Traynor	.317	.320	Robinson, B.	.218	.267
Robinson, J.	.317	.311	Aparicio	.200	.262
Vaughan	.302	.318			

Born 1927 or Before			Born 1928 or After		
Infield (cont.)	PAB	BA	*Infield*	PAB	BA
Sewell	.300	.312			
Doerr	.299	.288			
Frisch	.293	.316			
Lindstrom	.280	.311			
Appling	.270	.310			
Jackson	.267	.291			
Reese	.260	.269			
Herman	.254	.304			
Catcher	PAB	BA	*Catcher*	PAB	BA
Cochrane	.339	.320	None		
Dickey	.307	.313			
Berra	.297	.285			
Campanella	.295	.276			
Hartnett	.281	.297			
Lombardi	.239	.306			
Ferrell	.231	.281			

Just eyeball the above columns. Is there any doubt that offensive quality of the HOF player is slipping?

Hall of Fame standards are dropping at an accelerated pace for several reasons, some legitimate, some suspect.

1. Since Ted Williams, no superstars have appeared to enrich the averages. The best of the new crop show as much power as ever, but do not combine it with the contact hitting skills which characterize superstars.
2. Most newer players fall into average-to-low HOF molds which, together with the absence of superstars, depresses the average for the group.
3. Infielders are getting more recognition which, since they are not customarily the offensive equals of other players, has a tendency to pull general averages down.
4. Single-skilled power hitters are being recognized too often and too soon.

Are values changing? Will the HOF lose status if it continues to lower standards; to inflate good performance to great; elect single talents instead of broad ones? Is greatness being persistently reduced to the ability to hit a home run; the strength to play for twenty years?

Yes!

Pitchers

Similar to the fielders, only pitchers born after 1894 are included in this study. A great pitcher is a rare animal. Excluding old-timers (born before 1895), there are only 19 in the HOF as of 1987, elected as follows:

1940s

	ERA	W	L	%	Net Wins
Grove	3.06	300	141	.680	159
Hubbell	2.98	253	154	.622	99
Average	3.01	277	148	.652	129

Grove may have been the best pitcher that ever played the game, although some would offer a few others to compare him with. He didn't throw a ball in the major leagues until he was 25 years old, he pitched more innings than 11 of the selected HOF group, and he had more net wins than any of them. Hubbell was the stylish control master, probably remembered best for his All Star game performance of striking out God and his Apostles in succession — Ruth, Gehrig, Simmons, Foxx, and Cronin.

1950s

	ERA	W	L	%	Net Wins
Dean	3.04	150	83	.644	67
Lyons	3.67	260	230	.531	30
Average	3.36	205	157	.566	48

Dean had tough luck. He pitched fewer innings than any other pitcher in the group. After six straight superb seasons — during which he was the National League strikeout king five times — he had a freak accident which indirectly ruined his arm. Thereafter, he lived on wits. Lyons was a workhorse. Only four of the HOF group pitched more innings than he. His selection indicates the preoccupation of the press with pure quantity and longevity. Actually, Lyons was only marginally better than a .500 pitcher, and his selection set a low eligibility standard for others to meet.

1960s

	ERA	W	L	%	Net Wins
Feller	3.25	266	162	.621	104
Hoyt	3.59	237	182	.566	55
Ruffing	3.80	273	225	.548	48
Average	3.55	259	190	.577	69

Feller, along with Williams and Greenberg, is another example of a brilliant career being marred by war. At 23 years old, he entered military service and lost about four seasons as a consequence. For the two years prior to service, he won an average of 26 games; for the two years after service, he averaged 23 wins. Given those years to work with, Feller might have accumulated mind-boggling career stats. Hoyt and Ruffing had the good fortune to pitch for the Yankees during the Ruth/Gehrig years. If it were not for this stroke of good fortune, there is reason to doubt that either would be in the HOF today.

1970s

	ERA	W	L	%	Net Wins
Ford	2.74	236	106	.690	130
Koufax	2.76	165	87	.655	78
Spahn	3.08	363	245	.597	118
Lemon	3.23	207	128	.618	79
Gomez	3.34	189	102	.648	87
Roberts	3.40	286	245	.539	41
Wynn	3.54	300	244	.551	56
Average	3.16	249	165	.601	84

While they were doing it, Ford and Koufax did it as well as anybody. Lots of people might say Spahn was as good or better than Grove — which is saying plenty. Without question, he was one of the greatest and strongest to ever climb a mound. Lemon was a spot shy of superstar status. His Achilles' heel was control. Gomez, a pitcher of HOF quality, also had the good fortune to pitch for the Gehrig/DiMaggio Yankees. Roberts was a wonder boy for about six seasons, then tailed off to average for the balance of his career. He was the best control pitcher of the group. Wynn was a late starter, but a dependable workhorse type. Only Spahn and Roberts worked more innings than he.

1980s

	ERA	W	L	%	Net Wins
Marichal	2.89	243	142	.631	101
Gibson	2.91	251	174	.591	77
Drysdale	2.95	209	166	.557	43
Hunter	3.26	224	166	.574	58
Wilhelm (relief)	2.52	143	122	.540	21
Average	2.91	214	154	.582	60

Marichal didn't last as long as some, but had and used everything a pitcher needs to be known as brilliant—only Roberts and Hubbell equalled his control over a baseball. Gibson, the strikeout king of the select group, was a superb pitcher. Only Koufax, who pitched far fewer innings, allowed fewer hits per game than Gibson. Drysdale is another pitcher who had a relatively brief career. Next to Sandy Koufax and Bob Gibson, he is the strikeout master of the bunch. Catfish Hunter is the most recent addition to the HOF pitching corps. There is no doubt that he belongs in the HOF, but one wonders at the haste. Mostly a relief pitcher, Wilhelm is the first of his breed to get HOF recognition. He was a good one.

With the selection of Hoyt, Lyons, and Ruffing, HOF committees established standards that may permit mediocrity to creep into the HOF pitching corps of the future. Other than this, it appears that standards of eligibility have remained high, more so than in the fielder category. It was a healthy sign to see a pitcher like Wilhelm get the nod in 1985. Some old-time and several modern relief specialists should benefit from this during future years.

Part II
Classification of
Hall of Fame Members

Outfielders

We have seen when they were elected. An idea of relative class was demonstrated and briefly discussed. But a firmer feel for how players compare is needed, expressed in a form which facilitates identification of HOF candidates. This is where classification comes in.

Everybody would agree that catchers shouldn't be compared with first basemen, shortstops shouldn't be compared with outfielders, etc. Defensive positions have varying demands which influence offensive performance and expectations. Classifications by position strike proper groupings and comparisons. All analyses in Part II cover players born after 1894, and they are ranked in descending order according to their PAB. Once again, the columns for runs (R) and runs batted in (RBI) in this section do not include home runs, thus reflecting the players' true performance.

	AB	HR	R	RBI	PAB	BA	SA
Class 1 .360 +							
Ruth (N.Y. only)	7,287	.091	.179	.181	.451	.347	.708
Williams, T.	7,706	.068	.166	.171	.404	.344	.634
DiMaggio, J.	6,821	.053	.151	.172	.376	.325	.579
Class 2 .315–.359							
Wilson	4,760	.051	.134	.172	.358	.307	.545
Simmons	8,761	.035	.137	.173	.346	.334	.535
Ott	9,456	.054	.143	.143	.339	.304	.533
Averill	6,358	.037	.155	.146	.338	.318	.533
Goslin	8,654	.029	.143	.157	.329	.316	.500
Mantle	8,102	.066	.141	.120	.327	.298	.557
Klein	6,486	.046	.134	.139	.319	.320	.543
Class 3 .270–.314							
Cuyler	7,161	.018	.164	.131	.313	.321	.474
Hafey	4,625	.035	.133	.145	.313	.317	.526
Musial	10,972	.043	.134	.135	.312	.331	.559
Medwick	7,635	.027	.130	.154	.311	.324	.505
Kiner	5,205	.071	.116	.124	.311	.279	.548
Manush	7,653	.014	.154	.139	.307	.330	.479
Combs	5,748	.010	.196	.099	.306	.325	.462
Robinson, F.	10,006	.059	.124	.123	.305	.294	.537
Snider	7,161	.057	.119	.129	.305	.295	.540
Mays	10,881	.061	.129	.114	.304	.302	.557
Aaron	12,364	.061	.115	.125	.301	.305	.555
Slaughter	7,946	.021	.136	.143	.300	.300	.453
Waner, P.	9,459	.012	.160	.127	.298	.333	.473

	AB	HR	R	RBI	PAB	BA	SA
Class 3 (cont.)							
Youngs	4,627	.009	.166	.120	.295	.322	441
Kaline	10,116	.039	.121	.117	.277	.297	.480
Class 4 .269–							
Williams, B.	9,350	.046	.105	.112	.263	.290	492
Clemente	9,454	.025	.124	.113	.262	.317	.475
Brock	10,332	.014	.141	.073	.229	.293	.410
Waner, L.	7,772	.004	.151	.073	.228	.316	.394

This group covers some of the most prestigious names in the history of the game. No matter how figures are put together, some of these players appear at the top. Ruth is the best example. He was the second best contact hitter, the top home run hitter, he ties for second (with Gehringer) as a run scorer, and ranks third as an RBI man. Whatever a man can do with a bat in his hands Ruth did, and he did it expertly.

Batting average doesn't make a superstar. Neither does power. To hit consistently, but without power, will get HOF attention for a player, but he will rank low among his peers (e.g., Lloyd Waner). To concentrate solely on the home run will get HOF attention for a player who is extraordinarily successful in the enterprise, but he too will rank as a low producer (Killebrew). It's the combination of contact and power that makes the highly rated HOF producer. Many examples of this appear in the above listing.

A superstar outfielder must have a PAB of .360 + , as opposed to .351 + for all superstar-caliber players. To be known as a superstar outfielder, in other words, is a tougher job than being known as a general superstar. Three outfielders qualify as superstars: Ruth, Ted Williams, and Joe DiMaggio, or about 10 percent of the elite group. Seven players (24 percent) were better than average HOF outfielders.

Ruth, Williams, and Simmons are top contact hitters. Ruth, Kiner, and Williams lead the home run pack. Combs, Ruth, Williams and Youngs (tied) are leading run scorers. And Ruth, Simmons, DiMaggio and Wilson (tied) are the big RBI men.

A classification listing by PAB does not reflect the total value of a player because it does not consider durability; it rates skill alone, as if all players were active for the same amount of time. Since skill plus durability is the formula for greatness, a further step is needed to arrive at a ranking of relative greatness in the total sense. Such an exercise is beyond the purview of this book, but it would be unfair to the reader who, perhaps, sees his favorite player lowly graded in the above listing and is disposed, therefore, to pitch this book out of the nearest window.

So, a short-cut method has been devised which, hopefully, partially responds to this potential frustration.

Hall of Fame outfielders had careers of widely varying lengths. Generally accepted statistical procedure reveals that the average outfielder had between 6,046 and 10,013 at bats. Those above this range had unusually long careers; those below it, unusually short ones. Thus, we can group men into three career groups and, within each group, PAB-rank them, as follows:

	AB	HR	R	RBI	PAB	BA	SA
Long Careers							
Musial	10,972	.043	.134	.135	.312	.331	.559
Robinson, F.	10,006	.059	.124	.123	.305	.294	.537
Mays	10,881	.061	.129	.114	.304	.302	.557
Aaron	12,364	.061	.115	.125	.301	.305	.555
Kaline	10,116	.039	.121	.117	.277	.297	.480
Brock	10,332	.014	.141	.073	.229	.293	.410
Medium Careers							
Ruth	7,287	.091	.179	.181	.451	.347	.708
Williams, T.	7,706	.068	.166	.171	.404	.344	.634
DiMaggio, J.	6,821	.053	.151	.172	.376	.325	.579
Simmons	8,761	.035	.137	.173	.346	.334	.535
Ott	9,456	.054	.143	.143	.339	.304	.533
Averill	6,358	.037	.155	.146	.338	.318	.533
Goslin	8,654	.029	.143	.157	.329	.316	.500
Mantle	8,102	.066	.141	.120	.327	.298	.557
Klein	6,486	.046	.134	.139	.319	.320	.543
Medwick	7,635	.027	.130	.154	.311	.324	.505
Cuyler	7,161	.022	.160	.127	.309	.321	.486
Manush	7,653	.014	.154	.139	.307	.330	.479
Snider	7,161	.057	.119	.129	.305	.295	.540
Slaughter	7,946	.021	.136	.143	.300	.300	.453
Waner, P.	9,459	.012	.160	.127	.298	.333	.473
Williams, B.	9,350	.046	.105	.112	.263	.290	.492
Clemente	9,454	.025	.124	.113	.262	.317	.475
Waner, L.	7,772	.004	.151	.073	.228	.316	.394
Short Careers							
Wilson	4,760	.051	.134	.172	.358	.307	.545
Hafey	4,625	.035	.133	.145	.313	.317	.526
Kiner	5,205	.071	.116	.124	.311	.279	.548
Combs	5,748	.010	.196	.099	.306	.325	.462
Youngs	4,627	.009	.166	.120	.295	.322	.441

The above schedule does not select the best of the best, nor does it directly contrast players as the classification listing does. But it does recognize durability and, as such, moves the player evaluation process a step forward, providing for the interested fan one more argument for upgrading the rank of a favored player. In this book, it is as far as we go.

The analysis of HOF outfielders has provided the yardsticks against which active outfielders can be measured. It yields standards that HOF aspirants must meet. More specifically, it tells us the following:

1. A superstar HOF outfielder has a PAB of .360 + .
2. An above average HOF outfielder falls into the .315–.359 PAB range.
3. A below average HOF outfielder falls into the .270–.314 range.
4. A marginal HOF outfielder falls into the .228–.269 range.
5. An outfielder with a PAB below .228 does not belong in the HOF except under extraordinary circumstances.
6. A long career equals 10,014 + at bats; a short one equals less than 6,045 at bats; a normal career equals 6,046–10,013 at bats.

It's time to move to HOF infielders.

Infielders

We now move to the examination of the HOF infield corps. In the case of HOF outfielders, the average player had a PAB of .315, and the four-tier classification system was built upon that fact. For infielders, the average PAB is .284, and a classification structure was built on that fact, using the methodology previously explained. Results appear below:

	AB	HR	R	RBI	PAB	BA	SA
Class 1 .323 +							
Hornsby	8,173	.037	.156	.156	.349	.358	.577
Gehringer	8,860	.021	.179	.140	.340	.320	.480
Cronin	7,577	.022	.140	.165	.328	.302	.468
Class 2 .284–.322							
Traynor	7,559	.008	.149	.161	.317	.320	.435
Robinson, J.	4,877	.028	.166	.122	.317	.311	.474
Vaughan	6,622	.014	.163	.125	.302	.318	.433
Sewell	7,132	.007	.153	.140	.300	.312	.413
Doerr	7,093	.031	.123	.144	.299	.288	.461
Frisch	9,112	.012	.157	.125	.293	.316	.432
Mathews	8,537	.060	.117	.110	.287	.271	.509

	AB	HR	R	RBI	PAB	BA	SA
Class 3 .246–.283							
Lindstrom	5,611	.018	.141	.120	.280	.311	.449
Appling	8,857	.005	.144	.121	.270	.310	.398
Jackson	6,086	.022	.115	.130	.267	.291	.433
Boudreau	6,030	.011	.132	.120	.262	.295	.415
Reese	8,058	.016	.150	.094	.260	.269	.377
Herman	7,707	.006	.145	.103	.254	.304	.407
Kell	6,702	.012	.120	.118	.250	.306	.414
Class 4 .245–							
Robinson, B.	10,654	.025	.090	.102	.218	.267	.401
Aparicio	10,230	.008	.122	.069	.200	.262	.343

A superstar infielder must have a PAB of .323 + , as opposed to
.360 + for superstar outfielders. The offensive expectation of the
baseball world is lower for men who hold high-skill defensive positions.
Despite lower expectations, however, three superstar infielders could
compete head to head with all but the mightiest outfielders as offensive
performers.

Hornsby may have been the best pure hitter in history. Gehringer
was an offensive machine of remarkable consistency. Cronin was an RBI
hound, far more effective in this area than his BA indicates. The general
productivity of these men is historical evidence of the value of good and
gutsy contact hitters who do not employ outstanding home run tools.
The three superstar infielders also demonstrated — to those who would
see — the extent to which the home run is overstated as an offensive
weapon, unless it is accompanied as well by contact-hitting ability. For
example Hornsby, Gehringer, and Cronin — banjo hitters when compared to great sluggers — were more productive than the likes of Mantle,
Kiner, Mays, and Aaron, who were all prodigious home run hitters.

As home run hitters, Ed Mathews and Hornsby were superstar infielders; as scorers, Gehringer, Jackie Robinson and Vaughan were
superstars; as RBI men, Cronin, Hornsby, and Traynor were superstars.

Length of career varies as much with HOF infielders as it does with
their outfield brothers. The average man had 6180–9133 at bats. Players
with less than 6180 at bats had relatively short careers; those with more
than 9133 at bats had relatively long ones. As with outfielders, the table
below separates players into three career-length groups, and PAB rates
them within each grouping.

	AB	HR	R	RBI	PAB	BA	SA
Long Careers							
Robinson, B.	10,654	.025	.090	.102	.218	.267	.401
Aparicio	10,230	.008	.122	.069	.200	.262	.343

	AB	HR	R	RBI	PAB	BA	SA
Medium Careers							
Hornsby	8,173	.037	.156	.156	.349	.358	.577
Gehringer	8,860	.021	.179	.140	.340	.320	.480
Cronin	7,577	.022	.140	.165	.328	.302	.468
Traynor	7,559	.008	.149	.161	.317	.320	.435
Vaughan	6,622	.014	.163	.125	.302	.318	.453
Sewell	7,132	.007	.153	.140	.300	.312	.413
Doerr	7,093	.031	.123	.144	.299	.288	.461
Frisch	9,112	.012	.157	.125	.293	.316	.432
Mathews	8,537	.060	.117	.110	.287	.271	.509
Appling	8,857	.005	.144	.121	.270	.310	.398
Reese	8,058	.016	.150	.094	.260	.269	.377
Herman	7,707	.006	.145	.103	.254	.304	.407
Kell	6,702	.012	.120	.118	.250	.306	.414
Short Careers							
Robinson, J.	4,877	.028	.166	.122	.317	.311	.474
Lindstrom	5,611	.018	.141	.120	.280	.311	.449
Jackson	6,086	.022	.115	.130	.267	.291	.433
Boudreau	6,030	.011	.132	.120	.262	.295	.415

The analysis of HOF infielders is complete. Standards have been determined against which active infielders can be tested as follows:

1. A superstar HOF infielder has a PAB of .323 + .
2. An above average HOF infielder falls into the .284–.322 PAB range.
3. A below average HOF infielder falls into the .246–.283 PAB range.
4. A marginal HOF infielder falls into the .200–.245 range.
5. A long career equals 9,134 + at bats; a short one equals less than 6,180 at bats; normal careers are in the 6,180–9,133 at bat range.

Now we're ready for the first basemen.

First Basemen

It's time for first basemen. There aren't many in the HOF—only ten.

First basemen are commonly thought of as infielders. There's nothing wrong about that. But in this book they are separated from other infielders and treated as a separate category. There are reasons for this.

First base is a position that requires size — the taller the better. The reason is obvious. They are targets for throwing infielders; the bigger the target, the better. Since first basemen are usually big, power hitting is expected of them, and their offensive standards are completely different from those applied to higher skilled infield positions. Lou Gehrig is the prototype first baseman. To directly compare production output of first basemen with other infielders is, by definition, poor analytical procedure that results in distortion.

As a defensive position, first base is the final resting place for aging outfielders, infielders, and catchers. In a relative sense, it is the least demanding defensive position on the field. That isn't to say that fine athletes have not cavorted with great finesse around the initial sack, or that teams do not benefit when this is the case. But it is to say that if a team must be defensively weak somewhere, first base is a popular place to pick.

Hall of Fame outfielders have an average PAB of .315; infielders, .284. A four-tier classification system was built for each based upon those averages. For first basemen, the average PAB is .325 and a classification structure was built for them, using the same methods.

It should be noted that Gehrig, Foxx, and Greenberg were players of superhuman skill compared to successors. Since their performance figures are so excellent, and since they make up 30 percent of the HOF first basemen roster, their combined statistical weight results in a high-level classification system, higher than that for outfielders. Judging by the quality of recent appointments, standards will drop sharply in the years ahead as modern players are added.

	AB	HR	R	RBI	PAB	BA	SA
Class 1 .379 +							
Gehrig	8,001	.062	.174	.187	.423	.340	.632
Foxx	8,134	.066	.150	.171	.386	.325	.609
Greenberg	5,193	.064	.139	.182	.384	.313	.605
Class 2 .325–.378							
Mize	6,443	.056	.118	.152	.325	.312	.562
Class 3 .273–.324							
Bottomley	7,471	.029	.128	.161	.319	.310	.500
Terry	6,428	.024	.150	.144	.318	.341	.506
Kelly	5,993	.025	.112	.145	.282	.297	.452
Killebrew	8,147	.070	.087	.124	.282	.256	.509
McCovey	8,197	.064	.086	.126	.276	.270	.515
Class 4 .272–							
Banks	9,421	.054	.084	.119	.258	.274	.500

A superstar first baseman must have a PAB of .379 + , the highest in the HOF. The big three are responsible for this. Except for Ruth, Gehrig had no offensive superior; except for Ruth, Gehrig, and Ted Williams, the same can be said for Foxx and Greenberg. Greenberg was the last of the mighty trinity to retire (1947). Since that time, not a single first baseman has appeared to seriously challenge the productivity of these men.

The tragic Gehrig (he died prematurely) was the complete ballplayer, arguably more valuable to a team than the great Babe. Foxx was more powerful than Lou, and only a hair behind in productivity — close enough to infer that playing with Ruth was the factor that gave a productivity edge to Gehrig. Greenberg, a mighty basher, was also one of the great RBI hounds of baseball history. It's worth noting that all three combined great power with great contact hitting ability — the combination that produces superstars — the combination that is so lacking today.

The home run hitting superstar of the first basemen was Killebrew, challenged closely by Foxx, Greenberg, Gehrig, and McCovey. Gehrig was a superstar scorer, and also — along with Greenberg — a superstar RBI man. Superstar contact hitters were Gehrig and Terry.

Similar to players already examined, the men in this group had careers of varying length. They have been divided into three career-length groupings below, and within each group have been PAB rated. For first basemen, a long career equals 8563 + at bats; a short one equals less than 6123 at bats. The at bat range for a normal career is 6124–8562.

	AB	HR	R	RBI	PAB	BA	SA
Long Careers							
Banks	9,421	.054	.084	.119	.258	.274	.500
Medium Careers							
Gehrig	8,001	.062	.174	.187	.423	.340	.632
Foxx	8,134	.066	.150	.171	.386	.325	.609
Mize	6,443	.056	.118	.152	.325	.312	.562
Bottomley	7,471	.029	.128	.161	.319	.310	.500
Terry	6,428	.024	.150	.144	.318	.341	.506
Killebrew	8,147	.070	.087	.124	.282	.256	.509
McCovey	8,197	.064	.086	.126	.275	.270	.515
Short Careers							
Greenberg	5,193	.064	.139	.182	.384	.313	.605
Kelly	5,993	.025	.112	.145	.282	.297	.452

This finishes first basemen. Active players will be measured against de facto standards established by the ten HOF men:

1. A superstar HOF first baseman has a PAB of .379 + .
2. An above average HOF first baseman falls into the .325–.378 PAB range.
3. A below average HOF first baseman falls into the .273–.324 PAB range.
4. A marginal HOF first baseman falls into the .258–.272 PAB range.
5. A long career equals 8563 + at bats: a short one is less than 6124 at bats. Normal careers are in the 6124–8562 at bat range.

Bring on HOF catchers.

Catchers

Forty years ago, advice to a young player of promise was typically: "If you want to make the big time, put on catchers' pads and learn the job." The same advice is valid today, and would probably be ignored — as it always has been. There are only seven catchers in the HOF — seven men since 1936 — seven men in 50 years — and some would say there are at least two too many.

As with other players, a classification structure has been formed using methods previously explained. The HOF roster of catchers, classified, appears below:

	AB	HR	R	RBI	PAB	BA	SA
Class 1 .325 +							
Cochrane	5,169	.023	.178	.138	.339	.320	.478
Class 2 .284–.320							
Dickey	6,300	.032	.116	.160	.307	.313	.486
Berra	7,555	.047	.108	.142	.297	.285	.482
Campanella	4,205	.058	.092	.146	.295	.276	.500
Class 3 .249–.283							
Hartnett	6,432	.037	.098	.147	.281	.297	.489
Class 4 .248–							
Lombardi	5,855	.032	.070	.137	.239	.306	.460
Ferrell	6,028	.005	.109	.117	.231	.281	.363

In all other fielder classifications, more than one superstar was located but, alas, in this positional grouping, we find only Mickey Cochrane. Truly, he was a sterling performer capable of production performance never reached by more famous HOF personalities—Mantle, Musial, Kiner, Snider, Mays, and Aaron, for example. Similar to Hornsby, Gehringer, and Cronin, Cochrane was a superior contact hitter with modest power characteristics, talents which, when combined, equalled a formidable run producing machine.

About half of the HOF catchers fall into Class 2. Bill Dickey, almost as brilliant a hitter as Cochrane, was a deadly clutch hitter. Durable Berra was a serious home run threat. Campanella offset contact hitting weaknesses with superior demonstrations of power.

Campy is the home run superstar of the HOF catching corps; Cochrane, the superstar scorer; Dickey, the superstar RBI man. Cochrane and Dickey were superstar contact hitters.

An average career for a HOF catcher is 4964–6906 at bats; a long career, 6907 + at bats; a short one, less than 4964 at bats. Below, players are separated into career-length groupings, and are PAB rated within each group.

	AB	HR	R	RBI	PAB	BA	SA
Long Careers							
Berra	7,555	.047	.108	.142	.297	.285	.482
Medium Careers							
Cochrane	5,169	.023	.178	.138	.339	.320	.478
Dickey	6,300	.032	.116	.160	.307	.313	.486
Hartnett	6,432	.037	.098	.147	.281	.297	.489
Ferrell	6,028	.005	.109	.117	.231	.281	.363
Short Careers							
Campanella	4,205	.058	.092	.146	.295	.276	.500

As a result of this analysis, benchmarks have been set against which active players can be measured, as follows:

1. A superstar HOF catcher has a PAB of .321 + .
2. An above average HOF catcher falls into the .284–.320 PAB range.
3. A below average HOF catcher falls into the .249–.283 PAB range.
4. A marginal HOF catcher falls into the .231–.248 PAB range.
5. Over 6906 at bats equals a long career; under 4964 at bats equals a short one; 4964–6906 at bats equals a normal career.

With the completion of catchers, it is possible to summarize standards established by HOF players against which active players can be measured, as follows:

	Outfield	Infield	First Base	Catcher
PAB				
Superstar	.360 +	.323 +	.379 +	.321 +
Above average	.315–.359	.284–.322	.325–.378	.284–.320
Below average	.270–.314	.246–.283	.273–.324	.249–.283
Marginal	.228–.269	.200–.245	.258–.272	.231–248
Ineligible	.227 –	.199 –	.257 –	.230 –
Career at Bats				
Long	10014 +	9134 +	8563 +	6907 +
Medium	6046–10013	6180–9133	6124–8562	4963–6906
Short	6045 –	6179 –	6123 –	4962 –

The analysis of pitchers is next. The approach will be the same, but indicators of class and durability are changed. With pitchers, ERA (earned run average) = class; CG (complete games) = durability.

Pitchers

A good pitcher, like a good cup of coffee, is hard to find. The first HOF appointments were made in 1936. Only 18 live-ball era pitchers have made it in the last half century.

Earned run average has been selected as the quality determinant for pitchers — from a classification standpoint, it fills the same role the PAB factor did for fielders. Why use the ERA? The reason is basic and simple.

The pitcher's job is not to strike out people, or keep walks to a minimum, or minimize hits, or to win games (teams win games, not pitchers). Such things are worthy goals and, when present, admirable abilities and accomplishments. But they don't define the pitcher's job, which is to keep the other team from scoring, however his talents permit. He may be an intimidating power pitcher, a stuff artist, or a control magician. Who cares? As long as he keeps the runs down, he's a good pitcher. As long as his ERA is low, he has made his maximum contribution to the team. With a low ERA and a good team behind him, a pitcher will win big as a natural consequence. With a low ERA and a poor team behind him (something Walter Johnson contended with for most of his career), he may not win big. Either way, the quality of the pitcher remains the same.

It should be noted that ERA is not a good quality determinant for a relief pitcher. His role is different. His objectives are different. His operating environment is different. As a consequence Hoyt Wilhelm, the only relief pitcher in the HOF pitching corps, is excluded from the forthcoming analysis of HOF pitchers.

As was the case with the fielders, the classification of the HOF pitchers disregards time. Only ability, as shown by career ERAs, is measured. This typically results in some players being overrated; others, underrated. But this potential source of irritation to readers will be mitigated by presenting as well a schedule which sorts career length into three groups—long, medium, short. Hall of Fame pitchers are here ranked, in ascending order, by career ERA figures.*

	CG (equiv)	H	BB	BR	ERA	W	L	%	SO
Class 1 2.88–									
Ford	352.3	7.85	3.08	10.93	2.74	236	106	.690	5.55
Koufax	258.3	6.79	3.16	9.95	2.76	165	87	.655	9.27
Class 2 2.89–3.19									
Marichal	389.6	8.09	1.82	9.91	2.89	243	142	.631	5.91
Gibson	431.7	7.60	3.09	10.69	2.91	251	174	.591	7.22
Drysdale	381.3	8.09	2.24	10.33	2.95	209	166	.557	6.52
Hubbell	399.0	8.67	1.82	10.49	2.98	253	154	.622	4.20
Dean	218.4	8.79	2.10	10.89	3.04	150	83	.644	5.29
Grove	437.8	8.79	2.71	11.50	3.06	300	141	.680	5.18
Spahn	582.9	8.29	2.46	10.75	3.08	363	245	.597	4.43
Class 3 3.20–3.50									
Lemon	316.6	8.08	3.95	12.04	3.23	207	128	.618	4.03
Feller	425.3	7.69	4.15	11.84	3.25	266	162	.621	6.07
Hunter	383.1	7.72	2.49	10.21	3.26	224	166	.574	5.25
Gomez	278.1	8.23	3.94	12.17	3.34	189	102	.649	5.28
Roberts	521.0	8.79	1.73	10.53	3.40	286	245	.539	4.52
Class 4 3.51 +									
Wynn	507.3	8.46	3.50	11.96	3.54	300	244	.551	4.60
Hoyt	418.0	9.66	2.40	12.06	3.59	237	182	.566	2.89
Lyons	462.4	9.71	2.42	12.13	3.67	260	230	.531	2.32
Ruffing	482.4	8.90	3.19	12.09	3.80	273	225	.548	4.12

Two superstar pitchers dominate the 17-man listing. Ford represents the perfect blending of team and pitcher. He was great, as was the team he played with (he and the Yankees participated in 11 World Series). The consequence was the best winning percentage of all HOF pitchers. On a

*CG (equiv.) = equivalent complete games, H = hits, BB = bases on balls, BR = total baserunners allowed, ERA = earned run average, W = wins, L = losses, SO = strikeouts.

given day, Koufax may have been the greatest to ever throw a ball. Concerning hits allowed, base runners allowed, and strikeouts per game, Sandy was a superstar performer.

Seven pitchers fall into Class 2. Marichal and Hubbell were control masters. For combining durability with class, arguments could be made that nobody was ever any better than Gibson. Drysdale, a formidable power pitcher, had win/loss luck exactly opposite from Ford. Dizzy Dean was a skyrocket of balanced talent felled by a freak accident. Grove and Spahn contend with Gibson for the honor of being known as the best pitching investment in modern baseball history.

Spahn, Roberts, and Wynn were the physical supermen of the HOF pitching corps. Koufax and Gibson deprived offensive players of hits in superstar fashion. Roberts, Marichal, and Hubbell were superstar control masters. Overall baserunners allowed was the superstar specialty of Marichal, Koufax, and Drysdale. Superstar strikeout power was the forte of Koufax and Gibson. Ford and Grove were superstar clutch pitchers.

Dean had the shortest career. Lyons was easiest to hit. Feller was the wildest. Gomez allowed the most baserunners. Lyons had the weakest strikeout pitch. And Roberts was the poorest clutch pitcher.

Length of career differs greatly within the pitching corps. The following table separates men by career length, and ERA grades them within each group. The average HOF pitcher completed 310.8–494.3 games in his career; a long career is 494.4 + complete games; a short one, less than 310.7 complete games.

	CG (equiv)	H	BB	BR	ERA	W	L	%	SO
Long Career									
Spahn	582.9	8.29	2.46	10.75	3.08	363	245	.597	4.43
Roberts	521.0	8.79	1.73	10.53	3.40	286	245	.539	4.52
Wynn	507.3	8.46	3.50	11.96	3.54	300	244	.551	4.60
Medium Career									
Ford	352.3	7.85	3.08	10.93	2.74	236	106	.690	5.55
Marichal	389.6	8.09	1.82	9.91	2.89	243	142	.631	5.91
Gibson	431.7	7.60	3.09	10.69	2.91	251	174	.591	7.22
Drysdale	381.3	8.09	2.24	10.33	2.95	209	166	.557	6.52
Hubbell	399.0	8.67	1.82	10.49	2.98	253	154	.622	4.20
Grove	437.8	8.79	2.71	11.50	3.06	300	141	680	5.18
Lemon	316.6	8.08	3.95	12.04	3.23	207	128	.618	4.03
Feller	425.3	7.69	4.15	11.84	3.25	266	162	.621	6.07
Hunter	383.1	7.72	2.49	10.21	3.26	224	166	.574	5.25
Hoyt	418.0	9.66	2.40	12.06	3.59	237	182	.566	2.89
Lyons	462.4	9.71	2.42	12.13	3.67	260	230	.531	2.32
Ruffing	482.4	8.90	3.19	12.09	3.80	273	225	.548	4.12

	CG (equiv)	H	BB	BR	ERA	W	L	%	SO
Short Career									
Koufax	258.3	6.79	3.16	9.95	2.76	165	87	.655	9.27
Dean	218.4	8.79	2.10	10.89	3.04	150	83	644	5.29
Gomez	278.1	8.23	3.94	12.17	3.34	189	102	.649	5.28

Pitching standards have been determined. Active pitchers will be measured against them as the attempt to locate "The Pretenders" is made. Benchmarks are as follows:

ERA

Superstar	2.88 –
Above average	2.89–3.19
Below average	3.20–3.50
Marginal	3.51–3.80
Ineligible	3.81 +

Career Complete Games

Long career	494.4 +
Medium career	310.8–494.3
Short career	310.7 –

All benchmarks have been determined. But before putting them to work, a deeper look at fairness questions raised in the analysis is in order. How fair is the election system?

The Fairness Issue

Before moving to classification and evaluation of active players, a useful diversion is to examine questions raised as to why and when certain players were elected to the HOF, especially in recent years. The reason for questions is not to demean talents of those chosen, but rather to point out conflict between choices made and de facto performance standards established by accumulated previous choices. Consistency, not choice, is the issue.

Prior to Hartnett, for example, all HOF players hit .300 or better, and all had a PAB factor of .292 + . The selection of Hartnett opened a door. In the 1960s, three players who failed to meet one or both of the historical standards were accepted; in the 1970s, ten of the elected players (56 percent) did not meet one or both standards; most players selected in the 1980s don't meet historical standards. Obviously, standards are being lowered or changed, but more importantly, modern day players—with relatively weak records—are being chosen faster than older players with superior records, or are being chosen while older, superior players (who were measured against higher standards) continue to be ignored.

When one considers the value that retired players understandably place on HOF recognition, it is unfair and cruel to select modern players instead, or ahead, of them.

Most players are retired by the time they reach 40 years of age. If they played at HOF levels of excellence, all would agree that by the time they hit their fiftieth birthdays, they should be in the HOF. Below is a list of pitchers elected to the HOF after the fiftieth birthday:

	HOF	Age	ERA
Spahn	1973	52	3.08
Lemon	1976	56	3.23
Gomez	1972	64	3.34
Wynn	1972	52	3.54
Hoyt	1969	70	3.59
Lyons	1955	55	3.67
Ruffing	1967	62	3.80

The late selection of Spahn is understandable. He played forever, and you can't elect a man until he retires. But why did it take so long to elect the others? Assuming all had HOF quality to begin with (which is debatable), why did it take so long to recognize it? Could it be that modern baseball so rarely produces quality pitchers that selection committees constantly look to the past for talent, lowering standards of admission as they do? Whatever the reason for late selection, it raises questions about the recognition process. Greatness, which should be a common characteristic of all HOF players, is not difficult to recognize. Deserving players, like Wynn, should not have to wait so long. Undeserving ones should not be chosen in the first place.

Among fielders, instances of unfairness related to the time of election are even more blatant. The following list contains the names of players selected after they were 50 years old.

	HOF	Age	PAB	BA
Wilson	1979	79	.358	.307
Averill	1975	73	.338	.318
Goslin	1968	68	.329	.316
Mize	1981	68	.325	.312
Bottomley	1974	74	.319	.310
Klein	1980	76	.319	.320
Terry	1954	56	.318	.341
Hafey	1971	68	.313	.317
Medwick	1968	57	.311	.324

	HOF	Age	PAB	BA
Kiner	1975	53	.311	.279
Cuyler	1968	69	.309	.321
Manush	1964	63	.307	.330
Combs	1970	71	.306	.325
Snider	1980	54	.305	.295
Vaughan	1985	73	.302	.318
Slaughter	1985	69	.300	.300
Sewell, J.	1977	79	.300	.312
Doerr	1986	68	.299	.288
Youngs	1972	75	.295	.322
Kelly	1973	78	.282	.297
Hartnett	1955	55	.281	.297
Lindstrom	1976	71	.280	.311
Appling	1964	57	.270	.310
Jackson, T.	1982	79	.267	.291
Boudreau	1970	53	.262	.295
Reese	1984	65	.260	.269
Herman	1975	66	.254	.304
Kell	1983	61	.250	.306
Lombardi	1986	78	.239	.306
Ferrell	1984	79	.231	.281
Waner, L.	1967	61	.228	.316

Wilson, Averill, Goslin, and Mize were only a performance hair behind the most productive players in history. Thirteen other players produced a PAB of .300 or better, including Klein and Medwick. To withhold HOF recognition from such talent damns the selection system as blind or unfair. On the other hand, the late selection of the other players is understandable. Worthy though they may be, their records do not explode from the pages of baseball history.

By way of contrast, below is a selected list of players elected to the HOF before their fiftieth birthday:

	HOF	Age	PAB	BA
Mantle	1974	43	.327	.298
Robinson, F.	1982	47	.305	.294
Mays	1979	48	.304	.302
Aaron	1982	48	.301	.305
Berra	1972	47	.297	.285
Mathews	1978	47	.287	.271
Killebrew	1984	48	.282	.256
Kaline	1980	46	.277	.297
McCovey	1986	48	.276	.270
Williams, B.	1987	49	.236	.290
Clemente	1973	39	.262	.317

	HOF	Age	PAB	BA
Banks	1977	46	.258	.274
Robinson, B.	1983	46	.218	.267

Now, the issue here is not the selection of the above players to the HOF, but rather the time lag between when *they* were appointed, and when more highly skilled *veteran* players were chosen. There are no Ruths, Gehrigs, Hornsbys, Cronins, or Traynors in this list—no players who turned the baseball world on its ear with their feats. Why the rush with them and the slowness with the others?

The heavy smell of politics and favoritism hovers over a screening and selection process that creates such uneven results.

The Neglected Ones

The primary selection process to the HOF is managed by the Baseball Writer's Association of America (BBWAA). When a recently retired player (five years) of HOF skills is overlooked, they are responsible. The secondary selection process is controlled by the HOF. Its fundamental purpose is to clean up after the BBWAA—to recognize veteran players screened out by the BBWAA process. When a veteran player (retired 23 years or more) is finally recognized, credit belongs to the HOF committee.

It is fortunate for players, baseball, and the HOF that the veteran committee exists. The BBWAA does a poor and unfair job of selection. Too many fine players have been overlooked and too many ordinary players have been recognized too soon by the BBWAA. Belatedly, the HOF committee can and does correct many of these injustices.

But bad as it is to be chosen late, it is worse not to be chosen at all. An unknown number of deserving players fall into this classification.

It isn't the purpose of this book to locate them all. Since infielders are most abused by the home run and longevity preoccupations that color BBWAA selections, a sample of overlooked second basemen, shortstops, and third basemen appears below. They are referred to as "The Neglected Ones."

	AB	HR	R	RBI	PAB
Stephens	6,497	.038	.116	.143	.297
Pesky	4,745	.004	.179	.082	.265

	AB	HR	R	RBI	PAB
Boyer, K.	7,455	.038	.110	.115	.263
Hack	7,278	.008	.162	.080	.250
Dark	7,219	.017	.130	.087	.234
Bartell	7,629	.101	.138	.083	.232
Schoendinst	8,479	.101	.134	.081	.225
Fox	9,232	.004	.135	.082	.221

Standards for HOF infielders, determined a few pages back, are repeated below:

PAB

Superstar	.323 +
Above average	.284–.322
Below average	.246–.283
Marginal	.200–.245
Ineligible	.199 –

Career at Bats

Long career	9134 +
Medium career	6180–9133
Short career	6179 –

Vern Stephens

Stephens had a medium length career, and generated an above average PAB.

Vern was one of the best power hitting shortstops of modern baseball. If elected, only Eddie Mathews would rank ahead of him as a power hitting infielder. As a producer, he was superior to Frisch, Mathews, and Lindstrom. Could he field in HOF style?

	Fielding Average
Stephens	.962
Cronin	.953
Appling	.948
Reese	.962
Boudreau	.973
Aparicio	.971

If Cronin, Appling, and Reese were HOF defensive shortstops, so was Stephens.

Except for Cronin, Vern out-produced all shortstops. He played in more games than Lou Boudreau, Jack Robinson, Lindstrom, and Jackson. He retired in 1956 and should have been elected to the HOF in the 1960s. There is no logical reason for his absence.

John Pesky

John had a short career and produced a PAB below the average HOF infielder.

Pesky played in 12 American League seasons, two more than the minimum eligibility requirement. If elected to the HOF, his would be the shortest career of the group. For different reasons, he played about as little as Jackie Robinson. Should his short career disqualify him? No, on two counts. First, he did put his ten years in and that should settle the time question. Secondly, his career was short because he lost three full seasons to military service. For the two seasons prior to service, he averaged .328 at the plate. For the two seasons after service, he averaged .330. Obviously, the three seasons he lost would have been highly productive ones. If the reason for rejecting Pesky for the HOF is length of career, the reason is unseemly and unfair—unseemly because one does not penalize a man for serving his country; unfair because, despite military service, Pesky meets the time standard.

Pesky played shortstop and third base. He developed a fielding average of .967. For either position, this is HOF fielding. As a producer, largely due to his contact hitting ability, Pesky was the equal of Appling, and superior to recent infield appointees. Justice and fairness are not served by denying the HOF of the presence of this fine and talented baseball gentleman.

Boyer, Hack

Ken Boyer had a medium length career and developed a PAB below that of the average HOF infielder.

Boyer was a power hitting third baseman. With a fielding average of .957, he would be rated as an average fielder. As an offensive force, Boyer was 8 percent weaker than Mathews, and the equal of Boudreau. Under persistently lowered standards for infielders, equity is the argument that defends the Boyer claim to HOF status. Defensively adequate, he was offensively superior to five HOF infielders.

Stan Hack was similar to Boyer in career length and in his career PAB.

The same relational argument is made for Hack. The third baseman had a lifetime fielding average in the Mathews range. If Mathews was a HOF defensive third baseman, so was he. If Kell, Robinson and Aparicio were HOF offensively, so was he.

Dark, Bartell, Schoendinst, Fox

Dark, Bartell, and Schoendinst had normal career lengths, Fox had a long career.

All of the above were offensively superior to Robinson and Aparicio. Do they hold up defensively?

		Fielding Average
Dark	ss	.959
Bartell	ss	.955
Schoendinst	2b	.982
Fox	2b	.984

Dark and Bartell were not the defensive equals of Aparicio, but they were from 12 to 18 percent more effective offensively. The selection of Aparicio in 1984 makes logical the claim of such players for HOF recognition.

Robinson and Aparicio were elected to the HOF as defensive specialists—a look at their production records makes this conclusion obvious. Nobody played an infield position more defensively brilliant than Schoendinst and Fox played the second base position. And both were offensively superior to Robinson and Aparicio. If the newly elected third baseman and shortstop deserve to be in the HOF, so do Schoendinst and Fox.

As HOF admission standards continue to decrease, more players from the past will raise cries of unfairness. The above list is but a small sample of retired players who have a legitimate gripe against the selection system. Stephens should be immediately recognized as a HOF talent. Justice demands the recognition of Pesky. The case for the others is essentially comparative.

The audit of HOF selection committees is concluded. The primary committee headed by BBWAA gets poor marks. They have unnecessarily reduced standards of admission, they have unduly glamorized average skills, they have overlooked too many players of high skill and appointed too many players—too soon—of relatively average skill. The secondary committee headed by HOF appointees gets mixed marks. On the plus side, they have corrected many mistakes of the primary commit-tee. On the minus side, there are more oversights still to be mended. In the interests of fairness, the HOF selection system needs overhaul.

But warts and all, the HOF is where players want to end up. It's time to see how many legitimate candidates are on the field today.

Part III
Hall of Fame Pretenders

Outfielders

In the section of the book dealing with HOF players, standards were developed to be used when appraising the abilities of HOF aspirants. Analytical tools are in place. It's time to turn attention to active players. The objective is to locate "Pretenders" — those demonstrating skill levels at least equal to a HOF player who, while active, played the same position.

Methodology related to active players will use the same quality determinants, in the same way, as those used during the HOF analysis. Active players surviving the screening criteria will be listed and classified. Those with PABs below minimum HOF standards will be eliminated. Records of remaining men will be laid out in detail and analyzed. If they survive analysis, they will be designated "Pretenders." At the completion of the process, a classification listing of surviving Pretenders will be set forth.

The active player group will be approached in the same sequence used for HOF players. Only those who have played in 800 games or more through 1986 are considered. Although the statistical categories are the same, total runs batted in, runs and home runs are given in absolute numbers instead of the percent per at bat given in these categories for HOF members. Outfielders are analyzed first.

The abbreviation SD on the pretenders charts means "standard deviation," a statistical device used by this author to establish classification and normal performance ranges.

In typical numerical distributions like those in the charts, about two-thirds of all samples (for example, at bats) are within one standard deviation of the average of all samples. For example, a hitter with a career BA of .300 and a SD of .020 will usually hit in the .280–.320 range.

$$AVG + 1SD = HI; \ AVG - 1SD = LO.$$

In the language of the book, most of a player's seasons fall within his HI/LO range, his reasonably expected ability level. When his performance falls above this range, he's unusually hot; below it, unusually cold.

	G	AB	H	R	HR	RBI	BA	SA	PAB

Class 1 .360 +
None

Class 2 .315–.359
None

	G	AB	H	R	HR	RBI	BA	SA	PAB
Class 3 .270–.314									
Henderson, R.	1087	4071	1182	759	103	314	.290	.432	.289
Rice	1790	7127	2163	753	351	938	.303	.518	.287
Lynn	1537	5589	1632	665	241	685	.292	.496	.285
Winfield	1964	7287	2083	830	305	929	.286	.479	.283
Jackson, R.	2705	9528	2510	961	548	1111	.263	.493	.275
Murphy, D.B.	1360	5017	1388	547	266	556	.277	.491	.273
Parker	1779	6727	2024	731	247	846	.301	.491	.271
Guerrero	825	2842	865	309	139	322	.304	.514	.271
Class 4 .228–.269									
Kemp	1152	4022	1120	449	130	502	.278	.432	.269
Foster	1977	7023	1925	638	348	891	.274	.480	.267
Baylor	2072	7546	1982	826	315	864	.263	.442	.266
Evans, D.	1933	6661	1785	791	291	658	.268	.470	.261
Smith, L.	909	3148	915	530	41	248	.291	.406	.260
Raines	882	3372	1028	556	48	266	.305	.434	.258
Matthews	1944	6986	1972	839	231	724	.282	.441	.257
Griffey	1678	6126	1839	862	121	586	.300	.435	.256
Dawson	1443	5628	1575	603	225	613	.280	.476	.256
Downing	1586	5201	1382	597	166	568	.266	.413	.256
Thomas	1435	4677	1051	413	268	514	.225	.448	.256
McRae	2066	7186	2081	745	190	898	.290	.454	.255
Cedeno	2006	7310	2087	885	199	777	.285	.443	.255
Walling	903	2133	594	246	41	253	.278	.403	.253
Hendrick	1914	6840	1910	656	259	808	.279	.449	.252
Baines	992	3754	1077	352	140	449	.287	.468	.251
Murphy, D.K.	1131	3828	948	430	145	383	.248	.404	.250
Cruz, Jose	2189	7472	2147	827	153	879	.287	.423	.249
Moseby	974	3558	928	411	102	368	.261	.421	.248
Ward	831	3118	900	352	92	327	.289	.446	.247
Oglivie	1754	5913	1615	549	235	666	.273	.450	.245
Leonard	862	2964	808	298	81	347	.273	.418	.245
Jones	1246	4223	1056	479	139	412	.250	.415	.244
Baker	2039	7117	1981	722	242	771	.278	.432	.244
Roenicke	948	2443	611	220	111	264	.250	.440	.244
Dwyer	1043	2128	543	248	56	212	.255	.394	.242
Lemon	1467	5150	1429	581	166	500	.277	.451	.242
Easler	1053	3400	1000	332	113	378	.294	.461	.242
Henderson, S.	997	3324	933	376	65	349	.281	.415	.238
Cowens	1584	5534	1494	596	108	609	.270	.403	.237
Washington, C.	1529	5488	1524	632	130	535	.278	.421	.236
Mumphrey	1404	4618	1330	559	57	465	.288	.390	.234
Armas	1224	4513	1134	318	224	503	.251	.454	.232
Class 5 .221–									
Grubb	1365	4040	1130	447	97	365	.280	.416	.225
Wilson, W.	1267	4908	1457	745	30	327	.297	.391	.225
Lacy	1436	4291	1240	531	84	346	.289	.411	.224
Landreaux	1149	3919	1062	420	85	371	.271	.404	.224
Maddox	1749	6331	1802	660	117	637	.285	.413	.223
Mazzilli	1243	3758	987	430	84	322	.263	.389	.222

	G	AB	H	R	HR	RBI	BA	SA	PAB
Class 5 .227– (cont.)									
Paciorek	1365	4061	1145	405	83	408	.282	.414	.221
Sample	826	2516	684	325	46	184	.272	.384	.221
Wilson, M.	800	3015	834	411	40	209	.277	.390	.219
Youngblood	1180	3327	890	345	74	308	.268	.399	.219
Puhl	1155	4086	1150	522	57	306	.281	.394	.217
Bonnell	976	3068	833	307	56	299	.272	.389	.216
Beniquez	1377	4338	1193	511	70	351	.275	.377	.215
Herndon	1372	4478	1222	463	94	389	.273	.406	.211
Wohlford	1220	3049	793	328	21	294	.260	.343	.211
Moreno	1382	4992	1257	662	37	349	.252	.343	.210
Gross, G.	1537	3404	993	417	6	281	.292	.360	.207
Collins	1368	4484	1231	580	32	312	.275	.356	.206
Moore	1283	3926	1029	406	35	366	.262	.355	.206
Manning	1458	5134	1323	587	56	389	.258	.342	.201

Of the 61 outfielders, none meet HOF standards for Class 1 and Class 2; eight men meet HOF standards for Class 3; 33 meet the Class 4 test, and 20 have a PAB lower than the lowest rated HOF outfielder, Lloyd Waner.

Of the 20 players who fall into Class 5, several are good hitters but contact skills have not produced a PAB equal to the lowest in the HOF outfield group, nor are any sufficiently outstanding as contact hitters (as Lloyd Waner was, for example) to warrant HOF consideration on the basis of that single skill. All Class 5 players fail to meet minimum eligibility standards of the HOF and are, therefore, excluded from the rest of the study.

There are good active outfielders, but no superstars. As a group, they do not have the contact hitting expertise that was the foundation offensive talent of most HOF members until recent years. To the extent that fair PABs are being developed by modern players, it is the power swing that seems to be disproportionately responsible. *Homerunitis,* alive and well, is a general affliction which, for a few, is paying off in fair PABs; for many, it results in whiffs, double plays, and low PABs.

The motivating question of this book is: Who of the active players, based upon records through 1986, should be elected to the HOF after retirement and, incidentally, how do they rate when contrasted with other pretenders, and with current HOF members? In the broadest sense, the previous schedules answer the question posed. Now we proceed with a more microscopic analysis of claims to HOF recognition.

For visual purposes, each pretender analyzed will be compared with the highest and lowest-rated hall of famer in his position, and with the two hall of famers rated just above and below him.

Rick Henderson
Born 1958
Height 5'10"; weight 195
Throws left, bats right
HOF—Probable

Year	Age	G	AB	H	R	HR	RBI	BA	SA	PAB
1980	22	158	591	179	102	9	44	.303	.399	.262
1981	23	108	423	135	83	6	29	.319	.437	.279
1982	24	149	536	143	109	10	41	.267	.382	.299
1983	25	145	513	150	96	9	39	.292	.421	.281
1984	26	142	502	147	97	16	42	.293	.458	.309
1985	27	143	547	172	122	24	48	.314	.516	.355
1986	28	153	608	160	102	28	46	.263	.469	.289
Total		998	3720	1086	711	102	289	.292	.441	.296
Other*		89	351	96	48	1	25	.274	.336	.211
Career		1087	4071	1182	759	103	314	.290	.432	.289

*Less than 100 games: 1979

Standard Deviation		15	57	15	11	8	6			
Avg.		143	531	155	102	15	41	.292	.441	.296

Normal Performance Range (100 + games)

High		158	588	170	113	22	47	.289	.496	.310
Low		128	475	140	90	7	36	.296	.372	.280

Best Year (over 139 games): 1985

Super Years (PAB .360 +): None

Good Years (PAB .315–.359): 1985

Fair Years (PAB .270–.314): 1981, 1982, 1983, 1984, 1986

Avg.		139	516	147	97	14	39	.285	.434	.292

Other Years (PAB .269 –): 1980

Average Yearly Performance by Age

25 and under		140	516	152	98	9	38	.294	.408	.280
26–30		146	552	160	107	23	45	.289	.481	.317

Now in his late twenties, durability is the remaining question on Rick Henderson's HOF credentials. With eight seasons behind him, the case is in that he has HOF talent. But can he repeat year after year as the greats did?

Speed is his most publicized talent, but Henderson is more than a running machine. He fields his position well, is a sound contact hitter, and shows increasing power as he matures. The holder of the modern major league record for stolen bases in a season, Rick is also the most productive outfielder in the game. Considering the fact that he is usually positioned at the top of the batting order—thus being relatively deprived of RBI opportunties—this is an outstanding achievement.

The 1985 season was Rick's first with the Yankees. A good player looks even better when he plays for a good team. Certainly, Henderson benefitted from the move—as did the Yankees—and his style of consistent, quality performance should result in handsome numbers during his remaining seasons with the high-scoring Bombers.

Henderson's best power year was in 1986 when he hit 28 homers and generated a PAB of .289. His best production record was 1985, with a PAB of .355. This production was only a tad shy of superstar performance.

According to his 100 + game profile, Henderson is a Class 3 outfielder. In eight seasons, he has had no superstar years, one Class 2 year, five fair seasons, one bummer, and one partial year.

Similar to most of the greats, Rick showed his class immediately. In his early twenties, he sustained Class 3 performance levels. For the past two seasons, he has shown Class 2 talent and the capacity for a superstar year, or more, before he quits.

Henderson is a definite pretender. If he sustains his career numbers, he would fit into the HOF outfield corps as follows:

	HR	R	RBI	PAB	BA	SA
Ruth	.091	.179	.181	.451	.347	.708
Waner, P.	.012	.160	.127	.298	.333	.473
Youngs	.009	.166	.120	.295	.322	.441
Henderson	**.025**	**.186**	**.077**	**.289**	**.290**	**.432**
Kaline	.039	.121	.117	.277	.297	.480
Williams, B.	.046	.105	.112	.263	.290	.492
Waner, L.	.004	.151	.073	.228	.316	.394

Call him Henderson, the scorer. Only Earl Combs of the Ruthian Yankees crossed the plate with the frequency of Rick. This is the result of mating the considerable talents of Henderson with a hard-hitting team. If it continues, the speedy outfielder is a cinch for HOF honors.

Some analysts downgrade speed and base stealing ability, pointing out that a statistical correlation between such abilities and production can't be developed. But anyone who has played the game is fully aware of the upsetting influence that a player with Rick's talents can have on a defensive unit, including the pitcher. Measureable or not, many a game is directly or indirectly won by a rabbit on the basepaths.

Jim Rice
Born 1953
Height 6′2″; weight 205
Throws right; bats right
HOF — Probable

Year	Age	G	AB	H	R	HR	RBI	BA	SA	PAB
1975	22	144	564	174	70	22	80	.309	.491	.305
1976	23	153	581	164	50	25	60	.282	.482	.232
1977	24	160	644	206	65	39	75	.320	.593	.278
1978	25	163	677	213	75	46	93	.315	.600	.316
1979	26	158	619	201	78	39	91	.325	.596	.336
1980	27	124	504	148	57	24	62	.294	.504	.284
1981	28	108	451	128	34	17	45	.284	.441	.213
1982	29	145	573	177	62	24	73	.309	.494	.277
1983	30	155	626	191	51	39	87	.305	.550	.283
1984	31	159	657	184	70	28	94	.280	.467	.292
1985	32	140	546	159	58	27	76	.291	.487	.295
1986	33	157	618	200	78	20	90	.324	.490	.304
Total		1766	7060	2145	748	350	926	.304	.520	.287
Other*		24	67	18	5	1	12	.269	.373	.269
Career		1790	7127	2163	753	351	938	.303	.518	.287

*Less than 100 games: 1974

Standard Deviation		16	63	24	13	9	15			
Avg.		147	588	179	62	29	77	.304	.520	.287

Normal Performance Range (100 + games)

High		163	651	203	75	38	92	.312	.584	.314
Low		131	525	154	50	20	63	.294	.440	.252

Best Year (over 139 games): 1979

Super Years (PAB .360 +): None

Good Years (PAB .315–.359): 1978, 1979

Avg.		161	648	207	77	43	92	.319	.598	.326

Fair Years (PAB .270–.314): 1975, 1977, 1980, 1982, 1983, 1984, 1985, 1986

Avg.		148	592	180	64	28	80	.304	.511	.290

Other Years (PAB .269–): 1976, 1981

Avg.		131	516	146	42	21	53	.283	.464	.224

Average Yearly Performance by Age

25 and under		155	617	189	65	33	77	.307	.545	.284
26–30		138	555	169	56	29	72	.305	.523	.282
31–35		152	607	181	69	25	87	.298	.481	.297

Jim Rice was 33 years old in 1986, and the second highest rated active outfielder. With a PAB of .287, Rice would fit into the HOF as a Class 3 player. He has already paid his time dues having completed his thirteenth year in the majors, all with Boston. Jim is a legitimate pretender, probably a surer bet than Henderson.

It says something about modern baseball when the fact is dramatized that the top outfielders in the game today are of Class 3 quality when measured against HOF standards.

In terms of style, Rice is somewhat of a throwback to the old-timers. Although a power hitter of note, he is also a dependable contact hitter. More so than most modern hitters, Jim concentrates on hitting the ball, recognizing that size and good timing will bring him a fair share of home runs.

Jim's best power year was 1978 when, at 25 years of age, he hit 46 round trippers and generated a PAB of .316. But this wasn't his most productive year. This occurred in 1979, when he had 30 home runs and a .336 PAB. This is mid-level Class 2 performance. Rice has had seven .300 + BA years, and five .500 + SA seasons.

According to his 100 + game profile, Rice is a Class 3 outfielder. He hasn't had a superstar year, but did have two Class 2 years in 1978 and 1979. Also, he had eight Class 3 seasons, and two Class 4 years. For the past five straight seasons, his PAB has ascended.

At his present pace, Rice is a more effective producer than some HOF outfielders. If elected, his HOF position would be as follows:

	HR	R	RBI	PAB	BA	SA
Ruth	.091	.179	.181	.451	.347	.708
Waner, P.	.012	.160	.127	.298	.333	.473
Youngs	.009	.166	.120	.295	.322	.441
Rice	**.049**	**.106**	**.132**	**.287**	**.303**	**.518**
Kaline	.039	.121	.117	.277	.297	.480
Williams, B.	.046	.115	.102	.263	.290	.492
Waner, L.	.004	.151	.073	.228	.316	.394

Rice squeezes easily into Class 3. More powerful than Paul Waner or Youngs, he is not their equal as a contact hitter. Power plus good contact ability put him ahead of Kaline and Williams.

Rice is a good hitter, and a powerful one. The proposition is advanced that his PAB should be higher than it is because of his batting average. Ruth, Youngs, and the Waners had a 50 percent relationship between runs scored per at bat and BA. Kaline and Clemente had a 40 percent relationship, which is fairly typical. Rice runs 35 percent. The man is a good athlete. He runs well and smart. But he doesn't score— the weak element in his PAB. This is the breaks, and a comment on teammate RBI ability. Under more normal circumstances, Jim would have a PAB of about .302.

Fred Lynn

Born 1952
Height 6'1"; weight 190
Throws left, bats left
HOF — Probable

Year	Age	G	AB	H	R	HR	RBI	BA	SA	PAB
1975	23	145	528	175	82	21	84	.331	.566	.354
1976	24	132	507	159	66	10	55	.314	.467	.258
1977	25	129	497	129	63	18	58	.260	.447	.280
1978	26	150	541	161	53	22	60	.298	.492	.250
1979	27	147	531	177	77	39	83	.333	.637	.375
1980	28	110	415	125	55	12	49	.301	.480	.280
1982	30	138	472	141	68	21	65	.299	.517	.326
1983	31	117	437	119	34	22	52	.272	.483	.247
1984	32	142	517	140	61	23	56	.271	.474	.271
1985	33	124	448	118	36	23	45	.263	.449	.232
1986	34	112	397	114	44	23	44	.287	.499	.280
Total		1446	5290	1558	639	234	651	.295	.503	.288
Other*		91	299	74	26	7	34	.247	.371	.224
Career		1537	5589	1632	665	241	685	.292	.496	.285

*Less than 100 games: 1974, 1981

Standard Deviation		14	48	22	15	7	13			
Avg.		131	481	142	58	21	59	.295	.503	.288

Normal Performance Range (100 + games)

High		145	529	164	73	28	72	.310	.586	.328
Low		118	433	120	43	14	46	.276	.401	.239

Best Year (over 139 games): 1979

Super Years (PAB .360 +): 1979

Good Years (PAB .315–.359): 1975, 1982

Avg.		142	500	158	75	21	75	.316	.543	.341

Fair Years (PAB .270–.314): 1977, 1980, 1984, 1986

Avg.		123	457	127	56	19	52	.278	.473	.277

Other Years (PAB .269 –): 1976, 1978, 1983, 1985

Avg.		131	483	139	47	19	53	.288	.473	.247

Average Yearly Performance by Age

25 and under		135	511	154	70	16	66	.302	.495	.298
26–30		136	490	151	63	24	64	.308	.534	.308
31–35		124	450	123	44	23	49	.273	.475	.257

Fred Lynn, now in his mid-thirties, has completed the ten-year internship. With a PAB of .285, he is the third best producer of the active outfielders. Matched with Murray and Ripken in Baltimore in 1985, much was expected of him — but the good things didn't materialize. He had his poorest production season. In the last seven years Lynn, always injury prone, has only once played over 140 games. Either the fences are too hard, or his body is too soft. Fred may be the early burn-out type. He's a legitimate pretender, but may play himself out of contention before he quits.

Sweet-swinging Fred is one of the most graceful athletes ever to appear on the green, at the plate or in the field. His problem has been durability. In an average full season, a manager is fortunate to get 140 games out of the man.

Lynn has decent power, he's a reliable clutch hitter, and has had great contact hitting years. But his quality of performance can vary widely from year to year. Consistency is not a characteristic of the outfielder.

Lynn's best power year was 1979 with Boston. He hit 39 round trippers and generated a PAB of .375 — his best. This is superstar stuff. But he doesn't sustain it. In only three seasons has Lynn's PAB been .300 + .

According to his 100 + game profile, Lynn is a Class 3 outfielder. He has had one superstar year and two Class 2 seasons — a total of three years of better than average play as measured by HOF standards. For four more seasons he played Class 3 ball, and had four disappointing Class 4 years.

Lynn's career looks more stable when examined in five-year blocks. In his early twenties, he was a Class 3 player. He improved a bit in his late twenties, but not enough to change his Class 3 grade. In his thirties, he has slipped to Class 4. Will he come back — or fade out? Who knows?

If elected to the HOF, Fred would squeeze between Youngs and Kaline. Below, his career stats are compared with those of the highest and lowest rated HOF outfielders, as well as the two HOF outfielders who would rank just ahead of and just behind him.

	HR	R	RBI	PAB	BA	SA
Ruth	.091	.179	.181	.451	.347	.708
Waner, P.	.012	.160	.127	.298	.333	.473
Youngs	.009	.166	.120	.295	.322	.441
Lynn	**.043**	**.119**	**.123**	**.285**	**.292**	**.496**
Kaline	.039	.121	.117	.277	.297	.480
Williams, B.	.046	.105	.112	.263	.290	.492
Waner, L.	.004	.151	.073	.228	.316	.394

Lynn fits nicely into the HOF outfield roster. His style as a producer is certainly dissimilar to that of Paul Waner and Youngs, but he approaches the same marks with his own combination of talents. In many ways, Lynn is the mirror image of Kaline.

Dave Winfield

Born 1951
Height 6'6"; weight 220
Throws right, bats right
HOF—Possible

Year	Age	G	AB	H	R	HR	RBI	BA	SA	PAB
1974	23	145	498	132	37	20	55	.265	.438	.225
1975	24	143	509	136	59	15	61	.267	.403	.265
1976	25	137	492	139	68	13	56	.283	.431	.278
1977	26	157	615	169	79	25	67	.275	.467	.278
1978	27	158	587	181	64	24	73	.308	.499	.274
1979	28	159	597	184	63	34	84	.308	.558	.303
1980	29	162	558	154	69	20	67	.276	.450	.280
1981	30	105	388	114	39	13	55	.294	.464	.276
1982	31	140	539	151	47	37	69	.280	.560	.284
1983	32	152	598	169	67	32	84	.283	.513	.306
1984	33	141	567	193	87	19	81	.340	.515	.330
1985	34	155	633	174	79	26	88	.275	.471	.305
1986	35	154	565	148	66	24	80	.262	.462	.301
Total		1908	7146	2044	824	302	920	.286	.481	.286
Other*		56	141	39	6	3	9	.277	.383	.128
Career		1964	7287	2083	830	305	929	.286	.479	.283

*Less than 100 games: 1973

Standard Deviation		14	63	22	14	7	11			
Avg.		147	550	157	63	23	71	.286	.481	.286

Normal Performance Range (100 + games)

High		161	613	180	78	31	82	.293	.533	.311
Low		132	487	135	49	16	59	.277	.417	.255

Best Year (over 139 games): 1984

Super Years (PAB .360 +): None

Good Years (PAB .315–.359): 1984

Fair Years (PAB .270–.314): 1976, 1977, 1978, 1979, 1980, 1981, 1982, 1983, 1985, 1986

Avg.		148	557	158	64	25	72	.284	.489	.289

Other Years (PAB .269 –): 1974, 1975

Avg.		144	504	134	48	18	58	.266	.420	.245

Average Yearly Performance by Age

25 and under		142	500	136	55	16	57	.272	.424	.256
26–30		148	549	160	63	23	69	.292	.490	.283
31–35		148	580	167	69	28	80	.288	.503	.305

Dave Winfield of the Yankees is the number four active outfielder. Along with his major competitors, he carries the superstar label. He isn't one—but might have been had his case of *homerunitis* been less severe over the years. Winfield may be the most generally gifted player in the majors today. Dave had a great 1984 season, hitting .340 and producing a PAB of .330, unquestionably HOF territory. He did this by concentrating more on pure hitting and less on home run–hitting headlines. Over the past two years, Dave tailed off to PABs of .305 and .301, leaving the suspicion that we have seen his best.

Winfield has HOF talent and the time to cement his qualifications. His head, not his ability, will be the determinant—he will probably make it. But if he swings from the heels every time he's at the plate, he may not. It's up to him. Mark him a legitimate pretender.

Winfield has 14 seasons behind him, and he played in 100 + games in all but one. He's good for 147 games a year, which is typical of players of today. He's a balanced player—a solid clutch hitter.

As big as a moose, Winfield is nonetheless not primarily a power hitter. In the home run department, for example, he's roughly on a par with Lynn, but less formidable than Rice. His best power year was 1982 when, at 31 years of age, he hit 37 out of the park and generated a PAB of .284. But this was not his best production year, which occcurred in 1984—19 home runs, BA .340, PAB .330—solid Class 2 performance.

According to his 100 + game profile, Winfield is a Class 3 outfielder. He has never had a superstar year in HOF terms. He has had one Class 2, ten Class 3, and two Class 4 seasons.

Like good wine, Dave has improved with age. In his early twenties, he was a Class 4 outfielder. In his late twenties, he moved into Class 3. In his early thirties, he's in his prime. A huge man, he carried proportionate weight well, and is surprisingly fast and agile for one his size.

If elected to the HOF, Dave would squeeze into the same section of the HOF roster as Lynn and Rice, as follows:

	HR	R	RBI	PAB	BA	SA
Ruth	.091	.179	.181	.451	.347	.708
Waner, P.	.012	.160	.127	.298	.333	.473
Youngs	.009	.166	.120	.295	.322	.441
Winfield	**.042**	**.114**	**.127**	**.283**	**.286**	**.479**
Kaline	.039	.121	.117	.277	.297	.480
Williams, B.	.046	.105	.112	.263	.290	.492
Waner, L.	.004	.151	.073	.228	.316	.394

Winfield is not (but maybe could be) as good a contact hitter as his nearest competitors above, but overcomes this with power and clutch hitting skills. For the last four seasons, he has produced at better than the Waner/Youngs level.

The race for top dog position over the next few seasons will likely be among Henderson, Lynn, Rice, Winfield, and Dale Murphy (see p. 57). Experience runs with the middle three men—youth with the first and the last one. How do they compare for the past two seasons?

Average — 1985, 1986

	AB	R	HR	RBI	PAB	BA	SA
Henderson	1155	.194	.045	.081	.320	.289	.493
Rice	1164	.117	.040	.143	.300	.308	.489
Lynn	845	.095	.054	.105	.254	.275	.474
Winfield	1198	.121	.042	.140	.303	.269	.467
Murphy, D.	1230	.115	.054	.104	.273	.283	.508

It's Henderson, going away. Rice needs big years to stay ahead of the competition. Lynn is sinking fast—at a "cut-the-mustard" stage of his career. Winfield is going good—signs of age are appearing. Murphy had a relatively poor year in 1986.

Henderson looks like the outfielder of the future—and of the "now."

Reggie Jackson
Born 1946
Height 6'0"; weight 206
Throws left, bats left
HOF—Probable

Year	Age	G	AB	H	R	HR	RBI	BA	SA	PAB
1968	22	154	553	138	52	29	45	.250	.452	.228
1969	23	152	549	151	76	47	71	.275	.608	.353
1970	24	149	426	101	34	23	43	.237	.458	.235
1971	25	150	567	157	55	32	48	.277	.508	.238
1972	26	135	499	132	47	25	50	.265	.473	.244
1973	27	151	539	158	67	32	85	.293	.531	.341
1974	28	148	506	146	61	29	64	.289	.514	.304
1975	29	157	593	150	55	36	68	.253	.511	.268
1976	30	134	498	138	57	27	64	.277	.502	.297
1977	31	146	525	150	61	32	78	.286	.550	.326
1978	32	139	511	140	55	27	70	.274	.477	.297
1979	33	131	465	138	49	29	60	.297	.544	.297
1980	34	143	514	154	53	41	70	.300	.597	.319
1982	36	153	530	146	53	39	62	.275	.532	.291
1983	37	116	397	77	29	14	35	.194	.340	.196
1984	38	143	525	117	42	25	56	.223	.406	.234
1985	39	143	460	116	37	27	58	.252	.487	.265
1986	40	132	419	101	47	18	40	.241	.408	.251

	G	AB	H	R	HR	RBI	BA	SA	PAB
Total	2576	9076	2410	930	532	1067	.266	.498	.279
Other*	129	452	100	31	16	44	.221	.396	.201
Career	2705	9528	2510	961	548	1111	.263	.493	.275

*Less than 100 games: 1967, 1981

Standard Deviation

	G	AB	H	R	HR	RBI	BA	SA	PAB
	10	51	22	11	8	13			
Avg.	143	504	134	52	30	59	.266	.498	.279

Normal Performance Range (100 + games)

	G	AB	H	R	HR	RBI	BA	SA	PAB
High	153	556	156	63	37	73	.281	.570	.311
Low	133	453	112	40	22	46	.247	.410	.239

Best Year (over 139 games): 1969

Super Years (PAB .360 +): None

Good Years (PAB .315–.359): 1969, 1973, 1977, 1980

	G	AB	H	R	HR	RBI	BA	SA	PAB
Avg.	148	532	153	64	38	76	.288	.572	.335

Fair Years (PAB .270–.314): 1974, 1976, 1978, 1979, 1982

	G	AB	H	R	HR	RBI	BA	SA	PAB
Avg.	141	502	142	55	30	64	.282	.514	.297

Other Years (PAB .269 –): 1968, 1970, 1971, 1972, 1975, 1983, 1984, 1985, 1986

	G	AB	H	R	HR	RBI	BA	SA	PAB
Avg.	142	493	121	44	25	49	.245	.454	.241

Average Yearly Performance by Age

	G	AB	H	R	HR	RBI	BA	SA	PAB
25 and under	151	524	137	54	33	52	.261	.509	.265
26–30	145	527	145	57	30	66	.275	.507	.291
31–35	140	504	146	55	32	70	.289	.542	.310
36 +	137	466	111	42	25	50	.239	.440	.250

Reggie Jackson isn't the best player in the majors, but he's the best known. As a ballplayer, he's good. As a public relations man promoting projects related to himself, he's a superstar. He played for Charlie Finlay's A's, Baltimore, the Yankees, and the Angels.

But it isn't fair to athlete Jackson to suggest that his reputation is based only on puff developed by promoter Reggie Jackson. If he didn't have a product to sell, his promotion would fail. And Reggie had a product to sell, not as good as he would like you to believe, but as good as it had to be to get the attention of the HOF. He is a legitimate pretender.

With a PAB of .275, Jackson is the fifth most productive outfielder in the game. He's a homerun hitter of near superstar proportions, topped only by Schmidt among active players, and ranked above the likes of DiMaggio, Wilson, Ott, and Mize among HOF players. By way of contrast, his BA of .263 looks pretty sick when compared with HOF members. Only Killebrew and Aparicio were poorer contact hitters.

Newspaper reports suggest Jackson is proudest of the fact that he has hit more than 500 home runs, and believes this is his ticket to the HOF. Now the 500 home run situation is the result of talent plus durability, not talent alone. But, given the proclivity of selection committees to put too much weight on how a hitter gets runs rather than on overall productivity, it's probable that Jackson has calculated odds correctly and that he will not only be selected, but in near record time (note the rapid selection of McCovey in 1986).

Reggie, on a seasonal or career basis, is a durable man. In 1986, he completed his twentieth season. He has averaged 143 games a year, and played 132 games in 1986 — not bad for a 40-year-old.

In 18 of his 20 seasons, Jackson played in 100 + games. His 100 + game profile shows him to be Class 3 outfielder capable of broad variations in performance. He has never had a superstar year, but did have four Class 2 seasons, five Class 3, and nine Class 4 years.

Kiner was the first "home run or nothing" type hitter elected to the HOF. Reggie is of the same breed. His best power season was 1969 when, at 23 years of age, he hit 47 round trippers and developed a PAB of .353. This was also his best production year — he has had five seasons with a PAB of .300 + . Because of comparable styles, it's interesting to compare the career stats of Reggie with those of his HOF soulmate, Ralph Kiner.

	AB	R	HR	RBI	PAB	BA	SA
Kiner	5,205	.116	.071	.124	.311	.279	.548
Jackson	9,528	.100	.058	.117	.275	.263	.493

Jackson has one thing on Kiner — durability, by a wide margin (Kiner spent three years in the service). But in all of the offensive elements of the PAB, Kiner was superior to Reggie, especially in Reggie's favorite department — power.

Reggie has developed a large reputation as a situation hitter. It is deserved. Ability and luck have combined at various times in his career: He came up with the big hit when the biggest crowds were watching. Out of this knack for the sensational evolved a reputation as a clutch hitter. This is not deserved. Below are formulations used in this book to locate clutch hitting characteristics, applied to the top active outfielders and one of the best clutch hitters in baseball history, Al Simmons:

	Career		
	SA	RBI	%
Henderson	.432	.077	18
Rice	.518	.132	25
Lynn	.496	.123	25
Winfield	.479	.127	27
Jackson	.493	.117	24
Murphy, D.	.491	.111	23
Simmons	.535	.173	32

To get a feel for the relative meaning of the above numbers, keep in mind that if the same test were applied to Ruth, the answer would be 26 percent. Compared with the great RBI hunter, Simmons, it is quickly apparent that none of the top active outfielders rates as an RBI terror, and Jackson rates with the weakest of them. (It should be noted that Rick Henderson, a leadoff man, doesn't get the RBI chances of the others.)

Like Winfield, Reggie improved with age—up to a point. In his early twenties, he was a Class 4 outfielder despite good long ball production. In his late twenties, Jackson's contact hitting improved and his power production was normal. This combination moved him up to Class 3. The trend of improvement continued into his early thirties and moved him closer to the top of the Class 3 range. Now in his forties, Reggie has seen his best days and is a Class 4 performer sliding toward Class 5.

If elected to the HOF, Jackson would fit between Kaline and B. Williams, as follows:

	HR	R	RBI	PAB	BA	SA
Ruth	.091	.179	.181	.451	.347	.708
Youngs	.009	.166	.120	.295	.322	.441
Kaline	.039	.121	.117	.277	.297	.480
Jackson	**.058**	**.100**	**.117**	**.275**	**.263**	**.493**
Williams, B.	.046	.105	.112	.263	.290	.492
Clemente	.025	.124	.113	.262	.317	.475
Waner, L.	.004	.151	.073	.228	.316	.394

Jackson's last good year was 1982 (PAB .291). In the last four seasons, he has produced an average PAB of .237—well below his career average, and close to the lowest PAB in the HOF. Obviously, skills have leaked away.

It is entirely possible that Reggie's career record will deteriorate to

Class 4 quality before he quits. Will this affect his HOF chances? Probably not — because of the home run fetish of selection committees. But it should, at least, affect the timing.

Any true fan must suspect the quality of a game that continues to find room for athletes who are obviously all done — that continues to pay astronomical wages to over-the-hill jocks.

To hit the long ball and, at the same time, maintain an impressive BA is the toughest trick in sports, according to the old master, Ted Williams. Below is a schedule of the ten best power years of Ted and Reggie. Silently, it reveals the difference between the slugger of circa 1986 and a superstar.

	Williams			*Jackson*	
YR	BA	HR/PAB	YR	BA	HR/PAB
1941	.406	.081	1969	.275	.086
1942	.356	.069	1971	.277	.056
1946	.342	.074	1973	.293	.059
1947	.343	.061	1974	.289	.057
1949	.343	.076	1975	.253	.061
1950	.317	.084	1977	.286	.061
1954	.345	.075	1979	.297	.062
1955	.356	.088	1980	.300	.080
1957	.388	.067	1982	.275	.074
1960	.316	.094	1985	.252	.059

The label "superstar" should be used sparingly.

Dale Murphy

Born 1956
Height 6'5"; weight 215
Throws right, bats right
HOF — Possible

Year	Age	G	AB	H	R	HR	RBI	BA	SA	PAB
1978	22	151	530	120	43	23	56	.226	.394	.230
1979	23	104	384	106	32	21	36	.276	.469	.232
1980	24	156	569	160	65	33	56	.281	.510	.271
1981	25	104	369	91	30	13	37	.247	.390	.217
1982	26	162	598	168	77	36	73	.281	.507	.311
1983	27	162	589	178	95	36	85	.302	.540	.367
1984	28	162	607	176	58	36	64	.290	.547	.260
1985	29	162	616	185	81	37	74	.300	.539	.312
1986	30	160	614	163	60	29	54	.265	.477	.233
Total		1323	4876	1347	541	264	535	.276	.492	.275

	G	AB	H	R	HR	RBI	BA	SA	PAB
Other*	37	141	41	6	2	21	.291	.447	.206
Career	1360	5017	1388	547	266	556	.277	.491	.273

*Less than 100 games: 1976, 1977

Standard Deviation	23	92	33	21	8	16			
Avg.	147	542	150	60	29	59	.276	.492	.275

Normal Performance Range (100 + games)

	G	AB	H	R	HR	RBI	BA	SA	PAB
High	170	634	182	81	37	75	.288	.536	.305
Low	124	450	117	39	21	44	.260	.432	.232

Best Year (over 139 games): 1983

Super Years (PAB .360 +): 1983

Good Years (PAB .315–.359): None

Fair Years (PAB .270–.314): 1980, 1982, 1985

Avg.	160	594	171	74	35	68	.288	.519	.298

Other Years (PAB .269 –): 1978, 1979, 1981, 1984, 1986

Avg.	136	501	131	45	24	49	.262	.462	.236

Average Yearly Performance by Age

25 and under	129	463	119	43	23	46	.258	.444	.240
26–30	162	605	174	74	35	70	.288	.522	.296

Compared to HOF talent, Atlanta's Dale Murphy is a good player. Compared to his peers, and considering his age, he may be the most valuable investment in outfield talent on the field today. He is, without question, a pretender.

A power hitter with home runs per at bat of .060 + signifies a superstar in that department is afoot. Murphy approaches such talent. Concerning his HOF future, two questions remain: the ability to balance power hitting abilities with contact hitting requirements so that adequate PABs are developed; the strength and dedication to endure as a quality producer for the number of years necessary to make him competitive on the durability front.

From a home run standpoint, Murphy was in a 36 per year rut (three straight seasons) until 1985 when he finally got the extra one and posted 37 for the year—his best power season. But 1985 wasn't his best production year; this occurred in the 1983 season. Then 27 years old, Dale combined power hitting with his highest BA to date (.302), which enabled him to improve runs scored and RBI performance enough to lift his PAB for the year to .367—a superstar year—one of the few turned in by active outfielders. Murphy appears destined to move up in the classification structure. Only 30 years old, and plagued by none of the bad habits which ruin some baseball talents, Dale should have many good years ahead. The only cloud in his sky is the 1986 season which, for him, was a poor one.

Murphy completed his eleventh season in the majors in 1986. In nine of them, he played in 100 + games, averaging 147 games a year (for four consecutive years, Murphy played the full schedule).

Dale came up as a catcher, but some wise man in the Atlanta organization correctly appraised offensive potential and moved him to the outfield — a maneuver that could add several productive years to Dale's career and, perhaps, 20 + games per season.

In his first four years, there was good reason to suspect that Murphy was going to become another of the "home run or nothing" breed of hitter so prevalent today. His BA during those four early seasons was .263. But as the years passed, such fears were dissipated in the face of inclinings BAs. With improved contact hitting balanced with continuing power, Dale has shown himself capable of high-level production marks in each of the three elements of PAB: scoring, home runs, and RBIs. Before he's through, it's quite possible Dale Murphy will develop career performance numbers better than any of his current competitors. Rick Henderson will be his strongest competition.

According to his 100 + profile, Dale Murphy is a Class 3 outfielder. His career has been short, and the profile should improve as more current performance numbers begin to statistically overwhelm his slower beginning. He has had one superstar season, no Class 2 years, three Class 3 years, and five Class 4 seasons. To fatten up his numbers, Murphy needs more help from teammates and must boost his RBI numbers.

In his early twenties, Dale was a Class 4 talent. In his late twenties, he has been a high level Class 3 producer. Will he improve or deteriorate in his thirties? Time will tell.

Another way of demonstrating the style and potential of Murphy is to compare his best season to date with the best seasons turned in by other high rated active outfielders, as follows:

	Year	G	R	HR	RBI	PAB	BA	SA
Henderson	1985	143	.223	.044	.088	.355	.314	.516
Lynn	1979	147	.145	.073	.157	.375	.333	.637
Rice	1979	158	.126	.063	.147	.336	.323	.596
Winfield	1984	141	.153	.034	.143	.330	.340	.515
Jackson	1968	152	.138	.086	.129	.353	.275	.608
Murphy	1983	162	.161	.061	.145	.367	.302	.540

Of the above group, only Lynn and Murphy had superstar years. Coordinating power and contact hitting is the only formula for getting there. Henderson came close, and may yet do it—Jackson came close, but never hit consistently enough to make it. Rice is well balanced, but can't seem to get over the hump. When Winfield hits for average, power output drops—when he hits for power, BA drops. Murphy can do both. How often? Time will tell.

Dave Parker

Born 1951
Height 6'5"; weight 230
Throws right, bats left
HOF—Possible

Year	Age	G	AB	H	R	HR	RBI	BA	SA	PAB
1975	24	148	558	172	50	25	76	.308	.541	.271
1976	25	138	537	168	69	13	77	.313	.475	.296
1977	26	159	637	215	86	21	67	.338	.531	.273
1978	27	148	581	194	72	30	87	.334	.585	.325
1979	28	158	622	193	84	25	69	.310	.526	.286
1980	29	139	518	153	54	17	62	.295	.458	.257
1983	32	144	552	154	56	12	57	.279	.411	.226
1984	33	156	607	173	57	16	78	.285	.410	.249
1985	34	160	635	198	54	34	91	.312	.551	.282
1986	35	162	637	174	58	31	85	.273	.477	.273
Total		1512	5884	1794	640	224	749	.305	.498	.274
Other*		267	843	230	91	23	97	.273	.440	.250
Career		1779	6727	2024	731	247	846	.301	.491	.271

*Less than 100 games: 1973, 1974, 1981, 1982

Standard Deviation		8	43	19	12	7	11			
Avg.		151	588	179	64	22	75	.305	.498	.274

Normal Performance Range (100 + games)

High		160	631	198	76	30	85	.314	.568	.303
Low		143	546	160	52	15	64	.294	.417	.240

Best Year (over 139 games): 1978

Super Years (PAB .360 +): None

Good Years (PAB .315–.359): 1978

Fair Years (PAB .270–.314): 1975, 1976, 1977, 1979, 1985, 1986

Avg.		154	604	187	67	25	78	.309	.517	.280

Other Years (PAB .269 –): 1980, 1983, 1984

Avg.		146	559	160	56	15	66	.286	.425	.244

	G	AB	H	R	HR	RBI	BA	SA	PAB
Average Yearly Performance by Age									
25 and under	143	548	170	60	19	77	.311	.509	.283
26–30	151	590	189	74	23	71	.320	.527	.286
31–35	156	608	175	56	23	78	.288	.465	.259

Dave Parker has had 14 major league seasons. In ten of them, he played in 100 + games, averaging 151 per season. A few years ago, he was rated as one of the best outfielders in the business. But, in an injury wracked career—not entirely unrelated to personal habits—his performance has been choppy. In 1984, after being dropped by Pittsburgh, he had a pretty good year with Cincinnati, and showed even stronger stats in the past two seasons. With Pete Rose at the helm, it's sure that Parker will play hard—or not at all. He is a pretender with lots of "ifs" that the future will define.

Parker's 100 + game profile shows him to be a low level Class 3 outfielder comparable in ability to players just analyzed. He has had no superstar seasons, one Class 2 year, six Class 3 seasons and three Class 4 years.

Dave is a huge man, but not primarily a power hitter. His best power year was 1985 when, at 34 years of age, he hit 34 round trippers, combining this with a BA of .312 and a PAB of .282. But his best production year was 1978 when, at 27, he clocked 30, had a BA of .334, and a PAB of .325—his only .300 + PAB season. In ten full seasons, Dave has produced a BA of .300 + six times—.330 + in two of them.

After his big year in 1978, Parker lost the power stroke and his BA slipped as well, but in 1985, he showed signs of regaining both. Now in his mid-thirties, he still sits in Class 3—where he probably belongs. In his early and late twenties, Dave was a Class 3 producer. In his early thirties, he played Class 4 ball.

What is the fundamental difference between the great player of today and the greats of the HOF? In 1979, Lynn played at DiMaggio levels—but Joe did it 13 times (service credits allowed). In 1979, Rice played at Averill levels—but Earl did it seven times. In 1984, Winfield played at Goslin levels—but Goose did it nine times. In 1968, Jackson played at Wilson levels—but Hack did it six times. In 1983, Dave Murphy played at DiMaggio levels. In 1978, Parker played at Mantle levels. But only for a year. The greats did it year after year.

The greats of today rival accomplishments of the best in history—for a season. They are better than some of the greats of history—for a season. But the extraordinary year for the modern great was an ordinary one for greats of the past. Once they hit their stride, players of old continued high production until age finally ate away at skills.

What's the difference?
Repeatability!

Pedro Guerrero
Born 1956
Height 6'0"; weight 195
Throws right, bats right
HOF—Doubtful

Year	Age	G	AB	H	R	HR	RBI	BA	SA	PAB
1982	26	150	575	175	55	32	68	.304	.536	.270
1983	27	160	584	174	55	32	71	.298	.531	.271
1984	28	144	535	162	69	16	56	.303	.462	.264
1985	29	137	487	156	66	33	54	.320	.577	.314
Total		591	2181	667	245	113	249	.306	.525	.278
Other*		234	661	198	64	26	73	.300	.477	.247
Career		825	2842	865	309	139	322	.304	.514	.271

*Less than 100 games: 1978, 1979, 1980, 1981, 1986

Standard Deviation	8	38	8	6	7	7			
Avg.	148	545	167	61	28	62	.306	.525	.278

Normal Performance Range (100 + games)

High	156	584	175	68	35	70	.300	.565	.296
Low	139	507	159	55	21	55	.313	.479	.258

Best Year (over 139 games): 1983

Super Years (PAB .360 +): None

Good Years (PAB .315–.359): None

Fair Years (PAB .270–.314): 1982, 1983, 1985

Avg.	149	549	168	59	32	64	.307	.546	.283

Other Years (PAB .269 –): 1984

Average Yearly Performance by Age

25 and under	0	0	0	0	0	0	0	0	0
26–30	148	545	167	61	28	62	.306	.525	.278

A few years ago, nobody ever heard of Pedro Guerrero. Now, Tom LaSorda predicts a season to be good or bad depending on the health and availability of the talented Dominican.

Guerrero is a pretender with a durability problem that has been compounded by leg injuries. Now 31 years old, it is doubtful that he will play enough over his remaining years to draw HOF attention.

Pedro entered professional baseball at the tender age of 17. Functioning as an infielder/first baseman, he quickly demonstrated batting skill and power, but didn't get his first look at a big league uniform until 1978, when he was 22 years old. Still hitting like hell, he was back in the minors during the next season until the last few weeks, during which he had another cup of coffee with the Dodgers, and was finally in the bigs to stay.

Over the next two years, Pedro did everything but pitch and catch as he filled a utility role for LaSorda. In 1982, now 26 years old, the weak fielding Guerrero broke into the starting lineup and has become a fixture. In the 1986 season, a leg injury limited Pedro to a handful of games.

Pedro's best power year was 1985. He hit 33 homers and combined them with a BA of .320. This was also his best production year with the club—PAB .314.

According to his 100+ game profile, Guerrero is a Class 3 outfielder with but four relatively full seasons behind him—three in Class 3; one Class 4 year.

Guerrero is treated as an outfielder in this analysis. Actually, he has been a man without a permanent position for most of his career. This won't help him as a HOF candidate since it draws harsh attention to his questionable defensive skills. Adding this to his weak durability characteristics, Pedro is a very weak pretender with only a marginal chance at HOF recognition.

With the analysis of Pedro Guerrero, the detailed review of top outfielders in the game with 800+ games experience is finished. Readily conceding the talent of these men, and the fact that most have a good shot at HOF honors, nevertheless the dominant thrust of the performance data is discouraging. Except for quick flashes of general brilliance—as with Lynn and Murphy—there is no sign of genius, no hint that the sport has another genuine superstar in the wings.

Williams was the last. Will there ever be another?

There are 33 active outfielders in Class 4, the marginal HOF classification. Few deserve detailed examination. Except for the .300 hitters (Raines, Griffey), the review of them will be done in a briefer format.

Tim Raines
Born 1959
Height 5'8"; weight 170
Throws right, bats both
HOF—Possible

Year	Age	G	AB	H	R	HR	RBI	BA	SA	PAB
1982	23	156	647	179	86	4	39	.277	.369	.199
1983	24	156	615	183	122	11	60	.298	.429	.314

Year	Age	G	AB	H	R	HR	RBI	BA	SA	PAB
1984	25	160	622	192	98	8	52	.309	.437	.254
1985	26	150	575	184	104	11	30	.320	.475	.252
1986	27	151	580	194	82	9	53	.334	.476	.248
Total		773	3039	932	492	43	234	.307	.436	.253
Other*		109	333	96	64	5	32	.288	.414	.303
Career		882	3372	1028	556	48	266	.305	.434	.258

*Less than 100 games: 1979, 1980, 1981

Standard Deviation		4	27	6	14	3	11			
Avg.		155	608	186	98	9	47	.307	.436	.253

Normal Performance Range (100 + games)

High		158	635	192	113	11	58	.303	.457	.286
Low		151	581	181	84	6	36	.311	.413	.217

Best Year (over 139 games): 1983

Super Years (PAB .360 +): None

Good Years (PAB .315–.359): None

Fair Years (PAB .270–.314): 1983

Other Years (PAB .228–.269): 1982, 1984, 1985, 1986

Avg.		154	606	187	93	8	44	.309	.437	.238

Average Yearly Performance by Age

25 and under		157	628	185	102	8	50	.294	.411	.255
26–30		151	578	189	93	10	42	.327	.475	.250

Tim Raines got his first shot at the big leagues in 1979. Over the next two years, he played some second base and outfield for the Montreal club and showed the contact hitting talent that had flashed during his minor league career. In 1982, 23 years old, he cracked the starting lineup. For the past two seasons, he has functioned as a full time outfielder and has shown himself to be one of the best contact hitters in baseball.

In five full seasons, Tim has generated a production record better than that of Lloyd Waner, the lowest rated HOF outfielder, and has maintained a BA in excess of .300 while doing it. To have any chance at eventual HOF honors, Raines must repeat these characteristics while also duplicating the durability record of Waner (7,772 AB).

Except to say that his challenges are not impossible, and that he has made a good start on the long road to the museum, it's too early to come down with a hard verdict on Tim Raines.

Ken Griffey
Born 1950
Height 6'0"; weight 200
Throws left, bats left
HOF — Doubtful

Year	Age	G	AB	H	R	HR	RBI	BA	SA	PAB
1975	25	132	463	141	91	4	42	.305	.402	.296
1976	26	148	562	189	105	6	68	.336	.450	.319
1977	27	154	585	186	105	12	45	.318	.467	.277
1978	28	158	614	177	80	10	53	.288	.417	.233
1980	30	146	544	160	76	13	72	.294	.454	.296
1981	31	101	396	123	63	2	32	.311	.409	.245
1982	32	127	484	134	58	12	42	.277	.407	.231
1983	33	118	458	140	49	11	35	.306	.437	.207
1984	34	120	399	109	37	7	49	.273	.381	.233
1985	35	127	438	120	58	10	59	.274	.425	.290
1986	36	139	490	150	48	21	37	.306	.492	.216
Total		1470	5433	1629	770	108	534	.300	.433	.260
Other*		208	693	210	92	13	52	.303	.447	.227
Career		1678	6126	1839	862	121	586	.300	.435	256

*Less than 100 games: 1973, 1974, 1979

Standard Deviation		16	70	26	22	5	13			
Avg.		134	494	148	70	10	49	.300	.433	.260

Normal Performance Range (100 + games)

High		150	564	174	92	15	61	.308	.486	.298
Low		117	424	122	48	5	36	.288	.363	.209

Best Year (over 139 games): 1976

Super Years (PAB .360 +): None

Good Years (PAB .315–.359): 1976

Fair Years (PAB .270–.314): 1975, 1977, 1980, 1985

Avg.		140	508	152	83	10	55	.299	.439	.289

Other Years (PAB .269 –): 1978, 1981, 1982, 1983, 1984, 1986

Avg.		127	474	139	56	11	41	.293	.408	.227

Average Yearly Performance by Age

25 and under		132	463	141	91	4	42	.305	.402	.296
26–30		152	576	178	92	10	60	.309	.446	.280
31–35		119	435	125	53	8	43	.288	.412	.241
36 +		139	490	150	48	21	37	.306	.492	.216

Ted Williams claims that the most difficult single thing to do in professional sports is to consistently and safely hit a ball thrown by a major league pitcher under competitive conditions. Many agree. Certainly, HOF selection committees do. Rightfully so, they regard a player with a .300 + BA, who has lasted for awhile, with great respect.

If a player with decent career length posts a BA of .300 + , he is almost assured of HOF recognition. If the player also excels at some other highly regarded baseball skill (base running, defense, unusual leadership), HOF selection is almost guaranteed, regardless of PAB.

Class 4 HOF players met these qualifications. Clemente, a superior contact hitter, was also considered a superb defensive right fielder. Brock, a near .300 hitter, was as efficient a base stealer as ever played the game, and also joined the 10,000 + At Bats club, which has only eight members. Lloyd Waner was a more efficient contact hitter than about half of the HOF outfield corps. And Bill Williams, the most recent addition to the roster, was a durable player with commendable power and contact hitting credentials.

Active Class 4 outfielders must match the skill bank of the incumbents of Class 4 in the HOF if they expect to get HOF consideration. Otherwise, the definition of greatness, which should be characteristic of all HOF appointments, becomes cheapened.

Ken Griffey has completed 14 major league seasons, the greatest of which were spent with Sparky Anderson's Cincinnati Reds. Traded to Atlanta in 1986, after more than four career-tarnishing years with the Yankees, Ken has had some fair years but seems to be slipping. The end could be near for the player who turned 36 years old in 1986. Because of his BA, Griffey must be accepted as a pretender—but he's a weak prospect.

According to his 100 + game profile, Griffey is a Class 4 outfielder. He's had no superstar years, one Class 2 year, four Class 3 and six Class 4 seasons.

Griffey isn't a power hitter, averaging about six home runs a season. In 1980, at 30 years of age, he hit 13 homers to set the high mark in that department for his career. When he was 26 years old, he had his best PAB year at .319, a solid Class 2 performance. It's the only .300 + PAB year he ever had. Essentially a contact hitter in the Waner mode, Ken has hit .300 + six times, and has never been far from that mark.

Ken is one of the best active contact hitters. Against major league standards, he isn't regarded as superior in any other aspect of the game. It's doubtful that he'll play as long as any of the HOF Class 4 outfielders. Due to contact hitting ability, and assuming it holds up, Griffey may appear on HOF ballots, but it's doubtful he'll make it. A qualifier against his most outstanding characteristic (BA) is seasonal playing time—Ken has averaged only 134 games a year. This figure essentially reflects how he was used by the Yankees, not his ability or physical condition. It could well be that the move from the Reds (where he was appreciated) to New York (where he wasn't) will cost him his HOF seat.

To treat so skeptically the talents of a fine athlete like Griffey relative to HOF potential may seem to some to be cruel and arbitrary. On the contrary. To be even considered as a pretender to this exclusive club is a high compliment. For, you see, the HOF is not the haven for fine athletes, but for superior athletes. To make the point, below are some comparative statistics dealing with Griffey, the modern contact hitter, with contact hitter Lloyd Waner, the lowest rated HOF outfielder.

	Griffey	*Waner*
100 + game seasons	11	13
BA .350 +	0	2
.340 +	0	2
.330 +	1	5
.320 +	1	6
.310 +	3	8
.300 +	6	9

Kemp, Foster, Baylor, Evans, Smith

The above players have two things in common. They are rated as Class 4 outfielders, and they have PABs between .260 and .270. None are considered to be pretenders because they do not meet the de facto criteria established by the Class 4 HOF outfield corps.

Kemp turned 32 years old in 1986. In only one of the past six seasons has he played a reasonably full schedule. His numbers essentially reflect five good seasons with Detroit. It takes more than five good years to crack the HOF. Kemp is not a pretender.

Foster, 38 years old in 1986, has completed a sometimes brilliant major league career. He has seen 17 years go by. In 1977, at the age of 29, Foster had a season to brag about—52 homers, BA of .320, and a PAB of .359—high level Class 2. 1975 through 1981 was his hot period with the Reds. Then he went to the Mets—age took hold—he never produced more than 28 homers or generated a BA above .269. The talented slugger didn't get going until he was 27 years old. The late start ruined his HOF chances.

Baylor, 37 years old in 1986, functions as a DH, most recently with the Red Sox. With 17 seasons behind him, Don had a BA of .300 + in just one. He's good for 20-30 home runs a year. A valuable journeyman ballplayer, and an asset for any team, he is not HOF material.

Dwight Evans, 35 years old in 1986, is a superb defensive outfielder—perhaps the equal of Clemente in this respect. But Clemente also had a lifetime BA of .317. Evans has a career BA of .268. This is his problem and he has neither the time nor the ability to solve it. Unless selection committees suddenly go bananas over defensive ability in the outfield, Dwight is an unlikely HOF prospect.

Lonnie Smith can hit. Also, he is 32 years old with weak defensive credentials. He will not build a HOF durability record in the years left to him.

Matthews, Dawson, Downing, Thomas, McRae, Cedeno

The above Class 4 outfielders all have PABs of .255–.259. For some, there is small hope — for others, none.

Gary Matthews turned 36 in 1986. Recently, his playing time has been limited, and he will probably soon hang it up. His career BA reasonably reflects his contact hitting ability throughout 14 seasons in the majors. Matthews can give you 10–20 home runs a year. A good player, Gary does not have a HOF record.

Andre Dawson, 32 years old in 1986, has a career BA of .279. He has also been a formidable base stealer, although not in the Brock class in this respect (top season: 39). If he can boost the BA, Dawson would have an outside chance to get HOF attention. Hitting .255 in 1985, however, is not the way to go about it. He may be another of the modern players who fold in their early thirties. Count him out.

Brian Downing, 36 years old in 1986, doesn't have time to build a HOF durability record, nor does he have a HOF production record in other respects. The outfielder is a valuable team member, but not a HOF talent.

Gorman Thomas can hit home runs. That's it! When a player directs 100 percent of his energy to this skill, he must be superb at it to offset other weaknesses. Gorman has averaged 21 homers a year in a 13-season career. He not only should not go to the HOF, it would be a disgrace if, with his .225 BA, he did.

Hal McRae turned 41 years old in 1986 with a career BA of .290. Now functioning mostly as a DH, he has about had it. With over 7,100 at bats, McRae has hit .300 + in six of his 18 years in the big leagues. Since he started to play 100 + games in 1973, McRae had only one bad season at the plate (BA .234). As a contact hitter, he deserves attention. On the other hand, of his 13 relatively full seasons, Hal played less than 130 games eight times. There's no doubt that Hal can hit a ball, but his general activity level as a two-way player leaves much to be desired. He won't make it.

Cesar Cedeno, 35 years old in 1986, has a lifetime BA of .285. These days, he's essentially a part-time player. In his 17-year career, he played 100 + games in 12 seasons, averaging 123 games a year — poor durability. Cedeno faded early and will not make the HOF.

Walling, Hendrick, Baines, Murphy

The above Class 4 outfielders have career PABs of .250–.254.

Dennis Walling, a Houston outfielder, was 32 years old in 1986 with the durability characteristic of a player almost a decade younger. He won't be around long enough to create a HOF record.

George Hendrick, 37 years old in 1986, has a career BA of .279 with over 6,800 at bats in 16 seasons. He's about due to hang them up. Hendrick is a notch or two below HOF quality.

Relatively speaking, Baines is a baby in this group — 28 years old in 1986 with seven seasons under his belt. He hits with good power, and usually generates BAs over .300. Look for this young man to move up in classification over the next few years. He's an interesting prospect, but it's too early to label him a pretender.

Dwayne Murphy, 31 years old in 1986 isn't related to Dale either by blood or — unfortunately for Dwayne — by talent. With nine years and 3,828 at bats chalked up, Murphy has struggled to stay alive in the majors. He has given Oakland a PAB of .250 over the past several seasons. Murphy doesn't figure to get any better. He isn't a pretender.

Cruz, Moseby, Ward, Oglivie, Leonard

The above outfielders have PABs of .245–.249.

Jose Cruz, 39 years old in 1986, carries a career BA of .287. Jose has improved with age. Over the past 11 seasons, his BA was .296. If the slender outfielder can add a few more quality seasons to his 17 years in the majors, he may draw a surprising amount of HOF attention — but he is not a pretender.

Lloyd Moseby is a young outfielder with Toronto. Twenty-seven years old with seven seasons behind him in 1986, Lloyd has not demonstrated HOF talent.

Gary Ward, 33 years old in 1986, didn't get going in the majors until he was 29 years of age. To build the necessary durability characteristics, he'll have to be an amazing physical specimen. Don't bet on him.

Ben Oglivie turned 37 in 1986 with a career BA of .273. His home run stroke disappeared three years previously. He's about done. Ben put a few good seasons together in his day, but that's not enough to get into the HOF. He's another of the home-run-or-bust hitters who too often get the bust instead of the homer.

Jeff Leonard, 31 years old, moved into 800 + game territory during the 1986 season. He has neither the class nor the durability to earn HOF consideration.

Jones, Baker, Roenicke, Dwyer, Lemon, Easler

The above outfielders have PABs of .240–.244.

Ruppert Jones, 31 years old in 1986, played 126 games for California in 1986, with a BA of .229. The year before, he played in 125 games with a BA of .231—no HOF talent here.

Dusty Baker was a well-travelled 37-year-old in 1986. He started when he was 19, and has 19 seasons, over 7,100 at bats, and a career BA of .278 behind him. Dusty played in 100 + games in 13 seasons, hitting .300 + in two of them. He's capable of hitting 20–30 big ones a year. Baker's a good journeyman ballplayer, but not HOF material.

Gary Roenicke, 32 years old in 1986, is a part-time outfielder with Baltimore. He will not draw HOF attention.

Jim Dwyer, 36 years old in the same year, has been a part-time outfielder for most of his career. The HOF ignores part-time players.

Chet Lemon, was 31 years old with 12 major league seasons and a BA of .277 behind him in 1986. In nine years, Chet played in 100 + games. He is a top outfielder. The bat is his problem. Can he hit well enough to meet Class 4 standards? For three seasons, Lemon hit for .300 + , proving that he can, sometimes—but for six seasons, including 1985 and 1986, Chet hit below .300—sometimes well below. Doubt persists. Lemon can't make it on the glove alone. Rate him doubtful.

Mike Easler, 36 years old in 1986, has never been a full-time two-way player. Now hanging on as a DH, he is not a HOF talent.

Henderson, Cowens, Washington, Mumphrey, Armas

The above are the lowest-rated active Class 4 outfielders with PABs below .240.

In 1986, Steve Henderson was 34 years old with a .281 BA. Last year he played little. Mostly, Steve has been a part-time player. He is not HOF material.

Al Cowens was 35 years old the same year. A solid outfielder, he has played for 13 seasons, has about 5,500 at bats and a career BA of .270. His record does not meet Class 4 HOF standards. He's about to retire.

Claude Washington was 32 years old in 1986 with 13 seasons and a BA of .278 to look back on. He can give you ten home runs a year and is dangerous on the bases. Claude has already played in both leagues and for six teams in his career, which suggests that contemporary managers regard him as dispensable. Hall of Fame committees will probably take the same view.

Jerry Mumphrey turned 34 in 1986. That year, he completed his thirteenth major league season, and it was a fair one. Jerry has about 4,600 at bats to his credit—not much for a 34-year-older. Durability is a problem. His BA of .288 is within reach of Class 4 HOF territory, but it's doubtful that Mumphrey can improve it over the half dozen or more seasons he needs to get serious HOF attention.

Tony Armas was 33 years old with a BA of .251 in 1986. When his legs are working, he's a good defensive outfielder, and one of the most prolific home run hitters in baseball. Also, he's usually close to the top of the list in whiffs. Tony is hitting home runs at a .050 per at bat pace—about one in every 20 at bats. But the power hitter—so lionized in the world of active baseball—is old hat in the HOF world. Armas needs more than a long ball record to get into the museum.

Outfielders—The Pretenders

Active outfielders have been analyzed, some in great depth, some less so. Theoretically, all players in the first four classifications are pretenders, but not all survived the analysis. Some did, as follows:

	BA	PAB	Comment
Henderson, Rick	.290	.289	Possible
Rice	.303	.287	Probable
Lynn	.292	.285	Possible durability?
Winfield	.286	.283	Probable
Jackson	.263	.275	Very Probable
Murphy, Dale	.277	.273	Possible—improving
Parker	.304	.271	Possible

In the sample, there are 61 active outfielders. In the above list are ten pretenders—16 percent of the group. Only Reggie is a cinch. His career is in—and is adequate. Rice and Winfield are solid prospects. Lynn is fading—the others have durability problems to resolve.

Outfield analysis is complete. Pretenders have been located. Wish them luck. Now, it's on to the infielders in search of more HOF pretenders.

Infielders

In the active infielder group, 55 players are in the analysis sample. None qualifies as a superstar. By classification, the group breaks down as follows: Class 1—0; Class 2—2; Class 3—4; Class 4—37; Class 5—12.

Applicable standards against which to measure infielder performance are as follows:

	Standard
Quality—PAB	
Class 1	.323+
2	.284–.322
3	.246–.283
4	.200–.245
Durability—At Bats	
Long	9134+
Medium	6180–9133
Short	6179–

The 55 infielders who met the qualifications of this study are identified in the following schedule. All have played in more than 800 games through 1986.

	G	AB	H	R	HR	RBI	BA	SA	PAB
Class 1 .323+									
None									
Class 2 .284–.322									
Schmidt	2107	7292	1954	852	495	897	.268	.536	.308
Brett	1741	6675	2095	863	209	841	.314	.505	.287
Class 3 .246–.283									
Ripken	830	3210	927	396	133	339	.289	.483	.270
Cey	2028	7058	1845	653	312	816	.261	.446	.252
Harrah	2155	7402	1954	920	195	723	.264	.395	.248
Moreland	887	3082	880	280	83	394	.286	.421	.246

	G	AB	H	R	HR	RBI	BA	SA	PAB
Class 4 .200–.245									
Whitaker	1283	4705	1320	631	93	429	.281	.404	.245
Yount	1811	7037	2019	890	153	674	.287	.429	.244
Madlock	1698	6207	1906	713	146	657	.307	.442	.244
Grich	2008	6890	1833	815	224	640	.266	.424	.244
DeCinces	1512	5347	1397	491	221	594	.261	.450	.244
Lansford	1139	4478	1307	521	113	450	.292	.428	.242
Trammell	1289	4631	1300	612	90	414	.281	.403	.241
Molitor	1010	4139	1203	597	79	311	.291	.418	.238
Herr	873	3162	874	405	16	333	.276	.359	.238
Randolph	1494	5511	1511	858	39	412	.274	.355	.238
Nettles	2508	8716	2172	788	384	883	.249	.424	.236
Parrish, L.A.	1619	5829	1552	529	210	630	.266	.441	.235
Lopes	1765	6311	1661	865	154	454	.263	.389	.233
Orta	1734	5779	1610	602	128	613	.279	.412	.232
Garner	1732	5885	1543	647	104	610	.262	.392	.231
Bell	2133	8068	2273	869	177	816	.282	.409	.231
Mulliniks	822	2288	614	252	43	231	.268	.401	.230
Bernazard	925	3181	841	389	61	281	.264	.387	.230
Smalley	1543	5348	1369	558	155	505	.256	.395	.228
Ray	808	3053	880	334	32	305	.288	.395	.220
Brookens	927	2658	657	276	48	252	.247	.371	.217
White	1803	6100	1583	612	131	562	.260	.393	.214
Concepcion	2300	8247	2198	850	100	809	.267	.359	.213
Templeton	1423	5562	1578	659	44	475	.284	.382	.212
Knight	1240	3967	1102	343	67	430	.278	.399	.212
Cruz, Julio	1156	3859	916	534	23	256	.237	.299	.211
Washington, U.	897	2787	700	330	27	228	.251	.343	.210
Wallach	839	3031	771	228	110	296	.254	.425	.209
Gross, W.	1106	3125	727	252	121	275	.233	.395	.207
Royster	1287	3910	979	485	33	291	.250	.331	.207
Burleson	1284	4933	1358	582	48	387	.275	.362	.206
Hubbard	1055	3573	866	370	59	306	.242	.348	.206
Morrison	884	2744	730	205	97	254	.266	.433	.203
Oberkfell	1059	3423	970	388	20	283	.283	.371	.202
Ganter	1120	3871	1066	410	40	327	.275	.358	.201
Wilfong	957	2682	667	278	38	221	249	.345	.200
Garcia	931	3651	1046	429	32	269	.286	.374	.200
Class 5 .199 –									
Smith, O.	1317	4739	1169	570	13	361	.247	.309	.199
DeJesus	1355	4575	1162	573	21	302	.254	.327	.196
Almon	1148	3230	826	340	36	254	.256	.346	.195
Iorg	809	2140	568	200	16	192	.265	.356	.191
Speier	2039	6631	1634	600	98	563	.246	.347	.190
Russell	2181	7318	1926	750	46	581	.263	.338	.188
Trillo	1579	5533	1450	501	52	479	.262	.343	.187
Reynolds	1177	3742	968	374	35	286	.239	.351	.186
Griffin	1228	4408	1133	482	19	317	.257	.335	.186
Oester	980	3368	895	338	39	245	.266	.360	.185
Berra	834	2508	595	184	49	227	.237	.345	.183
Ramirez	871	3358	882	329	36	244	.263	.345	.181

According to the developed standards, a player with a PAB of less than .200 is ineligible for HOF consideration. It follows, therefore, that all Class 5 players are excluded from further analytical consideration. This poses a problem which should be addressed before moving along to the deeper appraisal of the careers of the other men.

Consensus is building that Ozzie Smith may be the most defensively brilliant shortstop ever seen. In recent years, the HOF selection committee has regarded defensive skill with increasing favor. If Smith continues to scintillate in the field, and if his recent BA improvement continues, he may break through offensive biases and get himself elected.

Generally speaking, infielders are a more impressive group than their outfield brothers. Schmidt and Brett are bona fide Class 2 players, and Ripken is a powerful young shortstop in the Cronin mold. Other Class 3 candidates are valuable producers and, given the recent appointment of Aparicio, some Class 4 players are also good bets for future HOF glory.

Who of the active infielders, based upon records through the 1986 season, should be considered as pretenders?

Let's find out.

Mike Schmidt
Born 1949
Height 6′2″; weight 203
Throws right, bats right
HOF — Probable

Year	Age	G	AB	H	R	HR	RBI	BA	SA	PAB
1973	24	132	367	72	25	18	34	.196	.373	.210
1974	25	162	568	160	72	36	80	.282	.546	.331
1975	26	158	562	140	55	38	57	.249	.523	.267
1976	27	160	584	153	74	38	69	.262	.524	.310
1977	28	154	544	149	76	38	63	.274	.574	.325
1978	29	145	513	129	72	21	57	.251	.435	.292
1979	30	160	541	137	64	45	69	.253	.564	.329
1980	31	150	548	157	56	48	73	.286	.624	.323
1981	32	102	354	112	47	31	60	.316	.644	.390
1982	33	148	514	144	73	35	52	.280	.547	.311
1983	34	154	534	136	64	40	69	.255	.524	.324
1984	35	151	528	146	57	36	70	.277	.536	.309
1985	36	158	549	152	56	33	60	.277	.532	.271
1986	37	160	552	160	60	37	82	.290	.547	.324
Total		2094	7258	1947	851	494	895	.268	.537	.309
Other*		13	34	7	1	1	2	.206	.294	.118
Career		2107	7292	1954	852	495	897	.268	.536	.308

*Less than 100 games: 1972

Standard Deviation	15	67	22	13	8	12			
Avg.	150	518	139	61	35	64	.268	.537	.309

Normal Performance Range (100 + games)

High	165	586	162	74	43	76	.276	.584	.329
Low	134	451	117	48	28	52	.258	.475	.282

Best Year (over 139 games): 1974

Super Years (PAB .323 +): 1974, 1977, 1979, 1980, 1981, 1983, 1986

Avg.	149	520	144	63	39	71	.278	.571	.332

Good Years (PAB .284–.322): 1976, 1978, 1982, 1984

Avg.	151	535	143	69	33	62	.267	.511	.306

Fair Years (PAB .246–.283): 1975, 1985

Avg.	158	556	146	56	36	59	.263	.527	.269

Other Years (PAB .245 –): 1973

Average Yearly Performance by Age

25 and under	147	468	116	49	27	57	.248	.478	.283
26–30	155	549	142	68	36	63	.258	.525	.305
31–35	141	496	139	59	38	65	.280	.571	.327
36 +	159	551	156	58	35	71	.283	.540	.298

Most members of the HOF were good combination hitters, that is to say, contact hitters with at least respectable power. Some were specialists, that is to say, great contact and little power—or great power and light in the contact department. Of the more modern players, Clemente is a good example of a contact specialist; Killebrew, a good example of a power specialist.

Mike Schmidt is a power specialist—historically, an unusual role for an infielder.

At 21 years of age, Mike began his two-year minor league career in 1971. In his second season, the power that was to be his trademark blossomed, and the Phillies took a look at him. In 1973, then 24 years of age, Mike took over the hot corner for the club and has occupied that position for the 15 years he has been in the majors.

Elsewhere in this book it has been noted that a player with a .060 + home run per at bat factor qualifies as a power superstar. Ruth, Williams, Mantle, Kiner, Mays, and Aaron are outfielders who have met this mark; Gehrig, Greenberg, Foxx, Killebrew, and McCovey were first basemen who did it; Ed Mathews is the only infielder in the club; no catcher has done the job.

Schmidt will join this elite group. He is, without question, a pretender who will end up in the HOF.

In 1986 Mike was 37 years old and, through that season, had 7,292 at bats to his credit—more than several of the HOF infielders. In short, durability is no longer a question with Schmidt. He's on his way to a career of at least average length.

Mike is no earthshaker as a contact hitter. In 12 full seasons, his BA was .300 + only once — only five times was it .280 + . Power is his game — home run or bust. His best power year was 1980 when, at 31 years of age, he dumped 48 over the wall — .088 per at bat — a homer every 11 times at bat. In three seasons, Schmidt hit 40 + home runs; in 12 seasons, 30 + . He has been consistent. His best overall production year was 1974 when, at 25 years of age, he had a PAB of .331 accompanied by 36 home runs and a BA of .282.

Good hit, no field — good field, no hit. Managers are haunted by the unbalanced player who is great at one side of the game but lousy at the other. Schmidt is not one of these. He's a solid performer at the hot corner. No active third baseman under consideration has handled more assists per game than Mike (including Brooks Robinson), and he is sure-handed as well. Perhaps Bell and Nettles have a defensive leg up on Mike, but few if any of the other third basemen can make the same claim. He is a complete ballplayer.

According to his 100 + game profile, Schmidt is a Class 2 infielder with superstar potential. He had seven superstar seasons (including, amazingly, 1986) and four Class 2 years — a total of 11 seasons of above-average baseball when measured against HOF standards — no active player competes with this level of sustained excellence. Also, Mike has had two Class 3 seasons and one Class 4 year. He will fit nicely into the HOF hierarchy, as follows:

	HR	R	RBI	PAB	BA	SA
Hornsby	.037	.156	.156	.349	.358	.577
Traynor	.008	.149	.161	.317	.320	.435
Robinson, J.	.028	.166	.122	.317	.311	.474
Schmidt	**.068**	**.117**	**.123**	**.308**	**.268**	**.536**
Vaughan	.014	.163	.125	.302	.318	.453
Sewell	.007	.153	.140	.300	.312	.413
Aparicio	.008	.122	.069	.200	.262	.343

For a guy with a .268 BA, this is swift company. Schmidt is an unorthodox performer for an infielder, but has earned his comparative stature his own way — the power way.

For a free swinger and a relatively weak contact hitter, Mike has been unusually consistent. In his early twenties, he was just below Class 3 quality. In his late twenties, he was a solid Class 2 performer. In his early thirties, Mike was a superstar — the most valuable player investment in the game. Now on the last lap, Mike is still averaging Class 2 production numbers.

The prime years of Mike Schmidt are still ongoing, as of the end of the 1986 season. His remarkable physical condition says that he might have a few more. Time will tell.

Some say career statistics of old-timers will never be matched because the game has changed. It is harder today than it used to be to get fat numbers; don't make comparisons — the argument continues — it isn't fair to modern players.

Balderdash!

In the analysis of outfielders, it was shown that individual players still have magnificent seasons — they don't sustain such levels of performance. Now we bump into Schmidt. He does both — great seasons, repeated. The truth is apparent. The general quality of offensive baseball has slipped badly over the last two decades, but some individual players continue to play at historical levels of excellence. The trouble is, the game doesn't have enough of them.

There aren't many Mike Schmidts on the field. Enjoy his talents while you can.

George Brett
Born 1953
Height 6'0"; weight 200
Throws right, bats left
HOF — Probable

Year	Age	G	AB	H	R	HR	RBI	BA	SA	PAB
1974	21	133	457	129	47	2	45	.282	.363	.206
1975	22	159	634	195	73	11	78	.308	.456	.256
1976	23	159	645	215	87	7	60	.333	.462	.239
1977	24	139	564	176	83	22	66	.312	.532	.303
1978	25	128	510	150	70	9	53	.294	.467	.259
1979	26	154	645	212	96	23	84	.329	.563	.315
1980	27	117	449	175	63	24	94	.390	.664	.403
1982	29	144	552	166	80	21	61	.301	.505	.293
1983	30	123	464	144	65	25	68	.310	.563	.341
1984	31	104	377	107	29	13	56	.284	.459	.260
1985	32	155	550	184	78	30	82	.335	.585	.345
1986	33	124	441	128	54	16	57	.290	.481	.288
Total		1639	6288	1981	825	203	804	.315	.509	.291
Other*		102	387	114	38	6	37	.295	.452	.209
Career		1741	6675	2095	863	209	841	.314	.505	.287

*Less than 100 games: 1973, 1981

Standard Deviation		17	85	33	18	8	14			
Avg.		137	524	165	69	17	67	.315	.509	.291

	G	AB	H	R	HR	RBI	BA	SA	PAB
Standard Deviation Profile (100 + games)									
High	154	609	198	87	25	81	.325	.581	.316
Low	119	439	132	51	9	53	.301	.409	.257
Best Year (over 139 games): 1985									
Super Years (PAB .323 +): 1980, 1983, 1985									
Avg.	132	488	168	69	26	81	.344	.602	.362
Good Years (PAB .284–.322): 1977, 1979, 1982, 1986									
Avg.	140	551	171	78	21	67	.310	.524	.301
Fair Years (PAB .246–.283): 1975, 1978, 1984									
Avg.	130	507	151	57	11	62	.297	.460	.258
Other Years (PAB .245 –): 1974, 1976									
Avg.	146	551	172	67	5	53	.312	.421	.225
Average Yearly Performance by Age									
25 and under	144	562	173	72	10	60	.308	.459	.254
26–30	135	528	174	76	23	77	.330	.569	.334
31–35	128	456	140	54	20	65	.306	.517	.303

George Brett was 33 years old in 1986, which gives him time to add durability to the talent levels he has already shown. Join him with brother third baseman Mike Schmidt as a legitimate pretender, almost sure to be elected to the HOF.

According to the classification of infielders by PAB, George joins Schmidt as the only other Class 2 infielder in baseball. No active infielder has a chance to join Hornsby, Gehringer, and Cronin in the superstar class.

Like many of the old-time stars, Brett entered organized ball when he was 18 years old. From the beginning, he showed skill at the plate. KC looked at him in 1973. In 1974, at 21 years of age, he was the regular third baseman for the club. George completed his fourteenth season in the big leagues in 1986.

Brett is essentially a contact hitter with enough power to keep defensive fielders honest. His best power year was 1985 when, at 32 years old, he hit 30 home runs. In half of his 12 full seasons, Brett has hit 20 + home runs. His best production year was 1985 — PAB of .345; BA of .335. In 1986, he played hurt again, appearing in just 124 games.

Brett has never had a BA lower than .282. In eight of 12 full seasons, his BA was .300 + — in three of them, .330 + . Given his contact hitting skills, it isn't surprising to find that as a scorer of runs, Brett ranks with the best in the game. He is also one of the more reliable clutch hitters — in 1979, 1980, and 1985, he was one of the superstar RBI men.

According to his 100 + game profile, George is a Class 2 infielder. He had three superstar years, four Class 2 years, three Class 3 and two Class 4 seasons. Wide swings in performance are directly related to his power stroke. When he hits 20 + home runs, he produces according to profile—when he does not, productivity slumps.

Brett is injury prone. This is his Achilles' heel. He is the Fred Lynn of infielders. In 1978, 1980, 1981, 1983, 1984, and 1986 (6 seasons) he played an average of 114 games a year. If anything keeps him out of the HOF, it'll be injuries and the impact they have on the durability and quality of his full career. In 12 full seasons, Brett has averaged 138 games a year—less than any of the prominent infielders. If elected to the HOF, Brett would fit between Ed Mathews and Fred Lindstrom.

	HR	R	RBI	PAB	BA	SA
Hornsby	.037	.156	.156	.349	.358	.577
Frisch	.012	.157	.125	.293	.316	.432
Mathews	.060	.117	.110	.287	.271	.509
Brett	**.031**	**.130**	**.126**	**.287**	**.314**	**.505**
Lindstrom	.018	.141	.120	.280	.311	.449
Appling	.005	.144	.121	.270	.310	.398
Aparicio	.008	.122	.069	.200	.262	.343

As a power hitter, Brett looks up to only Rajah Hornsby and Ed Mathews. He scores competitively—better than Mathews and Aparicio. Only Hornsby tops him as an RBI man. As a general producer, George should pass Mathews and, at least, crowd Frisch before he's through.

Like Schmidt, Brett is a modern player who can be unapologetically compared with the greats of history. The superstars? No! But there's nothing shabby about being joined with the likes of Traynor, Sewell, and Frisch. His career clearly indicates that, under modern conditions, men of talent can still produce numbers competitive with those of history.

Because of his imposing offensive credentials, Brett doesn't have to demonstrate superior defensive skills to qualify for HOF consideration. Nevertheless, it's useful to point out that George is an aggressive third baseman who covers reasonable ground with acceptable skill. It is likely, however, that the accumulated impact of injuries will cause him to move to first base or the outfield in the not-too-distant future.

When Brett completed the 1985 season, he moved from the short to the normal career zone. Along with Schmidt, George has already met quality and durability standards of the HOF. Despite the fact that he leads a low scoring team, Brett has posted impressive production statistics. He is one of the top offensive threats of his era, regardless of position.

Will the two top infielders in the game have to wait long before they join fellow HOF third basemen in the museum?

	AB	HR	R	RBI	PAB	BA	SA
Traynor	7559	.008	.149	.161	.317	.320	.435
Schmidt	**7292**	**.068**	**.117**	**.123**	**.308**	**.268**	**.536**
Mathews	8537	.060	.117	.110	.287	.271	.509
Brett	**6675**	**.031**	**.130**	**.126**	**.287**	**.314**	**.505**
Lindstrom	5611	.018	.141	.120	.280	.311	.449
Kell	6702	.012	.120	.118	.250	.306	.414
Robinson	10654	.025	.090	.102	.218	.267	.401

Schmidt will claim more durability than most. His home run hitting exceeds Mathews and all other third basemen. He scores as well as Mathews and better than Robinson. Only Traynor was a higher RBI and PAB man. Mike is a better contact hitter than Robinson, and the most formidable slugger of the third basemen. Certainly, he won't have to wait long for his place in the museum.

Brett has more at bats than Lindstrom. As a home run hitter, he bows only to Mathews. He scores better than all but Traynor and Lindstrom. Only Traynor is a better RBI man and contact hitter. Only Mathews is a stronger slugger. If George can stay healthy, his election to the HOF should be quick and smooth. If he can't, durability questions will be raised.

Brett and Schmidt can accept HOF honors with heads held high. They belong. They deserve it.

Cal Ripken
Born 1960
Height 6'4"; weight 200
Throws right, bats right
HOF—Possible

Year	Age	G	AB	H	R	HR	RBI	BA	SA	PAB
1982	22	160	598	158	62	28	65	.264	.475	.259
1983	23	162	663	211	94	27	75	.318	.517	.296
1984	24	162	641	195	76	27	59	.304	.510	.253
1985	25	161	642	181	90	26	84	.282	.469	.312
1986	26	162	627	177	73	25	56	.282	.461	.246
Total		807	3171	922	395	133	339	.291	.487	.273
Other*		23	39	5	1	0	0	.128	.128	.026
Career		830	3210	927	396	133	339	.289	.483	.270

*Less than 100 games: 1981

	G	AB	H	R	HR	RBI	BA	SA	PAB
Standard Deviation	1	21	18	12	1	10			
Avg.	161	634	184	79	27	68	.291	.487	.273
Normal Performance Range (100 + games)									
High	162	656	202	91	28	78	.308	.525	.300
Low	161	613	167	67	26	57	.272	.446	.245

Best Year (over 139 games): 1985

Super Years (PAB .323 +): None

Good Years (PAB .284–.322): 1983, 1985

Avg.	162	653	196	92	27	80	.300	.493	.303

Fair Years (PAB .246–.283): 1982, 1984, 1986

Avg.	161	622	177	70	27	60	.284	.482	.252

Other Years (PAB .245 –): None

Average Yearly Performance by Age

25 and under	161	636	186	81	27	71	.293	.493	.280
26–30	162	627	177	73	25	56	.282	.461	.246

Cal Ripken, Sr., is a Baltimore coach, and a favorite to fill the 1987 managerial job which will be vacated by Earl Weaver. Billy Ripken is a son of Cal Sr., and a minor league infielder with a chance to make the parent club in 1987. Bill Ripken, brother of Cal Sr., was a minor league outfielder for a couple of years. So it can be accurately said that baseball runs in the Ripken family blood. It's no surprise that Cal Jr. entered professional baseball at 18 years of age. At 21, he took his first look at the shortstop job of the Orioles and at 22, he owned it. Twenty-six years old in 1986, he is the most valuable infielder (considering his age) in professional baseball.

Cal had five full seasons behind him in 1986. In his early thirties, he will have gathered all basic durability credentials. According to his 100 + game profile, Ripken is a Class 3 infielder with Class 2 potential. With a little more help from his teammates, he could end up as the most productive shortstop to play the game since Joe Cronin hung them up.

Cal is a well-rounded offensive performer. In only his first season as a regular did he hit below .280 — twice his BA was above .300. He can be depended on for 25–30 home runs a year. This combination of contact hitting ability and power will make him an eye-popping producer if his teammates cooperate. In his first five full seasons, Ripken has posted two Class 2 years and three Class 3 performances.

It's too early to guarantee the HOF future of Ripken, but it does seem apparent that only injury can interrupt his direct flight to immortality. If he maintains his present average production, he'll fit between Luke Appling and Travis Jackson, as follows:

	HR	R	RBI	PAB	BA	SA
Hornsby	.037	.156	.156	.349	.358	.577
Lindstrom	.018	.141	.120	.280	.311	.449
Appling	.005	.144	.121	.270	.310	.398
Ripken	**.041**	**.123**	**.106**	**.270**	**.289**	**.483**
Jackson	.022	.115	.130	.267	.291	.433
Boudreau	.011	.132	.120	.262	.295	.415
Aparicio	.008	.122	.069	.200	.262	.343

It's a good bet that Ripken will overtake Appling. Will he then crowd Vaughan (PAB .302) and Cronin (PAB .328), the two highest ranked shortstops? The above numbers indicate that Cal has the BA and the power to do it. RBIs and scoring are his problems, and they will be resolved only if the hitters around him are equivalently productive.

As a bonus, Cal is a fine defensive shortstop. This man is one fine piece of young baseball talent.

Ron Cey
Born 1948
Height 5'9"; weight 185
Throws right, bats right
HOF—Possible

Year	Age	G	AB	H	R	HR	RBI	BA	SA	PAB
1973	25	152	507	124	45	15	65	.245	.385	.247
1974	26	159	577	151	70	18	79	.262	.397	.289
1975	27	158	566	160	47	25	76	.283	.473	.261
1976	28	145	502	139	46	23	57	.277	.462	.251
1977	29	153	564	136	47	30	80	.241	.450	.278
1978	30	159	555	150	61	23	61	.270	.452	.261
1979	31	150	487	137	49	28	53	.281	.499	.267
1980	32	157	551	140	53	28	49	.254	.452	.236
1982	34	150	556	141	38	24	55	.254	.428	.210
1983	35	159	581	160	49	24	66	.275	.460	.239
1984	36	146	505	121	46	25	72	.240	.442	.283
1985	37	145	500	116	42	22	41	.232	.408	.210
Total		1833	6451	1675	593	285	754	.260	.442	.253
Other*		195	607	170	60	27	62	.280	.481	.245
Career		2028	7058	1845	653	312	816	.261	.446	.252

*Less than 100 games: 1971, 1972, 1981, 1986

| *Standard Deviation* | | 5 | 33 | 14 | 8 | 4 | 12 | | | |
| Avg. | | 153 | 538 | 140 | 49 | 24 | 63 | .260 | .442 | .253 |

	G	AB	H	R	HR	RBI	BA	SA	PAB
Normal Performance Range (100 + games)									
High	158	570	153	58	28	75	.269	.490	.281
Low	147	505	126	41	20	51	.250	.388	.222

Best Year (over 139 games): 1974

Super Years (PAB .323 +): None

Good Years (PAB .284–.322): 1974

Fair Years (PAB .246–.283): 1973, 1975, 1976, 1977, 1978, 1979, 1984

Avg.	152	527	138	49	24	66	.262	.452	.264

Other Years (PAB .245 –): 1980, 1982, 1983, 1985

Avg.	153	547	139	46	25	53	.255	.438	.224

Average Yearly Performance by Age

	G	AB	H	R	HR	RBI	BA	SA	PAB
25 and under	152	507	124	45	15	65	.245	.385	.247
26–30	155	553	147	54	24	71	.266	.446	.269
31–35	154	544	145	47	26	56	.266	.458	.237
36 +	146	503	119	44	24	57	.236	.425	.247

Ron Cey minus some talent equals Mike Schmidt.

Although relatively short compared to most major leaguers, the muscular Cey follows the Schmidt rule: knock it out of the park, or to hell with it. The difference is, he doesn't do it as well as Mike does:

	AB	R	HR	RBI	PAB	BA	SA
Schmidt	7,272	.117	.068	.123	.308	.268	.536
Cey	7,058	.093	.044	.115	.252	.261	.446

Cey was never a gazelle on the bases and, now 38 years old, has slowed even more—this hurts him in the runs scored department. Although good for 24 home runs a year, Ron did not offset weaknesses as a contact hitter to the same extent as Schmidt does.

Cey handled fewer assists per game in recent years. He covered less ground, and in 1985, he led the league in errors. In 1986, he played in less than 100 games. Age is showing in his numbers. In prior years, however, Ron Cey demonstrated good range and sure hands. He's been an adequate hot-corner man. When offensive skills are not outstanding, however, it is helpful to a pretender if defensive talents are.

Cey is a legitimate pretender with problems. His PAB invites Class 3 consideration, but is on the way down. He is not a 10,000 at bat player. His defensive play has not been outstanding. Mark him a long shot for HOF honors.

Ron was 20 years old when he first appeared in organized ball in 1968. Los Angeles looked at him in 1972 and 1973, and he became their regular third baseman in 1974. Cey gave a dozen years to LA before being traded to the Cubs, at the age of 35, in 1983. Judging by current and recent performance, the end is near for Cey.

According to his 100 + game profile, Cey is a Class 3 infielder on average. Ron had no superstar years, one Class 2 year, seven Class 3 years, and four Class 4 seasons. A durable player on a seasonal basis, Ron averaged 153 games a season over 12 relatively full years.

In 1979 and 1980, Cey hit 28 home runs, the best power performances of his career. But his most balanced and best production year was 1974 when, at 26 years of age, he generated a PAB of .289 supported by a BA of .262 and 18 home runs. Year in and year out, Cey has been an unusually consistent player at his predictable level of skill.

In his early twenties, Cey was a Class 3 infielder. In his late twenties, he moved closer to the top of the same class. In his early thirties, Cey dropped to Class 4. Last year (1986), Cey was not a regular starter.

If elected to the HOF, Cey would fit between Herman and Kell, as follows:

	AB	R	HR	RBI	PAB	BA	SA
Hornsby	8,173	.156	.037	.156	.349	.358	.577
Reese	8,058	.150	.016	.094	.260	.269	.377
Herman	7,707	.145	.006	.103	.254	.304	.407
Cey	**7,058**	**.093**	**.044**	**.115**	**.252**	**.261**	**.446**
Kell	6,702	.120	.012	.118	.250	.306	.414
Robinson	10,654	.090	.025	.102	.218	.267	.401
Aparicio	10,230	.122	.008	.069	.200	.262	.343

Aparicio is in the HOF because of superior durability, baserunning, and defensive skills to which Cey can't lay claim. Had it not been for military service, Reese would have rivaled the durability of Aparicio. Robinson was a long-careered defensive genius. Relative to Reese, Robinson, and Aparicio, comparative durability knocks Cey out. How does Cey compare defensively with George Kell, the only third baseman in the above group with comparable durability?

	APG*	EPG	Total	EPG%
Kell	1.850	.094	1.944	4.84%
Cey (1986 excluded)	2.018	.111	2.129	5.21%

*APG = assists per game, EPG = errors per game.
EPG% = percent of EPG to total of APG and EPG.

If Cey has a HOF argument, it is that he is more durable than Kell, and competes well offensively and defensively. If Cey's PAB drops farther—goodbye argument.

Long careers are not unusual in baseball history. Many men play well into their late thirties—some into their early forties. So it is not unusual to see a 39-year-old Cey still answering the bell. Many have done the same.

What is becoming increasingly unusual is the lingering of older players on the baseball scene as full-time starters long after skills have obviously and substantially depleted.

Joe Morgan peaked in 1977 at 34 years old. Thereafter, he hit from .230 to .250 for seven years except for one season when his BA went up to .289 (134 games). Cey has been a shadow of himself for years. Why and how do they hang on for so long?

From the players' standpoint? Easy! Money! From management's standpoint? Older players with declined skills are better than newer players at 100% skill levels. This is a comment on the available talent pool today.

In its golden era, baseball had no competition from other sports. Today, football, hockey, basketball—even tennis and golf—draw on the pool of athletes. College educations are common, career options broad, minor leagues weak. In addition to these circumstances, baseball expanded. $%&*@#! That's why old jocks are still active.

Toby Harrah
Born 1948
Height 6'0"; weight 180
Throws right, bats right
HOF—Doubtful

Year	Age	G	AB	H	R	HR	RBI	BA	SA	PAB
1971	23	127	383	88	43	2	20	.230	.290	.170
1972	24	116	374	97	46	1	30	.259	.321	.206
1973	25	118	461	120	54	10	40	.260	.364	.226
1974	26	161	573	149	58	21	53	.260	.417	.230
1975	27	151	522	153	61	20	73	.293	.458	.295
1976	28	155	584	152	49	15	52	.260	.377	.199
1977	29	159	539	142	63	27	60	.263	.479	.278
1978	30	139	450	103	44	12	47	.229	.360	.229
1979	31	149	527	147	79	20	57	.279	.444	.296
1980	32	160	561	150	89	11	61	.267	.380	.287
1981	33	103	361	105	59	5	39	.291	.388	.285
1982	34	162	602	183	75	25	53	.304	.490	.254
1983	35	138	526	140	72	9	44	.266	.365	.238
1985	37	126	396	107	56	9	35	.270	.389	.253

	G	AB	H	R	HR	RBI	BA	SA	PAB
Total	1964	6859	1836	848	187	664	.268	.400	.248
Other*	191	543	118	72	8	59	.217	.333	.256
Career	2155	7402	1954	920	195	723	.264	.395	.248

*Less than 100 games: 1969, 1984, 1986

Standard Deviation	19	81	27	13	8	13			
Avg.	140	490	131	61	13	47	.268	.400	.248

Normal Performance Range (100 + games)

High	159	571	158	74	21	61	.276	.454	.273
Low	122	409	105	47	5	34	.256	.326	.212

Best Year (over 139 games): 1979

Super Years (PAB .323 +): None

Good Years (PAB .284–.322): 1975, 1979, 1980, 1981

Avg.	141	493	139	72	14	58	.282	.419	.291

Fair Years (PAB .246–.283): 1977, 1982, 1985

Avg.	149	512	144	65	20	49	.281	.460	.262

Other Years (PAB .245 –): 1971, 1972, 1973, 1974, 1976, 1978, 1983

Avg.	136	479	121	52	10	41	.253	.362	.215

Average Yearly Performance by Age

25 and under	120	406	102	48	4	30	.250	.328	.202
26–30	153	534	140	55	19	57	.262	.419	.246
31–35	142	515	145	75	14	51	.281	.417	.271
36 +	126	396	107	56	9	35	.270	.389	.253

Toby entered organized baseball at 19 years of age. He spent four years in the minors, mostly playing middle infield positions. In 1971, the Washington Senators brought him up and he played about three-quarters of a season for them at shortstop and third base. In 1972, he moved to Texas and in two injury-plagued seasons, covered shortstop and third base for them. Injuries behind him, Harrah then gave Texas five more years of solid play until traded, in 1979, to Cleveland. Continuing to play a variety of infield positions, Toby gave the Indians five workman-like years. Then came an unfortunate season with the Yankees, and finally the move back to Texas.

According to his 100 + game profile, Harrah is a consistent contact hitter with fair power. His best power year was 1982 with Cleveland when, at 34 years of age, he clocked 25 big ones combined with a BA of .304 and a PAB of .254. But this was not his best production year, which occurred in 1979. Then 31 years old, he hit 20 home runs, had a BA of .279, and a PAB of .296 — a solid Class 2 season.

In a 17-year career, Toby has played in 100 + games in 14 of them.

He never had a superstar season, but he has had four Class 2 years, three Class 3 seasons, and seven Class 4 seasons.

Toby was a slow starter. In his early twenties, he was a Class 4 infielder with an unsettled defensive position. In his late twenties, he moved to the low end of Class 3 and continued to play, less than brilliantly, several infield positions. In his early thirties, he was at his best — high level Class 3 — but still couldn't nail down a regular infield position. Now in his late thirties, Toby seems destined to finish as a part-time infielder — his regular playing days are over. In 1986, he appeared in 95 games for Texas as a second baseman.

In durability terms, Harrah has already had a career of average length. If elected to the HOF, he would fit between Robinson and Kell, as follows:

	AB	R	HR	RBI	PAB	BA	SA
Hornsby	8,173	.156	.037	.156	.349	.358	.577
Herman	7,707	.146	.006	.103	.254	.304	.407
Kell	6,702	.120	.012	.118	.250	.306	.414
Harrah	**7,402**	**.124**	**.026**	**.098**	**.248**	**.264**	**.395**
Robinson	10,654	.090	.025	.102	.218	.267	.401
Aparicio	10,230	.122	.008	.069	.200	.262	.343

Recent appointments to the HOF have legitimized the qualifications of journeyman players like Toby Harrah. On a comparative basis, he has earned consideration. But he will probably be rejected. Class 4 HOF infielders have two common characteristics: they were defensively brilliant; they were extraordinarily durable. Harrah is neither.

Keith Moreland
Born 1954
Height 6'0"; weight 200
Throws right, bats right
HOF — No

Year	Age	G	AB	H	R	HR	RBI	BA	SA	PAB
1982	28	138	476	124	35	15	53	.261	.399	.216
1983	29	154	533	161	60	16	54	.302	.460	.244
1984	30	140	495	138	43	16	64	.279	.422	.248
1985	31	161	587	180	60	14	92	.307	.440	.283
1986	32	156	586	159	60	12	67	.271	.384	.237
Total		749	2677	762	258	73	330	.285	.421	.247
Other*		138	405	118	22	10	64	.291	.420	.237
Career		887	3082	880	280	83	394	.286	.421	.246

*Less than 100 games: 1978, 1979, 1980, 1981

	G	AB	H	R	HR	RBI	BA	SA	PAB
Standard Deviation	9	46	19	11	1	14			
Avg.	150	535	152	52	15	66	.285	.421	.247

Normal Performance Range (100 + games)

	G	AB	H	R	HR	RBI	BA	SA	PAB
High	159	581	172	62	16	80	.296	.451	.273
Low	141	490	133	41	13	52	.271	.385	.216

Best Year (over 139 games): 1985

Super Years (PAB .323 +): None

Good Years (PAB .284–.322): None

Fair Years (PAB .246–.283): 1984, 1985

	G	AB	H	R	HR	RBI	BA	SA	PAB
Avg.	151	541	159	52	15	78	.294	.432	.267

Other Years (PAB .245 –): 1982, 1983, 1986

	G	AB	H	R	HR	RBI	BA	SA	PAB
Avg.	149	532	148	52	14	58	.278	.414	.233

Average Yearly Performance by Age

	G	AB	H	R	HR	RBI	BA	SA	PAB
25 and under	0	0	0	0	0	0	.000	.000	.000
26–30	144	501	141	46	16	57	.281	.428	.237
31–35	159	587	170	60	13	80	.289	.412	.260

Before he played a full season in the major leagues, Keith was 28 years old. All other considerations aside, this fact epitomizes Keith's problem — durability. Unless he's a physical superman, he will not accumulate enough competitive playing time to qualify for serious HOF attention.

In addition to the durability question, Moreland also presents a defensive record that is a turnoff. Except for his first year in organized baseball (1975), Keith has never played a single position for a team. Is he a catcher, an outfielder, or an infielder? Nobody knows. And the absence of an answer will keep him out of the HOF if nothing else does.

Moreland is a handy journeyman who swings a good bat with fair power. But he isn't a pretender.

The remaining Class 4 players, whether analyzed briefly or in detail, represent marginal skills which should get HOF attention as a result of the choices of Brooks Robinson and Luis Aparicio, which created HOF opportunities that never existed before.

Lou Whitaker
Born 1957
Height 5'11"; weight 160
Throws right, bats left
HOF — Possible

Year	Age	G	AB	H	R	HR	RBI	BA	SA	PAB
1978	21	139	484	138	68	3	55	.285	.357	.260
1979	22	127	423	121	72	3	39	.286	.378	.270
1980	23	145	477	111	67	1	44	.233	.283	.235
1981	24	109	335	88	43	5	31	.263	.373	.236
1982	25	152	560	160	61	15	50	.286	.434	.225
1983	26	161	643	206	82	12	60	.320	.457	.240
1984	27	143	558	161	77	13	43	.289	.407	.238
1985	28	152	609	170	81	21	52	.279	.456	.253
1986	29	144	584	157	75	20	53	.269	.437	.253
Total		1272	4673	1312	626	93	427	.281	.404	.245
Other*		11	32	8	5	0	2	.250	.281	.219
Career		1283	4705	1320	631	93	429	.281	.404	.245

*Less than 100 games: 1977

Standard Deviation		15	92	33	11	7	8			
Avg.		141	519	146	70	10	47	.281	.404	.245

Normal Performance Range (100 + games)

High		156	612	179	81	17	56	.293	.466	.252
Low		127	427	112	58	3	39	.264	.316	.235

Best Year (over 139 games): 1978

Super Years (PAB .323 +): None

Good Years (PAB .284–.322): None

Fair Years (PAB .246–.283): 1978, 1979, 1985, 1986

Avg.		141	525	147	74	12	50	.279	.412	.258

Other Years (PAB .245 –): 1980, 1981, 1982, 1983, 1984

Avg.		142	515	145	66	9	46	.282	.398	.235

Average Yearly Performance by Age

25 and under		134	456	124	62	5	44	.271	.367	.244
26–30		150	599	174	79	17	52	.290	.440	.246

There are several top defensive second basemen in baseball. Whitaker is one of them—he may be the best.

Lou has other things going for him. He was only 29 years old in 1986, and has ten seasons and over 4,700 at bats behind him. His lifetime BA is .281, but he has done better than that in five of his nine full seasons.

Lou plays for a fine team and a great manager. Such an environment helps the performance of any player. With maturity, his power hitting has picked up. Although he faltered in 1986, Lou's record should continue to improve. He's only halfway on the long journey to the HOF and, for that reason alone, Whitaker can't be ranked as better than a possibility. But he is a bona fide pretender with a good chance to make it—if he doesn't burn out.

In 1975, 18 years old, Lou moved into the minor leagues. Detroit took its first look at him in 1977, and in 1978, at 21 years of age, he became the regular second baseman of the Detroit team. In nine of his ten years, he played in 100 + games, averaging 141.

Whitaker is basically a good contact hitter who scores runs at a competitive rate. Although he pops them out now and then, he is not rated as a power hitter — ten homers a year over nine full seasons. He's improving in the power game, having averaged about 20 a year over the past two seasons. His best production year (over 139 games) was his first, when he posted a PAB of .260 supported by a BA of .285 and three home runs.

According to his 100 + game profile, Whitaker will swing between Class 3 and Class 4 in production performance. This, plus the BA, will have to improve. He's had four Class 3 and five Class 4 seasons so far. It's somewhat disturbing to note that his best production years were the earliest ones; his worst, the recent ones. One guesses that the fuller schedule he's now playing has confronted him more frequently with the left-handed curve ball, a situation that hurts the BAs of all but the greatest left-handed hitters.

If elected to the HOF, Lou would be ranked below Kell, as follows:

	AB	R	HR	RBI	PAB	BA	SA
Hornsby	8,173	.156	.037	.156	.349	.358	.577
Herman	7,707	.145	.006	.103	.254	.304	.407
Kell	6,702	.120	.012	.118	.250	.306	.414
Whitaker	**4,705**	**.134**	**.020**	**.091**	**.245**	**.281**	**.404**
Robinson	10,654	.090	.025	.102	.218	.267	.401
Aparicio	10,230	.122	.008	.069	.200	.262	.343

Lou can compete with HOF infielders in talent. Can he do so for a HOF career?

Robin Yount

Born 1955
Height 6'0"; weight 170
Throws right, bats right
HOF — Possible

Year	Age	G	AB	H	R	HR	RBI	BA	SA	PAB
1974	19	107	344	86	45	3	23	.250	.346	.206
1975	20	147	558	149	59	8	44	.267	.367	.199
1976	21	161	638	161	57	2	52	.252	.301	.174

Year	Age	G	AB	H	R	HR	RBI	BA	SA	PAB
1977	22	154	605	174	62	4	45	.288	.377	.183
1978	23	127	502	147	57	9	62	.293	.428	.255
1979	24	149	577	154	64	8	43	.267	.371	.199
1980	25	143	611	179	98	23	64	.293	.519	.303
1982	27	156	635	210	100	29	85	.331	.578	.337
1983	28	149	578	178	85	17	63	.308	.503	.285
1984	29	160	624	186	89	16	64	.298	.441	.271
1985	30	122	466	129	61	15	53	.277	.442	.277
1986	31	140	522	163	73	9	37	.312	.450	.228
Total		1715	6660	1916	850	143	635	.288	.430	.244
Other*		96	377	103	40	10	39	.273	.419	.236
Career		1811	7037	2019	890	153	674	.287	.429	.244

*Less than 100 games: 1981

| *Standard Deviation* | | 16 | 82 | 30 | 17 | 8 | 15 | | | |
| Avg. | | 143 | 555 | 160 | 71 | 12 | 53 | .288 | .430 | .244 |

Normal Performance Range (100 + games)

High		159	637	190	88	20	68	.298	.503	.276
Low		127	473	130	54	4	38	.274	.331	.201

Best Year (over 139 games): 1982

Super Years (PAB .323 +): 1982

Good Years (PAB .284–.322): 1980, 1983

| Avg. | | 146 | 595 | 179 | 92 | 20 | 64 | .300 | .511 | .294 |

Fair Years (PAB .246–.283): 1978, 1984, 1985

| Avg. | | 136 | 531 | 154 | 69 | 13 | 60 | .290 | .437 | .268 |

Other Years (PAB .245 –): 1974, 1975, 1976, 1977, 1979, 1986

| Avg. | | 143 | 541 | 148 | 60 | 6 | 41 | .273 | .368 | .197 |

Average Yearly Performance by Age

25 and under		141	548	150	63	8	48	.274	.389	.217
26–30		147	576	176	84	19	66	.305	.495	.294
31–35		140	522	163	73	9	37	.312	.450	.228

Yount is going to present problems to HOF selection committees that they haven't had to face since they elected Ernie Banks.

For about half of his career, Banks was an extraordinary shortstop. For the second half of his career, he was a less productive first baseman. He's listed as a first baseman despite the fact that it's his production numbers during his shortstop years that qualified him for consideration.

Yount has a bum arm. After 11 notable years as a shortstop with Milwaukee, he played outfield and first base in 1985 and 1986. How will the HOF treat him?

Robin Yount is a Class 4 infielder who, turning 31 years of age in

1986, has time to improve his productivity rating. He must do so to strengthen his marginal position as a pretender. Class 4 of the HOF is currently populated with defensive specialists of superior durability. Although a good fielder, Robin will not make anyone forget Aparicio. But he has a good chance to improve productivity, BA, and durability numbers.

Robin broke into minor leagues at 18 years of age in 1973. A year later, he was the dominant shortstop for Milwaukee. In 1975, at 20 years of age, Yount owned the job. Still only 31 years old (at the end of 1986), Robin already has 13 seasons behind him. In 12 of them, he played in 100 + games—an average of 143 games a year.

Yount is essentially a good contact hitter with credible power. As a scorer of runs, he has had four superstar years. Three times his BA has been .300 + ; in three other seasons, he has approached this BA level. He had one superstar RBI year, three others with an SA of .500 + , and in two years his PAB was .300 + . Robin ranks next to Ripken among active shortstops—a fine ballplayer. And it should be noted that, on a team which features clout rather than speed, Robin is a capable and dangerous base stealer.

In 1982, Robin had his best power and production year: PAB .337, 29 home runs, BA .331. In all except home runs, this was an across-the-board superstar season for the young man.

According to his 100 + game profile, Yount is a high level Class 4 shortstop. In his early twenties, Yount was a low level Class 4 infielder. In his late twenties, he was a Class 2 infielder. In 1986, he sunk again to Class 4, but the suspicion is that this reflects the deterioration of his team's offensive capabilities more than it hints at declining personal skills.

What will Yount be in future years? Will he self-destruct in his thirties as so many do these days, or will he continue for four to six years current (and HOF) performance levels? The HOF future of Robin Yount depends on how these questions are resolved.

Bill Madlock

Born 1951
Height 5'11"; weight 185
Throws right, bats right
HOF—Possible

Year	Age	G	AB	H	R	HR	RBI	BA	SA	PAB
1974	23	128	453	142	56	9	45	.313	.442	.243
1975	24	130	514	182	70	7	57	.354	.479	.261

Year	Age	G	AB	H	R	HR	RBI	BA	SA	PAB
1976	25	142	514	174	53	15	69	.339	.500	.267
1977	26	140	533	161	58	12	34	.302	.426	.195
1978	27	122	447	138	61	15	29	.309	.481	.235
1979	28	154	560	167	71	14	71	.298	.438	.279
1980	29	137	494	137	52	10	43	.277	.399	.213
1982	31	154	568	181	73	19	76	.319	.488	.296
1983	32	130	473	153	56	12	56	.323	.444	.262
1984	33	103	403	102	34	4	40	.253	.323	.194
1985	34	133	513	141	57	12	44	.275	.402	.220
1986	35	111	379	106	28	10	50	.280	.404	.232
Total		1584	5851	1784	669	139	614	.305	.438	.243
Other*		114	356	122	44	7	43	.343	.503	.264
Career		1698	6207	1906	713	146	657	.307	.442	.244

*Less than 100 games: 1973, 1981

Standard Deviation	15	56	25	13	4	14			
Avg.	132	488	149	56	12	51	.305	.438	.243

Normal Performance Range (100 + games)

High	147	544	174	69	15	65	.320	.487	.275
Low	117	431	123	43	8	37	.286	.376	.203

Best Year (over 139 games): 1982

Super Years (PAB .323 +): None

Good Years (PAB .284–.322): 1982

Fair Years (PAB .246–.283): 1975, 1976, 1979, 1983

Avg.	139	515	169	63	12	63	.328	.465	.267

Other Years (PAB .245 −): 1974, 1977, 1978, 1980, 1984, 1985, 1986

Avg.	125	460	132	49	10	41	.288	.412	.218

Average Yearly Performance by Age

25 and under	133	494	166	60	10	57	.336	.475	.257
26–30	138	509	151	61	13	44	.296	.435	.231
31–35	126	467	137	50	11	53	.292	.418	.244

History has shown that HOF selection committees look favorably on players who can maintain a .300 + BA over a career of 6,000–9,000 at bats. Bill Madlock, by 1986, had completed 14 major league seasons with about 6,200 at bats. His lifetime BA is .307. If he protects this BA achievement for at least three more seasons, he's a good bet to make the HOF. Thirty-five years old in '86, this assignment is not an easy one for him. He isn't aging well. For the past three seasons, his BA was below .300.

Madlock is a legitimate pretender who must show more durability, and protect his BA, to remain in contention.

Bill was 19 years old in 1970 when he joined organized baseball. In

1974, Texas looked at him and unflatteringly traded him to the Cubs. That fortunate club installed him at third base, and he proceeded to give them three gang-buster seasons. The team rewarded him by trading him to San Francisco for meeny, miny, and mo before the 1977 season. Still only 26 years old, Bill headed west and gave his new team the best part of three good seasons. The organization rewarded him with a trade, this time to the Pirates, where he resided for five + seasons until traded to Los Angeles in 1985.

Madlock has had twelve 100 + game seasons. In seven of them, his BA was .300 + — two of them, .330 + . Contact hitting is his bag. That he isn't one of the leading scorers in the league is partly due to the fact that he has averaged only 132 games a season, and to the fact that getting on base is only half of the scoring act — teammates must drive you in to complete the runs scored routine.

In 1982, Bill had his best power season, stroking 19 into the seats. This was also his most efficient production year — a PAB of .296 supported by a BA of .319.

According to his 100 + game profile, Madlock is a high level Class 4 infielder capable of broad swings in quality from year to year. He had no superstar seasons, one Class 2 season, four Class 3 years, five Class 4 seasons, and two bummers. As a producer, he's not exactly dependable.

If elected to the HOF at current production levels, Madlock would slip between Robinson and Kell, as follows:

	AB	R	HR	RBI	PAB	BA	SA
Hornsby	8,173	.156	.037	.156	.349	.358	.577
Herman	7,707	.145	.006	.103	.254	.304	.407
Kell	6,702	.120	.012	.118	.250	.306	.414
Madlock	**6,207**	**.115**	**.024**	**.105**	**.244**	**.307**	**.442**
Robinson	10,654	.090	.025	.102	.218	.267	.401
Aparicio	10,230	.122	.008	.069	.200	.262	.343

Madlock is nowhere near the glove man that Robinson was, nor does he figure to last as long as Robby did. So, to get into the HOF, Bill must compete favorably with Kell. If he does not maintain career quality for a few more years, he is in trouble.

In his early twenties, Madlock was a Class 3 infielder. In his late twenties, the batting eye slipped a notch, and so did his quality rating. Now in his mid-thirties, Bill is showing strong signs of deterioration.

Athletes of today are (or should be) better conditioned than they used to be — and they are taller and huskier. Diets are better. Doctors hover over them. Trained surgeons patch them up. They live in cleaner, better facilities when on the road. They don't run, throw, field, or hit when appropriate muscles aren't going ticktock like they're supposed to. Yet, flocks of them poop out when they're in their late twenties and early thirties. A few hot years and poof—skills vanish. Why?

A hungry man will work harder for a loaf of bread than a well-fed one will. When the hungry man gets his loaf, he's more apt to repeat the chores used to get it than his well-fed brother will. Don't you agree? There is a correlation between work and need.

Players of today get too rich, too quickly, for too little. Rich men don't bust their humps once the pocket is full. Neither do ballplayers.

Carney Lansford
Born 1957
Height 6'2"; weight 195
Throws right, bats right
HOF—Possible

Year	Age	G	AB	H	R	HR	RBI	BA	SA	PAB
1978	21	121	453	133	55	8	44	.294	.406	.236
1979	22	157	654	188	95	19	60	.287	.436	.266
1980	23	151	602	157	72	15	65	.261	.390	.252
1981	24	102	399	134	57	4	48	.336	.439	.273
1982	25	128	482	145	54	11	52	.301	.444	.243
1984	27	151	597	179	56	14	60	.300	.439	.218
1986	29	151	591	168	61	19	53	.284	.421	.225
Total		961	3778	1104	450	90	382	.292	.425	.244
Other*		178	700	203	71	23	68	.290	.449	.231
Career		1139	4478	1307	521	113	450	.292	.428	.242

*Less than 100 games: 1983, 1985

| *Standard Deviation* | | 19 | 87 | 20 | 14 | 5 | 7 | | | |
| Avg. | | 137 | 540 | 158 | 64 | 13 | 55 | .292 | .425 | .244 |

Normal Performance Range (100 + games)
| High | | 156 | 627 | 178 | 78 | 18 | 61 | .283 | .440 | .251 |
| Low | | 118 | 452 | 138 | 51 | 8 | 48 | .304 | .403 | .234 |

Best Year (over 139 games): 1979

Super Years (PAB .323 +): None

Good Years (PAB .284–.322): None

Fair Years (PAB .246–.283): 1979, 1980, 1981
| Avg. | | 137 | 552 | 160 | 75 | 13 | 58 | .289 | .420 | .263 |

Other Years (PAB .245 –): 1978, 1982, 1984, 1986
| Avg. | | 138 | 531 | 156 | 57 | 13 | 52 | .294 | .428 | .229 |

	G	AB	H	R	HR	RBI	BA	SA	PAB
Average Yearly Performance by Age									
25 and under	132	518	151	67	11	54	.292	.422	.254
26–30	151	594	174	59	17	57	.292	.430	.221

Carney is one of the best young infielders in the game. He is producing at Class 4 levels and, at 29 years of age in 1986, is in his prime (prime years of the better infielders are 24–32 years of age). Enough information on Lansford is already in to say that he's no Brooks Robinson with the glove. If he's going to make it, the bat will have to do it for him.

This means that Lansford will have to end up as a Class 3 infielder with a PAB in the .246–.283 range. In four of his seven full seasons to date, he has done so. Carney has demonstrated the ability to hit .300+ in a season. Unless an impressive power stroke comes to him soon—at no expense to his BA—he'd be wise to concentrate on this contact hitting ability, his only road to the museum.

Carney is a legitimate pretender, but too new on the scene to rate as better than a possibility for the HOF. If he develops further, it will probably be in the George Brett mold. Their comparative statistics appear below:

	AB	R	HR	RBI	PAB	BA	SA
Brett	6,675	.129	.031	.127	.287	.314	.505
Lansford	4,478	.116	.025	.101	.242	.292	.428

Lansford started at 18 years of age in 1975. In 1978, 21 years of age, he was the regular third baseman for California. He spent three seasons with that club, two with the Red Sox, and now seems to be settled down in Oakland. Carney is injury prone, and has appeared in an average of 137 games a year during his seven 100+ game years. He missed most of the 1983 and 1985 seasons, and must stay healthy soon if he hopes to build a competitive durability record.

According to his 100+ game profile, Carney is stuck at the Class 3–4 level—no Class 1 or Class 2 seasons. He is a competitive clutch hitter. To build the right numbers, he needs more extra base hits and more help from his teammates.

Carney has a long way to go, but if he maintains his production rate, he would fit into the HOF infield corps between Robinson and Kell, both third basemen, as follows:

	AB	R	HR	RBI	PAB	BA	SA
Hornsby	8,173	.156	.037	.156	.349	.358	.577

	AB	R	HR	RBI	PAB	BA	SA
Herman	7,707	.145	.006	.103	.254	.304	.407
Kell	6,702	.120	.012	.118	.250	.306	.414
Lansford	**4,478**	**.116**	**.025**	**.101**	**.242**	**.292**	**.428**
Robinson	10,654	.090	.025	.102	.218	.267	.401
Aparicio	10,230	.122	.008	.069	.200	.262	.343

Carney must either significantly improve his PAB, or boost his BA above .300, and accomplish such things over five more full seasons to seriously compete for HOF honors.

Lansford is the best of the young third basemen in this active player sample. He has never had better than a Class 3 year—yet another example of the deterioration of talent in major league baseball.

The number of major league teams has expanded greatly—a smaller pool of lesser-trained players are thinly layered around both leagues. No wonder the best young third baseman is a Class 4 player.

Alan Trammell
Born 1958
Height 6'0"; weight 170
Throws right, bats right
HOF—Possible

Year	Age	G	AB	H	R	HR	RBI	BA	SA	PAB
1978	20	139	448	120	47	2	32	.268	.339	.181
1979	21	142	460	127	62	6	44	.276	.357	.243
1980	22	146	560	168	98	9	56	.300	.404	.291
1981	23	105	392	101	50	2	29	.258	.327	.207
1982	24	157	489	126	57	9	48	.258	.395	.233
1983	25	142	505	161	69	14	52	.319	.471	.267
1984	26	139	555	174	74	14	55	.314	.468	.258
1985	27	149	605	156	66	13	44	.258	.380	.203
1986	28	151	574	159	86	21	54	.277	.469	.280
Total		1270	4588	1292	609	90	414	.282	.405	.243
Other*		19	43	8	3	0	0	.186	.186	.070
Career		1289	4631	1300	612	90	414	.281	.403	.241

*Less than 100 games: 1977

| *Standard Deviation* | | 14 | 65 | 24 | 16 | 6 | 9 | | | |
| Avg. | | 141 | 510 | 144 | 68 | 10 | 46 | .282 | .405 | .243 |

Normal Performance Range (100 + games): 1980

| High | | 155 | 575 | 168 | 83 | 16 | 55 | .291 | .469 | .268 |
| Low | | 127 | 444 | 120 | 52 | 4 | 37 | .269 | .324 | .209 |

Best Year (over 139 games): 1980

Super Years (PAB .323 +): None

	G	AB	H	R	HR	RBI	BA	SA	PAB

Good Years (PAB .284–.322): 1980

Fair Years (PAB .246–.283): 1983, 1984, 1986

| Avg. | 144 | 545 | 165 | 76 | 16 | 54 | .302 | .469 | .269 |

Other Years (PAB .245 –): 1978, 1979, 1981, 1982, 1985

| Avg. | 138 | 479 | 126 | 56 | 6 | 39 | .263 | .362 | .213 |

Average Yearly Performance by Age

| 25 and under | 139 | 476 | 134 | 64 | 7 | 44 | .281 | .386 | .240 |
| 26–30 | 146 | 578 | 163 | 75 | 16 | 51 | .282 | .438 | .246 |

Alan is the keystone partner of Sweet Lou Whitaker in the Detroit infield. They shared their first full big league season, Alan at 20 years of age, Lou at 21. In no small way, the strong defensive middle that they provide accounts for the success of the Tiger franchise in recent years.

Since the sore-armed Yount moved to the outfield, Alan Trammell is the only shortstop in the majors who competes decently against the talented Cal Ripken of Baltimore. In head-to-head competition, they look like this:

				Offense			
	AB	R	HR	RBI	PAB	BA	SA
100 + games:							
Ripken	634	.125	.042	.107	.273	.291	.487
Trammell	459	.133	.020	.090	.243	.282	.405
1986:							
Ripken	627	.116	.040	.090	.246	.282	.461
Trammell	574	.150	.030	.094	.280	.277	.469

Power and durability are the offensive differences between the two shortstops, with Trammell closing the gap in recent years.

			Defense		
	APG	EPG	Total	EPG%	FA
Career:					
Ripken	3.064	.135	3.199	4.22	.972
Trammell	2.783	.109	2.892	3.77	.976
1986:					
Ripken	2.975	.080	3.055	2.62	.982
Trammell	2.947	.146	3.093	4.72	.969

In 1986 Trammell was 28, Ripken 27. Trammell has played longer, and the defensive strain may be showing. Using Ozzie Smith's fielding average as the standard (.978), both are good glove men.

Offensively, Ripken is top dog and he is at least as good as Trammell with the glove. Overall, the vote goes to him.

Trammell was 18 when, in 1976, he joined the minor leagues. In 1977, Detroit brought him up for a few games. In 1978, at 20 years of age, Alan took over the demanding job of shortstop for the team. He has been there since.

Fundamentally, Alan is maturing into an adept contact hitter with growing power. But given the many examples of modern stars going *el foldo* after a few hot years, his 1985 season was worrisome — BA .258, PAB .203 — but he snapped back in 1986 with one of his best seasons.

In 1980, Alan had his best production year, with a Class 2 PAB of .291, accompanied by a BA of .300 and nine home runs. According to his 100 + game profile, he is a high level Class 4 infielder whose performance can range broadly from year to year. He has had no superstar years, one Class 2 season, three Class 3 years, four Class 4 seasons, and one bummer.

Alan is a legitimate pretender who hasn't been around long enough to rate as better than a possibility for HOF recognition. He has plenty of time to build the necessary durability record, and has shown streaks of HOF contact hitting and production talent. To make it, he must sustain higher levels of play for at least six more seasons.

If elected to the HOF, Alan would slip into the popular spot for modern infielders — between Kell and Robinson, as follows:

	AB	R	HR	RBI	PAB	BA	SA
Hornsby	8,173	.156	.037	.156	.349	.358	.577
Herman	7,707	.145	.006	.103	.254	.304	.407
Kell	6,702	.120	.012	.118	.250	.306	.414
Trammell	**4,631**	**.132**	**.019**	**.090**	**.241**	**.281**	**.403**
Robinson	10,654	.090	.025	.102	.218	.267	.401
Aparicio	10,230	.122	.008	.069	.200	.262	.343

Alan has a long way to go.

Graig Nettles
Born 1944
Height 6′0″; weight 187
Throws right, bats left
HOF — Probable

Year	Age	G	AB	H	R	HR	RBI	BA	SA	PAB
1970	26	157	549	129	55	26	36	.235	.404	.213
1971	27	158	598	156	50	28	58	.261	.435	.227
1972	28	150	557	141	48	17	53	.253	.395	.212
1973	29	160	552	129	43	22	59	.234	.386	.225
1974	30	155	566	139	52	22	53	.246	.403	.224
1975	31	157	581	155	50	21	70	.267	.430	.243
1976	32	158	583	148	56	32	61	.254	.475	.256
1977	33	158	589	150	62	37	70	.255	.496	.287
1978	34	159	587	162	54	27	66	.276	.460	.250
1979	35	145	521	132	51	20	53	.253	.401	.238
1981	37	103	349	85	31	15	31	.244	.398	.221
1982	38	122	405	94	29	18	37	.232	.402	.207
1983	39	129	462	123	36	20	55	.266	.446	.240
1984	40	124	395	90	36	20	45	.228	.413	.256
1985	41	137	440	115	51	15	46	.261	.420	.255
1986	42	126	354	77	20	16	39	.218	.379	.212
Total		2298	8088	2025	724	356	832	.250	.424	.236
Other*		210	628	147	64	28	51	.234	.419	.228
Career		2508	8716	2172	788	384	883	.249	.424	.236

*Less than 100 games: 1968, 1969, 1980

Standard Deviation		17	87	26	11	6	12			
Avg.		144	506	127	45	22	52	.250	.424	.236

Normal Performance Range (100 + games)

High		161	592	153	56	28	64	.258	.461	.251
Low		126	419	100	34	16	40	.239	.372	.216

Best Year (over 139 games): 1977

Super Years (PAB .323 +): None

Good Years (PAB .284–.322): 1977

Fair Years (PAB .246–.283): 1976, 1978, 1984, 1985

Avg.		145	501	129	49	24	55	.257	.446	.254

Other Years (PAB .245 –): 1970, 1971, 1972, 1973, 1974, 1975, 1979, 1981, 1982, 1983, 1986

Avg.		142	499	124	42	20	49	.248	.408	.225

Average Yearly Performance by Age

25 and under		0	0	0	0	0	0	.000	.000	.000
26–30		156	564	139	50	23	52	.246	.405	.220
31–35		155	572	149	55	27	64	.261	.454	.255
36 +		124	401	97	34	17	42	.243	.412	.233

It seems as though Nettles has been around forever—and he has. He was 23 years old when he first looked at the major leagues in Minnesota in 1967; 26 years old when he got his first starting job with Cleveland; 29 years old when he joined the Yankees; 40 years old when he went west to San Diego—and he's still going. But his playing time for

1986 and the preceding five years suggests that he's just keeping time, waiting for the clock to run out. Who can blame him for hanging on — he still gets the big bucks. But the fact that he can, says something nasty about the level of talent in baseball.

In his 20-year career, Graig had sixteen 100 + game seasons, averaging 144 games a year — good durability. He has about 8,700 at bats to his credit, more than most HOF infielders. Durability is no problem for Nettles.

Graig never had a BA of .300 + , or a SA of .500 + , or a PAB of .300 + . Yet he is a legitimate pretender. Why? Because he has impressive durability and other superior talents. What are the superior talents? He has more lifetime home runs than any other AL third baseman (nowhere near as many as Mathews of the HOF and the NL), he has a respectable Class 4 PAB, and he has been a superb defensive third baseman. It's better than a 50/50 bet that Graig will make it — sometime — no rush.

Is Nettles as good with the glove as Robinson was? Defensive comparisons by age brackets are shown below.

| | | | *Defense* | | | |
	G	APG	EPG	Total	EPG%	FA
25 and under						
Robby	781	2.014	.101	2.115	4.78	.968
Graig	121	.438	.033	.471	7.02	.980
26–30						
Robby	783	2.135	.082	2.217	3.69	.975
Graig	780	2.455	.130	2.585	5.01	.962
31–35						
Robby	785	2.205	.093	2.298	4.05	.971
Graig	777	2.251	.099	2.350	4.22	.969
36 +						
Robby	547	2.274	.088	2.362	3.72	.972
Graig	830	1.842	.130	1.972	6.59	.951
Career						
Robby	2896	2.148	.091	2.239	4.07	.971
Graig	2508	2.092	.116	2.208	5.25	.962

It could be argued that when both were 25–35 years old, the added range of Graig made him the more effective of the two despite a persistently higher error rate — he who gambles much often errs; he who gambles not at all, is error-free.

Both were poets of the hot corner. Robinson has been recognized for this skill. Probably, Nettles will be too.

According to his 100 + game profile, Nettles is a Class 4 infielder. He never had a superstar season. He had one Class 2 year, four Class 3 years, and 11 Class 4 seasons.

Nettles competes well with lower echelon Class 4 HOF infielders, as follows:

	AB	R	HR	RBI	PAB	BA	SA
Hornsby	8,173	.156	.037	.156	.349	.358	.577
Herman	7,707	.145	.006	.103	.254	.304	.407
Kell	6,702	.120	.012	.118	.250	.306	.414
Nettles	**8,716**	**.090**	**.044**	**.102**	**.236**	**.249**	**.424**
Robinson	10,654	.090	.025	.102	.218	.267	.401
Aparicio	10,230	.122	.008	.069	.200	.262	.343

Buddy Bell

Born 1951
Height 6'2"; weight 185
Throws right, bats right
HOF—Possible

Year	Age	G	AB	H	R	HR	RBI	BA	SA	PAB
1972	21	132	466	119	40	9	27	.255	.363	.163
1973	22	156	631	169	72	14	45	.268	.393	.208
1974	23	116	423	111	44	7	39	.262	.352	.213
1975	24	153	553	150	56	10	49	.271	.376	.208
1976	25	159	604	170	68	7	53	.281	.366	.212
1977	26	129	479	140	53	11	53	.292	.426	.244
1978	27	142	556	157	65	6	56	.282	.392	.228
1979	28	162	670	200	71	18	83	.299	.451	.257
1980	29	129	490	161	59	17	66	.329	.498	.290
1982	31	148	537	159	49	13	54	.296	.426	.216
1983	32	156	618	171	61	14	52	.277	.411	.206
1984	33	148	553	174	77	11	72	.315	.458	.289
1985	34	151	560	128	51	10	58	.229	.350	.213
1986	35	155	568	158	69	20	55	.278	.445	.254
Total		2036	7708	2167	835	167	762	.281	.408	.229
Other*		97	360	106	34	10	54	.294	.428	.272
Career		2133	8068	2273	869	177	816	.282	.409	.231

*Less than 100 games: 1981

Standard Deviation		13	66	23	11	4	13			
Avg.		145	551	155	60	12	54	.281	.408	.229

Normal Performance Range (100 + games)

High		159	617	178	70	16	68	.288	.449	.250
Low		132	485	132	49	8	41	.272	.357	.202

	G	AB	H	R	HR	RBI	BA	SA	PAB

Best Year (over 139 games): 1984

Super Years (PAB .323 +): None

Good Years (PAB .284–.322): 1980, 1984

	G	AB	H	R	HR	RBI	BA	SA	PAB
Avg.	139	522	168	68	14	69	.321	.477	.290

Fair Years (PAB .246–.283): 1977, 1979, 1986

	G	AB	H	R	HR	RBI	BA	SA	PAB
Avg.	149	572	166	64	16	64	.290	.442	.252

Other Years (PAB .245 –): 1972, 1973, 1974, 1975, 1976, 1978, 1982, 1983, 1985

	G	AB	H	R	HR	RBI	BA	SA	PAB
Avg.	146	550	148	56	10	48	.270	.382	.208

Average Yearly Performance by Age

	G	AB	H	R	HR	RBI	BA	SA	PAB
25 and under	143	535	144	56	9	43	.269	.372	.202
26–30	141	549	165	62	13	65	.300	.441	.254
31–35	152	567	158	61	14	58	.279	.418	.235

Buddy turned 35 years old in 1986. The 1985 season was one of his worst, but thanks to the confident support of his manager, Pete Rose, he snapped back with a good year in 1986. Will he prosper or fold during the next few years? His physical condition and record say he will have a few more good seasons.

Bell is one of the best defensive third baseman in baseball today. Additionally, with a career BA of .282, Bell is one of the best contact hitters of the active infielders and, for an infielder, a respectable power hitter too. With such an array of skills, Bell is a pretender. But he needs two or three more years of above average performance to make it. Imposing durability is an important characteristic for a Class 4 offensive talent.

A major problem for Buddy throughout his career has been the quality of teams with which he has been associated. Cleveland and Texas organizations gained far more from his presence than he did from them. Playing with better teams always improves statistical and actual performance of a competitor like Bell. Had this been the case, instead of the opposite, it is reasonable to project that Buddy would have produced more Class 2 and Class 3 seasons. And a succession of such seasons, combined with defensive skills, would have greatly enhanced his HOF chances.

Bell was 18 when he entered professional baseball in 1969. In 1972, he was the regular third baseman for the Cleveland Indians. After seven years with that hapless organization—years which featured steady personal growth—Buddy happily headed west and joined the Texas group, hoping that the competitive environment would improve. It did not. Although his personal play continued at high levels, the Texas organization was a long way from being a new baseball dynasty. In 1985, Pete

Rose rescued Bell from the Texas carpet to an organization that is often involved in post-season action. Bell should benefit from the move.

Buddy completed his fifteenth season in 1986. A sound contact hitter, he has enough power to keep the opposition honest. His top production season was 1984 when, at 33 years of age, he generated a PAB of .289 supported by a BA of .315 and 11 home runs. Bell has had five seasons with a BA of .290 + . Except for his first three years, and 1985, he never hit less than .270. Few with his BA have had worse luck scoring runs. Few active players with his BA and clutch hitting traits have fewer RBIs to show for it. This is a reflection of the banjo-hitting teams he has endured, and is an example of why HOF selection committees take a look at BAs as well as run production.

Bell shows up for 145 games a year, and has over 8,000 at bats behind him. This is good durability but, unless he improves his PAB, he figures to be compared with Robinson when the HOF dons do their pondering. A more impressive durability factor would help him greatly. Is he physically and mentally up to it? Time will tell.

The analysis of Bell's career, and that of many other players, points up the problem with which HOF selection committees will be increasingly faced during upcoming years. Player productivity is falling. This general slippage hurts the player with capacity to produce but who, at the same time, is dependent on the talents of teammates to fatten his numbers. Baseball, despite the increasing focus on the home run, is a team game. Hitters must have hitters behind them to score. Hitters must have hitters in front of them to get RBIs. Too often good hitters get little support — in front or in back. This reduces production of good hitters and increases the likelihood that historically minded members of selection committees will overlook deserving players.

Some active Class 4 infielders have been analyzed in depth because some aspect of their talent pool compares favorably with the records of the two lowest rated HOF infielders. Remaining Class 4 infielders will be treated more cursorily in the belief that selection committees will rarely choose players with PAB levels assigned to this classification unless they have demonstrated extraordinary capability in some highly regarded area of the game.

DeCinces, Grich, Molitor, Herr, Randolph

The above infielders have PABs in the .236–.245 range.

Doug DeCinces, the good-fielding California third baseman, has a high level Class 4 PAB. But Doug has a bad back and only about 5,300 at bats in his background. He will not play long enough to earn HOF backing. Waiting for Brooks Robinson to retire cost Doug the playing time he needed to build a durability record. He is no pretender.

If Grich, the California second baseman, had 10,000 + at bats to his credit, his superior defensive record and his adequate production history would draw HOF attention. With but 6,900 at bats behind him, however, the 37-year-older (as of '86) is not a pretender.

Durability is also the problem of Paul Molitor, the charismatic third baseman for Milwaukee. In his nine major league seasons, he has played 140 + games only four times. Thirty years old in 1986, it's too late for him to build the impressive durability record that he needs. Paul is not a pretender.

Tommy Herr, the St. Louis second baseman, has the same problem as Molitor, albeit for different reasons. According to HOF standards, his production record and BA are rather ordinary, and his excellent defensive skills won't get attention unless supported by imposing durability credentials—which he doesn't have. Tommy didn't have a regular job in the majors until he was 28. The late start killed his HOF chances.

It seems that Willie Randolph has been around forever. But he hasn't. He was only 32 years old in 1986. Willie has completed 11 major league seasons with about 5,500 at bats.

Willie got old when he was 26. Until then, he was good for 30 + stolen bases a year. Since then, his top has been 16. It shows in other ways too. From 1976 through 1980, Willie's production record showed upward progress. Since then, the production trend is down. Slippage in the field is also noticeable. During his first five seasons, Randolph averaged 139 games and 3.08 assists per game; during the past six, he has averaged 128 games and 2.82 assists per game. About the only thing in Willie's game that has held up is his BA. Like clockwork, Randolph will deliver a BA in the .270–.280 range.

The point is, Willie is fading fast. He'll have trouble developing acceptable durability characteristics. He's a good ballplayer, offensively and defensively, but won't be around long enough to get HOF attention. Statistically, Willie is a pretender—in the real world, chances are slim that he will make it.

Parrish, Lopes, Orta, Garner, Mulliniks, Bernazard, Smalley

These players have PABs in the .226–.235 range.

Larry Parrish, now with Texas, was 33 years old in 1986. He has averaged 125 games a year with two clubs over a 13-year career. No defensive genius, Parrish is a home run threat (16 per year, average) that some managers have found useful. In terms of durability or skill, Larry is not HOF caliber.

Davey Lopes turned 40 years old in 1986. Now with Houston, Davey had 15 years and about 6,300 at bats—a short career in HOF terms. As a full-time player, mostly at second base, Dave was through in 1980. Since then, he has floated around as a utility player. A good journeyman athlete, Davey is not a HOF infielder.

Jorge Orta, now with Kansas City, was 36 years old in '86. In his 15-year major league career, he has played for five clubs, averaging 116 games a year at six different positions. Obviously a part-time player with ordinary defensive ability, Jorge is not a pretender.

Phil Garner, now with Houston, saw his thirty-seventh year in 1986. In 14 years, Phil had played for four teams, averaging 124 games per year. Except for first base, Phil has played all infield positions. With about 5,900 at bats to his credit, the talented utility man will not build a HOF record.

Steve Mulliniks was, in 1986, a 30-year-old utility infielder for Toronto. A good journeyman ballplayer, Steve is not a pretender.

Tony Bernazard, 30 years old in '86, is the regular second baseman for the Indians. He is a good all-around ballplayer. A player with about 3,200 at bats behind him at Tony's age has little chance of building a durability record that might qualify him for consideration.

Roy Smalley, 34 years old in 1986, came up with Texas in 1975, moved to Minnesota for an extended stay, touched bases with New York and Chicago, and now plays several positions back in Minnesota. In 12 seasons, Smalley has averaged 129 games a year, mostly at shortstop. Since 1980, Smalley has been mostly a utility man who has lived by the bat—not the glove. With 5,300 at bats behind him, Roy is not a HOF player.

Ray, Brookens, White

The above players have PABs in the .216–.225 range.

Johnny Ray, the 29-year-old second baseman of Pittsburgh in 1986, is a good contact hitter who handles himself well defensively. Ray will not build an astounding durability record. Stuck with the Pirates, it's doubtful that his PAB will rise above the Class 4 range. He is not a major base-stealing threat. His only HOF chance is to fatten his BA—a slim chance.

Tom Brookens, 33 years old in '86, had a shot at third base with the Tigers and didn't make it. He's no pretender.

Frank White is a slick fielding second baseman. Over past seasons, Frank has fielded his position as well as the job can be done. But high level skills came late to White, and his career-long record, in the field and at the plate, will not be good enough to draw serious HOF attention. Now 36 years of age with 14 seasons and 6,100 at bats behind him, Frank hasn't time to build the durability record to join the Class 4 HOF infielders—no pretender here.

White is a media favorite. He will draw HOF support when his time comes. But, if the HOF is to remain as the home of the great—not the good—then the personable and talented White must be passed by. A direct comparison with Bobby Doerr should make this obvious.

	AB	R	HR	RBI	PAB	BA	FA
White	6,100	.100	.022	.092	.214	.260	.981
Doerr	7,093	.123	.031	.144	.298	.288	.980

Concepcion, Templeton, Knight, Cruz, Washington, Wallach, Gross, Royster, Burleson, Hubbard

The above infielders have PABs in the .206–.215 range.

Dave Concepcion has 17 seasons and about 8,200 + at bats behind him. Until 1986, when he turned 38, he had been a fully active player for the Cincinnati Reds. Dave will build a strong durability record before he's through, but not as good as Aparicio's. Dave doesn't cover the ground that Luis did, nor is he as sure-handed. Close might be good enough if the durability factor were as strong. But it isn't. And the higher PAB of Concepcion isn't strong enough to offset comparative weaknesses. Dave will be looked at as a HOF prospect, but he hasn't displayed enough tools long enough to be regarded as a pretender. Like Frank White, Dave has been a fine ballplayer in his era, but this isn't enough to draw HOF votes.

Garry Templeton, the 30-year-old San Diego shortstop in 1986, has about 5,600 at bats to his credit. His BA has not been .300 + since 1980. He is not a defensive or base-stealing genius. It's unlikely that his PAB will improve much, or that his final durability stats will be unduly impressive. Garry is not a pretender.

Ray Knight, 34 years old in 1986, is coming away from a good season with the Mets, mostly playing third base. A hot World Series seems to have made many forget that Ray has been a utility infielder with three clubs for most of his career. In 11 years, he has averaged 113 games a year. The HOF does not enshrine utility men.

Julio Cruz, 32 years old in '86, has been a hurt second baseman with the White Sox for the past two years. He may never be a regular again. In a ten-year career, Julio has averaged 116 games a season. Similar to the others above, Cruz is a journeyman ballplayer who does not have HOF talent.

U.L. Washington, 33 years old in 1986, has ten seasons and 2,800 at bats behind him. Durability alone eliminates this player from future HOF competition.

Tim Wallach turned 29 years old in 1986, and was the regular third baseman with Montreal for the preceding five years. He's a solid, but not outstanding, all-around ballplayer with better than average power. Tim has not shown HOF talent yet, and it's doubtful that he will in the future.

Thirty-four years old in '86, Gross averaged 101 games a season as a utility man for either Oakland or the Orioles. He played in only three major league games in 1986. Wayne is not a HOF candidate.

Jerry Royster has been a utility infielder for San Diego, and before that, Atlanta. In a 14-year career, he has averaged 92 games a year with three different clubs — not a HOF record.

Rick Burleson, 35 years old in 1986, is struggling to make a comeback with California. For all practical purposes, Rick's last season as a full-time player of considerable promise was 1980. Shortly after the trade which sent him from Boston to California, Burleson's arm blew. Absent the injury, Rick might have built a record of pretender quality — given the injury, he will not be considered.

Glenn Hubbard, 29 years old in 1986, has been the regular second baseman for Atlanta for the past five years. He's a solid fielder with modest batting skills. For his age, his durability stats aren't impressive. Glenn is not a HOF talent.

Morrison, Oberkfell, Gantner, Wilfong, Garcia

The above infielders have PABs in the .200–.205 range. The lowest rated HOF infielder is Aparicio, whose PAB was .200.

Jim Morrison, a 34-year-old utility man with Pittsburgh in '86, played a full season that year for the first time since 1980. This is not a HOF record.

Ken Oberkfell, 30 years old in '86, spent a 9-year utility man career with the Cardinals, and now plays regularly for Atlanta. He has averaged 106 games a season. With only 3,400 at bats behind him, Ken doesn't have a chance to build HOF numbers over the balance of his career.

Jim Gantner has been a steady infielder for the Brewers for the past seven years. Prior to that, he served as a utility man for the same club. Gantner has been active for 11 years, averaging 98 games a season. A talented batsman and a competent fielder, it's too late for Jim to build a HOF record.

Bob Wilfong is a utility infielder for California. In a ten-year career, he has averaged 96 games a year for Minnesota and California—he is no pretender.

Damaso Garcia, 29 years old in 1986, is the lowest rated active Class 4 infielder—but is more talented than many of them. The Yankees fooled around with him for two seasons, then traded him to Toronto. In 1980, he took over second base duties for that club and, except when injured in 1981, held the job through the 1985 season. In 1986, he shared the job with another. Damaso is a competent fielder. In the past five seasons, he hit .300 + twice, and never hit less than .280. Because of his late start, it's unlikely that Garcia will develop Aparicio-like durability characteristics. Unless he goes crazy with the bat, Damaso has no HOF future.

The review of active Class 4 infielders is complete. It has revealed a fact worth noting—a considerable number of key defensive positions throughout the baseball world are being manned by part-time players. Many managers, unable to find men who can both hit and field to standards, are manipulating rosters vigorously, trying to get adequate performance by platooning right against left, fast vs. slow, good defense vs. hard hands, long ball vs. contact hitter.

This, combined with the plethora of over-the-hill players who are still active, are a telling comment on the general quality of talent which populates the modern baseball universe.

Ozzie Smith

Under the methodology being used, Ozzie Smith has been eliminated as a pretender—he has a PAB lower than that of Aparicio, the lowest rated HOF infielder. Why resurrect him?

When Aparicio was appointed to the HOF, a new de facto standard of eligibility was established. Prior to that election, offensive characteristics essentially determined an infielder's fate. Luis clearly did not fit the offensive mold of HOF infielders. It follows that, for the first time, other characteristics were lifted to a weight equal to, or greater than, batsmanship. In Lou's case, it was durability, defensive genius, and speed that did the job.

Doors were opened (that the HOF may regret) when Lou was enshrined. And Smith may squeeze through one of these doors. Why? Because he is a highly skilled shortstop. Equal to Aparicio? How does he compare in durability and speed?

Ozzie Smith sports a PAB of .199. Aparicio made it with a PAB of .200. Except for Luis, the lowest PAB in the HOF infield corps is .250 (George Kell). Obviously, Aparicio didn't crash the gates with his production record. Smith is about as productive as Luis. If he makes the HOF, it won't be because of offensive talent either.

Over a long career, Aparicio developed a BA of .262. Smith hits .247. The HOF is inclined to honor players with .300 + BAs, and usually pays little attention to .250 hitters. Luis wasn't chosen for contact hitting ability nor will Ozzie.

Aparicio had 10,230 at bats when he retired. In 1986, Ozzie was 32 years old with 4,739 at bats. For the most recent two seasons, Ozzie averaged 526 at bats. To catch Luis, he needs 5,491 more at bats—over ten seasons' worth. It's highly doubtful that Ozzie will play full tilt until he is 43 years old, so he won't match Luis' durability record.

In nine seasons, Ozzie has stolen 303 bases—34 a year. Ozzie had two seasons of 40 + stolen bases. In 18 years, Luis stole 506 bases—28 a year. In five seasons, he stole 40 + . Both shortstops show speed. But Aparicio is the clear champ.

Ozzie has played for nine years (1986); Luis, for 18 years. For comparative purposes, below are some defensive statistics for the first nine years of each man's career:

	Smith				*Aparicio*			
	APG	%	Total	EPG%	APG	%	Total	EPG%
1	3.45	.16	3.61	4.4	3.12	.23	3.35	6.9
2	3.56	.13	3.69	3.5	3.14	.14	3.29	4.3
3	3.93	.15	4.08	3.7	3.19	.14	3.33	4.2
4	3.84	.15	3.99	3.8	3.03	.15	3.18	4.7
5	3.82	.09	3.91	2.3	3.60	.12	3.72	3.2
6	3.26	.13	3.39	2.8	3.12	.19	3.31	5.7
7	3.52	.10	3.62	2.8	2.95	.13	3.08	4.2
8	3.47	.09	3.56	2.5	2.76	.08	2.84	2.8
9	2.96	.10	3.06	3.3	2.99	.10	3.09	3.2
	3.53	.12	3.65	3.3	3.10	.14	3.24	4.3

In the previous figures, putouts are ignored. Major league infielders seldom make an error on a ball in the air — ground balls and errant throws account for most errors. By relating all errors to assists only, a better reading of defensive skill is obtained at no great sacrifice to accuracy.

Relative to the evolution of the fielding glove, Aparicio played in a different era. Error rates are not comparable. For example, in the 1950s, .91 errors per game were made; in the 1980s (1984), .84 errors per game — the figure has been dropping for years as gloves have improved.

According to the above, Smith covers more ground than Luis and is more sure-handed. Even after making a reasonable adjustment for the different eras, the inference is strong that Smith makes fewer errors than Aparicio did.

Is Smith a pretender? How does he stack up with Luis?

	Smith	Aparicio
PAB	.199	.200
BA	.247	.262
SB-Per yr.	34	28
APG	3.52	3.08
EPG	.12	.14
Total	3.64	3.22
EPG/Total	3.3%	4.4%
AB	4,739	10,230

If Ozzie equals Luis' durability, will he make it? Based on current numbers, he probably would — he's a better shortstop — so far. He competes well in other areas. But it's not likely that Smith will play as long as Luis — few have — or that his numbers will look as sweet down the line. The book is still open on Ozzie. His career is far from over. For this reason, and in recognition of his superb defensive talents, he must be considered a pretender, albeit a long shot.

Infielders — The Pretenders

Active infielders have been analyzed, some in depth, some lightly. Theoretically, all Class 1 and 2 fielders are above-average pretenders unless something negative is discovered in record analysis. And all Class 3 players are below-average pretenders unless aberrations are found during analysis. All Class 4 infielders who meet the standards set by existing HOF players in that Class qualify as pretenders. Finally, no Class 5 player earns pretender designation unless something outstanding in his record is discovered.

In the outfield section, 12 pretenders were found who have varying chances of success in their pursuit of HOF honors. None are super-stars—few appear to be guaranteed a place in the museum. The infield corps is similarly lean, as follows:

	BA	PAB	Comment
Schmidt	.268	.308	Probable
Brett	.314	.287	Probable
Ripken	.289	.270	Possible
Cey	.261	.252	Possible—long shot
Yount	.285	.245	Possible—position?
Whitaker	.281	.245	Possible—Durability?
Madlock	.307	.244	Possible—Durability?
Lansford	.292	.242	Possible—BA?
Trammell	.281	.241	Possible—Durability?
Nettles	.249	.236	Probable—Defense
Bell	.282	.231	Possible—Durability?
Smith	.247	.199	Possible—Durability?

Similar to the outfield analysis, 12 infielders have chances of vary-ing strengths to make the HOF if they last long enough and if career ac-complishments do not ultimately differ too much from present levels. Generally speaking, baseball is richer in infield talent than it is in out-field talent. Schmidt is certainly one of the most outstanding players of his time, regardless of position. Brett is a throwback to the skill mixture that used to pertain in the major leagues, and would have been a better producer had he played decades ago. Ripken may be Cronin reborn. Yount, Whitaker, Madlock, Lansford, and Trammell have demon-strated everything but durability. And Nettles, Bell, and Smith can play quality defense with the best infielders who ever pulled a glove on.

So it's a good crop of infielders who will be facing HOF selection procedures sometime in the next 15–20 years. But with the possible ex-ceptions of Schmidt and Brett, there should be no unseemly haste in electing them. None are superstars whose absence will make the museum seem bare. Others were better and only casually recognized—others were better who haven't been elected yet.

Throughout the infielder section, reference has been made to defensive skill. Using Aparicio, Doerr, and Robinson as reference points, below are the three best active fielders at each infield position who have played at least 50 percent of the games played by the respec-tive models.

	G	APG	EPG	Total	EPG%	FA
			Shortstop			
Concepcion	2300	2.924	.139	3.063	4.54	.971
Trammell	1289	2.783	.109	2.892	3.77	.976
Yount*	1671	3.095	.176	3.271	5.37	.964
Aparicio	2599	3.084	.141	3.225	4.37	.971

*Through 1984—positional future cloudy.

	G	APG	EPG	Total	EPG%	FA
			Second Base			
Grich	2008	2.934	.094	3.028	3.10	.983
Whitaker	1283	2.949	.083	3.032	2.74	.983
White	1803	2.838	.097	2.935	3.30	.981
Doerr	1865	3.062	.115	3.177	3.62	.980

	G	APG	EPG	Total	EPG%	FA
			Third Base			
Bell	2133	2.163	.113	2.276	4.96	.965
Nettles	2508	2.092	.116	2.208	5.25	.962
Schmidt	2107	2.174	.137	2.311	5.93	.961
Robinson	2896	2.148	.091	2.239	4.07	.971

The infield analysis is complete—no superstars. But legitimate pretenders were nonetheless located. Now it is time to explore the world of first base.

First Basemen

There are 20 players in the first baseman sample. In terms of PAB classifications, the group is slotted as follows:

Class	Number
1	0
2	0
3	5
4	4
5	11

To begin with, it's apparent that no superstars, or near superstars, are active today. On the surface, it appears that five strong candidates are in the flock, and four Class 4 talents deserve a look. Others are ineligible on production grounds, but will be scanned for attributes deserving of HOF consideration.

Applicable standards against which to measure the performance of active first basemen are set forth below:

	Standard
Quality — PAB	
Class 1	.379 +
2	.325–.378
3	.273–.324
4	.258–.272
Durability — at Bats	
Long	8563 +
Medium	6124–8562
Short	6123 –

First basemen are established as a category separate from other infielders because, historically, the position has been peopled by high producing sluggers who can't be fairly compared with traditionally lighter-hitting infielders. In modern baseball, this is less and less the case, as the above summary and the following classification listing demonstrate. Following is the analysis of active first basemen with at least 800 games played through the 1986 season.

	G	AB	H	R	HR	RBI	BA	SA	PAB
Class 1 .379 +									
None									
Class 2 .325–.378									
None									
Class 3 .273–.324									
Murray	1499	5624	1679	609	275	740	.299	.505	.289
Hernandez	1721	6090	1840	841	128	772	.302	.445	.286
Clark	1235	4405	1213	508	194	511	.275	.477	.275
Horner	960	3571	994	330	215	437	.278	.508	.275
Thornton	1529	5206	1332	531	253	637	.256	.457	.273
Class 4 .258–.272									
Johnson	1369	3945	1016	343	196	503	.258	.459	.264
Perez	2777	9778	2732	893	379	1273	.279	.463	.260
Cooper	1833	7099	2130	752	235	854	.300	.469	.259
Durham	862	3006	844	320	116	342	.281	.475	.259
Class 5 .257 –									
Evans, Darrell	2286	7761	1947	828	347	805	.251	.432	.255

	G	AB	H	R	HR	RBI	BA	SA	PAB
Class 5 (cont.)									
Thompson	1418	4802	1253	432	208	574	.261	.438	.253
Kingman	1941	6677	1575	459	442	768	.236	.478	.250
Upshaw	965	3198	857	373	97	323	.268	.431	.248
Driessen	1708	5419	1450	589	152	600	.268	.412	.247
Garvey	2305	8759	2583	867	271	1028	.295	.448	.247
Rose	3562	14053	4256	2005	160	1154	.303	.409	.236
Bochte	1538	5233	1478	543	100	558	.282	.396	.230
Buckner	2176	8424	2464	844	164	908	.292	.417	.227
Chambliss	2174	7570	2109	727	185	787	.279	.415	.224
Cabell	1688	5952	1647	693	60	536	.277	.370	.217

According to developed procedures, Class 5 players are to be dropped from the balance of the analysis as ineligible, unless outstanding characteristics other than production can be identified.

Hall of Fame selection committees react positively to batting averages in .300 territory, and are impressed as well by durability and "most of" records that oftentimes attach to that characteristic. Mindful of such attitudes, three Class 5 first basemen deserve a deeper look:

Steve Garvey — batting skill.
Pete Rose — batting skill; durability.
Bill Buckner — batting skill.

The remaining players in Class 5, several of them fine journeyman ballplayers, are dismissed from the balance of this analysis.

Eddie Murray
Born 1956
Height 6'2"; weight 200
Throws right, bats both
HOF — Probable

Year	Age	G	AB	H	R	HR	RBI	BA	SA	PAB
1977	21	160	611	173	54	27	61	.283	.470	.232
1978	22	161	610	174	58	27	68	.285	.480	.251
1979	23	159	606	179	65	25	74	.295	.475	.271
1980	24	158	621	186	68	32	84	.300	.519	.296
1982	26	151	550	174	55	32	78	.316	.549	.300
1983	27	156	582	178	82	33	78	.306	.538	.332
1984	28	162	588	180	68	29	81	.306	.509	.303
1985	29	156	583	173	80	31	93	.297	.523	.350
1986	30	137	495	151	44	17	67	.305	.463	.259
Total		1400	5246	1568	574	253	684	.299	.503	.288

	G	AB	H	R	HR	RBI	BA	SA	PAB
Other*	99	378	111	35	22	56	.294	.534	.299
Career	1499	5624	1679	609	275	740	.299	.505	.289

*Less than 100 games: 1981

Standard Deviation	7	37	9	12	5	9			
Avg.	156	583	174	64	28	76	.299	.503	.288

Normal Performance Range (100 + games)

High	163	620	183	75	33	85	.296	.528	.312
Low	148	546	165	52	23	67	.302	.474	.261

Best Year (over 139 games): 1985

Super Years (PAB .379 +): None

Good Years (PAB .325–.378): 1983, 1985

Avg.	156	583	176	81	32	86	.301	.530	.341

Fair Years (PAB .273–.324): 1980, 1982, 1984

Avg.	157	586	180	64	31	81	.307	.525	.300

Other Years (PAB .272–): 1977, 1978, 1979, 1986

Avg.	154	581	169	55	24	68	.292	.472	.253

Average Yearly Performance by Age

25 and under	160	612	178	61	28	72	.291	.486	.263
26–30	152	560	171	66	28	79	.306	.518	.310

The crown as king of active first basemen sits easily on the head of Eddie Murray. During recent years, Ed has out-produced Keith Hernandez, and passed him as a career producer during a powerful 1985 season. Also, Murray is a match for Keith as a defensive first baseman. With the glove, neither of these men need bow to peers or ancestors.

The following comparison of the past five seasons of Murray and Hernandez justifies the claim that Ed is the best piece of first base talent in the eligible group.

	Avg. AB	R*	HR*	RBI*	PAB	BA
Murray	560	.121	.047	.145	.313	.306
Hernandez	562	.129	.020	.131	.280	.305

* = per at bat.

Eddie was weaned on a baseball—four other Murrays are in organized baseball. In 1973, at 17 years of age, he was playing minor league ball; at 21, he was the regular first baseman for the Orioles; at 30, he was the best first baseman in the game. This is progress. At 35, who knows? King, maybe.

Murray is a throwback to the old masters, albeit not as skilled as some. He gives you contact hitting, power, and clutch hitting. His best power season was 1983 — 33 home runs, PAB .332, and a BA of .306 — a solid Class 2 performance. But his best production year was 1985 — PAB .350, BA .297, and 31 long shots.

If elected to the HOF at existing achievement levels, Murray would fit between Terry and Kelly.

	AB	HR	R	RBI	PAB	BA	SA
Gehrig	8,001	.062	.174	.187	.423	.340	.632
Bottomley	7,471	.029	.128	.161	.319	.310	.500
Terry	6,428	.024	.150	.144	.318	.341	.506
Murray	**5,624**	**.049**	**.108**	**.132**	**.289**	**.299**	**.505**
Kelly	5,993	.025	.112	.145	.282	.297	.452
Killebrew	8,147	.070	.087	.124	.282	.256	.509
Banks	9,421	.054	.084	.119	.258	.274	.500

Ed fits nicely. Durability should not be a major problem for him. He has the combined batting skills to open the spread between himself and Kelly, especially if his teammates perform well and give him more scoring and RBI opportunities.

According to his 100 + game profile, Murray averages out as a stable Class 3 first baseman. He has had no superstar years, two Class 2 years, three Class 3 years, two Class 4 seasons, and two bummers. In his early twenties, Ed was a Class 4 first baseman. By his early thirties, he was an established Class 3 performer, and will most probably end up as such.

Murray is not Gehrig reincarnated — as the press would like us to believe — nor is he a Foxx, or a Greenberg. But he is a quality first baseman who would have been recognized as such in any baseball era — a star of the day, fast earning HOF credentials.

Ed would be wise to keep an eye over his shoulder. Don Mattingly is challenging.

Keith Hernandez
Born 1953
Height 6'0"; weight 185
Throws left, bats left
HOF — Probable

Year	Age	G	AB	H	R	HR	RBI	BA	SA	PAB
1976	23	129	374	108	47	7	39	.289	.428	.249
1977	24	161	560	163	75	15	76	.291	.459	.296

Year	Age	G	AB	H	R	HR	RBI	BA	SA	PAB
1978	25	159	542	138	79	11	53	.255	.389	.264
1979	26	161	610	210	105	11	94	.344	.513	.344
1980	27	159	595	191	95	16	83	.321	.494	.326
1981	28	103	376	115	57	8	40	.306	.463	.279
1982	29	160	578	173	72	7	87	.299	.413	.287
1983	30	150	538	160	65	12	51	.297	.433	.238
1984	31	154	550	171	68	15	79	.311	.449	.295
1985	32	158	593	183	77	10	81	.309	.430	.283
1986	33	149	551	171	81	13	70	.310	.446	.298
Total		1643	5867	1783	821	125	753	.304	.448	.290
Other*		78	223	57	20	3	19	.256	.372	.188
Career		1721	6090	1840	841	128	772	.302	.445	.286

*Less than 100 games: 1974, 1975

Standard Deviation		17	78	30	15	3	18			
Avg.		149	533	162	75	11	68	.304	.448	.290

Normal Performance Range (100 + games)

High		167	611	192	90	14	87	.313	.486	.313
Low		132	455	133	59	8	50	.291	.398	.258

Best Year (over 139 games): 1979

Super Years (PAB .379 +): None

Good Years (PAB .325–.378): 1979, 1980

Avg.		160	603	201	100	14	89	.333	.504	.335

Fair Years (PAB .273–.324): 1977, 1981, 1982, 1984, 1985, 1986

Avg.		148	535	163	72	11	72	.304	.442	.290

Other Years (PAB .272 –): 1976, 1978, 1983

Avg.		146	485	135	64	10	48	.279	.415	.250

Average Yearly Performance by Age

25 and under		150	492	136	67	11	56	.277	.425	.272
26–30		147	539	170	79	11	71	.315	.465	.298
31–35		154	565	175	75	13	77	.310	.442	.292

Keith is one of the finest fielding first basemen in baseball. Aggressive, he often leads the league in putouts, assists, or both, and is almost unbelievably sure-handed—he has a FA of .994. Most will agree with this assessment. But some will not agree—or will be surprised to learn—that Hernandez is the number two producer among active first basemen as well.

Hernandez is probably one of the most underrated players in the game. Why? He is not a major home run hitter. The overall production value of a consistent hitter with some power (like Hernandez) is systematically overlooked by PR people. On the other hand, the overall production value of poor contact hitters with home run capability is regularly overvalued by the media—they confuse drama with excellence.

A perfect example of this over/under value phenomenon exists right on Keith's team, the Mets, where he is paired with catcher Garry Carter in the middle of the lineup. Judging by newspaper inches of publicity, it's obvious that many consider the slugging catcher to be the better producer of the two. Nothing could be further from the truth, as the below comparisons demonstrate.

	AB	HR	R	RBI	PAB	BA	SA
Career							
Hernandez	6,090	.021	.138	.127	.286	.302	.445
Carter	6,063	.045	.095	.120	.260	.271	.462
1986							
Hernandez	551	.024	.147	.127	.298	.310	.446
Carter	490	.049	.116	.165	.330	.255	.439

During the championship 1986 season, Carter was a more productive player, but over the long course the above graphic demonstrates that the first baseman has been the dependable producer.

Keith, 33 years old in 1986, had a PAB better than that of several HOF first sackers. He's a good bet to develop the necessary durability characteristics before he retires. His Class 3 season in 1986 is a good sign. Keith is a pretender with a good chance to get into the HOF, although certain personal problems may delay his selection.

Hernandez entered the game in 1972 at 19 years of age. In 1974 and 1975, he played a little first base for the Cardinals, then covered that position regularly for them from 1976 to 1982. In 1983, Keith was traded to the Mets where he plays today. For New York it was a great trade. For the St. Louis club—who got two pitchers, Tweedledee and Tweedledum—it was one of the those dumb deals for which baseball is famous.

Hernandez is not a great power hitter: He hits an average of 11 big ones a year. For production, he relies upon scoring and RBIs. His best production year was 1979 when, at 26 years of age, he generated a PAB of .344 supported by a BA of .344 and 11 home runs. This solid Class 2 season is one of the best turned in by a first baseman in recent years.

According to his 100 + game profile, Keith averages out as a Class 3 first baseman. He has had no superstar years, two Class 2 years, six Class 3 years, three Class 4 seasons, and two bummers. If elected to the HOF, Keith would fit between Terry and Kelly, as follows:

	AB	HR	R	RBI	PAB	BA	SA
Gehrig	8,001	.062	.174	.187	.423	.340	.632
Bottomley	7,471	.029	.128	.161	.319	.310	.500
Terry	6,428	.024	.150	.144	.318	.341	.506
Hernandez	**6,090**	**.021**	**.138**	**.127**	**.286**	**.302**	**.445**
Kelly	5,993	.025	.112	.145	.282	.297	.452
Killebrew	8,147	.070	.087	.124	.282	.256	.509
Banks	9,421	.054	.084	.119	.258	.274	.500

Except for Killebrew, Hernandez fits the general mold of his closest HOF competitors. The spread between him and Kelly/Killebrew should grow before he retires.

In his early twenties, Keith was a Class 4 producer, better at that age than most of his peers. In his late twenties, contact and clutch hitting abilities bloomed and moved him to Class 3. In his early thirties, he has remained at that level.

For over nine seasons, Hernandez labored in the obscure St. Louis environment. His association with the Mets will draw more media attention, important to a player with the undramatic style of Hernandez. He represents the kind of athlete that is often overlooked.

Jack Clark
Born 1955
Height 6'3"; weight 205
Throws right, bats right
HOF—Doubtful

Year	Age	G	AB	H	R	HR	RBI	BA	SA	PAB
1977	22	136	413	104	51	13	38	.252	.407	.247
1978	23	156	592	181	65	25	73	.306	.537	.275
1979	24	143	527	144	58	26	60	.273	.476	.273
1980	25	127	437	124	55	22	60	.284	.517	.314
1982	27	157	563	154	63	27	76	.274	.481	.295
1983	28	135	492	132	62	20	46	.268	.441	.260
1985	30	126	442	124	49	22	65	.281	.502	.308
Total		980	3466	963	403	155	418	.278	.483	.282
Other*		255	939	250	105	39	93	.266	.455	.252
Career		1235	4405	1213	508	194	511	.275	.477	.275

*Less than 100 games: 1975, 1976, 1981, 1984, 1986

Standard Deviation	12	63	23	6	4	13			
Avg.	140	495	138	58	22	60	.278	.483	.282

Normal Performance Range (100+ games)

High	152	558	161	63	27	72	.288	.526	.291
Low	128	432	115	52	18	47	.265	.427	.270

	G	AB	H	R	HR	RBI	BA	SA	PAB
Best Year (over 139 games): 1978									
Super Years (PAB .379 +): None									
Good Years (PAB .325–.378): None									
Fair Years (PAB .273–.324): 1978, 1979, 1980, 1982, 1985									
Avg.	142	512	145	58	24	67	.284	.503	.291
Other Years (PAB .272 –): 1977, 1983									
Avg.	136	453	118	57	17	42	.261	.425	.254
Average Yearly Performance by Age									
25 and under	141	492	138	57	22	58	.281	.489	.277
26–30	139	499	137	58	23	62	.274	.474	.287

Jack had a relatively slow road to the major leagues. In 1973, at 18 years of age, he entered organized ball and immediately showed contact hitting ability and power. After an impressive season in 1975, San Francisco took a quick look at him, but it was back to the minors again for most of the 1976 year. Finally, in 1977, he was in the bigs to stay.

Jack came up as an outfielder, and acquitted himself well in that role for San Francisco for seven years. For the next two years, he also dabbled with the first base position until traded to the Cardinals in time for the 1985 season. Clark could easily be classified as an outfielder rather than a first baseman, but since St. Louis has decided to employ him full time at the initial sack, he was included in the first baseman group.

In 1986, Jack completed his twelfth major league season, averaging 103 games a year. In seven relatively full years, he averaged 140 games per year. Seasonal durability figures point up Jack's biggest problem — in 1986 he was 31 years old with only 4,405 at bats behind him. Even to reach a short career standard, Clark needs about four more solid seasons. Given his history of injuries, it's doubtful he'll last the course. On durability grounds alone, Clark is not a pretender.

Clark is a decent contact hitter with better than average power. His best power year was 1982 when, at 27 years of age, he clocked 27 homers supported by a BA of .274, and a PAB of .295. This was also his most productive year in which he played 139 + games. Jack has never had a Class 1 or Class 2 year — he had five Class 3 seasons, one Class 4, and one bummer.

If elected to the HOF, Clark would fit between McCovey and Banks, as follows:

	AB	HR	R	RBI	PAB	BA	SA
Gehrig	8,001	.062	.174	.187	.423	.340	.632

	AB	HR	R	RBI	PAB	BA	SA
Killebrew	8,147	.070	.087	.124	.282	.256	.509
McCovey	8,197	.064	.086	.126	.276	.270	.515
Clark	**4,405**	**.044**	**.115**	**.116**	**.275**	**.275**	**.477**
Banks	9,421	.054	.084	.119	.258	.274	.500

Compared with relatively recent appointees to the HOF, Clark has HOF talent, but not HOF durability. Both are required. Hall of Fame committees are unduly impressed with career length and the "most of" records that naturally attach to it, but it is nevertheless sound to give sufficient weight to durability when making choices.

Bob Horner
Born 1957
Height 6'1"; weight 215
Throws right, bats right
HOF — Doubtful

Year	Age	G	AB	H	R	HR	RBI	BA	SA	PAB
1979	22	121	487	153	33	33	65	.314	.552	.269
1980	23	124	463	124	46	35	54	.268	.529	.292
1982	25	140	499	130	53	32	65	.261	.501	.301
1983	26	104	386	117	55	20	48	.303	.528	.319
1985	28	130	483	129	34	27	62	.267	.499	.255
1986	29	141	517	141	43	27	60	.273	.472	.251
Total		760	2835	794	264	174	354	.280	.513	.279
Other*		200	736	200	66	41	83	.272	.489	.258
Career		960	3571	994	330	215	437	.278	.508	.275

*Less than 100 games: 1978, 1981, 1984

Standard Deviation	13	42	12	8	5	6			
Avg.	127	473	132	44	29	59	.280	.513	.279

Normal Performance Range (100 + games)

High	139	514	144	52	34	65	.280	.557	.295
Low	114	431	121	36	24	53	.280	.459	.261

Best Year (over 139 games): 1982

Super Years (PAB .379 +): None

Good Years (PAB .325–.378): None

Fair Years (PAB .273–.324): 1980, 1982, 1983

Avg.	123	449	124	51	29	56	.275	.519	.303

Other Years (PAB .272 –): 1979, 1985, 1986

Avg.	131	496	141	37	29	62	.284	.507	.258

	G	AB	H	R	HR	RBI	BA	SA	PAB
Average Yearly Performance by Age									
25 and under	128	483	136	44	33	61	.281	.527	.287
26–30	125	462	129	44	25	57	.279	.497	.271

Bob Horner never spent a day in the minor leagues. In nine major league seasons, he never once played over 141 games. The first fact suggests HOF talent; the second, his durability problem.

Twenty-nine years old in 1986, Horner has defensively concentrated on first and third base—he's no great shakes with the glove. Apparently settled at the initial sack, he is included with the first basemen grouping under the assumption that he will finish his career at that position.

Horner will make his reputation with the bat, not the glove. From the beginning, he demonstrated home run power. His best power year was 1980 when, at 23 years of age, he belted 35 big ones, supported by a BA of .268 and a PAB of .292. His best production year (139 + games) was 1982. Then 25 years old, he developed a PAB of .301, a BA of .261, and hit 32 homers.

According to his 100 + game profile, Horner is a Class 3 first baseman. In three seasons, he played less than 100 games. In the other six years, he developed three Class 3, one Class 4, and two bum years— the most recent, 1985, 1986.

If elected to the HOF, Bob would fit between McCovey and Banks, as follows:

	AB	HR	R	RBI	PAB	BA	SA
Gehrig	8,001	.062	.174	.187	.423	.340	.632
Killebrew	8,147	.070	.087	.124	.282	.256	.509
McCovey	8,197	.064	.086	.126	.276	.270	.515
Horner	**3,571**	**.060**	**.092**	**.123**	**.275**	**.278**	**.508**
Banks	9,421	.054	.084	.119	.258	.274	.500

Mr. Horner is a piece of talent—when he plays. But he doesn't play enough. He needs six more full seasons to build a fair durability record. Gifted with HOF talent, Horner will probably miss the boat that considers strength and will, as well as talent, as part of the admission price.

Andre Thornton

Born 1949
Height 6'2"; weight 205
Throws right, bats right
HOF—Doubtful

Year	Age	G	AB	H	R	HR	RBI	BA	SA	PAB
1974	25	107	303	79	31	10	36	.261	.439	.254
1975	26	120	372	109	52	18	42	.293	.516	.301
1977	28	131	433	114	49	28	42	.263	.527	.275
1978	29	145	508	133	64	33	72	.262	.516	.333
1979	30	143	515	120	63	26	67	.233	.449	.303
1982	33	161	589	161	58	32	84	.273	.484	.295
1983	34	141	508	143	61	17	60	.281	.439	.272
1984	35	155	587	159	58	33	66	.271	.484	.267
1985	36	124	481	109	27	22	66	.227	.391	.239
1986	37	120	401	92	32	17	49	.229	.392	.244
Total		1347	4697	1219	495	236	584	.260	.465	.280
Other*		182	509	113	36	17	53	.222	.381	.208
Career		1529	5206	1332	531	253	637	.256	.457	.273

*Less than 100 games: 1973, 1976, 1980, 1981

| *Standard Deviation* | | 16 | 87 | 26 | 14 | 8 | 15 | | | |
| Avg. | | 135 | 470 | 122 | 50 | 24 | 58 | .260 | .465 | .280 |

Normal Performance Range (100 + games)

		G	AB	H	R	HR	RBI	BA	SA	PAB
High		151	557	148	63	31	73	.265	.509	.300
Low		118	382	96	36	16	44	.252	.400	.250

Best Year (over 139 games): 1978

Super Years (PAB .379 +): None

Good Years (PAB .325–.378): 1978

Fair Years (PAB .273–.324): 1975, 1977, 1979, 1982, 1983

| Avg. | | 139 | 483 | 129 | 57 | 24 | 59 | .268 | .480 | .289 |

Other Years (PAB .272 –): 1974, 1984, 1985, 1986

| Avg. | | 127 | 443 | 110 | 37 | 21 | 54 | .248 | .430 | .252 |

Average Yearly Performance by Age

	G	AB	H	R	HR	RBI	BA	SA	PAB
25 and under	107	303	79	31	10	36	.261	.439	.254
26–30	135	457	119	57	26	56	.260	.499	.304
31–35	152	561	154	59	27	70	.275	.470	.279
36 +	122	441	101	30	20	58	.228	.391	.241

Some people have a lot of luck. Andre is one of them — and most of his luck has been bad. Thirty-seven years old in '86, he may be through as a full-time player — in 1985 and 1986, he was a DH for Cleveland.

Although Thornton has 13 major league seasons behind him, he played in 100 + games in only ten, averaging 135 games a year. With only 5,200 at bats at this stage in his career, Andre will not establish adequate durability for HOF consideration. Statistically, he looks like a pretender; in fact, he is not.

During his full seasons, Thornton had a PAB of .280. He is

essentially a power hitter. His defensive credentials are not superior. His best power seasons were in 1978 and 1984, with 33 home runs in each. The first of these, 1978, was his best overall production year. He generated a PAB of .333 and a BA of .262.

According to his 100 + game profile, Andre is a Class 3 first baseman. He has had no superstar seasons, one Class 2 year, three Class 3 years, three Class 4 years, and three bummers. His comparative skill level is demonstrated in the following graphic:

	AB	HR	R	RBI	PAB	BA	SA
Gehrig	8,001	.062	.174	.187	.423	.340	.632
Killebrew	8,147	.070	.087	.124	.282	.256	.509
McCovey	8,197	.064	.086	.126	.276	.270	.515
Thornton	**5,206**	**.049**	**.102**	**.122**	**.273**	**.256**	**.457**
Banks	9,421	.054	.084	.119	.258	.274	.500

Despite a short, injury-riddled career, Thornton had more, or as many, high quality seasons as many players of much higher reputation, but not enough total action to meet HOF standards of durability.

Do it well; do it long. These are the basic demands imposed on HOF aspirants. Some athletes were overrated (and elected to the HOF) because they did it well for a few years; some were overrated (and elected to the HOF) because they did it long. It must be both. The HOF is not the place for Sam Skyrocket or Dan Durable. It's the home for the strong and the talented.

Tony Perez
Born 1942
Height 6'2"; weight 205
Throws right, bats right
HOF—Possible

Year	Age	G	AB	H	R	HR	RBI	BA	SA	PAB
1965	23	104	281	73	28	12	35	.260	.466	.267
1967	25	156	600	174	50	28	74	.290	.500	.253
1968	26	160	625	176	75	18	74	.282	.430	.267
1969	27	160	629	185	66	37	85	.294	.526	.299
1970	28	158	587	186	67	40	89	.317	.589	.334
1971	29	158	609	164	47	25	66	.269	.438	.227
1972	30	136	515	146	43	21	69	.283	.497	.258
1973	31	151	564	177	46	27	74	.314	.527	.261
1974	32	158	596	158	53	28	73	.265	.460	.258
1975	33	137	511	144	54	20	89	.282	.466	.319
1976	34	139	527	137	58	19	72	.260	.452	.283
1977	35	154	559	158	52	19	72	.283	.463	.256

Year	Age	G	AB	H	R	HR	RBI	BA	SA	PAB
1978	36	148	544	158	49	14	64	.290	.449	.233
1979	37	132	489	132	45	13	60	.270	.425	.241
1980	38	151	585	161	48	25	80	.275	.467	.262
Total		2202	8221	2329	781	346	1076	.283	.478	.268
Other*		575	1557	403	112	33	197	.259	.386	.220
Career		2777	9778	2732	893	379	1273	.279	.463	.260

*Less than 100 games: 1964, 1966, 1981, 1982, 1983, 1984, 1985, 1986

Standard Deviation		15	83	27	11	8	13			
Avg.		147	548	155	52	23	72	.283	.478	.268

Normal Performance Range (100 + games)

		G	AB	H	R	HR	RBI	BA	SA	PAB
High		161	631	182	63	31	85	.289	.522	.283
Low		132	466	128	41	15	59	.275	.419	.248

Best Year (over 139 games): 1970

Super Years (PAB .379 +): None

Good Years (PAB .325–.378): 1970

Fair Years (PAB .273–.324): 1969, 1975, 1976

		G	AB	H	R	HR	RBI	BA	SA	PAB
Avg.		145	556	155	59	25	82	.280	.484	.300

Other Years (PAB .272 –): 1965, 1967, 1968, 1971, 1972, 1973, 1974, 1977, 1978, 1979, 1980

		G	AB	H	R	HR	RBI	BA	SA	PAB
Avg.		146	542	152	49	21	67	.281	.466	.253

Average Yearly Performance by Age

		G	AB	H	R	HR	RBI	BA	SA	PAB
25 and under		130	441	124	39	20	55	.280	.489	.258
26–30		154	593	171	60	28	77	.289	.495	.277
31–35		148	551	155	53	23	76	.281	.474	.274
36 +		144	539	150	47	17	68	.279	.448	.246

Ernie Banks is in the HOF because he defensively commanded two positions with considerable skill during his career: While a shortstop he was one of the most devastating power hitters in infield history, and he lasted longer than any other HOF first baseman. He is the lowest rated of the HOF first sackers and represents the minimum production standard that must be met if further deterioration of HOF quality is to be avoided.

If Tony Perez is elected to the HOF, he will join Banks in the Class 4 section of the HOF. A logical, but not powerful, pretender, Tony probably has a better chance of doing it than other Class 4 first basemen, including Cecil Cooper, because of his durability.

	AB	HR	R	RBI	PAB	BA	SA
Cooper	7,099	.033	.106	.120	.259	.300	.469
Perez	**9,778**	**.039**	**.091**	**.130**	**.260**	**.279**	**.463**
Banks	9,421	.054	.084	.119	.258	.274	.500

Cooper must build his durability and protect his other qualifying numbers while doing it. Perez, on the other hand, has surpassed the durability standard of Banks, owns a marginally superior PAB, and is about to retire. Also, Tony has covered two positions, as Ernie did, and has been a more effective RBI man and clutch hitter.

Cecil Cooper

Born 1949
Height 6'2"; weight 190
Throws left, bats left
HOF—Possible

Year	Age	G	AB	H	R	HR	RBI	BA	SA	PAB
1974	25	121	414	114	47	8	35	.275	.396	.217
1975	26	106	305	95	35	14	30	.311	.544	.259
1976	27	123	451	127	51	15	63	.282	.457	.286
1977	28	160	643	193	66	20	58	.300	.463	.224
1978	29	107	407	127	47	13	41	.312	.474	.248
1979	30	150	590	182	59	24	82	.308	.508	.280
1980	31	153	622	219	71	25	97	.352	.539	.310
1981	32	106	416	133	58	12	48	.320	.495	.284
1982	33	155	654	205	72	32	89	.313	.528	.295
1983	34	160	661	203	76	30	96	.307	.508	.306
1984	35	148	603	166	52	11	56	.275	.386	.197
1985	36	154	631	185	66	16	83	.293	.456	.261
1986	37	134	542	140	34	12	63	.258	.373	.201
Total		1777	6939	2089	734	232	841	.301	.472	.260
Other*		56	160	41	18	3	13	.256	.369	.213
Career		1833	7099	2130	752	235	854	.300	.469	.259

*Less than 100 games: 1971, 1972, 1973

Standard Deviation		21	115	38	13	7	22			
Avg.		137	534	161	56	18	65	.301	.472	.260

Normal Performance Range (100 + games)

High		157	649	199	70	25	87	.307	.510	.280
Low		116	419	122	43	10	43	.292	.412	.230

Best Year (over 139 games): 1980

Super Years (PAB .379 +): None

Good Years (PAB .325–.378): None

Fair Years (PAB .273–.324): 1976, 1979, 1980, 1981, 1982, 1983

Avg.		141	566	178	65	23	79	.315	.509	.295

Other Years (PAB .272 –): 1974, 1975, 1977, 1978, 1984, 1985, 1986

Avg.		133	506	146	50	13	52	.288	.436	.228

		G	AB	H	R	HR	RBI	BA	SA	PAB
Average Yearly Performance by Age										
25 and under		121	414	114	47	8	35	.275	.396	.217
26–30		129	479	145	52	17	55	.302	.485	.258
31–35		144	591	185	66	22	77	.313	.492	.279
36 +		144	587	163	50	14	73	.277	.418	.234

Cooper had the bad luck to grow up in the Boston Red Sox organization. Since being bitten by the Jimmy Foxx bug back in the 1930s, the Red Sox have been looking for another big, right-handed, long ball–hitting first sacker. Cooper, a slender left-hander, was treated like he had rabies while in Boston because of the right-handed power fetish. He never got a fair shot at the first base job and, finally, was traded to Milwaukee.

The Brewers got one of the best first basemen of the times. The Sox got—and deserved to get—wild-swinging, and right-handed, George Scott, proving that the organization that traded Babe Ruth still had the magic touch.

Cooper, with a PAB of .259, is a Class 4 first baseman. His PAB is better than that of the solitary incumbent of the HOF Class 4, Ernie Banks. Additionally, Cooper has a career BA of .300. For these reasons, Cooper must be considered as a pretender with a possible chance to be invited into the HOF.

Cooper has 16 seasons behind him, and played in 100 + games in 13 of them. He has averaged 137 games during his relatively full seasons, a low seasonal durability characteristic caused by the way he was handled during the Boston phase of his career. In his full seasons with that club, he averaged only 116 games a year. With Milwaukee, except when hurt, Cecil has been a sturdy performer.

The six years with Boston took their toll in terms of career at-bats. Coop needs as many as he can get over the remainder of his career so as to strengthen this aspect of his credentials.

Cecil is basically a contact hitter who, at times, goes on a power splurge. Averaging 18 home runs a year, his best power season was 1983 when he delivered 30 big ones. But his best overall production year occurred in 1980 when, at 31 years of age, he produced a PAB of .310 supported by a BA of .352 and 25 home runs—an impressive Class 3 performance.

According to his 100 + game profile, Cooper is a Class 4 first baseman. He has had no superstar or Class 2 years, six Class 3 years, two Class 4 and five bummers.

If elected to the HOF, Cooper would fit between McCovey and Banks, as follows:

	AB	HR	R	RBI	PAB	BA	SA
Gehrig	8,001	.062	.174	.187	.423	.340	.632
Killebrew	8,147	.070	.087	.124	.282	.256	.509
McCovey	8,197	.064	.086	.126	.276	.270	.515
Cooper	**7,099**	**.033**	**.106**	**.120**	**.259**	**.300**	**.469**
Banks	9,421	.054	.084	.119	.258	.274	.500

Build durability; hold the .300 BA. That's the formula Cecil must follow to crack the HOF.

Johnson, Durham

The above two players are Class 4 first basemen. If their records compare favorably with that of Ernie Banks, they deserve HOF consideration.

Cliff Johnson, 39 years old in 1986, played in 107 games with Toronto as a first baseman. In his entire major league career (15 seasons), Cliff has appeared in 140 + games only once (1983). The unanimous verdict of modern managers has been that Johnson is not a great ballplayer. Hall of Fame selection committees will agree.

Leon Durham turned 29 in 1986. In a seven-year career, he has been the first baseman of the Cubs in all but one. Leon is a good hitter who has delivered 20 + home runs in four of the past five seasons. To be a HOF candidate, a player should have about 5,000 at bats by the time he's 30 years old. Durham falls far short of this, and it's highly doubtful that his durability record will be adequate to move his other numbers into consideration.

Johnson and Durham are the last of the Class 4 active first basemen. Theoretically, the remaining first base candidates should be eliminated from the study since their PABs are lower than that of the lowest rated HOF first sacker, Ernie Banks (PAB .258).

But HOF committees have shown a willingness in the past to recognize qualities other than productivity as qualifying characteristics: durability, BA, defensive talent, and base-stealing ability, for example.

In Class 5 of the active roster of first basemen are three men who will be appraised by HOF committees because they have developed imposing records in some of the above areas—Pete Rose, Steve Garvey and Bill Buckner. Rose brings durability and BA. Garvey offers imposing durability, BA, and power. Buckner brings durability and contact hitting talents.

Top productivity records are certainly supported by imposing personal talents, but luck also plays a roll. Some great contact hitters are weak scorers because teammates don't move them along—because they hit in the wrong batting order position. The same is true about RBI stats—great hitters can show poorly because of factors over which they have no control. Rose, Garvey, and Buckner should have generated good production numbers. Blame circumstances for their failure to do so. It is entirely appropriate that selection committees consider what a player's production might have been had circumstances been more favorable to him.

Steve Garvey
Born 1948
Height 5'10"; weight 190
Throws right, bats right
HOF—Possible

Year	Age	G	AB	H	R	HR	RBI	BA	SA	PAB
1973	25	114	349	106	29	8	42	.304	.438	.226
1974	26	156	642	200	74	21	90	.312	.469	.288
1975	27	160	659	210	67	18	77	.319	.476	.246
1976	28	162	631	200	72	13	67	.317	.450	.241
1977	29	162	646	192	58	33	82	.297	.498	.268
1978	30	162	639	202	68	21	92	.316	.499	.283
1979	31	162	648	204	64	28	82	.315	.497	.269
1980	32	163	658	200	52	26	80	.304	.467	.240
1981	33	110	431	122	53	10	54	.283	.411	.271
1982	34	162	625	176	50	16	70	.282	.418	.218
1983	35	100	388	114	62	14	45	.294	.459	.312
1984	36	161	617	175	64	8	78	.284	.373	.243
1985	37	162	654	184	63	17	64	.281	.430	.220
1986	38	155	557	142	37	21	60	.255	.408	.212
Total		2091	8144	2427	813	254	983	.298	.451	.252
Other*		214	615	156	54	17	45	.254	.397	.189
Career		2305	8759	2583	867	271	1028	.295	.448	.247

*Less than 100 games: 1969, 1970, 1971, 1972

Standard Deviation		22	105	35	12	7	15			
Avg.		149	582	173	58	18	70	.298	.451	.252

Normal Performance Range (100 + games)

High		171	686	209	70	25	85	.304	.491	.264
Low		127	477	138	46	11	55	.289	.394	.234

Best Year (over 139 games): 1974

Super Years (PAB .379 +): None

Good Years (PAB .325–.378): None

	G	AB	H	R	HR	RBI	BA	SA	PAB
Fair Years (PAB .273–.324): 1974, 1978, 1983									
Avg.	139	556	172	68	19	76	.309	.478	.292
Other Years (PAB .272 –): 1973, 1975, 1976, 1977, 1979, 1980, 1981, 1982, 1984, 1985, 1986									
Avg.	152	589	174	55	18	69	.295	.444	.241
Average Yearly Performance by Age									
25 and under	114	349	106	29	8	42	.304	.438	.226
26–30	160	643	201	68	21	82	.312	.479	.265
31–35	139	550	163	56	19	66	.297	.453	.257
36 +	159	609	167	55	15	67	.282	.402	.231

Steve Garvey during his 100 + game seasons has a PAB near that of Ernie Banks, the lowest rated HOF first baseman. He also has a near .300 + BA during his 14 full seasons and, on a season to season basis, is the most durable man to play the position since Gehrig. Thirty-eight years old in 1986, the well-conditioned Garvey may be seeing the end of the tunnel. But he's a legitimate pretender and a very good bet to make it all the way. The fact that Garvey is one of the great gentlemen of the game won't hurt his chances any. He projects a fine image for a sports world that has been soiled by get-rich-quick, arrogant, drug-snorting athletes of the day. The sports scene needs more Garveys, Seavers, Winfields, and Dr. Js.

Garvey and Bill Buckner (another fine first baseman) got in each other's way in the early days of their careers. Both members of the Los Angeles organization at the time, they competed for the same job. As a consequence, neither got full-time duty. Finally, Buckner was traded and doors opened for both. But the competition had its price. Garvey was 27 years old before he was securely placed as a first baseman. Due to injuries as well as competition, Buckner didn't really get going until he was 30 years old.

Garvey is a generalist. In profile, he is a classic HOF player who does everything a degree or so below the stars of history. In 14 full seasons, his BA has been .300 + seven times. He is a solid contact hitter who delivers better than average power. And he is one of the outstanding clutch hitters in the game. In five seasons, he has had 80 + RBIs — superstar territory for this production element.

In 1977, at 29 years old, Steve had his best power year — 33 home runs. But his best production season was 1974 when, at 26 years of age, he generated a PAB of .288 supported by a BA of .312 and 21 homers — impressive Class 3 performance.

According to his 100 + game profile, Garvey averages out as a Class 5 first baseman, a tad less productive than Ernie Banks. Scoring is the major weakness in Steve's production performance. Given his contact hitting skills, this is a reflection on the ability of his teammates to exploit his talents properly. He has had three Class 3, three Class 4, and eight Class 5 seasons.

Steve Garvey is a player with marginal skill levels. That is to say, if elected, he will make it by a hair; if he misses, it will be by a hair. The difference could be his final BA. He needs .300 + to be safe.

Pete Rose
Born 1941
Height 5'11"; weight 203
Throws right, bats both
HOF—Probable

Year	Age	G	AB	H	R	HR	RBI	BA	SA	PAB
1963	22	157	623	170	95	6	35	.273	.371	.218
1964	23	136	516	139	60	4	30	.269	.326	.182
1965	24	162	670	209	106	11	70	.312	.446	.279
1966	25	156	654	205	81	16	54	.313	.460	.231
1967	26	148	585	176	74	12	64	.301	.444	.256
1968	27	149	626	210	84	10	39	.335	.470	.212
1969	28	156	627	218	104	16	66	.348	.512	.297
1970	29	159	649	205	105	15	37	.316	.470	.242
1971	30	160	632	192	73	13	31	.304	.421	.185
1972	31	154	645	198	101	6	51	.307	.417	.245
1973	32	160	680	230	110	5	59	.338	.437	.256
1974	33	163	652	185	107	3	48	.284	.388	.242
1975	34	162	662	210	105	7	67	.317	.432	.270
1976	35	162	665	215	120	10	53	.323	.450	.275
1977	36	162	655	204	86	9	55	.311	.432	.229
1978	37	159	655	198	96	7	45	.302	.421	.226
1979	38	163	628	208	86	4	55	.331	.430	.231
1980	39	162	655	185	94	1	63	.282	.354	.241
1981	40	107	431	140	73	0	33	.325	.390	.246
1982	41	162	634	172	77	3	51	.271	.338	.207
1983	42	151	493	121	52	0	45	.245	.286	.197
1984	43	121	374	107	43	0	34	.286	.337	.206
1985	44	119	405	107	58	2	44	.264	.319	.257
Total		3490	13816	4204	1990	160	1129	.304	.412	.237
Other*		72	237	52	15	0	25	.219	.270	.169
Career		3562	14053	4256	2005	160	1154	.303	.409	.236

*Less than 100 games: 1986

Standard Deviation		15	88	35	20	5	12			
Avg.		152	601	183	87	7	49	.304	.412	.237

Normal Performance Range (100 + games)

High		167	689	218	106	12	61	.316	.466	.261
Low		136	512	147	67	2	37	.288	.339	.206

	G	AB	H	R	HR	RBI	BA	SA	PAB

Best Year (over 139 games): 1969

Super Years (PAB .379 +): None

Good Years (PAB .325–.378): None

Fair Years (PAB .273–.324): 1965, 1969, 1976

	G	AB	H	R	HR	RBI	BA	SA	PAB
Avg.	160	654	214	110	12	63	.327	.468	.283

Other Years (PAB .272 –): 1963, 1964, 1966, 1967, 1968, 1970, 1971, 1972, 1973, 1974, 1975, 1977, 1978, 1979, 1980, 1981, 1982, 1983, 1984, 1985

	G	AB	H	R	HR	RBI	BA	SA	PAB
Avg.	151	593	178	83	6	47	.300	.402	.230

Average Yearly Performance by Age

	G	AB	H	R	HR	RBI	BA	SA	PAB
25 and under	153	616	181	86	9	47	.294	.406	.231
26–30	154	624	200	88	13	47	.321	.464	.238
31–35	160	661	208	109	6	56	.314	.425	.258
36 +	145	548	160	74	3	47	.292	.373	.226

Durability, thy name is Rose. Combine this with the skill it takes to maintain a career BA of .303, and you've got the surefire HOF formula. Pete is a pretender who is a sure bet to get into the HOF.

Some HOF credentials can't be measured. But one can't write about Charlie Hustle without making comment about the spirit he brought to the field. He breathed life into the word "competitor." His zest for victory could be tasted. Every athlete who has regularly played with Rose has probably played somewhat better than would have otherwise been the case. No higher compliment than this could be paid to a baseball man.

Forgetting enthusiasm for a minute, the closest thing to Rose in terms of batting style is the recently retired Rod Carew. Both were wrist hitters, and although Pete was no great shakes as a base stealer, both were aggressive on the bases. They compare as follows:

	AB	R	HR	RBI	PAB	BA	SA
25 and under							
Rose	616	.140	.015	.076	.231	.294	.406
Carew	478	.115	.012	.091	.218	.299	.408
26–30							
Rose	624	.141	.021	.075	.238	.321	.464
Carew	565	.140	.009	.096	.245	.340	.435
31–35							
Rose	661	.165	.009	.085	.258	.314	.425
Carew	547	.156	.013	.120	.289	.342	.467

	AB	R	HR	RBI	PAB	BA	SA
36 +							
Rose	501	.132	.004	.088	.224	.286	.359
Carew	479	.150	.006	.083	.239	.314	.388

In their early twenties, Rose was almost as good a hitter, and was more productive than Carew. Pete's scoring made the difference. For the next ten years, the hitting of both improved, but more so for Carew. The scoring advantage of Rose decreased, and the RBI advantage of Carew became the factor that pulled him ahead as a producer.

Rose has a flock of "most of" records which impresses the hell out of some but which can all be wrapped up under a single name—durability. He has played for 24 years and in all but one (1986) of them has appeared in 100 + games, averaging 148 games a season. His body has been a truly remarkable tool.

As wallpaper is to a house, so Pete Rose is to baseball. He has been around for so long it would seem un–American somehow to exclude him from the HOF—it wouldn't be the same without Pete Baseball. That's the name he should have been born with.

Bill Buckner
Born 1949
Height 6'1"; weight 185
Throws left, bats left
HOF—Possible

Year	Age	G	AB	H	R	HR	RBI	BA	SA	PAB
1971	22	108	358	99	32	5	36	.277	.366	.204
1972	23	105	383	122	42	5	32	.319	.410	.206
1973	24	140	575	158	60	8	38	.275	.351	.184
1974	25	145	580	182	76	7	51	.314	.412	.231
1976	27	154	642	193	69	7	53	.301	.389	.201
1977	28	122	426	121	29	11	49	.284	.425	.209
1978	29	117	446	144	42	5	69	.323	.419	.260
1979	30	149	591	168	58	14	52	.284	.437	.210
1980	31	145	578	187	59	10	58	.324	.457	.220
1981	32	106	421	131	35	10	65	.311	.480	.261
1982	33	161	657	201	78	15	90	.306	.441	.279
1983	34	153	626	175	63	16	50	.280	.436	.206
1984	35	135	482	131	43	11	58	.272	.392	.232
1985	36	162	673	201	73	16	94	.299	.447	.272
1986	37	153	629	168	55	18	84	.267	.421	.250
Total		2055	8067	2381	814	158	879	.295	.420	.229
Other*		121	357	83	30	6	29	.232	.339	.182
Career		2176	8424	2464	844	164	908	.292	.417	.227

*Less than 100 games: 1969, 1970, 1975

	G	AB	H	R	HR	RBI	BA	SA	PAB
Standard Deviation	20	104	31	16	4	18			
Avg.	137	538	159	54	11	59	.295	.420	.229
Normal Performance Range (100 games +)									
High	157	641	190	70	15	77	.296	.453	.252
Low	117	434	128	39	6	40	.294	.371	.196

Best Year (over 139 games): 1982

Super Years (PAB .379 +): None

Good Years: (PAB .325–.378): None

Fair Years (PAB .273–.324): 1982

Other Years (PAB .272 –): 1971, 1972, 1973, 1974, 1976, 1977, 1978, 1979, 1980, 1981, 1983, 1984, 1985, 1986

	G	AB	H	R	HR	RBI	BA	SA	PAB
Avg.	135	529	156	53	10	56	.294	.418	.225
Average Yearly Performance by Age									
25 and under	125	474	140	53	6	39	.296	.384	.207
26–30	136	526	157	50	9	56	.297	.416	.218
31–35	140	553	165	56	12	64	.298	.441	.239
36 +	158	651	185	64	17	89	.283	.435	.261

In 1968, then 19 years old, Billy Buck burned up the minor leagues with a BA of .344. This earned him a look with Los Angeles in 1969, and he was to stay in 1970. Unfortunately, Steve Garvey was also destroying minor league pitching at the same time, and joined Buckner on the Los Angeles bench in 1970. To make the cheese more binding for both men, Wes Parker, the incumbent first baseman, had hit .319 in 1969, and wasn't about to sit down for either of the hotshots from the bushes.

Bill banged away at the competition for a few years. By 1973, he was playing a full season between first base and the outfield. Then came his second round of problems. In 1974, Garvey was awarded the first base job, which moved Buckner to the outfield. In 1975, he was hurt, and at the close of the 1976 season, was traded to Chicago. During the next two seasons, Bill again fought the injury jinx, but came back in 1979, won the BA title in 1980, and gave the Cubs four more good seasons before being traded to Boston in 1984.

Buckner has had to struggle to develop a major league career. He has strong durability characteristics — despite the obstacles — to go with a lifetime BA of .29? Thirty seven years old in 1986, limping around on bad legs, Bill is adding to HOF credentials, is drawing media attention, and must be regarded as a long shot pretender, especially if he protects his BA.

Consistency, thy name is Buckner. In his early twenties, he was a .296 hitter; in his late twenties, .297; in his early thirties, .298; so far, in his late thirties, .283. Given this steadiness and skill, it can be argued—as with Garvey—that his low PAB is a reflection of teammate support, not his own skills. A scrappy competitor in the Pete Rose mold, Buckner deserves a look for HOF honors.

First Basemen—The Pretenders

The records of 20 active first basemen have been examined. None qualify for Class 1 or Class 2. Assuming that the quality of play does not deteriorate between now and retirement, pre-analysis theory says Class 3 athletes are surefire HOF appointees sometime in the future; those in Class 4 should be hot prospects; Class 5s are weak prospects from a production standpoint who must demonstrate some other accomplishments which demand attention, to become pretenders.

Post-analysis results upset theory. Not all Class 3 players survive, weaknesses appear in the Class 4 group, and outstanding characteristics in some Class 5 players qualify them for pretender designation despite sub-par PABs. A list of survivors follows:

	BA	PAB	Comment
Murray	.299	.289	Probable
Hernandez	.302	.286	Probable
Perez	.279	.260	Possible
Cooper	.300	.259	Possible—durability?
Garvey	.295	.247*	Possible
Rose	.303	.236*	Probable
Buckner	.292	.227*	Long shot

*Below the lowest rated HOF first baseman, Ernie Banks.

There are three superstar first basemen in the HOF. Greenberg, with a BA of .313 and a PAB of .384, was the last of the big three to be elected. No Class 1 or Class 2 first baseman has appeared on the scene since—no superstars appear on the above list. The day of the great producer is over.

But the game still produces attention-getting players. Individual accomplishments, plus durability, make Rose the strongest pretender. Murray and Hernandez have but time and consistency left to conquer. The election of Banks opened the door for players like Cooper and Perez. Garvey and Bill Buckner are weak pretenders, but their personal skill levels deserve attention.

What do the active catchers look like? Read on!

Catchers

There are 17 catchers who qualify for the study, and they place within the classification system as follows:

Class	Number
1	0
2	0
3	5
4	0
5	12

No superstars—or near superstars—operate behind the plate today. On the surface, five candidates are strong and the others are out of contention unless characteristics other than production can be identified as superior.

The established HOF standards that active catchers must meet are set forth below:

	Standard
Quality—PAB	
Class 1	.321 +
2	.284–.320
3	.249–.283
4	.231–.248
Durability—at Bats	
Long	6907
Medium	4964–6906
Short	4963 –

Durable catchers with competitive production records have always been a rare commodity. It is no less the case today. As with other positions, catchers appearing in at least 800 games through 1986 are analyzed.

	G	AB	H	R	HR	RBI	BA	SA	PAB
Class 1 .321 +									
None									
Class 2 .284–.320									
None									
Class 3 .249–.283									
Fisk	1827	6521	1767	722	281	696	.271	.462	.261
Carter	1689	6063	1646	576	271	728	.271	.461	.260
Simmons	2305	8396	2402	806	242	1106	.286	.440	.257
Porter	1697	5409	1338	565	181	624	.247	.409	.253
Parrish, L.	1146	4273	1123	365	212	488	.263	.469	.249

	G	AB	H	R	HR	RBI	BA	SA	PAB
Class 4 .231–.248									
None									
Class 5 .230 –									
Kennedy	962	3373	916	265	82	395	.272	.403	.220
Wynegar	1343	4183	1069	422	64	429	.256	.349	.219
Whitt	835	2303	571	180	86	237	.248	.416	.218
Heath	853	2818	698	261	55	270	.248	.361	.208
Pena	801	2872	821	244	63	277	.286	.411	.203
Boone	1843	5982	1501	459	96	606	.251	.349	.194
Ashby	1150	3449	835	252	69	345	.242	.354	.193
Sunberg	1763	5590	1397	495	83	496	.250	.348	.192
Cerone	858	2796	665	223	43	261	.238	.338	.188
Dempsey	1419	3949	939	360	78	302	.238	.349	.187
Yeager	1269	3584	816	255	102	308	.228	.355	.186
Martinez	1049	2743	618	187	58	263	.225	.343	.185

Unless outstanding non-production characteristics can be found, rules of the game say that all Class 5 catchers are to be dropped from the analysis as ineligibles. Alas, no such special qualities appear. No unusually long careers are in view. None can lay claim to great contact hitting ability. A fine defensive catcher like Sunberg will not make it with the glove alone.

Carlton Fisk
Born 1947
Height 6'2"; weight 220
Throws right, bats right
HOF — Probable

Year	Age	G	AB	H	R	HR	RBI	BA	SA	PAB
1972	25	131	457	134	52	22	39	.293	.538	.247
1973	26	135	508	125	39	26	45	.246	.441	.217
1976	29	134	487	124	59	17	41	.255	.415	.240
1977	30	152	536	169	80	26	76	.315	.521	.340
1978	31	157	571	162	74	20	68	.284	.475	.284
1980	33	131	478	138	55	18	44	.289	.467	.245
1982	35	135	476	127	52	14	51	.267	.403	.246
1983	36	138	488	141	59	26	60	.289	.518	.297
1984	37	102	359	83	33	21	22	.231	.468	.212
1985	38	153	543	129	48	37	70	.238	.488	.285
1986	39	125	457	101	28	14	49	.221	.337	.199
Total		1493	5360	1433	579	241	565	.267	.462	.258
Other*		334	1161	334	143	40	131	.288	.459	.270
Career		1827	6521	1767	722	281	696	.271	.462	.261

*Less than 100 games: 1969, 1971, 1974, 1975, 1979, 1981

	G	AB	H	R	HR	RBI	BA	SA	PAB
Standard Deviation	15	53	23	15	6	15			
Avg.	136	487	130	53	22	51	.267	.462	.258
Normal Performance Range (100 + games)									
High	150	541	153	68	28	67	.284	.536	.301
Low	121	434	107	38	16	36	.247	.370	.206

Best Year (over 129 games): 1977

Super Years (PAB .321 +): 1977

Good Years (PAB .284–.320): 1983, 1978, 1985

| Avg. | 149 | 534 | 144 | 60 | 28 | 66 | .270 | .493 | .288 |

Fair Years (PAB .249–.283): None

Other Years (PAB .248 –): 1972, 1973, 1976, 1980, 1982, 1984, 1986

| Avg. | 128 | 460 | 119 | 45 | 19 | 42 | .258 | .437 | .230 |

Average Yearly Performance by Age

25 and under	131	457	134	52	22	39	.293	.538	.247
26–30	140	510	139	59	23	54	.273	.460	.267
31–35	141	508	142	60	17	54	.280	.450	.260
36 +	130	462	114	42	25	50	.246	.455	.253

If Rick Ferrell is a HOF catcher, so is Carlton Fisk. This phrase applies to all active catchers with durability equal to Ferrell's and with a PAB of .231 + .

Another phrase dramatizes the importance of Ferrell's selection to the HOF in 1984, to wit, if Ferrell were not in the HOF, it is probable that no active catcher, including Fisk, would be designated a pretender.

Prior to the election of Ferrell, Hartnett was the lowest rated HOF catcher. No active catcher has a BA, SA, or PAB the equal of his.

But Ferrell was elected, and a new and lower de facto minimum standard of eligibility was established with this act. Lombardi was the first beneficiary of comparisons with the Ferrell record. Fisk will be another. He is a pretender with a strong chance to make the HOF.

Pudge was 20 when, in 1967, he joined organized baseball. The Boston Red Sox took a look at him in 1969, and again in 1971. In 1972, then 25 years old, Fisk took over the catching duties for the team. He spent 11 years in a Boston suit, then moved to Chicago, where he has spent the past six seasons.

Fisk is the Fred Lynn of catchers—injury prone. In a 17-year major league career, he has had eleven 100 + game years, averaging 136 games a year. In his first two years, he played little, and he had four shortened seasons due to injuries. You won't find Pudge blocking the plate much these days.

According to his 100 + game profile, Fisk averages out as a Class 3 catcher, capable of wide swings in performance. He has had one superstar year, three Class 2 years, four Class 4 seasons, and three bummers. If elected to the HOF, Fisk would fit between Hartnett and Lombardi, as follows:

	AB	R	HR	RBI	PAB	BA	SA
Cochrane	5,169	.178	.023	.138	.339	.320	.478
Campanella	4,205	.092	.058	.146	.295	.276	.500
Hartnett	6,432	.098	.037	.147	.281	.297	.489
Fisk	**6,521**	**.111**	**.043**	**.107**	**.261**	**.271**	**.462**
Lombardi	5,855	.070	.032	.137	.239	.306	.460
Ferrell	6,028	.109	.005	.117	.231	.281	.363

Fisk's durability will be considered adequate. As a scorer and power hitter, he looks good against the above HOF players. Clutch hitting is not one of his strong points and his relatively poor performance in this area weakens what would otherwise be a strong PAB.

Career appraisal in five-year time blocks defines more closely the true abilities of a player. In his early twenties, Pudge was a Class 4 catcher. In his late twenties, more timely hitting moved him into Class 3. This is his normal level of play which he has sustained since.

Catchers work harder than they used to. Only one HOF catcher, for example, worked 130 + games a year. Fisk, not the hardest working active catcher, averages more games per season than any of the HOF greats. If a catcher is an offensive threat, history has shown that it's a mistake to overwork him behind the plate. They wear out fast under such conditions. More mileage at a slower pace should be the governing principle on how to use catching talent — 120 to 130 games a year is a sensible target.

Gary Carter
Born 1954
Height 6'2"; weight 215
Throws right, bats right
HOF — Possible

Year	Age	G	AB	H	R	HR	RBI	BA	SA	PAB
1975	21	144	503	136	41	17	51	.270	.416	.217
1977	23	154	522	148	55	31	53	.284	.525	.266
1978	24	157	533	136	56	20	52	.255	.422	.240
1979	25	141	505	143	52	22	53	.283	.485	.251
1980	26	154	549	145	47	29	72	.264	.486	.270

Year	Age	G	AB	H	R	HR	RBI	BA	SA	PAB
1981	27	100	374	94	32	16	52	.251	.444	.267
1982	28	154	557	163	62	29	68	.293	.510	.285
1983	29	145	541	146	46	17	62	.270	.444	.231
1984	30	159	596	175	48	27	79	.294	.487	.258
1985	31	149	555	156	51	32	68	.281	.488	.272
1986	32	132	490	125	57	24	81	.255	.439	.331
Total		1589	5725	1567	547	264	691	.274	.469	.262
Other*		100	338	79	29	7	37	.234	.331	.216
Career		1689	6063	1646	576	271	728	.271	.461	.260

*Less than 100 games: 1974, 1976

Standard Deviation		16	54	20	8	6	11			
Avg.		144	520	142	50	24	63	.274	.469	.262

Normal Performance Range (100 + games)

		G	AB	H	R	HR	RBI	BA	SA	PAB
High		160	575	163	58	30	74	.283	.520	.280
Low		128	466	122	42	18	52	.263	.406	.240

Best Year (over 129 games): 1982

Super Years (PAB .321 +): 1986

Good Years (PAB .284–.320): 1982

Fair Years (PAB .249–.283): 1977, 1979, 1980, 1981, 1984, 1985

Avg.		143	517	144	48	26	63	.278	.488	.264

Other Years (PAB .248 –): 1975, 1978, 1983

Avg.		149	526	139	48	18	55	.265	.427	.230

Average Yearly Performance by Age

		G	AB	H	R	HR	RBI	BA	SA	PAB
25 and under		149	516	141	51	23	52	.273	.462	.244
26–30		142	523	145	47	24	67	.276	.476	.262
31–35		141	523	141	54	28	75	.269	.465	.300

Ted Simmons has provided ten quality seasons (Class 1, 2, or 3) in his career. Porter, with five, may have pooped out. Fisk won't add to his present four. Carter, at 32 years of age (1986), has eight quality seasons behind him—he could overtake Simmons before he quits. But it's no cinch that he will.

History tells us that a catcher who works more than 120–130 games a year runs the risk of early burnout. Carter has worked an average of 144 games in eleven 100 + game seasons; in seven of them, Carter worked 145 + ; in five, 150 + games. He may have peaked because of shortsighted career planning. He may never have another Class 3 season. It's doubtful that he will overcome the quality record of Simmons. Nevertheless, Carter is a pretender. Time will clarify his credentials.

In 1972, Carter entered the minor leagues at 18 years of age. Primarily a catcher, he also played some first base and outfield. Montreal looked at him in 1975, and made him a regular the next year—he was 22 years old. He spent 11 years with Montreal, but opened the 1985 season with the New York Mets. He has a lifetime PAB of .260, about 13 percent higher than that of Rick Ferrell, the lowest rated HOF catcher.

Carter is a middle-class power and contact hitter. According to his 100 + game profile, he averages out as a Class 3 catcher. He had one superstar year, one Class 2 year, six Class 3 years, two Class 4 seasons, and one bummer.

Baseball is starving for heroes. Mostly because of his eye-catching home run hitting, Gary has been elected. He is probably one of the half dozen best publicized athletes in the game today. From a relative standpoint, and considering the fact that Simmons and Fisk are about done, this is quite legitimate because he is arguably the most valuable catcher in the game. But, to keep things in perspective, from a historical standpoint Carter, although more productive than Ferrell and Lombardi, is less productive than all other HOF catchers.

In many ways, Gary is a young Fisk. Below is a comparison of the average 100 + game season experienced by both men through their thirtieth birthdays:

	AB	R	HR	RBI	PAB	BA	SA
Carter	519	.094	.045	.115	.254	.275	.469
Fisk	484	.115	.049	.096	.260	.282	.499

Both are sound defensively with the edge, perhaps, going to Carter. Carter has been more active. Overall at the same age, Fisk was the better producer.

Ted Simmons
Born 1949
Height 6'0"; weight 200
Throws right, bats both
HOF—Probable

Year	Age	G	AB	H	R	HR	RBI	BA	SA	PAB
1971	22	133	510	155	57	7	70	.304	.424	.263
1972	23	152	594	180	54	16	80	.303	.465	.253
1973	24	161	619	192	49	13	78	.310	.438	.226
1974	25	152	599	163	46	20	83	.272	.447	.249
1975	26	157	581	193	62	18	82	.332	.491	.279
1976	27	150	546	159	55	5	70	.291	.394	.238
1977	28	150	516	164	61	21	74	.318	.500	.302
1978	29	152	516	148	49	22	58	.287	.512	.250

Year	Age	G	AB	H	R	HR	RBI	BA	SA	PAB
1979	30	123	448	127	42	26	61	.283	.507	.288
1980	31	145	495	150	63	21	77	.303	.505	.325
1981	32	100	380	82	31	14	47	.216	.376	.242
1982	33	137	539	145	50	23	74	.269	.451	.273
1983	34	153	600	185	63	13	95	.308	.448	.285
1984	35	132	497	110	40	4	47	.221	.300	.183
1985	36	143	528	144	48	12	64	.273	.402	.235
Total		2140	7968	2297	770	235	1060	.288	.445	.259
Other*		165	428	105	36	7	46	.245	.339	.208
Career		2305	8396	2402	806	242	1106	.286	.440	.257

*Less than 100 games: 1968, 1969, 1970, 1986

Standard Deviation		15	62	29	9	7	13			
Avg.		143	531	153	51	16	71	.288	.445	.259

Normal Performance Range (100 + games)

		G	AB	H	R	HR	RBI	BA	SA	PAB
High		158	593	182	60	22	84	.308	.516	.280
Low		127	470	124	42	9	58	.264	.356	.233

Best Year (over 129 games): 1980

Super Years (PAB .321 +): 1980

Good Years (PAB .284–.320): 1977, 1979, 1983

		G	AB	H	R	HR	RBI	BA	SA	PAB
Avg.		142	521	159	55	20	77	.304	.482	.292

Fair Years (PAB .249–.283): 1971, 1972, 1974, 1975, 1978, 1982

		G	AB	H	R	HR	RBI	BA	SA	PAB
Avg.		147	557	164	53	18	75	.295	.465	.261

Other Years (PAB .248 –): 1973, 1976, 1981, 1984, 1985

		G	AB	H	R	HR	RBI	BA	SA	PAB
Avg.		137	514	137	45	10	61	.267	.385	.225

Average Yearly Performance by Age

		G	AB	H	R	HR	RBI	BA	SA	PAB
25 and under		150	581	173	52	14	78	.297	.444	.247
26–30		146	521	158	54	18	69	.303	.479	.271
31–35		133	502	134	49	15	68	.268	.420	.264
36 +		143	528	144	48	12	64	.273	.402	.235

Simmons will probably go into the books as the most valuable catcher of his era. He is a definite pretender and the surest bet of the active catchers for earning HOF laurels.

In 1967, at the age of 18, Ted Simmons entered professional baseball. For three years, the St. Louis Cardinals diddled with him. In 1971, at the age of 22, he became a starting catcher for that club. Ted was with the Cards for 13 years, then switched leagues and joined Milwaukee in 1981. He was with that team for four seasons. Now serving Atlanta as a pinch hitter and utility man, Simmons has compiled a 19-year major league career. In all but his first three seasons and 1986, he has played in 100 + games, averaging 143 games a year.

The durability of Simmons has been helped by the fact that, like

Berra, he has played defensive positions other than catcher. In recent years, he has become decreasingly the catcher, and increasingly the DH/utility type player.

According to his 100 + game profile, Simmons averages out as a Class 3 catcher. He has had one superstar year, three Class 2 years, six Class 3 years, three Class 4 years, and two bummers. If elected to the HOF, Ted would fit between Hartnett and Lombardi, as follows:

	AB	R	HR	RBI	PAB	BA	SA
Cochrane	5,169	.178	.023	.138	.339	.320	.478
Campanella	4,205	.092	.058	.146	.295	.276	.500
Hartnett	6,432	.098	.037	.147	.281	.297	.489
Simmons	**8,396**	**.096**	**.029**	**.132**	**.257**	**.286**	**.440**
Lombardi	5,855	.070	.032	.137	.239	.306	.460
Ferrell	6,028	.109	.005	.117	.231	.281	.363

As the durability king of HOF catchers, Berra will have to step down when Ted appears. Unlike Fisk, Ted's scoring and power elements do not dominate his PAB. RBIs make Ted tick. He is a superior clutch hitter.

The essential difference between Simmons and Fisk is time — Ted did it as well, longer. Both arrived at the same PAB destination point by different roads as the following comparison of 100 + game seasons shows.

	AB	R	HR	RBI	PAB	BA	SA
Simmons	8,396	.096	.029	.132	.257	.286	.440
Fisk	6,521	.111	.043	.107	.261	.271	.462

Fisk, more the solo performer, generates his PAB primarily with scoring and power. Simmons, more the team man, offsets Pudge's areas of superiority with clutch hitting — and he has done it with about 29 percent more at bats.

Simmons averages out as a Class 3 catcher. From him, a Class 1 season is a pleasant surprise. When he checks in with repetitive seasons below Class 3, hindsight tells us that either a young boy or an aging athlete was at work. Like Nettles, Lopes, and others, he's just punching the clock now, collecting a ridiculous income for so long as the fools who own the game will pay it.

Darrell Porter

Born 1952
Height 6'1"; weight 195
Throws right, bats left
HOF—Possible

Year	Age	G	AB	H	R	HR	RBI	BA	SA	PAB
1973	21	117	350	89	34	16	51	.254	.457	.289
1974	22	131	432	104	47	12	44	.241	.377	.238
1975	23	130	409	95	48	18	42	.232	.418	.264
1976	24	119	389	81	38	5	27	.208	.288	.180
1977	25	130	425	117	45	16	44	.275	.452	.247
1978	26	150	520	138	59	18	60	.265	.444	.263
1979	27	157	533	155	81	20	92	.291	.484	.362
1980	28	118	418	104	44	7	44	.249	.342	.227
1982	30	120	373	86	34	12	36	.231	.402	.220
1983	31	145	443	116	42	15	51	.262	.431	.244
1984	32	127	422	98	45	11	57	.232	.363	.268
Total		1444	4714	1183	517	150	548	.251	.408	.258
Other*		253	695	155	48	31	76	.223	.413	.223
Career		1697	5409	1338	565	181	624	.247	.409	.253

*Less than 100 games: 1971, 1972, 1981, 1985, 1986

Standard Deviation		13	53	22	13	4	16			
Avg.		131	429	108	47	14	50	.251	.408	.258

Normal Performance Range (100 + games)

High		144	482	129	60	18	66	.268	.465	.298
Low		118	376	86	34	9	34	.229	.335	.206

Best Year (over 129 games): 1979

Super Years (PAB .321 +): 1979

Good Years (PAB .284 .320): 1973

Fair Years (PAB .249–.283): 1975, 1978, 1984

Avg.		136	450	110	51	16	53	.245	.411	.265

Other Years (PAB .248 –): 1974, 1976, 1977, 1980, 1982, 1983

Avg.		127	413	101	42	11	41	.245	.383	.227

Average Yearly Performance by Age

25 and under	125	401	97	42	13	42	.242	.398	.243
26–30	136	461	121	55	14	58	.262	.424	.275
31–35	136	433	107	44	13	54	.247	.398	.255

Porter is a statistical possibility for the HOF. He is also a rapidly slipping 35-year-old catcher (1986). In a 16-year career, Darrell has had eleven 100 + game years, averaging 131 games a season. In the other five seasons, including the last two, he played a light schedule. With his relatively light durability record, and his choppy production performance, Porter is a pretender with a doubtful chance of success.

This is too bad. In 1979, Porter had the best season to come out of a catcher for a long time. Mickey Cochrane, Bill Dickey, and Roy Campanella had better ones. But Yogi Berra and Gabby Hartnett never did, nor has any active catcher. In other words, Darrell demonstrated HOF talent—then lost it.

Porter had his year in the sun. For a season, he was a true superstar. A comparison of his best with that of the top HOF catchers, and with the active catchers just analyzed follows:

				Best Years			
	AB	R	HR	RBI	PAB	BA	SA
Cochrane	518	.184	.044	.172	**.400**	.293	.510
Berra	597	.147	.047	.161	.355	.322	.533
Dickey	454	.126	.060	.193	**.379**	.313	.568
Campanella	519	.120	.079	.194	**.393**	.312	.611
Hartnett	508	.093	.073	.167	.333	.339	.630
Fisk	536	.149	.049	.142	.340	.315	.521
Carter	490	.117	.049	.165	.331	.255	.439
Simmons	.495	.127	.042	.156	.325	.303	.505
Porter	**533**	**.152**	**.038**	**.173**	**.362**	**.291**	**.484**

For that magic year, damn few were ever any better than Darrell Porter. And he has had a few others that weren't too shabby.

Porter peaked in 1979. In the last seven seasons, it has been a downhill course for Darrell. He seems to have run out of the sap that moved him to the top of the hill for a brilliant moment.

Lance Parrish
Born 1956
Height 6'3"; weight 210
Throws right, bats right
HOF—Possible

Year	Age	G	AB	H	R	HR	RBI	BA	SA	PAB
1979	23	143	493	136	46	19	46	.276	.456	.225
1980	24	144	553	158	55	24	58	.286	.499	.248
1982	26	133	486	138	43	32	55	.284	.529	.267
1983	27	155	605	163	53	27	87	.269	.483	.276
1984	28	147	578	137	42	33	65	.237	.443	.242
1985	29	140	549	150	36	28	70	.273	.479	.244
Total		862	3264	882	275	163	381	.270	.481	.251
Other*		284	1009	241	90	49	107	.239	.433	.244
Career		1146	4273	1123	365	212	488	.263	.469	.249

*Less than 100 games: 1977, 1978, 1981, 1986

	G	AB	H	R	HR	RBI	BA	SA	PAB
Standard Deviation	7	43	11	7	5	13			
Avg.	144	544	147	46	27	64	.270	.481	.251

Normal Performance Range (100 + games)

	G	AB	H	R	HR	RBI	BA	SA	PAB
High	150	587	158	52	32	76	.269	.522	.274
Low	137	501	136	39	22	51	.272	.432	.224

Best Year (over 129 games): 1983

Super Years (PAB .321 +): None

Good Years (PAB .284–.320): None

Fair Years (PAB .249–.283): 1982, 1983

	G	AB	H	R	HR	RBI	BA	SA	PAB
Avg.	144	546	151	48	30	71	.276	.503	.272

Other Years (PAB .248 –): 1979, 1980, 1984, 1985

	G	AB	H	R	HR	RBI	BA	SA	PAB
Avg.	144	543	145	45	26	60	.267	.469	.240

Average Yearly Performance by Age

	G	AB	H	R	HR	RBI	BA	SA	PAB
25 and under	144	523	147	51	22	52	.281	.479	.237
26–30	144	555	147	44	30	69	.265	.482	.257

Parrish was 30 years old in 1986. He has two quality seasons behind him, but his last three weren't inspiring despite improved home run production. He could turn out to be another of the early burnouts so common today, especially given the lower back problems that sidelined him for much of 1986.

So far in his ten-year career, Lance has had six 100 + game seasons, averaging 144 games each. This is too much, and might shorten the number of quality years he eventually produces. It's doubtful that Parrish will overtake the Simmons record before retirement.

But Lance is a legitimate pretender with a chance to be elected to the HOF. With but 4,273 at bats to his credit, he has got a lot to prove yet.

Parrish is the most powerful of the active catchers. Campanella is the most powerful of the HOF catchers. Their records compare as follows:

	AB	R	HR	RBI	PAB	BA	SA
100 + Game Seasons							
Career							
Lance	544	.084	.049	.118	.251	.270	.481
Roy	436	.092	.060	.147	.299	.277	.506
Best year							
Lance	605	.088	.045	.143	.276	.269	.483
Roy	519	.120	.079	.194	.393	.312	.611

In all PAB elements, Roy was superior on average, and in the hot year. Campy was a better hitter, a more powerful one, and a far better clutch hitter.

The election of Rick Ferrell to the HOF was a seminal decision in that it established levels of eligibility that will activate the HOF dreams of many catchers who would have otherwise been content with less lofty goals. All of the above men would have a tough time in the election process had it not been for that single decision.

	AB	HR	R	RBI	PAB	BA	SA
Cochrane	5169	.023	.178	.138	.339	.320	.478
Campanella	4205	.058	.092	.146	.296	.276	.500
Hartnett	6432	.037	.098	.147	.282	.297	.489
Fisk	**6521**	**.043**	**.111**	**.107**	**.261**	**.271**	**.462**
Carter	**6063**	**.045**	**.095**	**.120**	**.260**	**.271**	**.461**
Simmons	**8396**	**.029**	**.096**	**.132**	**.257**	**.286**	**.440**
Porter	**5409**	**.033**	**.105**	**.115**	**.253**	**.247**	**.409**
Parrish	**4273**	**.050**	**.085**	**.114**	**.249**	**.263**	**.469**
Lombardi	5855	.032	.070	.137	.239	.306	.460
Ferrell	6028	.005	.109	.117	.231	.281	.363

Active Catchers — The Pretenders

Seventeen catchers qualified for the analysis. No active catcher fits Class 1 or Class 2 specifications. There are no superstar catchers on the field today. But it seems obvious that, given the lower standards, the HOF catching corps will be considerably fattened in the next decade.

Theoretically, Class 3 and Class 4 players should be designated pretenders unless something unusual appears in the analysis of records. No Class 5 catcher should qualify as a pretender unless some startling personal skills are deemed to be of sufficient importance to outweigh low production rates. It is worth repeating that the recent election of Ferrell to the HOF lowered considerably entry level qualifications. Had this appointment not been made, it is doubtful that Lombardi would have been elected or any active catcher would qualify as a pretender.

As a result of classification and analysis, several pretenders were identified, as follows:

	BA	PAB	Comment
Fisk	.275	.265	Probable
Carter	.273	.254	Possible
Simmons	.287	.256	Probable

	BA	PAB	Comment
Porter	.247	.254	Possible — doubtful
Parrish	.263	.246	Possible — durability?

There are only seven catchers in the HOF. Standards have been difficult to meet. Hartnett was the lowest rated catcher with a PAB of .281. Until the election of Berra, no relatively modern player was able to break through the eligibility wall that Gabby represented. None of the above would have been able to.

Apparently, HOF committees decided that the Hartnett standard was too high. Looking around at modern talent they concluded that the HOF might never get another catcher unless standards were lowered. So they reached into the past, in 1984, and appointed a catcher that the process — probably correctly — had ignored for about three decades, the 79-year-old Ferrell. The wall of eligibility represented by Hartnett tumbled down. As a consequence, the above players were immediately presented with a case that will be difficult to deny. Predictably, appointments of catchers to the HOF will increase rapidly starting in a few years. Puff boys will explain this as a reflection of superior athletes now playing the game. Don't believe it. Admissions will increase because the entrance exam is easier to pass.

Upcoming? Active pitchers!

Pitchers

Active fielder analysis is complete. To complete the primary mission, locating pretenders, only the active pitcher appraisal remains.

Active pitcher analysis will proceed in a consistent manner. As a starting point, pitchers with 1,000 + innings pitched (excluding relief pitchers) will be graded into five ERA classifications. Records of dominant players will be reviewed in detail in search of characteristics which either confirm, or place in question, original ERA classifications. The analysis will conclude with final identification of pretenders.

In grading HOF players, four classifications were used. In grading active fielders, five classifications were used, the fifth housing active fielders with PABs lower than that of the lowest rated HOF member at each position. In grading pitchers, five classifications will again be used, the fifth housing active pitchers with ERAs above that of the lowest classified HOF pitcher. Class 5 pitchers are automatically disqualified as pretenders unless some outstanding non–ERA skills emerge in analysis.

Logic requires the statement that when offensive talents are relatively weak, pitching talents become the statistical beneficiaries. It is so today. Indisputably, fine pitchers have been operating in baseball over recent years, good enough to compare with the greats of any era. It is likewise true, however, that offensive capabilities of major leaguers are in a state of deterioration, which makes pitchers look better than they are, in the comparative historical sense. In other words, Spahn operating in the current offensive climate would generate an even more imposing record, and Seaver operating in the offensive climate of 25 years ago would not appear so dominating. To what extent is the pitching record of modern players a reflection of competition level, or a reflection of personal skill? The answer to this interesting question is beyond the purview of this work, and is commended to others who may be teased to examine it.

Sixty-seven pitchers qualify for examination, as follows:

Class	*Number*
1	1
2	6
3	19
4	16
5	25
Total	67

True class finally rears its head in this analysis of active players. A superstar has appeared. Six others are performing at better than average HOF levels, 19 deserve a careful look, and 16 are still in the hunt—a total of 42 players who rate some level of attention.

Because durability is so very important in pitcher evaluation, it has been sensibly considered in setting the selection process for detailed analysis. As a consequence, players with relatively shallow durability records will not be appraised in detail unless their efforts have placed them in either Class 1 or Class 2. Pretenders are those who had pitched at least 1000 innings through the 1986 season.

	CG*	H	BB	BR	ERA	W	L	%	SOPG
Class 1 2.88 –									
Seaver	531.3	7.47	2.62	10.09	2.86	311	205	.603	6.85
Class 2 2.89–3.19									
Valenzuela	172.8	7.50	3.13	10.62	2.94	99	68	.593	7.37
Blyleven	443.1	8.14	2.42	10.55	3.08	229	197	.538	6.97
Carlton	561.7	7.99	3.10	11.09	3.11	323	229	.585	7.19
Candelaria	224.1	8.37	2.13	10.50	3.12	141	89	.613	5.69

	CG*	H	BB	BR	ERA	W	L	%	SOPG
Class 2 (cont.)									
Welch	174.2	8.19	2.75	10.94	3.13	100	77	.565	6.29
Ryan	457.2	6.54	4.96	11.50	3.15	253	226	.528	9.35
Class 3 3.20–3.50									
Sutton	555.9	7.92	2.29	10.21	3.20	310	239	.565	6.17
John	475.6	8.96	2.41	11.37	3.23	264	210	.557	4.38
Guidry	246.6	8.23	2.35	10.59	3.24	163	80	.671	6.69
Blue	371.6	7.91	3.19	11.10	3.26	209	161	.565	5.85
Tudor	149.2	8.38	2.45	10.84	3.26	85	58	.594	5.19
Niekro, P.	585.0	8.34	2.98	11.32	3.27	311	261	.544	5.60
Stieb	206.6	8.10	3.05	11.15	3.34	102	92	.526	5.18
Forsch, K.	236.2	8.77	2.48	11.25	3.37	114	113	.502	4.43
Soto	179.0	7.11	3.45	10.56	3.37	94	83	.531	7.84
Tanana	306.4	8.47	2.52	10.99	3.40	159	153	.510	6.28
Sanderson	146.0	8.51	2.25	10.76	3.40	78	69	.531	6.05
Reuschel	308.0	9.17	2.46	11.64	3.43	162	155	.511	5.36
Gullickson	159.0	8.77	2.19	10.96	3.43	87	73	.544	5.03
Knepper	238.4	8.84	2.69	11.54	3.44	114	118	.491	5.06
Rozema	122.8	9.16	2.10	11.26	3.47	60	53	.531	3.65
Rhoden	235.3	8.96	2.73	11.69	3.48	121	97	.555	5.00
Andujar	223.8	8.31	3.06	11.36	3.49	122	108	.530	4.31
Niekro, J.	380.7	8.66	3.12	11.78	3.50	213	190	.529	4.35
Reuss	357.7	8.96	2.85	11.81	3.50	194	163	.543	4.88
Class 4 3.51–3.80									
Witt	136.4	8.40	3.11	11.51	3.52	71	59	.546	6.02
Hough	241.0	7.63	3.81	11.44	3.54	131	115	.533	5.74
Montefusco	183.4	8.74	2.80	11.54	3.54	90	83	.520	5.89
Darwin	137.9	8.52	2.90	11.42	3.55	72	78	.480	5.72
Morris	235.8	8.04	3.20	11.24	3.57	144	94	.605	5.63
Denny	238.9	8.76	3.26	12.02	3.58	123	108	.532	4.80
Petry	167.1	8.26	3.42	11.68	3.58	98	74	.570	4.63
Forsch, B.	263.4	8.74	2.65	11.38	3.62	143	116	.552	3.61
Vuckovitch	161.6	9.00	3.37	12.37	3.66	93	69	.574	5.46
Eckersley	277.3	8.66	2.25	10.91	3.67	151	128	.541	5.87
Leonard	243.0	8.79	2.56	11.35	3.69	144	106	.576	5.44
Scott	128.9	8.63	2.82	11.44	3.70	65	62	.512	5.82
Alexander	300.9	8.95	2.67	11.62	3.71	160	135	.542	3.98
Ruhle	156.8	9.46	2.22	11.68	3.73	67	88	.432	3.71
Honeycutt	173.6	9.32	2.61	11.93	3.76	87	105	.453	3.74
Rawley	144.2	8.99	3.54	12.53	3.80	81	79	.506	4.94
Class 5 3.81 +									
Flanagan	232.2	9.00	2.82	11.82	3.84	136	103	.569	5.06
McGregor	226.6	9.30	2.10	11.40	3.84	136	98	.581	3.77
Krukow	206.6	9.00	3.25	12.25	3.84	108	104	.509	6.20
Sutcliffe	157.4	8.43	3.80	12.24	3.84	86	68	.558	5.95
Robinson	126.3	8.62	3.32	11.94	3.85	59	63	.484	6.11
Mahler	120.4	9.40	3.00	12.40	3.85	61	59	.508	4.39
McWilliams	137.8	8.92	3.08	12.00	3.91	68	67	.504	5.60
Trout	143.8	9.83	3.24	13.07	3.94	74	75	.497	3.94

	CG*	H	BB	BR	ERA	W	L	%	SOPG
Haas	179.4	9.25	2.38	11.63	3.97	98	81	.547	4.68
Whitson	143.9	9.28	3.32	12.59	3.98	69	73	.486	5.07
Hoyt	145.7	9.01	1.92	10.93	3.99	98	69	.587	4.68
Langford	165.7	9.48	2.51	11.99	4.01	73	106	.408	4.05
Dotson	143.9	8.90	3.54	12.45	4.01	83	76	.522	4.89
Slaton	298.2	9.30	3.37	12.67	4.03	151	158	.489	3.99
Bannister	203.6	8.70	3.34	12.04	4.03	101	117	.463	6.90
Wilcox	223.8	8.90	3.44	12.34	4.08	119	113	.513	5.08
Lacoss	131.0	9.34	3.72	13.06	4.09	61	67	.477	3.72
Clancy	196.4	8.88	3.50	12.38	4.13	102	116	.468	4.78
Ruthven	234.3	9.20	3.27	12.47	4.14	123	127	.492	4.93
Burris	240.7	9.46	3.12	12.59	4.16	106	132	.445	4.39
Keough	132.2	9.00	3.86	12.86	4.17	58	84	.408	4.46
Beattie	127.6	9.20	3.61	12.81	4.17	52	87	.374	5.17
Martinez, T.	208.1	9.25	2.94	12.19	4.18	111	99	.529	4.43
Hurst	111.6	9.93	3.03	12.96	4.31	55	54	.505	6.16
Viola	121.1	9.40	2.92	12.32	4.38	63	64	.496	5.66

*CG = equivalent complete games; H = hits; BB = bases on balls;
BR = baserunners; ERA = earned run average; W = wins; L = losses; SOPG = strikeouts per game.

Applicable standards applied to active pitchers are set forth below:

		Standard
Quality — ERA		
Class 1		2.88 –
2		2.87–3.19
3		3.20–3.50
4		3.51–3.80
Durability — Complete Games		
Long		494.3 +
Medium		310.9–494.2
Short		310.8 –

Class 5 active pitchers will be eliminated from further consideration unless some outstanding skill other than ERA can be identified. Although the group contains some of the best known (and paid) names in the game, there appears to be no justification for waiving the elimination rule in any particular case. There are no signs of unusual durability. Impressive strikeout capabilities of pitchers like Bannister, Krukow, and Robinson become uninteresting when mated with high ERAs.

Before getting into player analysis, a disturbing factor exists in baseball which should be mentioned. Most students of the game accept ERA as the best single indicator of talent in a pitcher. Until 1976, this standard could be applied to the baseball universe with measured confidence because both leagues played by the same rules. Additionally,

HOF players could be compared using the ERA yardstick because they too played under the same rules.

Desperate to offset declining offensive production in the major leagues (due to *homerunitis* and declining talent), the American League, in 1976, adopted the DH (designated hitter) rule. Under it, a pitcher ceased being a two-way player, and a one-way specialist was substituted for him in the offensive lineup. The National League refused to adopt the same rule. As a consequence, since 1975, playing conditions between the two leagues have differed in a fundamental way, and the difference attacks the future acceptability of ERA as a universal quality standard. Consider the following:

	NL	*ERA* AL	AL/NL
1973–1975*	3.64	3.74	103%
1976–1979	3.66	3.79	104
1980–1982	3.64	4.11	113
1983–1985	3.60	4.07	113

*Prior to DH rule in AL.

This snapshot of the impact of the DH rule on pitchers tells us a number of things of importance:

1. Playing under common rules, NL pitching was slightly better than in the AL (3 percent), but the difference was not consequential.
2. On average, both leagues were producing Class 4 pitching quality, according to historical standards.
3. People are slow to change. For the first three years of the DH rule, impact on pitchers was small.
4. The impact of the matured DH rule on ERAs is now distortive from a historical standpoint.
5. As a practical matter, an AL pitcher has a poorer chance to qualify for HOF recognition than does a NL pitcher. To avoid unfairness, HOF selection committees will be forced to develop separate qualification standards for both leagues. Comparisons of pitching talent from era to era, or from league to league, is no longer possible absent sophisticated statistical techniques.

The loss of historical perspective is no small thing to a game so filled with myths, so reliant upon statistical measurements or performance. What has been the profit? Is the trade-off worthwhile?

| | *Runs Per Game* | | | *Home Runs Per Game* | | |
	NL	AL	AL/NL	NL	AL	AL/NL
1973–1975*	4.14	4.21	102%	.70	.75	107%
1976–1979	4.12	4.23	103	.69	.74	107
1980–1982	4.11	4.54	111	.69	.87	126
1983–1985	4.08	4.52	111	.70	.89	127

*Prior to DH rule in AL.

By introducing a ninth offensive player, the AL has increased total scoring by 9 percent — an inconsequential amount. Home run production in the AL has increased by 20 percent — a significant change. It can be concluded, therefore, that for those who equate baseball quality with long ball drama, the DH rule was a modest success. As payment for this drama, the AL has negated the impact of managerial skill on game outcome by rendering useless various inside baseball tactics, has tacked .37 runs per game on the ERAs of its pitchers, has confused attempts at comparative analysis by sportswriters and analysts, and has destroyed comparative baseball history. For those interested in immediate thrills, or for those preoccupied with profit, the DH is a good rule. For the rest of us, it stinks.

Tom Seaver
Born 1944
Height 6'1"; weight 210
Throws right, bats right
HOF — Probable

Year	Age	CG	H	BB	SO	W	L	%	ERA	Per Game SO	Per Game BR
1967	23	27.9	224	78	170	16	13	.552	2.76	6.1	10.8
1968	24	30.9	224	48	205	16	12	.571	2.20	6.6	8.8
1969	25	30.3	202	82	208	25	7	.781	2.21	6.9	9.4
1970	26	32.3	230	83	283	18	12	.600	2.81	8.8	9.7
1971	27	31.8	210	61	289	20	10	.667	1.76	9.1	8.5
1972	28	29.1	215	77	249	21	12	.636	2.92	8.6	10.0
1973	29	32.2	219	64	251	19	10	.655	2.08	7.8	8.8
1974	30	26.2	199	75	201	11	11	.500	3.20	7.7	10.4
1975	31	31.1	217	88	243	22	9	.710	2.38	7.8	9.8
1976	32	30.1	211	77	235	14	11	.560	2.59	7.8	9.6
1977	33	29.0	199	66	196	21	6	.778	2.59	6.8	9.1
1978	34	28.9	218	89	226	16	14	.533	2.87	7.8	10.6
1979	35	23.9	187	61	131	16	6	.727	3.14	5.5	10.4
1983	39	25.7	201	86	135	9	14	.391	3.55	5.3	11.2
1984	40	26.3	216	61	131	15	11	.577	3.95	5.0	10.5
1985	41	26.6	223	69	134	16	11	.593	3.16	5.0	11.0
Total		462.3	3395	1165	3287	275	169	.619	2.72	7.1	9.9
Other*		69.0	576	225	353	36	36	.500	3.80	5.1	11.6

								Per Game		
	CG	H	BB	SO	W	L	%	ERA	SO	BR
Career	531.3	3971	1390	3640	311	205	.603	2.86	6.9	10.1
*Less than 22 CG: 1980, 1981, 1982, 1986										
Standard Deviation	2.5	11	11	51	4	2				
Avg.	28.9	212	73	205	17	11	.619	2.72	7.1	9.9
Normal Performance Range										
High	31.4	224	84	257	21	13	.620	2.86	8.2	9.8
Low	26.4	201	61	154	13	8	.619	2.56	5.8	9.9

Best Year (over 27 CG): 1971

Super Years (ERA 2.88 –): 1967, 1968, 1969, 1970, 1971, 1973, 1975, 1976, 1977, 1978

Avg.	30.5	215	74	231	19	10	.643	2.42	7.6	9.5

Good Years (ERA 2.89–3.19): 1972, 1979, 1985

Avg.	26.5	208	69	171	18	10	.646	3.07	6.5	10.5

Fair Years (ERA .320–3.50): 1974

Other Years (ERA 3.51 +): 1983, 1984

Avg.	26.0	209	74	133	12	13	.490	3.75	5.1	10.8

Average Yearly Performance by Age

25 and under	29.7	217	69	194	19	11	.640	2.38	6.5	9.6
26–30	30.3	215	72	255	18	11	.618	2.53	8.4	9.4
31–35	28.6	206	76	206	18	9	.659	2.69	7.2	9.9
36 +	26.2	213	72	133	13	12	.526	3.55	5.1	10.9

No active player has combined durability and skill better than Tom Seaver. He is a highly qualified pretender who should be elected to the HOF five years after retirement.

Tom is a superstar — the only one on the field today. In any era, he would have been great, perhaps as great as he is against current competition. When elected to the HOF, he will fit between Koufax and Marichal in the ERA category, as follows:

	CG	ERA	BR	SO	W	L	%	NW
Ford	352.3	2.74	10.93	5.55	236	106	.690	130
Koufax	258.3	2.76	9.95	9.27	165	87	.655	78
Seaver	**531.3**	**2.86**	**10.09**	**6.85**	**311**	**205**	**.603**	**106**
Marichal	389.6	2.89	9.91	5.91	243	142	.631	101
Gibson	431.7	2.91	10.69	7.22	251	174	.591	77
Ruffing	482.4	3.80	12.09	4.12	273	225	.548	48

By any form of measurement, Seaver is a standout. Forty-two years old in 1986, he just completed what could be his final season with the Boston Red Sox.

After one year in the minors, Tom joined the New York Mets in 1967 at the age of 23. He was an instant winner and league leader. After 11 seasons with that club, he was traded to Cincinnati in 1977, then 33 years old. Slowing down by this time, he didn't turn the world upside down during the years with Cincinnati and was traded back to the Mets for one season. In 1984, at 40, Tom headed for Chicago where he did a hard day's work for the White Sox until traded to Boston during the 1986 season.

Seaver does it all: he's tough to hit, has good control, and is one of the better power pitchers. His best power season was 1971 when, at 27 years of age, he whiffed 289 hitters. It was also his best performance year as a pitcher, with an ERA of 1.76. He allowed only 8.5 runners per game. How could anyone be more effective? In 1968, Bob Gibson had an even better year. It's interesting to compare the two best seasons of these two magnificent right-handers:

	CG	H	BB	BR	ERA	SO	W	L	%
				Best Year					
Seaver	31.8	6.60	1.92	8.52	1.76	9.09	20	10	.667
Gibson	33.9	5.84	1.83	7.67	1.12	7.91	22	9	.710

During these seasons, no better pitcher ever strode to the mound than these two. The result of their efforts, an average of 21 wins, is an object lesson on the folly of using the win/loss record of pitchers as the critical quality determinant. For example, Dean and Grove had years in which they won 30 or 31 games. Does that mean that, during those seasons, both pitched better than Seaver and Gibson did when they, in their best seasons, won an average of 21 games? See for yourself!

	CG	H	BB	BR	ERA	SO	W	L	%
				Best Year					
Seaver	31.8	6.60	1.92	8.52	1.76	9.09	20	10	.667
Gibson	33.9	5.84	1.83	7.67	1.12	7.91	22	9	.710
Dean	34.7	8.30	2.16	10.46	2.65	5.62	30	7	.811
Grove	32.1	7.76	1.93	9.69	2.06	5.45	31	4	.886

As great as Dean and Grove were in their best years, Seaver and Gibson were better. They allowed fewer hits, fewer walks, fewer base-runners, and had a better power pitch, but they didn't win as many games. Winning games isn't a pitcher's job — it's a team job. A pitcher's job is to keep men off the bases and to stop those who get there from scoring.

According to his 100 + game profile, Seaver averages out as a superstar pitcher. He has had ten superstar years, three Class 2 years, one Class 3 year, one Class 4 season, and one bummer.

Seaver is beyond his prime. But for most of his career, he was something to see. In his early twenties, he was the best in baseball. In his late twenties and early thirties, he continued to turn in superstar performances. In his late thirties, the well-conditioned veteran continued to be a formidable force.

Fernando Valenzuela
Born 1960
Height 5'11"; weight 180
Throws left, bats left
HOF — Possible

| | | | | | | | | | Per Game | | |
Year	Age	CG	H	BB	SO	W	L	%	ERA	SO	BR
1982	22	31.7	247	83	199	19	13	.594	2.87	6.3	10.4
1983	23	28.6	245	99	189	15	10	.600	3.75	6.6	12.0
1984	24	29.0	218	106	240	12	17	.414	3.03	8.3	11.2
1985	25	30.2	211	101	208	17	10	.630	2.45	6.9	10.3
1986	26	29.9	226	85	242	21	11	.656	3.14	8.1	10.4
Total		149.3	1147	474	1078	84	61	.579	3.04	7.2	10.9
Other*		23.4	148	66	196	15	7	.682	2.26	8.4	9.1
Career		172.8	1295	540	1274	99	68	.593	2.94	7.4	10.6

*Less than 22 CG: 1980, 1981

Standard Deviation		1.1	14	9	22	3	3				
Avg.		29.9	229	95	216	17	12	.579	3.04	7.2	10.9

Normal Performance Range

High		30.9	244	104	237	20	15	.573	3.28	7.7	11.2
Low		28.8	215	86	194	14	10	.589	2.79	6.7	10.4

Best Year (over 27 CG): 1985

Super Years (ERA 2.88–): 1982, 1985

Avg.		30.9	229	92	204	18	12	.610	2.67	6.6	10.4

Good Years (ERA 2.89–3.19): 1984, 1986

Avg.		29.4	222	96	241	17	14	.541	3.09	8.2	10.8

Fair Years (ERA 3.20–3.50): None

Other Years (ERA 3.51 +): 1983

Average Yearly Performance by Age

25 and under		29.9	230	97	209	16	13	.558	3.01	7.0	11.0
26–30		29.9	226	85	242	21	11	.656	3.14	8.1	10.4

Valenzuela, who turned 26 years old in 1986, already has eight major league seasons behind him. In five of them, he pitched 198 +

innings—two superstar years, two Class 2 years, and one Class 4 season. Working for Tommy LaSorda, a former pitcher, Fernando has been used intelligently. It's doubtful that he'll be put on an early burnout schedule by crafty Tom.

Valenzuela is a legitimate pretender. He has HOF skills which now must endure the tests of time and stability. He's a strong bet to make it all the way if he keeps his head on straight—and his belly trim.

Fernando had about 1,555 innings pitched at the end of the 1986 season. The graphic below shows how he compares with other prominent HOF lefties in this respect:

| | Innings Pitched | |
	Total	Age 26
Ford	3171	530
Koufax	2325	948
Hubbell	3591	392
Grove	3940	455
Spahn	5246	432
Valenzuela	?	1555

According to his 22 + game profile, Valenzuela is a Class 2 pitcher with superstar potential. As it was with the above southpaws, his best years should be ahead of him. Certainly he must be rated as the best proven-pitching investment in baseball today. If elected to the HOF at his present efficiency level, Fernando would fit between Gibson and Drysdale, as follows:

	CG	ERA	BR	SO	W	L	%	NW*
Ford	352.3	2.74	10.93	5.55	236	106	.690	130
Marichal	389.6	2.89	9.91	5.91	243	142	.631	101
Gibson	431.7	2.91	10.69	7.22	251	174	.591	77
Valenzuela	**172.8**	**2.94**	**10.62**	**7.37**	**99**	**68**	**.593**	**31**
Drysdale	381.3	2.95	10.33	6.52	209	166	.557	43
Hubbell	399.0	2.98	10.49	4.20	253	154	.622	99
Ruffing	482.4	3.80	12.09	4.12	273	225	.548	48

*Net wins.

Bert Blyleven

Born 1951
Height 6'3"; weight 205
Throws right, bats right
HOF—Probable

									Per Game		
Year	Age	CG	H	BB	SO	W	L	%	ERA	SO	BR
1971	20	30.9	267	59	224	16	15	.516	2.82	7.3	10.6
1972	21	31.9	247	69	228	17	17	.500	2.73	7.1	9.9
1973	22	36.1	296	67	258	20	17	.541	2.52	7.1	10.1
1974	23	31.2	244	77	249	17	17	.500	2.66	8.0	10.3
1975	24	30.7	219	84	233	15	10	.600	3.00	7.6	9.9
1976	25	33.1	283	81	219	13	16	.448	2.87	6.6	11.0
1977	26	26.1	181	69	182	14	12	.538	2.72	7.0	9.6
1978	27	27.1	217	66	182	14	10	.583	3.02	6.7	10.4
1979	28	26.3	239	92	172	12	5	.706	3.61	6.5	12.6
1980	29	24.1	219	59	169	8	13	.381	3.82	7.0	11.5
1984	33	27.2	204	74	170	19	7	.731	2.87	6.2	10.2
1985	34	32.7	264	75	206	17	16	.515	3.15	6.3	10.4
1986	35	30.2	262	58	215	17	14	.548	4.00	7.1	10.6
Total		387.7	3142	930	2707	199	169	.541	3.04	7.0	10.5
Other*		55.4	463	142	383	30	28	.517	3.39	6.9	10.9
Career		443.1	3605	1072	3090	229	197	.538	3.08	7.0	10.6

*Less than 22 CG: 1970, 1981, 1982, 1983

Standard Deviation		3.3	32	10	29	3	4				
Avg.		29.8	242	72	208	15	13	.541	3.04	7.0	10.5

Normal Performance Range

High		33.1	273	81	238	18	17	.522	3.09	7.2	10.7
Low		26.5	210	62	179	12	9	.572	2.96	6.7	10.2

Best Year (over 27 CG): 1973

Super Years (ERA 2.88–): 1971, 1972, 1973, 1974, 1976, 1977, 1984

Avg.		30.9	246	71	219	17	14	.535	2.73	7.1	10.2

Good Years (ERA 2.89–3.19): 1975, 1978, 1985

Avg.		30.1	233	75	207	15	21	.561	3.06	6.9	10.2

Fair Years (ERA 3.20–3.50): None

Other Years (ERA 3.51+): 1979, 1980, 1986

Avg.		26.9	240	70	185	12	11	.536	3.82	6.9	11.5

Average Yearly Performance by Age

25 and under		32.3	259	73	235	16	15	.516	2.76	7.3	10.3
26–30		25.9	214	72	176	12	10	.545	3.28	6.8	11.0
31–35		29.9	243	69	197	18	12	.589	3.02	6.3	10.3

Blyleven is hurting from *walterjohnsonitis,* a disease suffered by the old fireballer during most of his career. Its statistical symptom is a poor winning percentage despite superior pitching performance. The ethical abstraction from this phenomenon is: Hard work doesn't pay off.

If elected to the HOF, Bert would show a winning percentage poorer than any HOF pitcher except Ted Lyons, who had a career ERA of 3.67 and, perhaps, deserved no more wins than he got. On the other hand, as a HOF member, Blyleven will show an ERA (3.08) better than nine of the HOF pitchers. In other words, Bert is a hell of a pitcher who has been—and is—saddled with teams that have produced poorly for him. He is an outstanding pretender who will end up in the HOF. Bert Blyleven has already met the test of time. His durability characteristics are more than adequate.

The fickle finger of fate has been out to lunch as far as Bert is concerned. Don't ask him for tips on the next horse race. He is snake bit. In seven superstar performance years with an average ERA of 2.73, Blyleven averaged 17–14, a winning percentage of .535. In 1971, with an ERA of 2.82, he was 16–15; in 1972, with an ERA of 2.73, he was 17–17; in 1974, with an ERA of 2.66, he was 17–17; unbelievably, in 1976, with an ERA of 2.87, he was 13–16. No sir! Don't ask Bert for any tips on the races.

Blyleven joined Minnesota in 1970 at 19 years of age. His performance during a part year, plus a brilliant minor leagues record, suggested that a new and major pitching talent had arrived. A long and successful career was in early bloom.

In 1971, Bert became numero uno of the Minnesota Twins pitching staff. He labored long and well for the club during six full seasons. His average ERA was 2.82—superstar stuff. Only twice during that period was his ERA 3.00 + —the highest was 3.18. His win/loss record with that team must have been fantastic. Right? Wrong! Despite superstar performances, Blyleven left Minnesota for Texas during the early part of the 1976 season with a six-year 95–85 record, for a winning rate of .528.

In about two seasons with Texas, he compiled an average ERA of about 2.80. Things turned around for him, right? Wrong! With Texas, his superstar efforts earned him a 28–22 record—a winning rate of .560.

When he moved to Pittsburgh in 1978 at the age of 27, he was lugging a 123–107 (.535) record with him despite the fact that for eight seasons he'd been a pitching superstar. In his three years with the Pirates, Bert pitched relatively poorly, turning in an average ERA of about 3.48. His win/loss record went to hell with that kind of an ERA. Right? Wrong! He was 34–28 (.548) with that club—he pitched worse and won more.

With this revolutionary formula in mind, Bert rode his lucky hot streak to the pits of Cleveland in 1981, then 30 years old. For three seasons, he pitched little, probably figuring that this course of action was less laborious, and kept him out of trouble. Then in 1984, he decided to try again. He had another superstar year at the age of 33 and, presto, his record was 19–7 (.731). Has the wheel turned for battered Bert? Will long-awaited wins come his way? It doesn't look like it. Mother Nature was fooling him in 1984. Poor Bert. Poor battered Bert. In 1985, he was 17–16 despite an ERA of 3.16. In 1986, Bert did better (17–14) with a higher ERA (4.01).

If elected to the HOF, Blyleven would fit between Spahn and Lemon in the ERA classifications, as follows:

	CG	ERA	BR	SO	W	L	%	NW
Ford	352.3	2.74	10.93	5.55	236	106	.690	130
Grove	437.8	3.06	11.50	5.18	300	141	.680	159
Spahn	582.9	3.08	10.75	4.43	363	245	.597	118
Blyleven	**443.1**	**3.08**	**10.55**	**6.97**	**229**	**197**	**.538**	**32**
Lemon	316.6	3.23	12.04	4.03	207	128	.618	79
Feller	425.3	3.25	11.84	6.07	266	162	.621	104
Ruffing	482.4	3.80	12.09	4.12	273	225	.548	48

Bert rates the HOF. The fetish of selection committees for "most of" records, however, could hurt his chances. The only thing he has "most of" is lousy luck.

Steve Carlton
Born 1944
Height 6'5"; weight 219
Throws left, bats left
HOF—Probable

									Per Game		
Year	Age	CG	H	BB	SO	W	L	%	ERA	SO	BR
1968	24	25.8	214	61	162	13	11	.542	2.99	6.3	10.7
1969	25	26.2	185	93	210	17	11	.607	2.17	8.0	10.6
1970	26	28.2	239	109	193	10	19	.345	3.72	6.8	12.3
1971	27	30.3	275	98	172	20	9	.690	3.56	5.7	12.3
1972	28	38.4	257	87	310	27	10	.730	1.98	8.1	8.9
1973	29	32.6	293	113	223	13	20	.394	3.90	6.8	12.5
1974	30	32.3	249	136	240	16	13	.552	3.22	7.4	11.9
1975	31	28.3	217	104	192	15	14	.517	3.56	6.8	11.3
1976	32	28.1	224	72	195	20	7	.741	3.13	6.9	10.5
1977	33	31.4	229	89	198	23	10	.697	2.64	6.3	10.1
1978	34	27.4	228	63	161	16	13	.552	2.84	5.9	10.6
1979	35	27.9	202	89	213	18	11	.621	3.62	7.6	10.4
1980	36	33.8	243	90	286	24	9	.727	2.34	8.5	9.9
1982	38	32.9	253	86	286	23	11	.676	3.10	8.7	10.3
1983	39	31.6	277	84	275	15	16	.484	3.11	8.7	11.4
1984	40	25.4	214	79	163	13	7	.650	3.58	6.4	11.5

	CG	H	BB	SO	W	L	%	ERA	SO	BR
Total	480.8	3799	1453	3479	283	191	.597	3.07	7.2	10.9
Other*	80.9	688	289	561	40	38	.513	3.39	6.9	12.1
Career	561.7	4487	1742	4040	323	229	.585	3.11	7.2	11.1

*Less than 22 CG: 1965, 1966, 1967, 1981, 1985, 1986

Standard Deviation	3.4	28	18	47	5	4				
Avg.	30.0	237	91	217	18	12	.597	3.07	7.2	10.9

Normal Performance Range

	CG	H	BB	SO	W	L	%	ERA	SO	BR
High	33.4	266	109	264	22	16	.588	3.24	7.9	11.2
Low	26.7	209	73	170	13	8	.613	2.85	6.4	10.6

Best Year (over 27 CG): 1972

Super Years (ERA 2.88 –): 1969, 1972, 1977, 1978, 1980

Avg.	31.5	228	84	233	21	11	.669	2.37	7.4	9.9

Good Years (ERA 2.89–3.19): 1968, 1976, 1982, 1983

Avg.	29.6	242	76	230	18	11	.612	3.08	7.8	10.7

Fair Years (ERA 3.20–3.50): 1974

Other Years (ERA 3.51 +): 1970, 1971, 1973, 1975, 1979, 1984

Avg.	28.8	240	99	193	15	13	.527	3.66	6.7	11.8

Average Yearly Performance by Age

	CG	H	BB	SO	W	L	%	ERA	SO	BR
25 and under	26.0	200	77	186	15	11	.577	2.58	7.2	10.6
26–30	32.4	263	109	228	17	14	.548	3.21	7.0	11.5
31–35	28.6	220	83	192	18	11	.626	3.15	6.7	10.6
36 +	30.9	247	85	253	19	11	.636	2.99	8.2	10.7

Left-handers always look better than right-handers. When they're tough, they seem to pitch the invisible ball. There have been some great ones—Carlton is one more. Below is a comparison of Steve's best year with the best years of other famous southpaws:

	Best Season								
	CG	H	BB	BR	ERA	SO	W	L	%
Spahn	29.6	7.13	2.37	9.50	2.10	5.00	23	7	.767
Ford	27.2	7.79	2.10	9.89	2.13	6.32	17	6	.739
Koufax	35.8	6.71	2.15	8.86	1.73	8.83	27	9	.750
Grove	32.1	7.76	1.93	9.69	2.06	5.45	31	4	.886
Carlton	38.4	6.69	2.27	8.96	1.98	8.07	27	10	.730

A few interesting thoughts emerge from this schedule. The first: Carlton is an outstanding pretender deserving of quick entry into the HOF. The second: Carlton at his best could pitch with any left-hander in history. The third: What idiots Koufax and Carlton were to pitch so much in a single season. In the case of the peerless Koufax, the story of his tragically short career is well known. In the case of Steve Carlton, it took four years to shake off the effects of his superman performance in 1972. In 1977 he fortunately returned to the superstar form almost burned out of him in a single season.

According to his 22 + complete game profile, Carlton averages out as a Class 2 pitcher. He has had five superstar seasons, four Class 2 years, one Class 3 year, five Class 4 years, and one bummer. When elected to the HOF, Steve will fit between Spahn and Lemon in the ERA classifications, as follows:

	CG	ERA	BR	SO	W	L	%	NW
Ford	352.3	2.74	10.93	5.55	236	106	.690	130
Grove	437.8	3.06	11.50	5.18	300	141	.680	159
Spahn	582.9	3.08	10.75	4.43	363	245	.597	118
Carlton	**561.7**	**3.11**	**11.09**	**7.19**	**323**	**229**	**.585**	**94**
Lemon	316.6	3.23	12.04	4.03	207	128	.618	79
Feller	425.3	3.25	11.84	6.07	266	162	.621	104
Ruffing	482.4	3.80	12.09	4.12	273	225	.548	48

Carlton, 43 years old in '86, is slipping. The end is near—he hasn't been healthy since 1984. But he's destined to appear as one of the most durable quality pitchers of this or any other day. One of the great strikeout artists of baseball history, Lefty's best power year was 1972 when, at 28, he sent 310 hitters back to the bench muttering to themselves.

In 16 seasons, Carlton pitched 198 + innings. He averaged 30.0 complete games, an ERA of 3.04, and 217 whiffs a year (7.23 strikeouts per game). In one year, Steve whiffed 300 + ; in half of them, 200 + went down swinging; in the entire 16-year period, he never struck out less than 161.

Except for short-careered Koufax, right-hander Bob Gibson is the top strikeout artist of the HOF pitching corps. Below is a comparison of the career records of Gibson and Carlton:

	CG	H	BB	BR	ERA	SO	W	L	%
Carlton	561.7	7.99	3.10	11.09	3.11	7.19	323	229	.585
Gibson	431.7	7.60	3.09	10.69	2.91	7.22	251	174	.591

The winner? Carlton—he's almost as good and more durable.

John Candelaria

Born 1953
Height 6'7"; weight 232
Throws left, bats both
HOF—Doubtful

| | | | | | | | | | Per Game | | |
Year	Age	CG	H	BB	SO	W	L	%	ERA	SO	BR
1976	23	24.4	173	60	138	16	7	.696	3.15	5.6	9.5
1977	24	25.7	197	52	133	20	5	.800	2.34	5.2	9.7
1979	26	23.0	201	41	101	14	9	.609	3.22	4.4	10.5
1980	27	25.9	246	50	97	11	14	.440	4.02	3.7	11.4
Total		99.0	817	203	469	61	35	.635	3.18	4.7	10.3
Other*		125.1	1059	274	807	80	54	.597	3.06	6.5	10.7
Career		224.1	1876	477	1276	141	89	.613	3.11	5.7	10.5

*Less than 22 CG: 1975, 1978, 1981, 1982, 1983, 1984, 1985, 1986

Standard Deviation		1.2	26	7	18	3	3				
Avg.		24.8	204	51	117	15	9	.635	3.18	4.7	10.3
Normal Performance Range											
High		25.9	231	58	136	19	12	.605	3.66	5.2	11.1
Low		23.6	178	44	99	12	5	.689	2.66	4.2	9.4

Best Year (over 27 CG): None

Super Years (ERA 2.88 –): 1977

Good Years (ERA 2.89–3.19): 1976

Fair Years (ERA 3.20–3.50): 1979

Other Years (ERA 3.51 +): 1980

Average Yearly Performance by Age											
25 and under		25.1	185	56	136	18	6	.750	2.73	5.4	9.6
26–30		24.4	224	46	99	13	12	.521	3.64	4.1	11.0

John was 22 years old when, in 1975, he joined the Pittsburgh Pirates. At 33 years of age (1986) it's doubtful that he can build an adequate durability record. By that year, he had 12 major league seasons and 224 complete games behind him. In only four seasons has he worked 22 + complete games. He was hurt in 1981, and hasn't carried a full pitching load since.

According to his 22 + game profile, Candelaria averages out as a Class 2 pitcher with unimpressive durability. He had one superstar year, and one each of classes 2, 3, and 4. He showed early promise, then ran out of gas.

The HOF honors the strong and the talented — durability plus skill. John is not the first to show adequate skill but, for one reason or another, inadequate staying power.

Bob Welch
Born 1956
Height 6'3"; weight 190
Throws right, bats right
HOF — Doubtful

Year	Age	CG	H	BB	SO	W	L	%	*Per Game*		
									ERA	SO	BR
1980	24	23.8	190	79	141	14	9	.609	3.28	5.9	11.3
1982	26	26.2	199	81	176	16	11	.593	3.36	6.7	10.7
1983	27	22.7	164	72	156	15	12	.556	2.65	6.9	10.4
1986	30	26.2	227	55	183	7	13	.350	3.28	7.0	10.8
Total		98.9	780	287	656	52	45	.536	3.16	6.6	10.8
Other*		75.3	647	192	440	48	32	.600	3.09	5.8	11.1
Career		174.2	1427	479	1096	100	77	.565	3.13	6.3	10.9

*Less than 22 CG: 1978, 1979, 1981, 1984, 1985

Standard Deviation		1.6	23	10	17	4	1				
Avg.		24.7	195	72	164	13	11	.536	3.16	6.6	10.8

Normal Performance Range

High		26.3	218	82	181	17	13	.565	3.39	6.9	11.4
Low		23.2	172	62	147	9	10	.492	2.89	6.4	10.1

Best Year (over 27 CG): None

Super Years (ERA 2.88 –): 1983

Good Years (ERA 2.89–3.19): None

Fair Years (ERA 3.20–3.50): 1980, 1982, 1986

Avg.		25.4	205	72	167	12	11	.529	3.31	6.6	10.9

Other Years (ERA 3.51 +): None

Average Yearly Performance by Age

25 and under		23.8	190	79	141	14	9	.609	3.28	5.9	11.3
26–30		25.0	197	69	172	13	12	.514	3.12	6.9	10.6

Bob Welch, 30 in 1986, has nine major league seasons and about 174 complete games behind him. For two of the previous three seasons, he has carried less than a full pitching load.

Welch has shown HOF talent, but not HOF dedication. He's still young enough to make a charge at worthy goals, but the record says the drive to excel is missing or, at best, too late in coming. It is doubtful that Bob will make it.

Since hitting the majors in 1978 at the age of 22, Bob has been an unstable performer. In a nine-year career, he has had four 22 + complete game seasons, averaging 24.7 complete games a year. He averages out as a Class 2 hurler—one superstar year; no Class 2 years; three Class 3 seasons. Statistically, he is borrowing on his superstar 1983 year (ERA 2.65), the mathematical weight of which has kept him in Class 2. As he continues to perform at normal rates of efficiency, Bob's position in the classification structure will drop.

Everybody has some talents—some seem loaded with it. Most

apply modest talents in a constructive way with varying degrees of fervor in the pursuit of modest success. Some have success handed to them and abuse the gifts that draw attention to them. It's sad to see beauty sliced up by the hand of the owner thereof. For awhile, Bob seemed to be doing that. But that's behind him. Future years may be brighter.

Nolan Ryan
Born 1947
Height 6'2"; weight 195
Throws right, bats right
HOF—Probable

Year	Age	CG	H	BB	SO	W	L	%	ERA	Per Game SO	BR
1972	25	31.6	166	157	329	19	16	.543	2.28	10.4	10.2
1973	26	36.2	238	162	383	21	16	.568	2.87	10.6	11.0
1974	27	37.0	221	202	367	22	16	.579	2.89	9.9	11.4
1975	28	22.0	152	132	186	14	12	.538	3.45	8.5	12.9
1976	29	31.6	153	183	327	17	18	.486	3.36	10.4	10.6
1977	30	33.2	198	204	341	19	16	.543	2.77	10.3	12.1
1978	31	26.1	183	148	260	10	13	.435	3.71	10.0	12.7
1979	32	24.8	169	114	223	16	14	.533	3.59	9.0	11.4
1980	33	26.0	205	98	200	11	10	.524	3.35	7.7	11.7
1982	35	27.8	196	109	245	16	12	.571	3.17	8.8	11.0
1985	38	25.8	205	95	209	10	12	.455	3.80	8.1	11.6
Total		322.0	2086	1604	3070	175	155	.530	3.16	9.5	11.5
Other*		135.2	904	664	1207	78	71	.523	3.14	8.9	11.6
Career		457.2	2990	2268	4277	253	226	.528	3.15	9.4	11.5

*Less than 22 CG: 1968, 1969, 1970, 1971, 1981, 1983, 1984, 1986

Standard Deviation		4.7	26	38	69	4	2				
Avg.		29.3	190	146	279	16	14	.530	3.16	9.5	11.5
Normal Performance Range											
High		34.0	216	184	348	20	16	.548	3.04	10.2	11.8
Low		24.6	163	108	211	12	12	.502	3.31	8.6	11.0

Best Year (over 27 CG): 1972

Super Years (ERA 2.88 –): 1972, 1973, 1977

Avg.		33.7	201	174	351	20	16	.551	2.65	10.4	11.1

Good Years (ERA 2.89–3.19): 1974, 1982

Avg.		32.4	209	156	306	19	14	.576	3.01	9.4	11.2

Fair Years (ERA 3.20–3.50): 1975, 1976, 1980)

Avg.		26.5	170	138	238	14	13	.512	3.38	9.0	11.6

Other Years (ERA 3.51 +): 1978, 1979, 1985

Avg.		25.6	186	119	231	12	13	.480	3.70	9.0	11.9

	CG	H	BB	SO	W	L	%	*Per Game* ERA	SO	BR
Average Yearly Performance by Age										
25 and under	31.6	166	157	329	19	16	.543	2.28	10.4	10.2
26–30	32.0	192	177	321	19	16	.543	3.03	10.0	11.5
31–35	26.2	188	117	232	13	12	.520	3.45	8.9	11.7
36 +	26.1	205	95	209	10	12	.455	3.76	8.0	11.5

Steve Carlton, a southpaw, has more career strikeouts than Walter Johnson. Nolan Ryan, a right-hander, has more career strikeouts than Carlton. That makes Ryan king of the "most of" strikeout records for a career. But those with "most of" records are not necessarily the best at their specialties. Often, it is durability rather than skill which serves as the underpinning for the "most of" title. What is Ryan? Is he king because of durability, or because of comparatively superior skill? The career strikeout record of Nolan is compared with that of other prominent power pitchers below:

Career Strikeouts

	CG	SO	SOPG
Koufax	258.3	2396	9.28
Gibson	431.7	3117	7.22
Feller	425.3	2581	6.07
Seaver	485.2	3403	7.01
Carlton	561.7	4040	7.19
Ryan	**457.2**	**4277**	**9.35**

Walter Johnson had 3,508 career strikeouts. Ryan, Carlton, and Seaver are beyond this point. Ryan has the edge and figures to open up the difference between himself and the others before he retires. On a per game basis, or a career basis, Ryan is the most awesome strikeout artist in the history of baseball.

To test this conclusion further, below is the record of the above players for the three seasons during which they had the most strikeouts:

Strikeouts — Best Three Years

	CG	SO	SOPG
Koufax	107.8	1005	9.32
Gibson	100.8	813	8.07
Feller	114.9	869	7.56
Seaver	96.3	823	8.55
Carlton	105.1	882	8.39
Ryan	**106.4**	**1091**	**10.25**

Based upon these schedules, players can be ranked under two headings: Durability (career) and skill (three years).

Durability	Skill
Ryan	Ryan
Carlton	Koufax
Seaver	Seaver
Gibson	Carlton
Feller	Gibson
Koufax	Feller

There you have it. Ryan is the legitimate king of the whiffers. Added to the fact that he is also an overall Class 2 pitcher, the strikeout title is Nolan's automatic ticket to HOF immortality. He is a pretender guaranteed to enter the HOF.

According to his 22 + complete game profile, King Ryan averages out as a Class 2 pitcher. He has had three super years, two Class 2 years, three Class 3 years, and three Class 4 seasons. When elected to the HOF, he will fit between Spahn and Lemon in the ERA classification structure, as follows:

	CG	ERA	BR	SO	W	L	%	NW
Ford	352.3	2.74	10.93	5.55	236	106	.690	130
Grove	437.8	3.06	11.50	5.18	300	141	.680	141
Spahn	582.9	3.08	10.75	4.43	363	245	.597	118
Ryan	**457.2**	**3.15**	**11.50**	**9.35**	**253**	**226**	**.528**	**27**
Lemon	316.6	3.23	12.04	4.03	207	128	.618	79
Feller	425.3	3.25	11.84	6.07	266	162	.621	104
Ruffing	482.4	3.80	12.09	4.12	273	225	.548	48

Ryan was pitching for the Mets, in 1968, at 21 years of age. During his four years with that team, New York was a contender in only one season (1969). In his eight years in a California uniform, the team was one of the worst in baseball except for 1979 and, perhaps, 1978. By the time he went to Houston, in 1980, Nolan was 33 years old with his best years behind him. In 1980 the team was a contender, but otherwise was not a major competitive force in the league. Playing for such an array of losers explains the unimpressive win/loss record of Ryan—his skills deserved better associates. Like Blyleven, Nolan has been riding the wrong horse for most of his career.

Does luck influence the win/loss record of a player?

Five Best Seasons

	Ryan				Ruffing		
Year	ERA	Win/Loss	%	Year	ERA	Win/Loss	%
1972	2.28	19/16	.543	1939	2.94	21/7	.750
1977	2.77	19/16	.543	1937	2.99	20/7	.741
1973	2.87	21/16	.568	1932	3.09	18/7	.720
1974	2.89	22/16	.579	1935	3.12	16/11	.593
1982	3.17	16/12	.571	1938	3.32	21/7	.750
Avg.	2.80	19/15	.559		3.09	19/8	.704

With an ERA of over three runs per game, Ruffing won 70 percent of his decisions. With an ERA of less than three runs per game, Ryan won about 56 percent. Luck!

Judging pitchers by their winning records is a risky business that can bring weird results. For example, on that basis Gomez is the number four pitcher in the HOF, better than the likes of Marichal, Gibson, Drysdale, Hubbell, and Dean. Was he?

Per Game

	W/L %	H	BB	BR	ERA	SO
Gomez	.649	8.23	3.94	12.17	3.34	5.28
Marichal	.631	8.09	1.82	9.91	2.89	5.91
Gibson	.591	7.60	3.09	10.69	2.91	7.22
Drysdale	.557	8.09	2.24	10.33	2.95	6.52
Hubbell	.622	8.67	1.82	10.49	2.98	4.20
Dean	.644	8.79	2.10	10.89	3.04	5.29

Except for Hubbell and Dean, Gomez gave up more hits than the others. He was the wildest. He allowed the most baserunners. He allowed the most runs. Except for Hubbell, he had the weakest strikeout pitch. In short, Gomez wasn't as good a pitcher as the others, which is another way of saying that winning percentages and quality pitching are not synonymous.

Don Sutton

Born 1945
Height 6'1"; weight 190
Throws right, bats right
HOF — Probable

| | | | | | | | | | *Per Game* | | |
Year	Age	CG	H	BB	SO	W	L	%	ERA	SO	BR
1966	21	25.1	192	52	209	12	12	.500	2.99	8.3	9.7
1967	22	25.9	223	57	169	11	15	.423	3.94	6.5	10.8
1968	23	23.1	179	59	162	11	15	.423	2.60	7.0	10.3
1969	24	32.6	269	91	217	17	18	.486	3.47	6.7	11.1
1970	25	28.9	251	78	201	15	13	.536	4.08	7.0	11.4
1971	26	29.4	231	55	194	17	12	.586	2.55	6.6	9.7
1972	27	30.3	186	63	207	19	9	.679	2.08	6.8	8.2
1973	28	28.4	196	56	200	18	10	.643	2.43	7.0	8.9
1974	29	30.7	241	80	179	19	9	.679	3.23	5.8	10.5
1975	30	28.2	202	62	175	16	13	.552	2.87	6.2	9.4
1976	31	29.8	231	82	161	21	10	.677	3.06	5.4	10.5
1977	32	26.7	207	69	150	14	8	.636	3.19	5.6	10.4
1978	33	26.4	228	54	154	15	11	.577	3.55	5.8	10.7
1979	34	25.1	201	61	146	12	15	.444	3.82	5.8	10.4
1980	35	23.6	163	47	128	13	5	.722	2.21	5.4	8.9
1982	37	27.8	224	64	175	17	9	.654	3.06	6.3	10.4
1983	38	24.4	209	54	134	8	13	.381	4.09	5.5	10.8
1984	39	23.7	224	51	143	14	12	.538	3.76	6.0	11.6
1985	40	25.1	221	59	107	15	10	.600	3.86	4.3	11.2
1986	41	23.0	192	49	116	15	11	.577	3.74	5.0	10.5
Total		538.2	4270	1243	3327	299	230	.565	3.21	6.2	10.2
Other*		17.7	132	29	104	11	9	.550	2.60	5.9	9.1
Career		555.9	4402	1272	3431	310	239	.565	3.20	6.2	10.2

*Less than 22 CG: 1981

Standard Deviation		2.7	25	12	31	3	3				
Avg.		26.9	214	62	166	15	12	.565	3.21	6.2	10.2

Normal Performance Range

High		29.6	239	74	198	18	14	.557	3.48	6.7	10.5
Low		24.2	188	50	135	12	9	.579	2.89	5.6	9.9

Best Year (over 27 CG): 1972

Super Years (ERA 2.88 –): 1968, 1971, 1972, 1973, 1975, 1980

Avg.		27.2	193	57	178	16	11	.595	2.45	6.5	9.2

Good Years (ERA 2.89–3.19): 1966, 1976, 1977, 1982

Avg.		27.3	214	67	174	16	10	.621	3.07	6.4	10.3

Fair Years (ERA 3.20–3.50): 1969, 1974

Avg.		31.6	255	86	198	18	14	.571	3.35	6.3	10.8

Other Years (ERA 3.51 +): 1967, 1970, 1978, 1979, 1983, 1984, 1985, 1986

Avg.		25.3	219	58	146	13	13	.500	3.86	5.8	10.9

Average Yearly Performance by Age

25 and under		27.1	223	67	192	13	15	.475	3.45	7.1	10.7
26–30		29.4	211	63	191	18	11	.627	2.63	6.5	9.3
31–35		26.3	206	63	148	15	10	.605	3.18	5.6	10.2
36 +		24.8	214	55	135	14	11	.556	3.69	5.4	10.9

Everybody knows Tom Terrific Seaver. Jockey shorts Palmer is all over television. Not-so-well publicized Don Sutton was still doing a journeyman job at 41 years of age in 1986, and has been quietly building one of the best pitching records in modern baseball history.

Don was 21 years old when, in 1966, he moved right into the starting rotation of Los Angeles. For 15 years — until he became a free agent in 1980 — Sutton was the mainstay of the LA pitching corps. Moving on to Houston at 36, he cut down on his mound appearances but gave the club two solid seasons. At the end of the 1982, Don was traded to Milwaukee where he played for three years, and in 1986, after a few months in Oakland, went back with LA while winding the clock down. Don is still carrying a full pitching load.

From a durability standpoint, Sutton has gone beyond Seaver, passed Carlton in 1987, and could possibly outwork Phil Niekro and surpass the mighty Spahn before he quits. It is interesting to note that, like Tom Seaver, Don has never pitched 300 + innings in a season. He has paced his career magnificently. An obvious pretender, Sutton should have no trouble getting HOF votes.

Don has not been the equal of peerless Tom over the years, but they are much alike in many respects in terms of style and durability. In age blocks, their careers are matched below.

22 + Complete Game Seasons

	Yrs	CG	H	BB	BR	ERA	SO	W	L	%
25 and under										
Don	5	27.1	8.23	2.47	10.70	3.45	7.09	13	15	.475
Tom	3	29.7	7.37	2.32	9.69	2.38	6.53	19	11	.640
26–30										
Don	5	29.4	7.18	2.14	9.32	2.63	6.50	18	11	.621
Tom	5	30.3	7.10	2.38	9.48	2.53	8.42	18	11	.621
31–35										
Don	5	26.3	7.83	2.40	10.23	3.18	5.63	15	10	.605
Tom	5	28.6	7.20	2.66	9.86	2.69	7.20	18	9	.659
36 +										
Don	6	23.6	8.49	2.16	10.65	3.55	5.50	13	11	.542
Tom	7	21.1	8.23	2.99	11.22	3.66	5.10	11	10	.524

Tom got up to speed sooner than Don. In their early twenties, he was clearly the superior pitcher, despite the fact that Don had the better power pitch. LA didn't have much of a team during the early 1970s, which accounts for Don's poor win/loss record. Both men were hot in their late twenties. Tom was harder to hit, Don had better control; Tom's power increased with age, Don's diminished. By a hair, Tom was the better man. In their early thirties, both men slipped a notch, but Don more so. Tom continued to pitch superstar ball; Don slipped to Class 2 levels. Now in the twilight of their careers, Don seems to be holding up a tad better. Notice the sensible pace of both careers. This is a key to longevity, something which both know and expertly practice.

The most informative aspect of the above comparison to many people is the implied status it gives to Don Sutton. Everybody acknowledges the greatness of Tom, but for some reason there seems to be a reluctance to give to Sutton an equivalent level of admiration. Beyond argument, the above comparison makes clear that Sutton has earned it.

According to his 22 + complete game profile, Don averages out as a Class 2 pitcher. He has had six superstar years, three Class 2 years, three Class 3 years, four Class 4 years, and four bummers. When elected to the HOF, he'll fit between Spahn and Lemon in the ERA classifications, as follows:

	CG	ERA	BR	SO	W	L	%	NW
Ford	352.3	2.74	10.93	5.55	236	106	.690	130
Grove	437.8	3.06	11.50	5.18	300	141	.680	141
Spahn	582.9	3.08	10.75	4.43	363	245	.597	118
Sutton	**555.9**	**3.20**	**10.21**	**6.17**	**310**	**239**	**.565**	**71**
Lemon	316.6	3.23	12.04	4.03	207	128	.618	79
Feller	425.3	3.25	11.84	6.07	266	162	.621	104
Ruffing	482.4	3.80	12.09	4.12	273	225	.548	48

Sutton is a durability competitor of the indestructible Spahn. Only two HOF pitchers (Sandy Koufax, Juan Marichal) allowed fewer baserunners per game. The Achilles' heel of Don is pitching with men on base—31 percent of his baserunners score. Only Roberts and Ruffing of the HOF pitching corps were weaker in this area. It is this chink in his pitching armor that keeps Sutton from superstar ranks. Ford, for example, allowed more baserunners (10.93), but fewer earned runs 2.74 (25 percent).

How many baserunners are allowed? How many baserunners score? The ERA of a pitcher is a reflection of how a pitcher confronts both of these hurdles. Don is strong in the skill game (baserunners); not so strong at the clutch pitching game (percent of baserunners scored). Because of his strength in the first area, he is a HOF pitcher; because of his relative weakness in the second, he is not a superstar.

Below is a chart which lists pitchers so far analyzed in clutch pitching order (career to date):

	Career	*Best Year*
Ryan	27.4%	22.4%
Valenzuela	27.7	23.8
Carlton	28.0	22.2
Seaver	28.3	20.7
Welch	28.6	25.5
Blyleven	29.3	25.0
Candelaria	29.7	24.1
Sutton	**31.3**	**25.4**

Tommy John
Born 1943
Height 6′3″; weight 203
Throws left, bats right
HOF — Possible

									Per Game		
Year	Age	CG	H	BB	SO	W	L	%	ERA	SO	BR
1966	23	24.8	195	57	138	14	11	.560	2.62	5.6	10.2
1969	26	25.8	230	90	128	9	11	.450	3.26	5.0	12.4
1970	27	29.9	253	101	138	12	17	.414	3.28	4.6	11.8
1971	28	25.4	244	58	131	13	16	.448	3.62	5.1	11.9
1973	30	24.2	202	50	116	16	7	.696	3.10	4.8	10.4
1976	33	23.0	207	61	91	10	10	.500	3.09	4.0	11.7
1977	34	24.4	225	50	123	20	7	.741	2.78	5.0	11.3
1978	35	23.7	230	53	124	17	10	.630	3.30	5.2	12.0
1979	36	30.7	268	65	111	21	9	.700	2.97	3.6	10.9
1980	37	29.4	270	56	78	22	9	.710	3.43	2.6	11.1
1982	39	24.7	239	39	69	14	12	.538	3.69	2.8	11.3
1983	40	26.1	287	49	65	11	13	.458	4.33	2.5	12.9
Total		312.1	2850	729	1312	179	132	.576	3.29	4.2	11.5
Other*		163.4	1413	415	771	85	78	.521	3.11	4.7	11.2
Career		475.6	4263	1144	2083	264	210	.557	3.23	4.4	11.4

*Less than 22 CG: 1963, 1964, 1965, 1967, 1968, 1972, 1974, 1975, 1981, 1984, 1985, 1986

Standard Deviation		2.5	27	17	26	4	3				
Avg.		26.0	238	61	109	15	11	.576	3.29	4.2	11.5

Normal Performance Range

High		28.5	265	78	135	19	14	.577	3.50	4.7	12.0
Low		23.6	210	44	84	11	8	.574	3.04	3.6	10.8

Best Year (over 27 CG): 1979

Super Years (ERA 2.88 −): 1966, 1977

Avg.		24.6	210	54	131	17	9	.654	2.70	5.3	10.7

	CG	H	BB	SO	W	L	%	Per Game ERA	SO	BR
Good Year (ERA 2.89–3.19): 1973, 1976, 1979										
Avg.	26.0	226	59	106	16	9	.644	3.04	4.1	11.0
Fair Years (ERA 3.20–3.50): 1969, 1970, 1978, 1980										
Avg.	27.2	246	75	117	15	12	.561	3.32	4.3	11.8
Other Years (ERA 3.51 +): 1971, 1982, 1983										
Avg.	25.4	257	49	88	13	14	.481	3.88	3.5	12.0
Average Yearly Performance by Age										
25 and under	24.8	195	57	138	14	11	.560	2.62	5.6	10.2
26–30	26.3	232	75	128	13	13	.495	3.31	4.9	11.7
31–35	23.7	221	55	113	16	9	.635	3.05	4.8	11.6
36 +	27.7	266	52	81	17	11	.613	3.57	2.9	11.5

Forty-three years old in 1986, Tommy should be all through, but it looks as though he'll throw a few more for the Yankees in 1987. A legitimate pretender, he should be in the HOF in a decade. When elected, he'll fit between Lemon and Feller in the ERA classifications, as follows:

	CG	ERA	BR	SO	W	L	%	NW
Ford	352.3	2.74	10.93	5.55	236	106	.690	130
Spahn	582.9	3.08	10.75	4.43	363	245	.597	118
Lemon	316.6	3.23	12.04	4.03	207	128	.618	79
John	**475.6**	**3.23**	**11.37**	**4.38**	**264**	**210**	**.557**	**54**
Feller	425.3	3.25	11.84	6.07	266	162	.621	10
Hunter	383.1	3.26	10.21	5.25	224	166	.574	58
Ruffing	482.4	3.80	12.09	4.12	273	225	.548	48

Of the above players, only Spahn and Ruffing pitched more. Tommy has earned his HOF slot.

Tom was 18 when he entered organized ball in 1961. In 1963, he was brought up by Cleveland and pitched a little for that club before being traded, in 1965, to the Chicago White Sox. He had six good seasons with Chicago who traded him for Richie Allen before the 1972 season began. Then 29, Tom gave LA two plus good seasons, quit to have surgery performed on an arm that had suddenly gone bad, and came back to have three more good years with the team before joining the Yankees, in 1979, as a free agent. John played more than three years for the Bombers, ran the string out with the California Angels, and surprisingly returned to the pitching-starved Yankees in 1986 for a cup of coffee. Tom has had a 23-year major league career, and pitched 22 + complete games in 12 of them.

According to his 22 + complete game profile, Tommy John

averages out as a Class 3 pitcher—two superstar years, three Class 2 years, four Class 3 years, two Class 4 years, and one bummer. Essentially a control pitcher with the ability to punch a hitter out in tight situations, John is a lot like Carl Hubbell in style. A comparison of the careers of the two stylish southpaws follows:

22 + Complete Game Seasons

	Yrs	CG	H	BB	BR	ERA	SO	W	L	%
Tom	12	26.0	9.15	2.35	11.50	3.29	4.19	15	11	.576
Carl	10	30.5	8.56	1.77	10.33	2.85	4.30	19	11	.641

John, of course, was not as good as King Carl, but his approach to the job was the same. Neither relied upon the big strikeout pitch; both relied upon control and finesse—Carl was a control master. When Tommy John is elected, he will be one of the top six control pitchers in the HOF.

Tommy was in his prime at 23–36 years of age. During that 14-year period, he had nine 22 + complete game years averaging about 26 complete games a season, and posting a Class 2 ERA of 3.11. When he was on his game, John was one of the most proficient craftsmen to ever practice the art of pitching—the Willie Pep of the pitching mound.

Vida Blue
Born 1949
Height 6'0"; weight 200
Throws left, bats both
HOF—Doubtful

									Per Game		
Year	Age	CG	H	BB	SO	W	L	%	ERA	SO	BR
1971	22	34.7	209	88	301	24	8	.750	1.82	8.7	8.6
1973	24	29.3	214	105	158	20	9	.690	3.27	5.4	10.9
1974	25	31.3	246	98	174	17	15	.531	3.26	5.6	11.0
1975	26	30.9	243	99	189	22	11	.667	3.01	6.1	11.1
1976	27	33.1	268	63	166	18	13	.581	2.36	5.0	10.0
1977	28	31.1	284	86	157	14	19	.424	3.83	5.0	11.9
1978	29	28.7	233	70	171	18	10	.643	2.79	6.0	10.6
1979	30	26.3	246	111	138	14	14	.500	5.01	5.2	13.6
1980	31	24.9	202	61	129	14	10	.583	2.97	5.2	10.6
Total		270.3	2145	781	1583	161	109	.596	3.10	5.9	10.8
Other*		101.2	794	404	592	48	52	.480	3.71	5.8	11.8
Career		371.6	2939	1185	2175	209	161	.565	3.26	5.9	11.1

*Less than 22 CG: 1970, 1972, 1981, 1982, 1983, 1984, 1985, 1986

Standard Deviation		2.9	26	17	47	3	3				
Avg.		30.0	238	87	176	18	12	.596	3.10	5.9	10.8

								Per Game		
	CG	H	BB	SO	W	L	%	ERA	SO	BR
Normal Performance Range										
High	33.0	264	104	223	21	15	.581	3.46	6.8	11.2
Low	27.1	213	69	128	14	9	.621	2.66	4.7	10.4
Best Year (over 27 CG): 1971										
Super Years (ERA 2.88 –): 1971, 1976, 1978										
Avg.	32.1	237	74	213	20	10	.659	2.29	6.6	9.7
Good Years (ERA 2.89–3.19): 1975, 1980										
Avg.	27.9	223	80	159	18	11	.632	2.99	5.7	10.8
Fair Years (ERA 3.20–3.50): 1973, 1974										
Avg.	30.3	230	102	166	19	12	.607	3.26	5.5	10.9
Other Years (ERA 3.51 +): 1977, 1979										
Avg.	28.7	265	99	148	14	17	.459	4.37	5.1	12.7
Average Yearly Performance by Age										
25 and under	31.8	223	97	211	20	11	.656	2.74	6.6	10.1
26–30	30.0	255	86	164	17	13	.562	3.34	5.5	11.3
31–35	24.9	202	61	129	14	10	.583	2.97	5.2	10.6

Blue has 371.6 complete games behind him. He weighs in as a Class 3 pitcher. In terms of durability and class, he must be considered as a pretender. To get serious attention, he must compare favorably with other short-career players.

	CG	ERA	BR	SO	W	L	%	NW
Ford	352.3	2.74	10.93	5.55	236	106	.690	130
Koufax	258.3	2.76	9.95	9.27	165	87	.655	78
Dean	218.4	3.04	10.89	5.29	150	83	.644	67
Lemon	316.6	3.23	12.04	4.03	207	128	.618	79
Hunter	383.1	3.26	10.21	5.25	224	166	.574	58
Gomez	278.1	3.34	12.17	5.28	189	102	.649	87
Blue	**371.6**	**3.26**	**11.10**	**5.85**	**209**	**161**	**.565**	**.48**

The above comparison supports the position that Blue is a legitimate pretender—not to be elected as soon as a Seaver, but to be seriously considered within a decade or so.

The Blue career was mishandled. Some of this falls at his own feet—his personal history will not add to the desire of committees to single him out. But in addition to personal problems, Blue was worked like a horse from the beginning. Awesome young talent leaked from his fingers in the sweat of overwork, subtracting from both the quality and durability of his career.

Blue entered professional baseball in 1968, at the age of 19. In

1970, Oakland took a look at him. In 1971, he pitched 312 innings for that team, and won 24 games with an ERA of 1.82 (in his long career, Tom Seaver never worked 300 + innings in a season). This was Vida's best year. Never again did he approach that level of excellence.

In a 17-year career, Blue has had nine 22 + game seasons — three superstar years, two Class 2s, two Class 3s, and two bummers. He averages out as a high level Class 3 pitcher.

If elected to the HOF, Vida would fit between Hunter and Gomez, as follows:

	CG	ERA	BR	SO	W	L	%	NW
Ford	352.3	2.74	10.93	5.55	236	106	.690	130
Feller	425.3	3.25	11.84	6.07	266	162	.621	104
Hunter	383.1	3.26	10.21	5.25	224	166	.574	58
Blue	**371.6**	**3.26**	**11.10**	**5.85**	**209**	**161**	**.565**	**48**
Gomez	278.1	3.34	12.17	5.28	189	102	.649	87
Roberts	521.0	3.40	10.53	4.52	286	245	.539	41

A man who could have been better, Blue did well enough to be considered as a long shot contender for HOF honors.

Phil Niekro
Born 1939
Height 6'2"; weight 195
Throws right, bats right
HOF — Probable

									Per Game		
Year	Age	CG	H	BB	SO	W	L	%	ERA	SO	BR
1967	28	23.0	164	55	129	11	9	.550	1.87	5.6	9.5
1968	29	28.6	228	45	140	14	12	.538	2.59	4.9	9.6
1969	30	31.6	235	57	193	23	13	.639	2.57	6.1	9.3
1970	31	25.6	222	68	168	12	18	.400	4.27	6.6	11.3
1971	32	29.9	248	70	173	15	14	.517	2.98	5.8	10.6
1972	33	31.3	254	53	164	16	12	.571	3.06	5.2	9.8
1973	34	27.2	214	89	131	13	10	.565	3.31	4.8	11.1
1974	35	33.6	249	88	195	20	13	.606	2.38	5.8	10.0
1975	36	30.7	285	72	144	15	15	.500	3.20	4.7	11.6
1976	37	30.1	249	101	173	17	11	.607	3.29	5.7	11.6
1977	38	36.7	315	164	262	16	20	.444	4.04	7.1	13.1
1978	39	37.1	295	102	248	19	18	.514	2.88	6.7	10.7
1979	40	38.0	311	113	208	21	20	.512	3.39	5.5	11.2
1980	41	30.6	256	85	176	15	18	.455	3.63	5.8	11.3
1982	43	26.0	225	73	144	17	4	.810	3.62	5.5	11.5
1983	44	22.4	212	105	128	11	10	.524	3.97	5.7	14.1
1984	45	24.0	219	76	136	16	8	.667	3.08	5.7	12.3
1985	46	24.4	203	120	149	16	12	.571	4.09	6.1	13.2
1986	47	23.3	241	95	81	11	11	.500	4.33	3.5	14.4

								Per Game		
	CG	H	BB	SO	W	L	%	ERA	SO	BR
Total	554.0	4625	1631	3142	298	248	.546	3.27	5.7	11.3
Other*	31.0	256	112	136	13	13	.500	3.32	4.4	11.9
Career	585.0	4881	1743	3278	311	261	.544	3.27	5.6	11.3

*Less than 22 CG: 1964, 1965, 1966, 1981

| *Standard Deviation* | 4.7 | 37 | 28 | 42 | 3 | 4 | | | | |
| Avg. | 29.2 | 243 | 86 | 165 | 16 | 13 | .546 | 3.27 | 5.7 | 11.3 |

Normal Performance Range

High	33.9	280	113	207	19	17	.524	3.45	6.1	11.6
Low	24.4	206	58	123	12	9	.582	3.03	5.1	10.8

Best Year (over 27 CG): 1974

Super Years (ERA 2.88 –): 1967, 1968, 1969, 1974, 1978

Avg.	30.8	234	69	181	17	13	.572	2.50	5.9	9.9

Good Years (ERA 2.89–3.19): 1971, 1972, 1984

Avg.	28.4	240	66	158	16	11	.580	3.04	5.6	10.8

Fair Years (ERA 3.20–3.50): 1973, 1975, 1976, 1979

Avg.	31.5	265	94	164	17	14	.541	3.30	5.2	11.4

Other Years (ERA 3.51 +): 1970, 1977, 1980, 1982, 1983, 1985, 1986

Avg.	27.0	239	101	158	14	13	.519	3.98	5.9	12.6

Average Yearly Performance by Age

25 and under	0.0									
26–30	27.7	209	52	154	16	11	.585	2.38	5.6	9.4
31–35	29.5	237	74	166	15	13	.531	3.14	5.6	10.5
36 +	29.4	256	101	168	16	13	.542	3.56	5.7	12.1

Because he is as old as Moses and a knuckleball hurler, it is easy to forget that Niekro has been one of the most durably effective pitchers of his era. Phil is a pretender with a strong chance to get HOF recognition.

Phil was 20 years old when, in 1959, he entered professional baseball. Milwaukee was the first team to look at him in 1964, but he didn't land a steady major league job until 1967 when Atlanta brought him up to stay. He was 28 years old. In five years he was all done. Right? Wrong!

Niekro, despite the late beginning, has 23 major league seasons and 585 + complete games pitched behind him. In 19 of those years, he pitched 22 + complete games, averaging 29.2 complete games per year. Over the years, he has exhibited the whole gamut of skills from strikeout power to control. His best power year was 1977 when, at 38, he had 262 strikeouts (7.14 per game). But his most effective pitching performance occurred in 1974 when, at 35, he posted a 2.38 ERA assisted by 195 strikeouts.

According to his 22 + game profile, Phil averages out as a high level Class 3 pitcher. He had four superstar years, four Class 2 years, four Class 3 years, two Class 4 seasons, and five bummers. Forty-seven years old in 1986, Niekro is struggling. The end is near.

When elected to the HOF, Phil will fit between Hunter and Gomez in the HOF classification structure, as follows:

	CG	ERA	BR	SO	W	L	%	NW
Ford	352.3	2.74	10.93	5.55	236	106	.690	130
Feller	425.3	3.25	11.84	6.07	266	162	.621	104
Hunter	383.1	3.26	10.21	5.25	224	166	.574	58
Niekro, P.	**585.0**	**3.27**	**11.32**	**5.60**	**311**	**261**	**.544**	**50**
Gomez	278.1	3.34	12.17	5.28	189	102	.649	87
Roberts	521.0	3.40	10.53	4.52	286	245	.539	41
Ruffing	482.4	3.80	12.09	4.12	273	225	.548	48

Despite reliance on the crazy knuckleball, Phil has better control than several HOF hurlers, shows strongly in durability comparisons, has allowed fewer baserunners than eight HOF pitchers, and falls neatly into the high level Class 3 ERA classification structure.

Niekro wasn't active in the major leagues during his early twenties. In his late twenties, he was a superstar—comparable to the best in the game. In his early thirties, Phil was a Class 2 pitcher. Since, he averages out as a Class 3 hurler—at 45 years of age, Niekro had a Class 2 season. Amazing!

Phil was in his prime from 28 to 39 years of age. During that 12-year period, he functioned as a solid Class 2 pitcher. When elected to the HOF, he will stand next to Pete Rose and Warren Spahn as one of the monuments to athletic durability.

Joe Niekro
Born 1944
Height 6'1"; weight 190
Throws right, bats right
HOF—Possible

										Per Game	
Year	Age	CG	H	BB	SO	W	L	%	ERA	SO	BR
1969	25	24.6	237	51	62	8	8	.500	3.71	2.5	11.7
1970	26	23.7	221	72	101	12	13	.480	4.06	4.3	12.4
1978	34	22.6	190	73	97	14	14	.500	3.86	4.3	11.7
1979	35	29.3	221	107	119	21	11	.656	3.00	4.1	11.2
1980	36	28.4	268	79	127	20	12	.625	3.55	4.5	12.2

| | | | | | | | | | Per Game | | |
Year	Age	CG	H	BB	SO	W	L	%	ERA	SO	BR
1982	38	30.0	224	64	130	17	12	.586	2.47	4.3	9.6
1983	39	29.3	238	101	152	15	14	.517	3.48	5.2	11.6
1984	40	27.6	223	89	127	16	12	.571	3.05	4.6	11.3
1985	41	25.0	211	107	121	11	13	.458	3.84	4.8	12.7
Total		240.4	2033	743	1036	134	109	.551	3.41	4.3	11.5
Other*		140.2	1262	446	620	79	81	.494	3.65	4.4	12.2
Career		380.7	3295	1189	1656	213	190	.529	3.50	4.4	11.8

*Less than 22 CG: 1967, 1968, 1971, 1972, 1973, 1974, 1975, 1976, 1977, 1981, 1986

Standard Deviation		2.6	20	19	24	4	2				
Avg.		26.7	226	83	115	15	12	.551	3.41	4.3	11.5

Normal Performance Range

High		29.3	246	101	139	19	14	.577	3.39	4.7	11.8
Low		24.1	206	64	91	11	10	.513	3.43	3.8	11.2

Best Year (over 27 CG): 1982

Super Years (ERA 2.88 –): 1982

Good Years (ERA 2.89–3.19): 1979, 1984

Avg.		28.4	222	98	123	19	12	.617	3.02	4.3	11.3

Fair Years (ERA 3.20–3.50): 1983

Other Years (ERA 3.51 +): 1969, 1970, 1978, 1980, 1985

Avg.		24.8	225	76	102	13	12	.520	3.79	4.1	12.1

Average Yearly Performance by Age

25 and under		24.6	237	51	62	8	8	.500	3.71	2.5	11.7
26–30		23.7	221	72	101	12	13	.480	4.06	4.3	12.4
31–35		25.9	206	90	108	18	13	.583	3.37	4.2	11.4
36 +		28.1	233	88	131	16	13	.556	3.26	4.7	11.4

Joe, baby brother of Phil, was 42 years old in 1986. He carried a full pitching load in 1985, but went down with injuries during the 1986 season. Like Phil, Joe relies on the knuckleball to get the job done.

Each HOF appointment sets or confirms HOF qualification standards. Joe must be considered as a pretender because his record is competitive with some incumbents. Given his genes, there's no reason to doubt he'll be effectively wobbling his funny ball up to the plate for another season or more. Joe shouldn't be rushed into the HOF, but equity says he should eventually get there.

Joe has had a 20-year major league career. In nine seasons he pitched 22 + complete games, averaging about 27 complete games a year. Until he was 33 years old, Joe was a conventional pitcher who, in ten years, compiled a 68–75 record. From 1977 on, Joe has been a knuckler like brother Phil and, during this ten-year period, compiled a record of 145–115. Obviously, Joe wasn't going anyplace until brother Phil taught him the mysteries of flutter ball; with it, he has a shot at immortality.

According to his 22 + complete game profile, Joe averages out as a Class 3 pitcher. If elected to the HOF, he'd fit between Roberts and Wynn in the ERA classification structure, as follows:

	CG	ERA	BR	SO	W	L	%	NW
Ford	352.3	2.74	10.93	5.55	236	106	.690	130
Gomez	278.1	3.34	12.17	5.28	189	102	.649	87
Roberts	521.0	3.40	10.53	4.52	286	245	.539	41
Niekro, J.	**380.7**	**3.50**	**11.78**	**4.35**	**213**	**190**	**.529**	**23**
Wynn	507.3	3.54	11.96	4.60	300	244	.551	56
Hoyt	418.0	3.59	12.06	2.89	237	182	.566	55
Ruffing	482.4	3.80	12.09	4.12	273	225	.548	48

With the obvious exception of Ford, the selection of some of the above pitchers to the HOF did not represent the finest hour of selection committees. Had they not been a part of the Ruth/Gehrig/DiMaggio Yankee Bombers, Gomez, Hoyt, or Ruffing might not be in the HOF. Robin Roberts was a boy wonder who faded into a journeyman with masterful control—a marginal choice. Nevertheless, these men made it, and their presence gives Joe and others a shot. If he can last as long as brother Phil, it could be a good shot.

Jerry Reuss

Born 1949
Height 6'5"; weight 217
Throws left, bats left
HOF—Possible

									Per Game		
Year	Age	CG	H	BB	SO	W	L	%	ERA	SO	BR
1971	22	23.4	228	109	131	14	14	.500	4.78	5.6	14.4
1973	24	31.0	271	117	177	16	13	.552	3.74	5.7	12.5
1974	25	28.9	259	101	105	16	11	.593	3.50	3.6	12.5
1975	26	26.3	224	78	131	18	11	.621	2.54	5.0	11.5
1976	27	23.2	209	51	108	14	9	.609	3.53	4.7	11.2
1977	28	23.1	225	71	116	10	13	.435	4.11	5.0	12.8
1980	31	25.4	193	40	111	18	6	.750	2.52	4.4	9.2
1982	33	28.3	232	50	138	18	11	.621	3.11	4.9	10.0
1983	34	24.8	233	50	143	12	11	.522	2.95	5.8	11.4
1985	36	23.7	210	58	84	14	10	.583	2.92	3.5	11.3
Total		258.2	2284	725	1244	150	109	.579	3.36	4.8	11.7
Other*		99.4	922	293	500	44	54	.449	3.86	5.0	12.2
Career		357.7	3206	1018	1744	194	163	.543	3.50	4.9	11.8

*Less than 22 CG: 1969, 1970, 1972, 1978, 1979, 1981, 1984, 1986

| | | | | | | | | | *Per Game* | |
	CG	H	BB	SO	W	L	%	ERA	SO	BR
Standard Deviation	2.6	22	26	24	3	2				
Avg.	25.8	228	73	124	15	11	.579	3.36	4.8	11.7
Normal Performance Range										
High	28.4	250	99	149	18	13	.574	3.68	5.2	12.3
Low	23.2	207	46	100	12	9	.587	2.97	4.3	10.9

Best Year (over 27 CG): 1982

Super Years (ERA 2.88 –): 1975, 1980

	CG	H	BB	SO	W	L	%	ERA	SO	BR
Avg.	25.9	209	59	121	18	9	.679	2.53	4.7	10.3

Good Years (ERA 2.89–3.19): 1982, 1983, 1985

	CG	H	BB	SO	W	L	%	ERA	SO	BR
Avg.	25.6	225	53	122	15	11	.579	3.00	4.8	10.8

Fair Years (ERA 3.20–3.50): 1974

Other Years (ERA 3.51 +): 1971, 1973, 1976, 1977

	CG	H	BB	SO	W	L	%	ERA	SO	BR
Avg.	25.2	233	87	133	14	12	.524	4.02	5.3	12.7

Average Yearly Performance by Age

	CG	H	BB	SO	W	L	%	ERA	SO	BR
25 and under	27.8	253	109	138	15	13	.548	3.95	5.0	13.0
26–30	24.2	219	67	118	14	11	.560	3.36	4.9	11.8
31–35	26.2	219	47	131	16	9	.632	2.86	5.0	10.2
36 +	23.7	210	58	84	14	10	.583	2.92	3.5	11.3

Jerry was 37 years old in 1986 with about 358 complete games behind him. In 1984 he didn't carry a full pitching load; he snapped back in 1985 with a quality performance; in 1986, he was again disabled. He may be all done. By virtue of past HOF appointments, and his own competitive record, Reuss must be regarded as a pretender.

In an 18-year career, Jerry had ten 22 + complete game years, averaging about 26 complete games a season — he averages out as a Class 3 pitcher. He had two superstar years, three Class 2 seasons, one Class 3 year, two Class 4 seasons, and two bummers. If elected to the HOF, he would fit between Roberts and Wynn, as follows:

	CG	ERA	BR	SO	W	L	%	NW
Ford	352.3	2.74	10.93	5.55	236	106	.690	130
Gomez	278.1	3.34	12.17	5.28	189	102	.649	87
Roberts	521.0	3.40	10.53	4.52	286	245	.539	41
Reuss	**357.7**	**3.50**	**11.81**	**4.88**	**194**	**163**	**.543**	**31**
Wynn	507.3	3.54	11.96	4.60	300	244	.551	56
Hoyt	418.0	3.59	12.06	2.89	237	182	.566	55
Ruffing	482.4	3.80	12.09	4.12	273	225	.548	48

Jerry is competing with some long-winded athletes of comparable skill. If he can hang on for a few more seasons he could make it.

Guidry, Tudor

These pitchers have ERAs in the 3.20–3.29 range. Both are Class 3 pitchers who have not yet met the de facto minimum durability standard of the HOF (310.8 complete games—page 152).

Ron Guidry turned 36 years old in 1986. That year, he was out of action for about a month and had—for him—a poor year. In six of the last seven years, his ERA has been higher than his current career average. Guidry has shown HOF talent. His problem is durability. Yankee management didn't see fit to get Ron going until he was 27 years old. This didn't leave him enough time to build a competitive durability record, something which the HOF does (and should) demand. Although he still has an outside chance, it's not likely that Ron will make up the quality innings required in the time left to him.

John Tudor of the Cardinals was in 1986, 32 years old. In five seasons with Boston he was no whizz. A single year with the Pirates was fairly impressive. And for the last two seasons with the Cardinals, he's been one of the best in the game. A consequence of late-blooming skill is a poor durability record. Although he had plenty of opportunity, Tudor didn't really go to work until he was 29 years old. It's highly unlikely that he'll be around long enough to boost his 149 + complete games to a competitive figure. John is not a pretender.

Stieb, Ken Forsch, Soto

The above pitchers have ERAs in the 3.30–3.39 range. All are Class 3 pitchers with inadequate durability characteristics.

For five years, Dave Stieb of Toronto was one of the finest pitchers in baseball—then came 1986, arm trouble, and an ERA of 4.74. Then 29 years old, his 206 + complete games is not much of a durability record for a sore-armed hurler. Dave still has time to get going again, but as of now he looks like another skilled pitcher who won't last the course.

In 1986, Ken Forsch of the Angels was 40 years old, and hadn't pitched much since 1983. To reach his age without the necessary durability stats erases all HOF hopes. During his 16-year career Ken has been a useful journeyman, but he is not a pretender.

Mario Soto, a right-hander for Cincinnati, was 30 years old with 179 complete games to his credit in 1986 — about half of what he needs to get HOF attention. That year, he was relatively inactive with arm trouble. The two previous seasons suggested slippage. In a ten-year career, Mario has pulled a full load only four times. The HOF is for the strong and the talented. Soto has shown only the talent. He is no pretender.

Tanana, Sanderson, Reuschel, Gullickson, Knepper, Rozema, Rhoden, Andujar

The above pitchers have ERAs in the 3.40–3.49 range. All are Class 3 pitchers with inadequate durability characteristics.

Frank Tanana has a career going that brings back memories of Robin Roberts — short, brilliant beginnings; slow years of mediocrity.

	22 + *Game Years*	
	Tanana	Roberts
2.50 –	1	0
2.51–2.75	2	2
2.76–3.00	0	2
3.01–3.25	2	3
3.26–3.50	0	2
3.51–3.75	1	1
3.76–4.00	0	0
4.01 +	2	4
Total	8	14
Other years	6	6
Total years	14	20
ERA	3.40	3.40

Up to 1986, Frank had five full seasons during which he achieved an ERA equal to or better than his career ERA — for the other nine seasons he has been either a less effective pitcher, or a part-time one. In Robin's case, he had seven years in which he equalled or bettered his career ERA — in the other 13, he was either less active or less effective. Roberts was a marginal choice to the HOF. For Tanana to be as lucky, he must retain quality and match the durability record of Roberts. He won't do it.

Scott Sanderson, a right-hander with the Cubs, was 30 years old with 146 complete games charged to his account in '86. In his nine-year career, he has carried a full pitching load only twice, the last time in 1982. Scott isn't strong enough to make the HOF.

Rick Reuschel, 37 years old in 1986, has been with Pittsburgh since 1984. In 1986, he had a losing season while posting an ERA of 3.96. His last full season prior to 1986 was in 1980. If he ever had a chance, injuries ruined him in his early thirties. It's too late to catch up now. Rick is not a pretender.

Bill Gullickson, 27 years old in 1986, has 159 complete games to his credit. In 1986, with Cincinnati, he posted an ERA of 3.38. If the move from Montreal to Cincinnati does for him what a similar move did for John Tudor, Gullickson could possibly build a HOF record. He's young enough to keep his chances alive, but it's too early to rate him as a pretender.

Bob Knepper, Houston's southpaw, was 33 in 1986. He pitched well that year, and in four of his past six seasons, he has bettered his career ERA. To get competitive on the durability front, Bob needs about five more full seasons at career ERA rates. He may do it, but it's highly doubtful — the chances are too slim to rate him a pretender.

Dave Rozema, a Texas right-hander, is down as often as he's up. Thirty years old in 1986, Dave hasn't carried a full load since 1978. He's no pretender.

Rick Rhoden, 33 years old in 1986, is with Pittsburgh. He has 13 seasons and about 235 complete games behind him. He had six 22 + complete game years — two Class 1, one Class 2, one Class 4, and two Class 5. On durability grounds, Rhoden's record is in trouble. But he will be playing for the Yankees in 1987, and that may extend his effective career considerably. The odds are against Rick, he's not a pretender; but the gods have given him a second chance to build some competitive numbers.

Joaquin Andujar, 34 years old in 1986, was traded to Oakland at the end of the 1985 season by St. Louis — and promptly got hurt. In the majors for ten seasons, Joaquin has only carried a full load in four — one Class 1, two Class 3, one Class 5. Andujar has demonstrated HOF talent, but stability and durability are big question marks, especially for a man his age. He isn't a pretender.

With the appraisal of Andujar, the analysis of Class 3 pitchers is complete. Statistically, all have shown better than average ability when measured against HOF standards, but deeper analysis has discovered that most are fragile, and will not complete the HOF durability course. In the forthcoming analysis of Class 4 pitchers, it will be seen again that the ability to repeat quality performance year after year is the barrier that most active pitchers can't hurdle.

Witt, Hough, Montefusco, Darwin, Morris, Denny, Petry

The above pitchers have ERAs in the 3.51–3.59 range. All are Class 4 pitchers with deficient durability characteristics.

Mike Witt, 26 years old in '86, is a promising right-hander with California. That year he had a superstar season. Can he do it again? Can he put another decade of quality pitching together? He's young enough to keep his HOF hopes alive, but too inexperienced to rate the pretender designation.

Charlie Hough turned 38 years old in 1986 while with Texas. For the previous five seasons, the knuckleballer has operated as a full-time starter with one Class 2, one Class 3, two Class 4, and one Class 5 seasons. Charlie has about 241 complete games behind him — not much for his age. Even if he lasts as long as Phil Niekro, it is doubtful Charlie will pitch enough to get HOF attention. He is not a pretender.

John Montefusco, 36 years old in 1986, has been used mostly as a fireman for the last half dozen years. His injury-spotted career is not of HOF caliber.

Danny Darwin, 31 years old in 1986, spent that year with Milwaukee and Houston. In a nine-year career, he has but two 22 + complete game years. This isn't HOF performance. Danny is no pretender.

Jack Morris, 31 years old in 1986, is with Detroit. For the previous eight years, he carried a full load — Class 1 — 0; Class 2 — 1; Class 3 — 4; Class 5 — 3. Much of the credit for his relatively impressive win/loss ratio is owed to the fine offensive lineup that supports him. Jack has about 236 complete games to his credit — not enough. Can he hold quality and build sufficient durability? — possible, but doubtful. Jack has not yet earned pretender status.

John Denny, at 34, moved to Cincinnati from Philadelphia in 1986 and had a poor year with the Reds. John's light on durability — 239 complete games. In a career of 13 seasons, he had five 22 + complete game years — two Class 1s, one Class 2, and two Class 5s. John's brittle. He won't last the course — he's not a pretender.

Dan Petry, 28 years old in 1986 is with Detroit. He has about 167 complete games to his credit. That year, his arm went bad. All Class 4 HOF pitchers have one thing in common: a durability problem. At best, Petry seems destined to post a Class 4 career ERA but it's unlikely that his durability will be competitive. Still young enough to improve, Dan has a chance. But he hasn't yet earned pretender status.

Forsch, Vuckovitch, Eckersley, Leonard

The above pitchers have ERAs in the 3.60–3.69 range. All are Class 4 pitchers with weak durability stats.

Bob Forsch (brother of Ken), was 36 years old in 1986 while with St. Louis. That year he carried a full pitching load for the first time since 1982. It was a good Class 3 performance. Bob is another of the many journeyman pitchers in this group but, with only 263 complete games behind him at his age, he isn't a pretender.

Pete Vuckovitch was with Milwaukee in 1986, when he turned 34. Due to a bad arm, Pete has pitched little since 1982. He's probably through and is no pretender.

Dennis Eckersley, 32 years old in 1986, is with the Cubs. In 1985 he had arm trouble; in 1986 he pitched poorly. He has about 277 complete games behind him. Dennis is one of those who probably should have regularly performed at high HOF levels, but didn't. It's highly doubtful that Eckersley has the dedication or endurance to complete the HOF course. He is not a pretender.

Dennis Leonard played for Kansas City in 1986 at 35 years of age. Because of injury, he hasn't carried a full pitching load since 1981. He took another comeback shot in 1986, but didn't look so hot (ERA 4.44). The book is probably closed on Leonard. He has about 243 complete games behind him. Neither the quality nor quantity of his performance will draw HOF attention. He is not a pretender.

Scott, Alexander, Ruhle, Honeycutt, Rawley

The above pitchers also have ERAs in the 3.60–3.69 range. All are Class 4 pitchers with weak durability stats.

Mike Scott, 31 years old in 1986, waited too long to find the magic. In 1986, the Houston right-hander had an Alice-in-Wonderland year (ERA 2.22, 306 whiffs). He was probably the best pitcher in the game for that season. But a season doesn't make a HOF career. Mike won't chalk up enough innings to get HOF attention.

Doyle Alexander, 36 years old in 1986 moved back to the National League with Atlanta that season. He gave that club a Class 5 performance. Doyle has 301 complete games pitched behind him and has a chance to accumulate minimum durability stats before he quits. But that's not enough for high ERA pitchers—long durability is what he needs, and won't have. The much traveled Alexander is not a pretender.

Vern Ruhle, 35 years old in '86, hasn't pitched enough to get HOF attention. Operating mostly out of the bullpen since the mid–1970s, Vern is not a pretender.

Rick Honeycutt, 32 years old in 1986, has been with Los Angeles for the previous four seasons. The southpaw doesn't pitch enough to get HOF attention. Like so many others, he has not demonstrated the strength demanded of HOF players.

Shane Rawley was a 31-year-old left-hander for the Phillies in 1986 and gave them good work until his arm went bad. In nine seasons, Shane has worked a full load only twice. He will not build a competitive durability record and may well slide into Class 5 before he retires.

A scanning of Class 5 pitchers doesn't reveal anything that should cause the rule to eliminate such men from further consideration to be waived. Some famous names are in this group—Flanagan, McGregor; some big power pitchers—Krukow, Robinson, Bannister. But none has pitched long enough or well enough to demand close analysis.

More than any other position, it is worth noting that active pitchers fall victim to durability requirements. Many meet HOF ERA standards for a few seasons, but few have the strength, determination, and savvy to repeat quality work over the period required to compete with the greats of history.

Active Pitchers—The Pretenders

In theory, players in Class 4 and above are pretenders. In practice, analysis reveals that all men with qualifying ERAs are not HOF material. In theory and in practice, Class 5 pitchers are rejected as pretenders. They have failed to demonstrate HOF skill; it would be unwise to reduce further the standards of the HOF by selecting such men.

Some Class 5 pitchers are famous. Some are highly paid. Some have winning records. Some are strikeout artists. Why aren't they pretenders?

Fame is in the hands of the mythmakers. Average players are sometimes blown up by the media while other, better players are ignored. Players from New York, and other media centers, get more attention than those from less glamorous cities. Fame is tinsel. Talent is substance. Pretenders, famous or not, are players of substance.

Salary level should be an indicator of talent levels, but it isn't. Why do some clubs pay as much as they do for a pitcher who can't win unless his team gets over four runs? The answer to that question is easy. Pitchers with a high ERA are overpaid for the same reason that hitters with a BA of .240 who hit 25–30 home runs a season are overpaid. Why are such hitters overpaid? Because the world has gone mad, that is why. Mad! Mad! Mad! Madness doesn't govern the identification of pretenders.

A winning record is the marriage between luck and the efforts of all team members. A journeyman pitcher with a great team will have a winning record—luck will determine how big. Red Ruffing is a good example of this. A great pitcher with a lousy team may have an unimpressive win/loss record. Walter Johnson is a good example of this. Winning is a consequence of team effort that has no imperative relationship to pitching skill. Pretenders are players with superior skills who, in the right setting, would be winners—whether or not in fact they actually were.

Strikeout artists are the home run hitters of the pitching world—the glamour boys. In fact, a strikeout gets a batter out. So does a fielded ground ball, fly ball, pop-up, etc. An out is an out, however a pitcher gets it. Who cares how outs come to be so long as they indeed do come to be? Strikeout power is a tool that every pitcher wants to have in his toolbox. It's an important power to have in the squeaky situations that pitchers face. But it's only one of the tools. By itself, it isn't enough. Pretenders are men with varying levels of strikeout power who also command the other tools necessary to keep baserunners at a minimum, to keep them from scoring.

The active pitching corps is superior to the active fielders. A superstar exists, and more men legitimately compare with the greats of history. As a result of classification and analysis, the pitching pretenders have been identified as follows:

	CG	ERA	Comment
Seaver	531.3	2.86	Probable—superstar
Valenzuela	172.8	2.94	Possible—durability?
Blyleven	443.1	3.08	Probable
Carlton	561.7	3.11	Probable
Ryan	457.2	3.15	Probable
Sutton	555.9	3.20	Probable
John	475.6	3.23	Possible—good chance
Neikro, P.	585.0	3.27	Probable
Blue	371.6	3.26	Possible—doubtful
Niekro, J.	380.7	3.50	Possible
Reuss	357.7	3.50	Possible

It should be noted that all but Valenzuela already meet the de facto minimum HOF durability standard.

Of the 67 candidates, eleven are pretenders. Six will have little trouble moving into the HOF—Seaver, Blyleven, Carlton, Ryan, Sutton, and Phil Niekro. The others have chances ranging from good to doubtful. Most pretenders are older men at, or near, the retirement point. But the younger generation is well represented by Valenzuela, who may well become one of the greats of history before he quits.

Some very talented men do not appear in the above group. Candelaria is as tough on a given day as anyone. Welch can be a handful for any hitter. For a few years, Guidry bowed to nobody. Tudor has been brilliant recently. Stieb is viciously effective when healthy, as is Soto. On and on—the brilliant young Tanana ... the mercurial luster of Andujar. But all lack one thing. Compared to the greats of history, they just dropped in for a cup of coffee—they haven't pitched enough—and don't figure to. Short-term brilliance is not the road to the museum (although a few exceptions have been made)—long-term greatness is the ticket.

Conclusion

The principal objective of this book was to examine the records of a large sample of active players who meet minimum service standards, and to locate those who show HOF talent sufficiently to mark them as probable or possible additions to the HOF after retirement. This has been done.

Identified pretenders are listed below. The chart shows the position, the number of seasons played at each of the four HOF classification levels, the career PAB/ERA, and the best PAB/ERA (at certain activity levels) for each man.

Player	POS	Class				Career PAB/ERA	Best PAB/ERA
		1	2	3	4		
Henderson	of	0	1	5	1	.289	.355
Rice	of	0	2	8	1	.287	.336
Lynn	of	1	2	4	4	.285	.375
Winfield	of	0	1	10	2	.283	.330
Jackson	of	0	4	5	8	.275	.353
Murphy	of	1	0	3	4	.273	.367
Parker	of	0	1	6	3	.271	.325
Schmidt	inf	7	4	2	1	.308	.331
Brett	inf	3	4	3	2	.287	.345
Ripken	inf	0	2	3	0	.270	.312
Cey	inf	0	1	7	4	.252	.289
Whitaker	inf	0	0	4	5	.245	.260

Player	POS	*Class* 1	2	3	4	*Career* PAB/ERA	*Best* PAB/ERA
Yount	inf	1	2	3	2	.244	.337
Madlock	inf	0	1	4	5	.244	.296
Lansford	inf	0	0	3	4	.242	.266
Trammell	inf	0	1	3	4	.241	.291
Nettles	inf	0	1	4	11	.236	.287
Bell	inf	0	2	3	8	.231	.289
Smith	inf	0	0	0	5	.199	.235
Murray	1b	0	2	3	2	.289	.350
Hernandez	1b	0	2	6	1	.286	.344
Perez	1b	0	1	3	6	.260	.334
Cooper	1b	0	0	6	2	.259	.310
Garvey	1b	0	0	3	3	.247	.288
Rose	1b	0	0	3	1	.236	.297
Buckner	1b	0	0	1	3	.226	.279
Fisk	c	1	3	0	4	.261	.340
Carter	c	1	1	6	2	.260	.285
Simmons	c	1	3	6	3	.257	.325
Porter	c	1	1	3	3	.253	.362
Parrish	c	0	0	2	3	.249	.276
Seaver	p	10	3	1	1	2.86	1.76
Valenzuela	p	2	2	0	1	2.94	2.45
Blyleven	p	7	3	0	1	3.08	2.52
Carlton	p	5	4	1	5	3.11	1.98
Ryan	p	3	2	3	3	3.15	2.28
Sutton	p	6	4	2	3	3.20	2.08
John	p	2	3	4	2	3.23	2.97
Blue	p	3	2	2	0	3.26	1.82
P. Niekro	p	5	3	4	2	3.27	2.38
J. Niekro	p	1	2	1	2	3.50	2.47
Reuss	p	2	3	1	2	3.50	3.11

In this survey, records of 220 active players were examined. One hundred forty have production records as good or better than HOF members who played the same position, but only 41 of them emerged as pretenders. Most pretenders join satisfactory durability levels to go with exceptional skills. Some demonstrate durability and special skills which will attract selection committees. Others are still in the midst of the long race to the museum, and have yet to prove they can maintain skill levels over the full course. In classification terms, the 42 pretenders can be summarized as follows:

| | | | | *Class* | | |
	Total	1	2	3	4	5
Outfield	7	0	0	7	0	0
Infield	12	0	2	2	7	1
First Base	7	0	0	2	2	3
Catcher	5	0	0	5	0	0
Pitcher	11	1	4	6	0	0
Totals	42	1	6	22	9	4

The lone superstar is Tom Seaver. He produced 15 HOF seasons — 13 better than average HOF quality. Infielders and pitchers dominate Class 2 (better than average HOF quality). Schmidt is the dominant fielder in the game, with Brett the challenger. Valenzuela continues to fight the test of time. Blyleven, Carlton, Ryan, and Sutton have nothing left to prove. Most players fall into Class 3 and Class 4 — below average HOF grades. Finally, Smith, Garvey, Rose, and Buckner were resurrected from Class 5 because of superior skills other than production.

Which of the above players have displayed the most skill so far in their careers? A fair way of answering this question is to compare the number of Class 1 and Class 2 years (above HOF average). Under this test, the big three at each position are as follows:

Outfield	Jackson (4), Lynn (3), Rice (2).
Infield	Schmidt (11), Brett (7), Yount (3).
First Base	Hernandez (2), Murray (2), Perez (1).
Catcher	Simmons (4), Fisk (4), Carter (2).
Pitcher	Seaver (13), Sutton (10), Blyleven (10).

The dominant athletes of the group are Seaver, Schmidt, Sutton, and Blyleven, the only pretenders with a decade or more of above-average HOF performance under their belts.

Analysis is complete. Pretenders have been identified, HOF election processes evaluated and graded. The purposes of the book have been achieved. Final observations are in order.

Defensive baseball appears to be as good, perhaps better, than ever. The best of the active pitchers would have been recognized as such in any era. Tom Seaver, for example, richly deserves his ultimate place beside the greatest hurlers of history.

But baseball is hurting badly in the hitting department.

Ted Williams maintains that hitting a baseball safely, when it's thrown by a major league pitcher determined to foil the attempt, is the most difficult single athletic task in sports. Certainly, history proves only a handful of players mastered the act as he did.

Always a relatively rare skill, superior hitting today is almost totally absent from the scene. Of the 153 fielders included in this survey, ten have a BA of .300 + . The fielders examined in this book represent the offensive backbone of modern baseball in both leagues. Below is a profile of their contact hitting ability:

	Total	.300 +	.270– .299	.240– .269	.239 –
Outfield	61	5	39	16	1
Infield	55	2	18	32	3
First base	20	3	10	6	1
Catcher	17	0	5	8	4
Total	153	10	72	62	9

These players have all played in 800 + games—five or more seasons. Except for the new kids on the block, they represent the best that baseball has to offer—6 percent can't hit, 41 percent hit poorly, 47 percent are good hitters, and 6 percent are expert.

The offensive talent pool has slipped. The DH rule, which destroys strategic baseball, was an ill-advised attempt by the American League to bolster production—it hasn't been worth the damage it caused. *Homerunitis* isn't the answer either. The PR men of the game can huff and puff about the home run production of Joe Muscles—who probably hits .250—all they want. Alert fans know that overpriced sluggers often contribute more to accelerating ticket prices than to the quality of the game.

It is surprising to learn that, contrary to media hype, there are no superstar fielders today—we haven't had any for some time. Dismissing, out of hand, arguments of those who claim this loss reflects the increased skill requirements of the modern game, one must be concerned about the absence of superior talent, and the accompanying tendency of apologists to hide this by redefining greatness in a manner which overstates the very ordinary (by HOF standards) talents of today. This, of course, is an insult to retired players who developed the sport to high levels of excellence. In fairness to them—and to the many fine players overlooked by the HOF because they did not meet such high standards—qualifying standards must not be lowered further—active talents must be realistically appraised. In this respect, extraordinary admiration of the ordinary seems, recently, to be too characteristic of the media, and of HOF selection committees.

In Seaver, the examination revealed that we not only have a hall-of-famer, but also a superstar, and that in Sutton, Ryan, and Carlton, we have three greats of history. No doubt, some pitching excellence revealed is related to the offensive inferiority also exposed. But this is conjecture — sour grapes. Several active pitchers will be prestigious additions to the HOF within a decade. Given trends in the game, it is projected that a relatively huge number of qualified hurlers will be elected in years to come.

Modern baseball tends to reward flashy performers and ignore generalists who are largely responsible for victories — the long-term life blood of sports organizations. This is an unfortunate trend of long duration which hurts the game. Baseball men and selection committees should give more thought to what constitutes value in player performance. Those who spend so much time counting the gate, collecting TV receipts, and blowing good cash on ridiculous salary offers, would do everybody a favor if they gave equal time to plans and projects designed to rejuvenate the quality of the game. Good baseball will always draw crowds — at a fair price.

America is its form of government, the freedom of its people, its beautiful and varied landscapes, its jazz, swing, and musical comedies — and its green-sweatered baseball diamonds spread from coast to coast, populated by strong young men/boys swinging Babe Ruth bats. Hustlers try to sell fans on the idea that the high salaries of today equal the talents of yesterday. In the long pull, it won't sell. They are playing with Mother Nature — she will get them if they don't watch out. Baseball is a love affair, not a sideshow. It's not just a game. It's the national game — Babe's game.

Why is it important to keep baseball pure, to preserve for the average American the integrity of the game? A French-born historian, Jacques Barzun, perhaps gave the best answer to such questions: "Whoever wants to know the heart and mind of America had better learn baseball ... it fitly expresses the powers of the nation's mind and body."

Bibliography

Einstein, Charles, *The Baseball Reader*. New York: McGraw-Hill, 1983.

Guilfoile, Bill. *National Baseball Hall of Fame & Museum Yearbook*. Cooperstown, New York: National Baseball Hall of Fame and Museum, 1987.

MacFarlane, Paul. *Daguerreotypes of Great Stars of Baseball*. St. Louis: The Sporting News, 1981.

Neft, David S., et al. *The Sports Encyclopedia Baseball*. New York: St. Martin's/Marek, 1985.

Reichler, Joseph L. *The Baseball Encyclopedia*. New York: Macmillan, 1985.

Siegel, Barry. *Official Baseball Register, 1986 Edition*. St. Louis: The Sporting News, 1986.

_____. *Official Baseball Register, 1987 Edition*. St. Louis: The Sporting News, 1987.

Player Index

197

For Peter and
alicia,

How delightful
to meet you
both at the
MASA vigil, I
wish you well
in all you do.

Donna

DONNA L, Friess, PhD

4-22-95

Cry The Darkness

CRY THE DARKNESS
One Woman's Triumph Over
The Tragedy Of Incest

Donna L. Friess, Ph.D.
Foreword by Susan Forward, Ph.D.

Health Communications, Inc.
Deerfield Beach, Florida

Library of Congress-in-Publication Data

Friess, Donna L.
    Cry the darkness: one woman's triumph over the tragedy of incest/
Donna L. Friess; with foreword by Susan Forward.
      p.   cm.
    Includes bibliographical references.
    ISBN 1-55874-258-1
    1. Friess, Donna L.   2. Incest victims — United States-Biography.
3. Adult child sexual abuse victims — United States-Biography.
I. Title.
HV6570.7.F75   1993
362.7′64′092—dc20   92-38929
(B)   CIP

©1993 Donna L. Friess
ISBN 1-55874-258-1

Publisher: Health Communications, Inc.
              3201 S.W. 15th Street
              Deerfield Beach, FL 33442-8190

Cover design by Robert Cannata

Dedication

For my husband Ken,
my partner,
my soul mate.

Acknowledgments

Life's journey sometimes surprises us. One of the most incredible discoveries for me was that the many people in my life — friends, relatives, colleagues and students at Cypress College, my fellow scholars at the United States International University and my many neighbors in San Juan Capistrano — did not run away from me when they learned of my secret. Quite the contrary, I felt protected and accepted by them all. It shocked me to be cared for by so many dear people. That made this book possible, and I want to thank all of you. You helped hold me together through a difficult time.

Without the daily encouragement from my husband, Ken, when the pain of remembering was overwhelming, and without his intelligent critical thinking, the manuscript might never have been completed. My three children, Rick, Julie and Dan, provided a framework of strength from which I have drawn. My mother, Dorothy McIntyre, provided a constant flow of affection and encouragement, and I want to thank her for making the effort to grow. I appreciate my sister, Jacqueline L. Stack, for her clarity and strength through difficult times. My sister, Dee Dee, had the courage to change. I want to acknowledge Leanne Anteau whose friendship sustained me.

Barbara Nichols of Health Communications was a major motivating force behind this book. Many thanks for her commitment to it, and her thoughtful, sensitive editorial efforts.

Kevin Cooper and Creative Artists, Inc., Ron Anteau, Art Horan and Nina Ryan believed in this project. Stu Samuels created the title, Patrick O'Brien reminded me in critical moments to "just tell your story." My mother-in-law and friend, Helen Darby Holland, who passed away in March 1992, provided love and support.

I want to thank the staff at the *Los Angeles Times* for their sensitivity and courage in reporting the story, and especially Lynn Smith, Donna Frazier and John Archer. Bill Penzin and Jim Brown played special roles in this effort, as did Marsha MacWillie, Amy Zehnder and Roslyn Schryeur.

Peter Vegso and Gary Seidler, founders of Health Communications, had the faith to make the project a reality.

There have been many brilliant minds who have influenced my life. I want to acknowledge my appreciation to them for sharing their wisdom with me, especially Susan Forward, Sylvia Lane, Darryl Freeland, Herbert Baker, Alice Miller, Mary Catherine Bateson, Maya Angelou, John Bradshaw, M. Scott Peck and Eric Berne.

Lastly, I want to pay tribute to all my brave and beautiful brothers and sisters, nieces and nephews, sisters- and brothers-in-law, who stood tall and resolute. I love you all.

Introduction

The tricky part of the human journey is to transform ourselves continually as our life directions change. Erich Fromm says that we are in the constant process of giving birth to ourselves. We do it from childhood, through the challenges of puberty, adulthood, parenthood and, if we are lucky, old age. Re-creating ourselves is a lifetime effort.

Today life is moving faster than it ever has before, forcing us to alter our courses frequently or risk being lost at sea. We must use our imaginations to improvise new ways of being. I hope we will make decisions with the knowledge that we have the power and freedom to choose lives that are rich and full. Then we will truly become the captains of our ships.

My wish is that by sharing myself with you, you will come away with another perspective on the human condition and will understand better what happens to so many of us and our children at home. There is great strength in self-knowledge.

In the most personal sense, we are defined by our decisions, and, as a people, we are delineated, in part, by how we treat each other. My dream is that as you live out your own life, you will make conscious choices to make our world a better, more gentle place, that you will act to protect the children, all of our children, for they are our hope for the future.

Foreword
Susan Forward, Ph.D.

Susan Forward, Ph.D., is an internationally renowned therapist, lecturer and author of several books, including the *New York Times* bestsellers, *Toxic Parents* and *Men Who Hate Women and the Women Who Love Them.* In addition to her private practice, she hosted a daily radio talk show for five years. A pioneer in the field, Dr. Forward formed the first private sexual abuse treatment centers in California.

Incest is the most devastating betrayal a child can endure. It is perhaps the cruelest, most baffling of human experiences. It is a violation of the most basic trust between child and parent or caretaker. These children have nowhere to run, no one to run to. The child is caught as a hostage by a powerful terrorist. The protector becomes the persecutor and reality becomes a prison of dirty secrets. It is estimated that there are 60 million adult victims of childhood sexual abuse in America today.

A little child who has to keep a secret cannot imagine that the big person, the parent, is doing anything wrong. The child survives by turning the feelings of badness inward; their world is orchestrated around this core feeling of shame. Every adult who was molested as a child brings from childhood pervasive feelings of being hopelessly inadequate. All adult victims of incest share a legacy of tragic feelings: they feel Dirty, Damaged and Different — the Three Ds.

Incest leads to a form of psychological cancer. It is usually not terminal, but treatment is necessary and sometimes painful. This is not something that gets better by itself.

There is hope. When the secret of incest is exposed to the light of day and the victims are made to see that the shame is not theirs, they have a chance to stand up and hold their heads high. They have an opportunity to put their past behind them and to make their lives work. They can learn to rebuild their lives and their self-images and can develop a new dignity and sense of personal value. They can learn to lead happy, productive lives.

With *Cry The Darkness,* Donna Friess tells the story of her incredible struggle to expose the dark evil of incest to the light of truth. It was a war to save her four-year-old niece's life and the lives of the children dwelling in the adult victims of her father's tyranny. I applaud her courage and her strength.

Family Members

Raymond Landis, Sr. (Big Ray) — Donna's grandfather

Vera-May Landis (Maymie) — Donna's grandmother

Raymond Landis, Jr. — Donna's father and father of Sandy, Cee Cee, Trey, Chad, Diedre and Connie

Cecelia Burwick Landis — Donna and Sandy's mother, Ray Jr.'s first wife

Sandy — Donna's full younger sister

Bernice Landis — Raymond Landis, Jr.'s second wife, mother of Cee Cee, Trey, Chad, Diedre and Connie

Cee Cee Landis — Donna's oldest half-sister

Trey Landis — Donna's oldest half-brother

Chadwick Landis — Donna's half-brother

Connie Landis — Donna's half-sister

Diedre Landis — Donna's youngest half-sister

Anne Landis — Cee Cee's firstborn daughter

Jesse — Cee Cee's oldest son

Russ — Cee Cee's son

Nick — Cee Cee's son

Keely — Cee Cee's youngest daughter

Kyle — Cee Cee's baby boy

Rand — Cee Cee's husband

Crystal — Ray Landis, Jr.'s third wife and mother of step-daughter, Jamie

Ken Friess — Donna's husband

Donna and Ken's children: Rick, Julie and Daniel.

Sandy's two children: Joanne and Mindy

Prologue

January 18, 1990
Municipal Court
West Los Angeles

I couldn't watch when they brought him into the court-room in shackles, but I know I'll hear the sound of those chains for the rest of my life. How could I bear seeing my father restrained like some mad dog?

I was torn between the desire to run over and unlock those cruel handcuffs and hug my dad and the need to sit still while legal wheels turned to send him away to prison, maybe for the rest of his life. Breathless with anxiety, I finally mustered the courage to glance up at him. Plastic surgery had left his eyes pulled up into a peculiar slant that made him seem inhuman, demonic, and he looked like an aged satyr glaring at me with icy fury. The full force of his riveting blue eyes went through me like a sword.

I was terrified. My heart pounded in my chest and the agony I felt shook me to my soul. A small voice inside was crying out, "I love you, Daddy. How will I ever live without your love?"

The four-year-old voice within was drowned out by the threats he'd made a thousand times: "Donnie, people who talk end up six feet under. Betrayers are executed. People who tell have accidents." I could still hear him as if it were yesterday.

No, I didn't ever want to tell. I didn't want anyone to know, didn't want to be in this courtroom going through this scaring pain of shame and embarassment. And I was terrified that one day he would carry out his threats. After all, he kept a gun with him all the time.

The secret that I'd kept for a lifetime might have gone with me to the grave, but now I knew he hadn't stopped. He wouldn't stop until someone stopped him. I forced my attention away from the conflicting feelings within to focus on the harsh details of reality. Now there was another four-year-old girl living in terror. Who else could protect little Keely but me? I remembered how I'd felt the thousands of nights when I'd prayed that someone, somehow would protect me. But no one had.

The vision of Keely standing in front of me so paralyzed with fear that she could not speak loomed sharply into focus. She had stood there coughing and choking and stuffing, always stuffing her handkerchief into her tiny mouth.

And just last month she haltingly had choked out what Grandpa had been doing to her.

PART I
Growing Up

As I look at the image in the faded photograph, I can hardly believe the lovely little girl, all blond and sun-kissed, is really me and the handsome man holding me so proudly is my dad. We've been through so much since the photographer captured this tender moment almost half a century ago, yet there we are, having our day in the sun, forever smiling.

This picture of a precious child and her strong young father suggests the idyllic family life in California one envies on snowy winter days back East. It's not hard to fill in the details: endless ocean reaching beyond the horizon, miles of pristine golden sand under an intense blue sky, that clean salt-air smell, gulls circling overhead. Trips to the water's edge to splash in the gentle surf. Sand pails, sea shells, joy, love, laughter.

Yes, from the pictures taken that January day in 1949, I can see how the Landis family might be the envy of everyone. At least until the whole truth of who we were came out.

April 1948
Venice, California

"Wake up, Donna," my own voice comforted me as I came
into consciousness. "You're only having that same old dream."

I awoke feeling breathless and out of sorts again. It was
the dream I'd had during so many afternoon naps, the one
in which the peach blanket on my bunk bed was all messed
up and I couldn't stand the rumples down near my feet. In
my dream I couldn't get the blanket to be perfectly smooth
no matter how hard I tried.

I rolled over on my back to breathe more easily, and soon
my thumb and index finger were rubbing the satiny corner
of my blanket while I stared at the ceiling. I was vaguely
aware of the squeak of the oil pump next door dipping up
and down, up and down, pumping oil from under the sand.
A slight breeze wafted through, bringing the faint aroma of
oil along with sea air.

My mind drifted back to Sunday. It had been an especially
nice beach day. Usually the surf rolled right up to the front-
yard fence, but Sunday the tide was so low that the beach
seemed to go on forever, glistening jewel-like against the
receding water.

Our whole family had fanned out to see what we could
find in the wet sand. Daddy was walking barefoot with my
little sister Sandy on his shoulders. I went ahead near Mom,
hoping to get beautiful shells.

"Donnie, come over here," she yelled excitedly. I looked up
and saw her bending over something in the sand, and for an
instant I felt so much love for her. She was slim, girlish and
beautiful in her flowered bathing suit, with her long blond
hair falling around her face as she examined something in
her hand.

I raced over in response to her urgent tone and peered at the strange object.

"What is it?"

Mom held a perfect sand dollar in her palm. The design on the front looked like a beautiful flower. She turned it over.

"What do you see?" Her tone was warm and encouraging. She liked to teach us about our world.

"The purple bottom is all wiggly. Mommy, why is it wiggly?"

"Because it's still alive, Donnie. The ones we usually find are dead. The purple shows us its life."

"Can I touch it?"

"Be very gentle."

The thrill of discovering this wonderful new creature bubbled up in me and I had to run and get Sandy and Dad. He put Sandy down so she could touch it, too.

"Sandy, it's alive," I squealed as the reluctant three year old tested it gingerly with one tiny finger.

Daddy led us single file out near the waterline and carefully buried our sand dollar in the sand so it would have a chance to live.

It had really been the best afternoon! Mommy helped us build sand castles and put baby sand crabs in the courtyard so that the castle would have some people in it, and Daddy skipped stones over the surface of the sea while we watched enthralled. One, two...seven skips. Mom and Sandy and I tried but none of us could get close. Daddy was the champion stone skipper. He was so handsome and muscular, he could do anything. Everyone was always saying he and Mom were a beautiful couple and on this sun-drenched afternoon they were, in every sense of the word. We seemed to be a magic family living in an enchanted circle of love. And still, deep inside, I was holding my breath, hoping it would last.

It didn't seem to matter that we didn't even have a real house and lived in a one-room beach bungalow. But when we got back there that night, it seemed pathetically small and confining with its green couch in the middle and two sets of bunk beds along the walls. Sandy and I took our bath almost too tired to giggle at our usual game of slippery bumping cars in the tub.

Mom and Dad got through the evening without yelling at each other, but later that night when they thought we were asleep, I heard Dad swearing under his breath at Mom when he pushed his way into the lower bunk with her. Then came the muffled sounds of struggle and surrender that were so familiar, yet so upsetting.

I found myself trying to push the scene from my mind as I lay in my bunk that Tuesday afternoon and became aware that I had been rubbing the satin edge of my peach blanket back and forth furiously all this time. I didn't know why I should have to sleep in the afternoon like a baby anyway, but our baby-sitter Mimi made us. She seemed bored taking care of us. I didn't like weekdays at all. I usually felt lonely but there was nothing I could do about it. Dad had to go to work at his auto body shop and Mom had to take her opera lessons.

I should have been in kindergarten, but the class was full by the time Mom took me to register at Nightingale Elementary. I was so disappointed. I was five and longed to go to school, ached to get away from our dingy cottage and make new friends. But I was stuck at home for another year, doomed to taking dumb naps and staring around the room at uneven seams of tape Daddy had used to put up the drywall.

"Aristocrats," my dad had always called us. "Never forget you're an aristocrat, Donna. Your name means 'gracious lady' for a reason. You're going to be somebody some day." His voice still lingers in my ears.

The Landis family was a rare species, real native Californians in a state rapidly becoming populated with outlanders from other states. World War II had ended and people who had shipped out of California ports to the Pacific or had come to work in its defense plants decided to settle here for good. But my parents were born and raised in Los Angeles, a true son and daughter of the Golden State.

On my father's side, the Landises were pharmacists who had owned the first chain of drug stores in Los Angeles. Family legend has it that they were so rich my great aunt was nicknamed "Hats" at Los Angeles High in the 1890s because she owned more hats, the status symbol of the times, than any other girl in school. My grandfather, Big Ray, still owned a drugstore and went to work every day. In the great Landis tradition, his only child, my father, had been sent to pharmacy college at the University of Southern California.

My mother was Cecelia Burwick, and her father had a modest house-painting business. His daughters were the first generation to go to college. Mom was the third girl in the family and was to go to UCLA with the intention of becoming a teacher like her sisters before her.

My mom and dad had that born-for-each-other look and, in fact, had known each other since they were in sixth grade and started dating in high school. It might have been a foregone conclusion that they would marry but not as soon as they did. With the war and the draft looming, my father insisted that they get married right away or he would break up with Mom. They were only 17 at the time, and she wanted that teaching credential, but she didn't want to lose him. Surprisingly her parents went along with it. He seemed to love her so intensely.

Over the years when Dad and I had our special talks, he often told me the story of how much he'd loved my mom — "Crazy in love," was how he put it. He didn't think he could face college without her.

Mom was just 18 when she was married and became my mother the night she turned 19. She had managed to get in a semester at UCLA even though she was pregnant with me and Dad got in a year of pharmacy college. Mom's father died suddenly when I was six months old. Not long afterwards, Dad was drafted in spite of his status as a married student and Mom was left to manage on her own. Two years later Dad's bleeding ulcers earned him a medical discharge from the army. The family story is that he just couldn't tolerate the strain of regimentation or loneliness of life away from his family, and apparently he couldn't take more pharmacy college either.

By the time they were 25, my parents' lives seemed to have taken a serious detour. Instead of facing a promising future as the teacher and pharmacist they had intended to become, they had nothing. Full of fury, my father insisted that my grandmother let him build a tiny prefab house on her lot at the beach. He would become an auto body man and raise his family there. That was that.

It was there at the beach that the lines were drawn that delineated my life, there that my parents loved and raged, that my sister and I left our tiny footprints in the sand every day and watched them wash out to sea. And there that I set out full of excitement for my first day of school — a day that will be etched in my memory forever.

May 1948
Hollywood

"I have the prettiest girls in Hollywood," Dad used to tell us when he drove us to spend a weekend with our grandparents, Maymie and Big Ray. We must have made a charming sight, my movie-star handsome dad at the wheel of our new Ford sedan with his beautiful wife by his side and two wide-eyed little blonds in the back seat.

Sandy and I loved the drive from the beach to town. On a clear day we could see the mountains off in the distance, beyond the enormous flat basin of L.A., with its tall palms reaching toward blue sky. We never got tired of that trip into the sprawling city and the warmth of our grandparents' home. Maymie and Big Ray lived in a fine one-story English Tudor house in the stylish Wilshire District, right across from Farmers' Market.

The house was surrounded by an inviting green lawn and good climbing trees where birds liked to nest. I remember loving all that green so much. And when Maymie opened the oversized oak door of the house, she always greeted us girls with a big smile and hug as she drew us into the wonders of her world, so different from our house at the beach. Shiny oak floors were covered with Persian rugs, and every room was furnished with antiques. China cabinets were everywhere. Maymie was a tireless world traveler who had brought home beautiful antique dolls, fine bone china and other treasures from the corners of the earth. She displayed them in every room of the house except Big Ray's.

My grandfather was 66 years old, 20 years older than his vivacious wife. He was toothless and balding, but his role of family leader guaranteed everyone's tolerance of his eccentricities. He didn't like dentists, or doctors for that matter, and had never learned to drive. He slept in a small room behind the breakfast nook — the room that was meant for a live-in maid. Apparently it had been a long time since he and Maymie had shared a bedroom, and no one thought it was strange at all that he'd made this tiny room his own while Maymie had the biggest bedroom with the most elaborate furniture and best rugs in the house. Her headboard was unforgettable: a sunset depicted in fine inlaid cherry wood.

It was always so much fun to stay with Maymie and Big Ray. Sandy and I got to share a huge bedroom, just the two of us. We loved to snuggle under the blue down comforter in the carved oak bed and listen to the birds chirping outside the windows.

"Wake up, you little sleepy heads. Time to get up," Maymie called in her rich musical voice as she opened the door of our room. The smoky smell of bacon made us want to bounce out of bed.

"Donna, hurry up and you can pick out the dishes for breakfast."

Maymie knew how I loved to look at her beautiful china. I quickly set the table with plates decorated with bright roses and got out the funny glasses our grandfather had brought home especially for Sandy and me. We had shared conspiritorial giggles when Big Ray whispered how "naughty" those glasses were. There was a girl on the front dressed in a maid's uniform, but from the back her uniform disappeared as we drank our milk, leaving her backside naked.

Then it was time to wake up Big Ray. I knocked softly at his door, "Big Eyes, it's time to eat." Members of our family had many affectionate names for one another.

Big Ray always came out fully dressed, ready for his day. He wore a long-sleeved shirt and dark slacks, with his glasses perched on his prominent nose. He was tall and thin, over 6 foot 2, and I was sure he was the kindest man in the world.

"Hi, Princess! How are you this beautiful morning?" He gently picked me up and hugged me to his chest as he seated himself at the table. He always made me feel special and I loved him so much.

"You had a bad night, didn't you?" He looked into my eyes with concern. "You were gnashing your teeth something terrible again. It can't be good for your teeth."

"I don't remember, Big Ray." I was mystified.

Grandpa went on, "I tried to wake you up so that you would stop. Don't you remember, I patted your back for a while until you quieted down."

"Eat up, everyone," Maymie interrupted. "I'm taking the girls to Orbach's today for some new clothes. Their clothes look like they belong to the ragpickers. Then we're going to stop at the Farmers' Market for ice cream."

"You girls have fun. I'm going to the park to play checkers," Big Ray responded. No one was surprised. That's what he did every weekend.

It didn't take too much encouragement to get Sandy and me ready for a trip to the store. We often went shopping with Maymie and came home with something wonderful. I think she bought us most of our clothes.

Sometimes we went to Big Ray's drugstore with him, and especially loved twirling around on the stools at the soda fountain. Bernie, the teenager who worked behind the counter, made us extra big drinks and we thought she was neat.

On summer evenings when we stayed in town, Sandy and I loved to wait outside for Big Ray to come home from the drugstore on the bus. In the gathering dusk we played on the steel guard bar that protected the street light in front of the house. It was just the right height for us to somersault over, though it was easier for me than for my little sister. In the glow of the street lamp, I would place my hands on the bar, lift my right leg over it, straddle the bar, then go over. I'd whirl over and over on the bar as fast as I could until I could see Big Ray's tall form approaching in the pale light of streetlights across the street.

We squealed and jumped up and down with excitement as he got closer, but obediently waited on our side of the street. Finally he would scoop us up in his arms and carry us both inside.

"Whoa, there! Slow down, girls."

We could hardly wait for him to sit down and show us the treat he'd brought. We'd race to get on his lap.

"Donna, you climb up on this knee. Sandy you climb up over here. Hold this bag. I've got a surprise for my girls inside. No peeking!"

Big Ray was as delighted with our little treats as we were, and we loved his big toothless grin as he watched us joyfully dig inside the bag for candy or toys.

After a light dinner, which always included easy-to-chew milk toast, he loved to tell us bedtime stories. We'd climb on his lap once again and the stories would go on until Maymie insisted that we get ready for bed.

His stories were fabulous. We heard tales of horse-and-buggy days in Los Angeles, how he outsmarted teachers at Los Angeles High in 1901, how he handled robbers in a holdup at his drug store.

Though he passed away years ago, I can still hear Big Ray's voice telling the stories that let us know we had a real place in this city. I felt anchored and at home on visits to my grandparents' house. I don't know who I would have grown up to be if it hadn't been for their love and influence. To this day collecting antiques and hand painting china are important activities that enrich my life. I know I got my love of beautiful things from Maymie.

But there was something that didn't make sense about our living on the edge of poverty at the beach while my grandparents had so much. In my child's mind I couldn't formulate the questions and would probably have been afraid to ask them anyway. I always felt threatened by the ferocity of rage my father could summon. He was totally charming, yet capable of flying off the handle unexpectedly at all of us — his wife, his children, his parents.

Years later, when the whole story came to light, I knew I could not have handled the truth until I was much older and wiser and had a solid support system. I was already dealing with as much as I could.

January 1949
First Grade
Venice Beach

Early in the morning at the body shop, I was nervous
while my parents were working. I kept Sandy out of their
way, but my thoughts were on school. Today was the first
day of first grade. It was finally here! I was careful not to let
the dust and masking tape on the floor stick to my new
maroon oxfords. I wanted them to still look new by the time
I got to school. It was bad enough having to get Daddy to
show me which one fit on my right foot...when would I get
them straight?

As the time to leave for school drew near, I overheard my
parents arguing over who was going to take me. Mom insisted that she would but Dad overruled her.

"Goddamit, Cecelia, you haven't even finished sanding
the right fender yet. I've got to spray this thing this afternoon. I can't do everything around here myself, for God's
sake! I'll take Donnie while you finish up. Make sure those
windows are properly masked too."

I climbed up into the front seat of our car, a brand-new
light green Ford, and said goodbye to Mommy. As she kissed
my cheek, she seemed kind of sad. I knew she wished she
could take me.

I waved a last goodbye. I felt so special. A big girl at last!
As we drove away from the shop, I thought about making
new friends, about all the fun I would have with the kids at
recess. I always watched them hitting a big red ball against
the schoolyard fence.

Suddenly I looked up. This was not the way to school.
This was the way back to our house. I could see the small
stucco and frame cottages that made up the beach-front

housing area. It was mostly empty lots and oil wells, with an occasional estate owned by a Hollywood mogul oddly juxtaposed against the ugly wells.

I could see dozens of wells set between little beach bungalows. Some of the wells had tall derricks and others were squat. All had rusty corrugated fencing surrounding their machinery.

Venice was desolate on this bleak January day. Sparsely populated at best on the weekends of the summer, now in winter there was no one around except an occasional workman, dressed in oil-stained coveralls and a metal construction hat.

"Daddy, I have to get to school, why are we going to our house?" I asked. I was alarmed.

"There's plenty of time. I forgot something."

I was not reassured. When we got to the house, I pressed back against the seat, not wanting to get out of the car.

"Come on, Donnie!" urged Dad in silky tones.

"Daddy, I have to get to school," I pleaded.

"There is plenty of time."

It was his "no-nonsense" voice. I knew better than to argue with that voice. Reluctantly I climbed out of the car as Daddy unlocked the door to the house. Once inside, he pulled me into a hug. "I love you more than anything, my little bugger," he whispered into my ear. Perhaps he sensed my frustration, for he immediately started to tickle my tummy. I always liked to play tickle. Giggling, and breathless from squirming around, I soon forgot the time. I loved my Daddy's attention.

"Donna, betcha can't hide from me," he laughed.

"Betcha I can!" I taunted between giggles. "Close your eyes, Daddy. No! You have to cover them with your hands!" I reached for his hands and placed them over his eyes. "Now count to ten real slow!"

Hide and seek was our favorite game and I was good at it. I sneaked past him with light footsteps, and hid under our dinette table. The long oilcloth came down over my face. I held my breath. Dad pretended he couldn't find me and looked in all the corners.

Too soon, he discovered my hiding place. "Got you, you little bugger."

I was giggling so hard I could not stop. It was so funny. Daddy was tickling me and laughing. Suddenly he stopped laughing and his mood seemed to change. He became serious and agitated. I noticed a faint line of perspiration across his brow and his hands were shaking. What was going on? I was afraid.

He got weird, and started touching me in a strange way. It was not tickles now. It was under my panties.

"Hey, no!" I yelled, my laughter dead in my throat. "Hey, no...," I cried out. "What're you doing?" I pulled my legs together and tried to get up from where he'd pinned me down in our tickling match.

"Daddy, no! Stop touching me!" I protested, but my six-year-old cries did no good. This was a hulk of a man who lifted weights before dinner. This was a man who flexed his muscles as he ripped the six-inch phone book down the middle. This was a man who called himself a 180-pound gorilla. I was no match for Dad.

I grew still but it was not his strength that quieted me. It was a ferocity I sensed behind his eyes. He ignored me, said nothing and began to rub me under my panties while he did something funny to himself with his other hand. In spite of my pleas, he would not stop. It was exactly as if he had not heard me at all.

He seemed to be staring off into the distance when I briefly caught his eye. He stood up, zipped his pants and said in deadly serious tones, "Donnie, you're not to tell anyone about this. Not your mother or Maymie or Big Ray, not Sandy or your Aunt Margie. No one! You are to tell no one!"

His words were clear, and some deep, unspoken force communicated with an intensity that words never could. I was not to tell. His icy blue eyes threatening me, warning me, demanding that I never tell, put such a spell on me that I froze to the borders of my being.

I would not tell, but the fear I felt was like a big lump in my throat. Somewhere near my heart, I felt an ugly hole of shame opening. I would never tell. But I would always feel the searing edges of that hollow opening deep within.

Finally Daddy took me to school. I was upset and I was late. But mostly I was terrified. School was never as wonderful as I had dreamed it would be. It was dark somehow when I had yearned for light. I knew that I never really fit in. I felt so different, I might as well have had a mark across my forehead.

Eventually I was able to make one friend, Geraldine Renee. We enjoyed orange juice and graham crackers at recess and got especially good at twirling around in circles. The spinning was so neat! I had three dresses, but my favorite was a soft green one with a full skirt and sash that Aunt Margie, my mother's sister, had bought me. I washed it out at night so that it was ready again for twirling. When we twirled, my skirt would spread out in a floating arc. I loved to twirl. It helped me forget.

In the evenings before I went to bed, I pulled the dinette chair up to the kitchen sink and washed out my green dress and ankle socks. I noticed that the other girls had clean dresses and bright white socks, and I tried hard to be like them. I only had one pair of socks so I washed them carefully and hung them to dry on the back of the chair near the portable floor heater. I even learned to iron my dress. On special days I pinned my hair into what I hoped would be curls so that I would be pretty for twirling. Mommy praised me for all this activity and said I was a big girl, but she never helped.

Even with Geraldine, the graham crackers and twirling, first grade had many dark days. I was not sure why.

The worst day was May Day when the teacher told all of us to form a big circle on the playground to learn the May Day dance. I felt embarrassed and ugly when the children on either side of me recoiled when they saw my warts. Neither child would take my hand.

"She's got cooties! She's got cooties," they jeered.

The teacher ordered them to hold hands with me, but it really didn't make me feel better.

March 1950
Venice Beach

"For chrissake, Cecelia, the girls have green teeth." Dad's voice rose to a full-decibel shout. "Their necks are dirty. Why the hell can't you even keep them clean?"

"Why can't you keep Bernie out of our house?" Mom yelled back.

"At least she wouldn't dress the girls in blue jeans," Dad shot back. "You keep my girls out of those goddam things! They're going to grow up to be ladies. And ladies do not wear jeans."

My mother seemed to get smaller when Dad yelled at her. My parents had always argued about everything — especially about us kids. But when Bernie came to live in our driveway, their arguments became especially vicious. I wasn't sure exactly why, because Bernie seemed like a nice enough girl, but that seemed to be a turning point for our family. Mom had always been a little distant, but she seemed to lose her commitment to family life after that and never seemed sharply focused on us again. She retreated further into her world of singing lessons and college classes.

Dad had dragged a battered old wooden house trailer into our driveway and moved Bernie into it. She was 17, overweight and had mouse-colored braids pinned on the top of her head. She wore little makeup and never looked nearly as good as my glamorous mother. Bernie had worked at Big Ray's soda fountain, which my parents were now running, and Dad decided that she would make a good baby-sitter. At least that's what he told us. I was just seven, Sandy was five, and we still needed someone to take care of us.

Bernie and Mom sat together sometimes and shared Ovaltine at our little dinette table. Usually they commiserated with each other about my dad. Even so, Mom was always complaining to Dad about Bernie's coming into our house at all hours to use the bathroom. It was hard to understand the world of grown-ups. I found the best way to handle it was to be quiet and do what I was told.

I got along fine with Bernie. She was much better than any of our other baby-sitters, and I grew quite comfortable with her. She seemed to like me, too, and as time went on, we came to love each other.

Dad took care of Sandy and me quite often and liked to take us on excursions to the fun places on the beach. We always looked forward to going to the fun zone at Venice Pier and to the amusement center at Ocean Park where we played in the rolling barrels and laughed ourselves sick in front of the curvy mirrors. Sandy and I liked to run back and forth, watching ourselves turn from short and fat to tall and thin and back again. Dad seemed to enjoy it as much as we did, and we all laughed when the mechanical fat lady cackled.

One weekend Daddy packed me into our car and we drove all the way to Big Bear Lake, just the two of us. We drove for miles across the Los Angeles basin, then headed out east of the city toward Palm Springs, through country that looked more and more like desert with every passing mile.

On the way he talked about Bernie and Mom, and I listened hard.

"Donnie, you understand why I have Bernie, don't you? Your mother is frigid."

I didn't have any idea what that meant, but I nodded sagely. I was used to my parents talking to me as if I understood what they meant.

Dad reached over and patted my hand. "That's my girl, Donnie. You know, Bernie is lucky to have me. I could have anyone I want, but I want to stay with your mother for the sake of you girls."

I was glad to hear they were going to stay together, and I nodded again, this time with more enthusiasm.

"I could have married really old money. Mary Blank, the candy heiress, man did she want me. She's a fine lady. A real aristocrat," he lectured on, caught up in his reverie. His eyes narrowed and his tone changed as he continued, "Bernie is lower class. I'm not hurting her. She doesn't have such good chances. She'll let me stay with your mother."

At the base of the San Bernardino Mountains we found the steep, winding road up to Big Bear, and Dad grew quiet as he negotiated the switchback curves. The air got cooler as we got closer to the top and pine forests edged the road. At the top of the mountain, we saw huge granite boulders strewn along the shore of the lake as if a crazy giant had hurled them from the sky.

We stopped at a country store that looked like something out of a Wild West movie. A faded wooden sign across the tattered screen door announced, "Coca-Cola." Inside it was dimly lit but my eyes fell on a jar of fresh oatmeal cookies sitting on the counter. They looked delicious!

Dad noticed my interest right away. "Honey, do you want one of those big ol' cookies?"

"May I? I love them."

Dad nodded to the storekeeper and she asked me with a smile, "Which one would you like?"

My eyes were just at the level of the cookie jar and I surveyed them seriously.

"The one right there with the most raisins, please." I pointed out the biggest cookie in the jar.

Dad and the storekeeper laughed and seemed to be enjoying this as much as I was.

"You sure have a polite little girl, Mister," she commented.

Dad paid for the cookie and it was fresh and fragrant. It turned out to be the best thing about that trip. I ate it slowly, savoring its crunchy goodness for as long as I could. I had an idea of what was coming.

We checked into a rustic log cabin that had just one creaky bed, and I tried to think about that wonderful cookie when Dad did things to me in the dark.

When I resisted him, he caught my small wrist and twisted my arm hard enough to break the elbow, easily pinning me down. But I believed him when he told me I was his special girl and he loved me more than anything. He hurt me but said over and over that all this special attention was proof that he loved me. I pushed my scared feelings away, trying very hard not to have them, and remembered that cookie again.

I didn't have to be warned anymore. I would never tell on Daddy. Somewhere in the back of my mind I knew if I told Mommy, she would go crazy and I would lose her forever. That idea scared me even more than the awful things Daddy was doing to me.

We had many weekend trips after that, just the two of us, but the trip to Big Bear is the one I remember most clearly.

> Years later, when I was in my 40s, my husband and I took our three children up there on a family ski trip, and we passed that same log cabin. A flash of that trip with Dad crowded my consciousness and that awful night came back, leaving me panicked, breathless, smelling that oatmeal cookie again as if it were only yesterday. I gulped air to maintain my equilibrium. My husband and children must not know anything was wrong. No, I would not tell. I would never tell.

Spring 1950
Venice Beach

"Mommy, look what I got for you." My heart was full as I skipped in the door with a big red rose wrapped in newspaper. Our neighbor down the beach had noticed me admiring her rose bushes and had cut the most beautiful flower for me to give to my mother. I was so proud. I just knew it would make her smile.

But no one was home at our house. The sound of angry voices coming from Bernie's trailer broke into my happy fantasy.

"Who knocked you up, you goddam whore?" Dad's voice grew louder and louder. "I know you've been out screwing around every time I turn my back," he yelled.

I ran to the trailer in time to see Bernie's face contort with anguish. "No! No! I didn't. No one," was all she could manage between sobs.

"Don't lie, you stupid bitch. It was the lifeguard. I know you, always hanging around those muscleheads." He looked as if he were about to take a swing at her.

"Stop yelling! Do you want the whole world to know?" Mom chimed in.

"You stay out of this, Cecelia. It's between Bernie and me. She's gotta take a lie detector test, goddam it. I know she's been out screwing around."

He turned his fury back to Bernie and she cowered under its force. "You go take that lie detector test or you're never going to see me again. I'll throw you right out on the street. Let your lifeguard take care of you."

If they had asked me, I would have told them that Bernie only talked about the undertow with Skip, the lifeguard who manned the tower near our house. I knew, I had been with her. But no one asked me. They raged on, the three of them, until Mom turned on her heel and left Bernie's trailer, and I went with her.

"I don't know why I get into these things," she muttered to no one in particular. "It really doesn't matter to me."

I didn't know what that meant, but it must have been something terrible that happened to poor Bernie. Mom seemed awfully unhappy about it. I put the rose in a glassful of water for her and she hugged me, but she didn't really smile.

Later that night Mom brought up Bernie again when she thought we were asleep.

"Who's going to support your bastard?" she whispered furiously to Dad. "It's not bad enough you have to park your girlfriend in the driveway and make her pregnant, now you're going to have to support another child. And with what?"

Dad didn't care whether we were awake or asleep. "I told you, it wasn't me. Bernie's been screwing around," he shouted. "Besides, my family's rich. They'll always come through with the money."

"I haven't seen much around here for your real family, much less Bernie's baby."

Dad was quiet for a minute.

Mom went on, "She can't keep that baby around here, Ray, she just can't. Everyone will know you're screwing her."

"Get off my back, Cecelia. I'll do whatever I want to Bernie, and you can't stop me. Now shut the fuck up."

I couldn't tell whether Mom was crying or not. Mostly when Dad yelled at her, she just looked sad, so very sad. I wished with all my heart that the rose had made her smile.

"Listen, Sandy! I can hear a baby cry." I shook my little sister's shoulder with excitement. "Can you hear it?"

Sandy looked puzzled, and her eyes rolled upward as she listened intently.

"There it is again. You can hear it, Sandy. Just listen harder."

Between the sounds of cars whizzing by on Washington Boulevard, I was sure I could hear the faint cry of a baby.

Sandy and I stood outside the hospital, pressed against the windows, trying to stay cool under the overhanging roof. The heat was incredible for a June day. We weren't allowed to go into the hospital when Mom and Dad went to see Bernie, so we stood outside the window, cupped our hands against the dusty screen and tried to peer in. I could barely make out shapes in the shadows, but as my eyes became accustomed to the gloom, I was pretty sure I saw four women lying in beds along the walls. One of them waved to me so I guessed that must be Bernie. Was that her baby I could hear?

Sandy and I liked to play dolls, but we had never had a real baby to play with. I was so excited I couldn't stand still. "A real baby, Sandy. We have a real baby!"

When we got home I got out my Betsy Wetsy doll, gave her a bottle and changed her diaper when she wet on cue. I had to practice as hard as I could for when Bernie's baby came home. I had never held a real baby and could only imagine how it would feel.

A few days later Mom and Dad went back to the hospital to pick up Bernie and her new baby. But they didn't come home to our house — Dad had found a new apartment for Bernie in a garage facing an alley off a back street. When we went in, it seemed really tiny, and I noticed right away it didn't have a bathroom. There was a white porcelain pan behind a curtain for Bernie to go to the bathroom in. I thought that was odd. There was no sink and the water came from a hose in the backyard.

Bernie sat down with the baby, and I got to look at her. She had brown hair like Bernie's, a pink wrinkled face and the tiniest little hands I'd ever seen.

"What's her name, Bernie?" I whispered.

"Cee Cee. That's short for Cecelia," Bernie replied, smiling down at her infant daughter with great tenderness.

I had to think about that for a minute. I wondered why Bernie's baby was named after my mom, but decided not to ask questions. I wasn't sure how relationships worked, but in some deep way I knew that Cee Cee and I were family.

Cee Cee started to cry. So much noise from such a little girl! Mom took her from Bernie and rocked her gently, but Cee Cee kept right on crying.

Mom handed her back to Bernie who tried to soothe her tears.

"Come on, Donnie," Mom said, taking my hand and leading me outside. "Let's go to the store and buy Cee Cee some blankets and clothes. It doesn't look like there's anything here for that poor little baby at all."

Mom was gentle and loving with Cee Cee, but her voice was always filled with anger when she spoke to my father. The whole feeling in our home changed and there was a noticeable lack of warmth between Mom and Dad. Gone were the long sunny days when the four of us skipped stones on the beach.

Mom spent less and less time with us. She had a job now on the playground and still kept up with her opera classes. Some nights she didn't get in until very late. Once we overheard her telling Dad all about her new boyfriend, and he did not seem to mind. They confided secrets in the dark sometimes, like old friends, in contrast to their fierce arguments by day. I felt uneasy, unsure about what was happening to our family, but I knew better than to ask.

Not long after Cee Cee was born, Dad took me aside and warned me in those now familiar grave tones, "Donnie, if anyone asks you about this new baby, you are to tell them her name is Cee Cee Davis, and her father was killed in a taxi cab crash in Chicago."

It was a hard speech to remember but I tried to keep all the "c" words together as we had been taught in school — cab, crash, Chicago. I could do it.

"You'd better remember, Donnie."

I nodded, "Okay."

"I'm not kidding, Donnie. It's a secret who her real father is. You are to tell the truth to no one."

I wasn't sure about her real father, but I understood about not telling the truth. He could count on me. I wasn't going to tell. I always behaved like a good little girl — a good little girl who grew warts on her hands, ground her teeth at night and occasionally wet the bed.

I ground my teeth and wet my bed alone, so no one knew, but the warts were different. They made my hands so ugly, and it was hard to keep them hidden. I wondered where those warts came from. I didn't have them when I was younger, before first grade, before Daddy started to take me to school in the mornings.

February 1951
Venice Beach

"Let us in! Please let us in. We'll be good."

Sandy and I were shivering and crying but the door wouldn't open. We were locked out again on the pitch black beach with the angry surf pounding a few yards away and nothing but spooky oil wells to keep us company. They looked like a herd of metal dinosaurs dipping up and down in the eerie light of the new moon, creaking and moaning, "kuh plump, kuh plump," as they brought up thick, foul-smelling oil.

My little sister and I were no strangers to the night. We were often locked out as punishment for making noise or playing too spiritedly. It was always scary out there with the night sounds.

It was also frightening to be left in charge of Sandy and Cee Cee at Bernie's new apartment, but I was often the baby-sitter when my dad took Bernie out. She had moved to a new place when Cee Cee was seven months old. I loved it during the day: it had a stove, a little patio and even a real bathroom. There were about 12 children to play with in the family next door and we had all kinds of fun. They were poor, but their house echoed with laughter and smelled of homemade bread. After dark, though, if I got frightened, it would never occur to me to knock on their door and ask for help.

I worried about Cee Cee's wobbly little head and tried hard to handle her gently. She was a darling baby and I loved to hug her and play with her, but I was concerned about hurting her and about making her bottle right. Turning the gas on seemed dangerous if I didn't hurry to strike the match, I would have blown us up. And I didn't want to overheat the milk and scald her mouth.

Sandy would usually come with me when I took care of Cee Cee. If Bernie and Dad stayed out late, we'd be afraid of every sound outside. After I'd lay Cee Cee in her crib, I'd shush Sandy and tiptoe to the back door to make sure it was bolted. Eventually Sandy and I would fall asleep clinging to each other in a big chair, listening hard for strange noises over the sound of the oil wells and the wind rustling through the palm trees.

We stayed at Bernie's apartment a lot while my mother was busy, and she was busy almost every day with her job and with practice for the opera. On Saturdays when she was home, she'd lie on the floor with our huge dictionary perched on her diaphragm while she vocalized.

"May, me, mou, mu-u-u-u-u," Mom sang out, holding her notes as long as possible to strengthen her abdominal muscles.

"May, me, mou, mu," Sandy and I echoed as we ran through the house giggling.

"Enough noise," Dad shouted. "You girls get the hell out of here and go play. Don't bother your mother."

We were used to not bothering Mom, so we went outside to the driveway where we found the beautiful old 1936 Chevrolet they were restoring. Mom had meticulously painted it by hand. It had four doors that opened from the center post, and was the perfect place to play stagecoach.

Sandy and I hid from Indian attacks in the back seat. As imaginary desperados and Indians stalked us from behind the oil well next door, we grew excited.

"They're coming. Look out!" I screamed.

"Get down!" squealed Sandy, slamming the door to keep the bad guys out.

As the game heated up, we slammed the doors over and over, and by the end of the day, each of us had managed to break our index finger.

Mom was furious. She could not believe that we would be so stupid. My sister and I chalked it all up to a rough day on the range, but Mom shook her head at us as she tried to fix our broken fingers. Our oddly curved fingers would attest to that Indian attack for years.

Decades later Sandy demanded that Mom explain why she let us play in that dangerous way and why our fingers were not set by a doctor. I never gave it a second thought. Perhaps I did not expect much from anyone.

I was usually careful to be a good girl but sometimes Sandy and I played dangerous games, especially after she started afternoon kindergarten at Nightingale and we spent our after-school hours together. I'm not sure why I needed to be daring. Perhaps it was because I had so little control over my own body that I felt pushing my limits gave me a sense of being in charge of my life.

During the years that Mom was a playground leader, Sandy and I used to walk up to Venice Beach where she worked after school. On the way we'd skip along Windward Avenue on the covered sidewalks of the quietly decaying buildings with their once majestic colonnades, now home to an odd collection of winos, bums and other bizarre characters.

Everyone along the boardwalk knew us, two little tow-headed girls holding hands, making their way to the playground where their mother worked, where it was safe. We never talked to strangers even though they talked to us. We had been warned time and time again about bad men who would lure little girls into cars with candy, and we took those warnings very seriously. I did not want to get yelled at or get locked out in the night, and I certainly did not want anything bad to happen to little Sandy.

Mom would wait for us at the entrance to the playground, which was just in front of the rotting old pier at Venice Beach, but after that, she'd have to ignore us, not wanting her supervisor to get angry at her for having her children hanging around. We pretended we were not her children. We practiced being invisible.

Once I did have an important question. I sneaked over to the office and stood staring at the floor until Mom wasn't busy. The red cement of the game area was covered with a fine white layer of sand. I tried to be quiet, but I couldn't wait any longer.

"Mommy, what religion am I? That big girl over on the swings wants to know."

"You're Protestant, Donnie," she answered matter of factly.

It didn't mean anything to me, but at least I had a category to fit into.

One day Sandy and I sneaked off the fenced-in play yard with Elsa, an 11-year-old who often came to the playground with her little dog, a small brown dachshund named Hans. We darted past "No Trespassing" signs and the boarded-up entrance to the pier, which had long since been considered too dangerous for visitors. Elsa picked up her dog and ran out on the pier, along the narrow walkway between the old arcade building and the sheer drop to the pounding surf below.

"Come on, Donna. It's fun!" she dared.

I was frightened. "It's too high! It's scary," I yelled across the distance to her. I noticed poor little Hans was shaking in her arms.

"Chicken, chicken," she taunted.

Sandy was silently standing next to me. I looked at the surf rising and falling beneath me. I could see white sea foam between the rough boards of the rickety pier, which shook under the pounding of the waves.

"There's no rail. What if I fall?" I yelled into the winter afternoon.

"Just be careful, you yellow chicken."

With that I took a deep breath and stepped out onto the splintery foot-wide ledge. Gingerly I placed one foot in front of the other, taking tiny steps, inching my way along the length of the building. It seemed to take an eternity. I looked up at Elsa once, but it was a mistake. She looked mean, as if she hoped I would fall into the ocean and get swept away. My heart began to pound even harder but I couldn't stop now. I speeded up, taking the last few steps quickly. I made it!

I looked back at my little sister, and shouted, "Don't try it, Sandy! Don't come out here."

I don't know whether she could hear me over the sound of the wind and surf, but from the terrified look on her face, I knew she wouldn't try.

Elsa's little dachshund was shivering, seeming to understand that one false step and we could be killed. Without saying anything to Elsa I gathered my courage and started back. With the wind gusting around me, I put one foot in front of the other very carefully and, step by step, made my way back toward safety.

At last I was at my sister's side. We were both petrified. We both looked back at the big girl clutching her little dog, trying to make her way to safety, too, no longer taunting, but as terrified as we were. Finally they arrived at the safe end of the pier, and we all raced back to the security of the playground, never to venture up there again. We never played with Elsa again, nor did we ever tell a soul what we had done.

For months afterward, I would sit on the swing and stare at that narrow little catwalk. The next year the city tore down that dangerous pier, but I remembered it always and that death-defying walk. I wondered whatever made me take such a big chance.

Summer 1952
Culver City, California

"Come on, Donnie. I want to show you our new house."
Dad was beaming. "You'll really like it, Honey. It's a beauty.
And it's much sunnier than at the beach."

We climbed into the car and shivered as we drove inland
through the chill fog that hugs the coast in June. After a
few miles, we broke through into the fading sunshine of late
afternoon as we reached the little wood-fronted stucco
house in Culver City.

I was so excited, I could hardly wait to see it. I brought
my new plastic vanity set with me, even though our furniture would not be delivered until the next day. I had bought
the little blue comb, brush and mirror with my own money
so that I would have something special for my new bedroom.

I skipped up the sidewalk across the tiny green lawn and
jumped up and down as Dad unlocked the door. I started to
run through the house but he would not let me.

"In a minute you can see it all," he said in that familiar
threatening voice.

"Daddy, I want to see everything." I was miserable, knowing what was coming.

"Please, Daddy," I begged.

But he ignored my pleas and led me into the bedroom he
would share with Mommy. He made me kneel and bend forward on my hands and knees, with my head inside the closet.

"Hold still," he demanded.

I was used to hearing "hold still." He always said that to
me, since the first day of school when we played hide and
seek.

I clutched my hair brush in my hand while he touched me
with his fingers under my panties. I prayed it would be over

soon. I had trained myself to separate away from myself and concentrate on something else while Daddy did what he always did to himself with his other hand. This time I kept my mind focused on the new house.

Later Daddy let me see all the rooms.

Even though my excitement was diminished by the holding-still episode, I still felt amazed when I walked through the house. It was so much like other children's homes. In the dusky light I could see a real bathroom, real closets and a private room just for Sandy and me.

I was nine years old, and for the first time it looked as if I might have a normal life — at least a life that looked normal. Underneath it all, I felt anything but normal. But I had become good at pretending. I would act as if I did not feel dirty, pretend I did not feel as if I had a mark on my forehead. Pretense was my first line of defense. I could not think of anything else to do.

September 1952
Culver City, California

Now that I was nine, I was excited about starting fourth grade. I was surprised to see that I had a male teacher, Mr. Good. I wasn't too sure what to expect from him and started out the year sitting at the back of the room, staring at the old inkwell hole. But Mr. Good lived up to his name, and soon I began to feel comfortable.

When we shared about our summer vacations, some of the children talked about trips they had taken. I didn't want to tell about any of the day trips Dad had made me take with him, but told about moving from the beach to our new house in Culver City.

When a redhead named Leanne got up and told about sailing on *Sea Gypsy*, her parents' new 32-foot sailboat, I thought she was the most beautiful girl I had ever seen. She had freckles all over and a long pony tail with three ringlets in it. I wished I could be like her: beautiful, freckled, red-headed, sweet and self-assured. More than anything, I wished she would be my friend.

Before long, we did become friends. Leanne lived right across the street from our school and invited me over all the time after class. I'll never forget the first time I walked into her house. It was clean like my grandparents' house and smelled of furniture polish. Her mother was always happy to see us. She would smile, laugh with us and interrupt her housework to get us cookies and milk. So this was how other mothers behaved!

I took mental notes all the time at Leanne's house. There were stacks of clean, neatly folded clothes at the foot of Leanne's bed, shiny kitchen cabinets, no dust and toys neatly stowed away. When Leanne and her mom took me shopping with them at a department store, I was really impressed. I had been going by myself on the bus to W.T. Grant's dime store when I needed something new to wear.

Having Leanne for a friend was the happiest experience of my childhood. I loved her and felt safe and secure at her house. I was there almost every day, and we had great fun playing with her brother's baseball cards, playing jacks or just giggling like crazy about funny things that happened at school. All the other kids thought we were hilarious. We were always laughing until our sides hurt.

That was the year my warts disappeared. I'm not sure I understood what it meant when I read that warts might be psychosomatic, but when my friendship with Leanne brought such happiness into my life, the warts went away.

I had to invite Leanne to visit my home eventually, but I put it off as long as I could. The day before she came, I got very busy, raking up leaves in the backyard, sweeping dust and hundreds of candy wrappers from under the twin beds in the room I shared with Sandy. What a mess! Before school I was up early making all the beds and dusting. I ran a load of laundry, folded some of my clothes and stacked them on the end of my bed. I wanted Leanne to think that my mom took care of me the way hers did.

I had learned so much about how normal households worked at Leanne's home, it made it easier to pretend our family was like hers. In fact, it made it imperative. I even wondered out loud what was in my brown paper lunch bag with the rest of the kids in the school lunchroom. Of course, I always knew I had a baloney sandwich and an apple. I made my own lunch every morning and didn't really mind. It just took a minute. But I was envious of the other kids who had someone make their lunches for them. And their breakfasts.

I made many friends that wonderful year in fourth grade, and before long the other girls invited me to join their Brownie troop. It was exciting to think about having a cute little Brownie outfit and going to meetings, and I begged my mother to call the troop leader right away.

When the Brownie leader explained that each girl had to host one meeting and that her mother had to be there for it, my mother looked crestfallen. She still had her job at the park and could not be home to conduct a Brownie meeting. In those "Leave It To Beaver" days of the '50s, working mothers were rare and looked down on, and their children were often excluded.

"Donnie, sweetheart, I'm so sorry."

"I know, Mom. It's okay." It was hard, but I knew Mom felt as bad as I did about it, and I tried to be brave.

"Honey," she continued, "you've talked about nothing but Brownies for weeks now, but I'll make it up to you. We'll do something fun. While I teach crafts next summer, you can join the class. The ladies will love you! We'll make those fiber flowers you like so much. Your very own flowers for your room. You'll like that, won't you, Honey?"

I didn't want Mom to feel more sorry for me. She could not help it if she had to work to help support our family.

"Don't worry so much about the Brownies, Mom. The girls are still my friends. I see them every day at school. Leanne still has lots of time to play."

I understood why I could not be a Brownie. I had always understood these things and pretended that I felt okay. I knew I wasn't like the other kids, but I wasn't always so sure why. Even though I was a little confused, I never complained, not even on Thursdays, Brownie day, when the other girls wore their uniforms to school and went to their meeting without me. I wanted so much to be part of that group. Especially when the Brownies had their monthly pajama party at one of the girl's houses. I'd hear in vivid detail how the party had gone and all about their nutty tricks. I acted enthusiastic and laughed at their antics, but deep inside, where the truth hid, I was in terrible pain.

Summer 1953
Culver City

We were glad when summer arrived, and we spilled out of class right into vacation time with its promise of long afternoons at the beach. But that summer between the fourth and fifth grade something happened that sent shock waves through my soul and dimmed the luster of my life.

It started with a fishing trip, an overnight with Dad, up the coast north of Malibu to Sycamore Cove where there was a nice fishing pier.

It began well enough. I was getting good at fishing and caught five fish on one multiple hook at the same time. Five Lucky Joes at once made me feel really proud, and Dad was shouting in excitement so all the other fishermen on the pier could hear. I think I was the only girl there, and I had proved my excellence as a fisherman. I even caught a shark, which was quite a lot for a nine year old to land.

Later we had a campfire and ate hot dogs. We always threw the fish back. The Pacific was beautiful that night and stars were visible overhead, even before the sun sank into the lavender waves. As we watched the sky grow dark, Dad moved closer and took my face in his hands. Looking into my eyes he smiled softly.

"You're my special girl, Donnie," he whispered, nuzzling me with his face. "I love you more than anything."

I knew what was coming. He was going to have me bend over and hold still for him. I glanced up and down the beach to be sure no one could see us. I didn't want anyone to know how he touched me.

But I was wrong. That isn't what he wanted at all.

Tonight he seemed stronger than ever before as he hugged me to him. He was in his bathing suit, and I could smell the aroma of sweat in the hair on his chest.

Later that night, after I went to sleep in the front bunk, Daddy woke me up. He was naked, which I was used to, but this time he was different. He pushed up my nightie, lay down beside me and began to touch me. I tried not to breathe, tried to fake sleep, but he did not stop for a long time. Then he rolled over on to me, his big naked body right on top of my little one. I felt panicked as he began to breathe faster, but still I did not call out. What he did to me hurt terribly between my legs. It seemed to go on forever, but at last he was through.

"You're a real woman now, Donnie," he sighed.

But I wasn't. Not at all. I was a frightened nine year old who had just been raped by her own father, too terrified to cry out for help. If I had, he would have been furious, would have bent my wrists back until my elbows cracked, shouted, glared at me until ice formed on my soul, left me out all night on the beach and never let me back into the house. If I had tried to defend myself, no punishment would have been too terrible. And it wouldn't have done any good. There was no one there to help me.

I lay there in pain and terror afterwards. My father went back to sleep in his bunk as if nothing had happened. I was so sore I had trouble walking for several days. Was this what it meant to be a real woman?

I wondered about that all summer long. While Leanne and my other classmates were chattering about leaving Brownies behind and becoming Girl Scouts, it was hard for me to be with them. My mind seemed stuck in the pain and humiliation of becoming a real woman.

Daddy was after me a lot that summer. He never let me forget.

When September came and it was time to go back to school, I didn't want to go. I didn't want to face all the other children, didn't want them to see me, to look into my face. I was sure that someone would look into my eyes and discover that I was a real woman now. I thought I would die if anyone found out.

September 1953
Culver City

"Don't fuck with me, Donnie," Dad shouted, his face livid with rage. "Get back to work on that car."

"I don't want to," I shouted back. "Working on cars is for boys."

"Don't you dare defy me, goddamit. You're not going to be some bag of fluff, some helpless broad who doesn't know a carburetor from a commode."

As usual, Dad won the argument, and I went back under the hood.

Dad had bought me an old Hudson which needed a new engine. He decided that not only was it time for me to be a real woman, it was also time for me to learn how to rebuild a car. If my friends in fifth grade ever wondered about my family being weird before, this proved it. Whoever heard of buying a girl an old jalopy for her tenth birthday anyway?

The plan was for me to take the engine apart after school and on weekends, and I proceeded to do it through most of the fifth grade. Dad was adamant that I should understand the principles of internal combustion and be able to fix an engine. I hated working on that car. I wanted to ride bikes or talk about lipstick, Kotex or bras to Leanne on the phone, or read Nancy Drew mysteries. But I was afraid to take a stand against my dad's wishes, so I worked on the Hudson.

I missed more school than any other student in fifth grade and didn't care. Leanne was in a different class that semester, so I couldn't see her during the day anyway. And surprisingly, my parents said it was my decision whether I went to school. My new teacher, Mrs. Ferguson, ridiculed me so mercilessly for poor attendance that I preferred to stay home. Besides, it was easier to avoid the other kids than defend myself against them when they teased me about my old car.

Besides the Hudson, I had a new pink sewing machine Dad bought for me at the pawn shop and I liked to sew myself skirts and dresses. I made some for Cee Cee, too, because Bernie didn't know how and the poor little three-year-old was running around in tatters. Mom gave me regular sewing lessons and I was proud that I could make a beautiful gathered cotton skirt. Secretly I dreamed that Mom would sew something pretty for me, but she was too busy making her opera costumes and clothes for Sandy, who was too young to make her own.

As strange as things might have seemed around our house, there were good days, too. Some of the craziness even had payoffs. The Hudson, for example, really turned out great. Dad and I sold it at the end of the school year, and I got to keep the money. Dad wanted me to understand the value of a dollar and how dollars can be earned. I got the message — and the money — but hated working on that car and being treated like a boy almost as much as I hated being treated like a real woman.

Mother's opera career progressed and she became the lead soprano for the Santa Monica Civic Light Opera Association. Dad sometimes had singing parts and often Sandy and I were on stage as "spear carriers." We had fun performing our small silent parts. Mom was Gilda in Verdi's *Rigoletto* and Musetta in *La Boheme*. She sang like an angel!

Being in opera was almost overwhelming, especially the tragic operas when Mom had to die on stage. The worst was the impassioned death scene in *Rigoletto* with its crashing cymbals and wailing violins, which helped her hit a C sharp in a difficult aria. It was intense when the stage darkened as she sang her last note and breathed her last breath.

But how wonderfully beautiful she looked up there under the klieg lights, radiant in her rich brocades and satin, her blond good looks dazzling the eager hordes. The star!

Later, after an eternity of curtain calls and armloads of long-stemmed red roses, Sandy and I would hang around her dressing room while she was taking off the heavy stage makeup. Her opera friends whirled around her, enamored with her talent, hoping some of her glamour would rub off on them. Some were like aging opera groupies. Eventually their commotion would wind down and their attention would turn to her two little daughters who stood quietly in the shadows. They pinched our cheeks and clucked appreciatively over us, but no one ever really took the time to get to know us.

Besides becoming an opera extra, an auto mechanic and a real woman in fifth grade, I also became a swimming enthusiast.

My dad bought our family a brand new 14-foot house trailer which we left all winter in a trailer park near Palm Springs. It was there that I perfected my swimming ability in the warm pool.

Compared with the rest of my life, the time in the desert was wonderful. My parents seemed to like each other better out there so I was happy. Still I worried a lot about their getting a divorce. A few years earlier, after one of their ugliest fights, I made Daddy promise that he would never divorce Mommy. He cuddled me and promised, "Donnie, I will never leave your mother, and I certainly will never leave you." I knew he would never leave me.

Once before, when I was in third grade, they separated for a short time. Dad rented an apartment, moved me in with him and called me "the lady of the house." I hated that. It was hard trying to cook dinner and I missed Mommy and Sandy. So I was very much relieved when my parents got back together and seemed happy with each other.

On the way home from these idyllic weekends at the trailer, we'd drive down the Hollywood Freeway through Los Angeles, listening to the Jack Benny Show or George

Burns and Gracie Allen on the radio. I would lay my head in my mother's lap while she stroked my forehead and I'd day-dream, sun-burned, tired and happy from swimming in the sun. I dreamed of that wonderful pool.

I liked the feel of my mother's cool fingers against my sun-burned brow. It felt so nice. What would I be when I grew up? Would I be a radio celebrity like Gracie Allen? No, she acted too dumb. A pharmacist like Big Ray's mother, Lydia? Maybe. A mother? Yes, I would be a mother. Maybe a famous swimmer like Esther Williams...I drifted to sleep, smiling contentedly, visualizing all the laps I had done in the swimming pool.

Spring 1954
Culver City

Dad began to teach Sandy and me his distorted views of
the world very early, attempting to shape our beliefs about
the meaning of life and women's place in it to suit his own
purposes.

It began when Dad taught us about Darwin and evolution. We took field trips to the Museum of Natural History
to see fossils. We saw ape-like Cro-Magnon men and women
and compared their skulls with the skulls of modern people.
Dad explained that human beings were simply animals who
had not evolved far from the cave.

"I decided long ago to allow myself anything that dogs do,"
he told me more than once.

Exhibits showing the life of frogs, from their tadpole beginnings to their walk on land, was clear evidence of how
things evolved. I was fascinated with the lungfish, which
made itself a papery cocoon for the dry season. It would lie
still in the cocoon, breathing through a lung-like structure,
until the rainy season returned. Then when a lake formed
on top, it would be set free. I often thought about that little
fish. Perhaps I, too, could be set free some day if I could just
keep still long enough.

We went to the La Brea Tar Pits near Maymie and Big
Ray's house and saw bones of dinosaurs that had roamed
through their neighborhood long before there were people
on earth. By the age of ten I was proud to be an expert on
evolution, and convinced that humans were merely animals
at the top of the evolutionary ladder.

After we learned about evolution, our lessons began in
earnest. While Mom was at opera rehearsal several nights

each week, Dad taught us that there was no God. He read
Robert Ingersoll's arguments against the possibility of a Su-
preme Being and expected us to discuss and support them
with our own thinking in the nights to follow. It seemed
logical to me. Indeed, how could there be a God? I could not
see God.

Then came Bible lessons. Dad told us how ridiculous it
was to believe God created the Earth and its inhabitants in
six days — after all, we already knew about evolution. And
how could those old Biblical heroes live for centuries beget-
ting all those offspring? And what about a talking serpent?
How dumb!

Dad explained that religion was to keep the miserable, ig-
norant lower classes in line; it was the "opiate of the masses."
Of course I could not know he was quoting Karl Marx. He
never let us forget that Mom's grandfather had been an Evan-
gelical minister, which proved the ignorance of her family.

Then Dad would turn right around and teach us the Ten
Commandments, stressing "Honor thy father." He told us
that Eve was created from Adam's rib and her purpose was
to serve Adam. Sandy and I learned that women were inferior and that we were on earth for the convenience of men.
We were to understand that we were "lucky to be alive,"
especially me. He told me over and over that my mom's
parents wanted her to get an abortion when she was pregnant with me because she was so young, but he had fought
and saved me. I owed him my life.

Our lessons went on for years. Besides learning that the
world's religions and values were nonsense, we heard in
great detail about South Sea Islanders who were superior to
us because they did not subscribe to incest taboos. Dad
explained that it was necessary to teach young female children of the tribe all about sexual practices so they would be
good wives. He taught us that it was necessary for girls to
make themselves worthy of men. He even read us the pas-

sage in the Bible over and over about daughters who filled the father with wine and lay with him to save his seed.

My father controlled our bodies, minds and spirits. As our primary caretaker, he gave us intense affection, but it was combined with brainwashing, abuse and the strict admonition to *never tell*. We lived in fear, under threat of violence. We never knew what form it would take — outbursts of rage, bent-back wrists, abandonment outside in the darkness. We were so ashamed, how could we ever tell anyone what was happening to us? How could we even talk about it with each other? Besides, who would want to help us when we were so dirty, different and disgusting? No, his authority over our lives was complete. There was no higher power.

I wanted so desperately just to be a dear little girl like my friends, to have my parents love me and take care of me. So I pretended everything was all right even though Dad was always getting me off alone, away from Mom and Sandy.

Spring 1955
Culver City

"I can't take it any longer, Ray," Mom said through her tears. "I'm leaving. I'll get an apartment and take the girls with me. You can have Bernie and Cee Cee."

"You can move out for all I care, but Donnie and Sandy are staying with me," Dad thundered back at her. "And quit that sniveling."

I hated it when Mom cried. It made me feel powerless so I just cowered down in the corner of the back seat. We had just turned into our driveway and the car was stopped, but I was too afraid to get out.

Dad was just getting wound up. "I've told you what will happen if you buck me on this," he shouted. "It will be over — your career, your little romance. It's all over if you go against me. Not only that, I will see that your fuckin' boyfriend loses his cushy job, too. I've already hired the best attorney in L.A., and if you want a fight, I'll give you one you'll never forget. I'll have your little ass in a sling."

Mom dissolved into sobs as Dad went on, his voice an octave lower. "I'll take Donnie and Sandy out of the state," he snarled. "You'll never see them again."

From my vantage point in the back seat I could see Mom shrink up against the door of the car, her determination stripped away. Tears were pouring down my cheeks, too, but I didn't dare do anything to stop the fight. I only hoped that Mom wouldn't go.

But finally, she did. Before she left, she explained how much she loved Sandy and me but could not stand Dad's insistence on having Bernie and Cee Cee. She told me she had a room for us girls in her new apartment and hoped we would come often. She'd rented right across the street from our junior high to make it easy for us to see her. I had helped her find the apartment, but all along I kept reassuring myself that she would not really go. There was still time for her to change her mind.

I was frightened and ashamed about our family's breaking up but would not have dreamed of telling her. Instead, I did my best to comfort her. She always seemed unhappy and I never wanted to add to that. My role was not to make waves.

"Don't worry, Mommy," I reassured her. "Sandy and I will be all right."

"Are you sure, Donnie?" she asked over and over as if she needed permission.

I put on my best adult act for her. "Of course, Mom. You know I can cook and clean. And we can see you after school. It will be just fine."

I told her this, but I wasn't sure at all. How could I get along without her? How could she leave me?

The last day Mom ever lived with us inevitably arrived and it was awful. I awoke with my stomach in a tight clump, remembering this was the last morning we would ever be a family. I took a deep breath, put on a happy face and went out to the kitchen where she was packing boxes.

"Oh, Donnie, I'm glad you are up." She sparkled with excitement. I could feel a new aura of energy around her.

"Good morning, Mom. So this is the big day." I used my cheery grown-up voice to conceal how scared I felt.

"Would you hurry and get dressed? The movers will be here around noon and I still have so many boxes to pack. Would you be a dear and pitch in?"

"Yeah, sure," I mumbled, aware that my bravado was slipping. Helping her pack was the last thing in the world I wanted to do. In my heart I wished she would unpack everything and stay. I took one last look around before everything changed. The old-fashioned upright piano Mom had inherited from her mother was flanked by a green print sofa and our new black-and-white TV set. Dad's green plastic lounge chair stood on a pretty wool area rug.

The kitchen was cheery and clean, a pretty blue room that Mom had painted. She had selected a darker blue for the spindly chairs and table from a secondhand store, creating the illusion of a set. I had been comfortable in this little house — it was so much homier than our place at the beach. Now what would happen? Sandy and I were used to taking care of ourselves, but with Mom leaving to start her new life, who would make us beautiful Easter baskets? Give us hugs?

I couldn't blame her for leaving Dad, though. I was old enough to understand why she couldn't stand having Bernie around because she was always getting pregnant. I remembered how upset Mom had been the night Bernie flopped down on our green sofa just a year before, huge with another baby, telling Dad it was time. She and Dad left together and came back a few days later without the baby. They said it was a beautiful boy and they'd given him up for adoption. I wondered whether they would have given the baby away if it had been another girl put on this earth to serve men. And I always wondered where my baby brother might be.

Then a few months later Bernie got pregnant again. This time Dad and Sandy drove her to Tijuana for an abortion. They brought her back to our house and I put fresh sheets on the couch so Bernie could sleep there for a few days to recuperate. Mom was furious with Dad that time and screamed about Bernie's bleeding on our couch.

But the worst fight they ever had was when Mom's diaphragm was missing. She told me the story over and over again, apparently having trouble believing it herself.

"Donnie, when I asked your dad where it was, he just looked at me with an insolent smile on his face. All he could say was, 'Well, you didn't want me to get Bernie pregnant again, did you?' I don't know how I'll ever forgive him."

I brought my mind back to the present and began to help Mom pack. I never knew what to do about the problems my parents had — there was no way to help.

The movers came and loaded everything onto the van except Dad's green chair, the TV set and our beds and dressers. We could hear our voices echoing around the empty rooms. Mom went off to start her new life and after she left, my heart felt empty, too. Deep inside I was afraid of living with Dad without Mom around.

In the year after Mom's move, Sandy and I used to sit together in the big green lounge chair watching the Mouse-keteers and waiting for Dad. He had a job as a design engineer now with an aerospace company down in El Segundo, and even though he always got home promptly at 5:30, the afternoons stretched out endlessly. Mom lived close to our school but it was a long bus ride from our house so we didn't see her very often.

I decided to cover up my embarrassment about my parents' divorce by not telling anyone. I knew I could keep this secret — it was just another secret, another part of me I could never share with anyone. If people knew the real truth about me, I knew I'd never have a single friend.

I was especially careful to keep the truth from Leanne. Her friendship meant so much to me. I don't think I would have done so well without the fun, companionship and protection she offered me, and the safe oasis of her home.

I spent at least two nights a week with Leanne, mostly at her house. Once when I accidentally broke a Johnny Mathis album belonging to a friend of her mother's, Leanne saw how frightened I was and decided to take the blame herself. I was amazed to find that someone cared enough to stand up for me.

"What can they do to me?" she asked. She was confident and bold.

I was startled at the question. She wasn't afraid of punishment at all, but I knew so much about it that it petrified

me. We ended up paying for the record but were not really
in trouble. Leanne's mother was understanding and treated
us like responsible human beings. I decided that if I ever had
children, I wanted to be just like Leanne's mother.

Leanne and I became the closest of friends and as we
rounded that difficult corner into adolescence, we shared
secrets — at least, Leanne told me all of her secrets. She
was sensitive and tender-hearted, loving and good, and cried
more easily than I. But then I seldom cried at all. I longed to
tell her everything but I knew how serious my secrets were.

We did talk about boys, though. That was the most exciting topic of all! We discussed who was "cute" and how exciting it would be to wear one-inch heels at junior high
graduation. We could hardly wait. As our girlish giggles and
guesses about boys, kissing, and dating inevitably became
more grown-up, I pretended to be just as innocent as she
was. I had to be very careful to follow her lead so I would
sound like a normal adolescent.

On July 15, Leanne and I went with her parents to spend
a week with friends of theirs down on the Palos Verdes
peninsula. It was beautiful there in the hills overlooking the
Pacific. However, there wasn't much for us girls to do, so our
host, who was a Boy Scout leader, invited his whole troop
over to meet us. Leanne and I were beside ourselves, nervous
and giggly all day. A whole troop of boys coming to meet us!

One by one they arrived. One in particular, Kenny Friess,
was very special. I was drawn to him the moment I saw his
handsome face and solid body through the glass of the door.
He was dressed immaculately in a fresh white button-down
shirt and dark cotton slacks and had a short up-to-the-min-
ute haircut. I was usually talkative and funny, but suddenly
got silent with this serious-minded boy. My mouth went dry,
my face felt hot, and I worried that he might not like me.
What if he could tell what my father did to me? That I didn't
have a normal family? I couldn't bear it if he thought I was
awful. He was the most handsome boy I had ever seen.

We all had a pleasant afternoon drinking Cokes and getting to know one another. That night when I was alone with Leanne, I spun around and around and flopped on the bed.

"Lee, isn't he cute? Did you notice how strong his arms are? Wasn't he funny when he said, 'What are we all going to do? Just sit around and listen to each other breathe?' Wasn't he clever? Isn't he just adorable?"

"Donna, I've never seen you like this before." Leanne could hardly get a word in edgewise.

"He's so neat! I'm really shook." But Leanne wasn't listening any more. She had fallen asleep, leaving me with only a tankful of tropical fish to share my silent thoughts of Kenny Friess.

As days went on, my thoughts stayed focused on Ken. I could not eat or sleep. Our friend's mother noticed my condition and delighted in teasing, "The love bug's bitten you and you can't hold still."

I laughed with her hoping everyone would pass it off as some kid stuff. But I knew better, knew something powerful and real had happened in my life. It was scary and exhilarating. *And as it happened, I never did get over it.*

When we got back I could hardly wait to tell Dad.

"I'm going to die, Daddy! I know it. I'm so gone, I can't even eat!"

"Huh? Honey, slow down and tell me all about this boy. I couldn't get it all from your phone call the other night, you were talking so fast." Daddy's words were laced with curiosity and approval.

"Oh, Daddy! He is so cute!" My words danced out of me.

"So tell me! Tell me everything."

"Well, he is just so neato and perfect. The right everything. I love his arms. They are real muscley and he smells so good." I paused for a moment. "Maybe I could send him a funny birthday card or something."

Daddy smiled over at me. "Honey, you know they talk about puppy love and kind of make fun of kids and their crushes, but I fell crazy in love with your mother in the sixth grade. I think puppy love is very real."

I grinned at Daddy. "Do you really? You don't think I'm goofy? I feel silly being so excited about a boy I've only known for one week. Besides that, he shakes me up so much, I can hardly even talk to him. I think he's shy, too." I paused. "It's so fabulous to be alive."

"Donnie, trust your instincts. Do you feel all light-headed? Does he make your breath go away?"

"Oh my gosh! I can't even breathe around him!"

"Just go slow, you have all the time in the world. Choosing a mate will be the most important decision you'll ever make."

"Oh, Daddy. I'm not even allowed to date for two years. I'm not looking for a husband!"

"You never know!" He turned to look at me. His eyes were serious. "Donnie, you are the single most wonderful thing that ever happened to me. I want the best for you. Now tell me all the rest." Daddy's voice was warm with enthusiasm. As I talked nonstop, he listened to every single word I had to say. Daddy made me feel very special at times like this, never young or silly. He had a way of showing me that my ideas mattered. He seemed as thrilled about Kenny as I was, and I was relieved that he didn't seem jealous.

It was always Dad who was so interested in my friends and what they were doing, all my assignments at school and my plans for the future. It was always Dad.

Spring 1956
Venice Beach

The year after Mom left, Dad and Sandy and I moved
back to the beach house. The State of California had purchased our home in Culver City because they needed the
land for the San Diego Freeway, which was about to be built
right through our living room.

Once the three of us moved back to the beach, Daddy
took time to give Sandy and me a lot of attention. He was
concerned that we completed our homework, knew how
machinery operated and how cultures evolved. There were
wonderful days when his eyes shone with love for us. When
he was happy, the whole world seemed to smile and I felt
warm and safe.

When he was in a terrible mood, though, it was a very
serious matter. To "cross him," as he liked to put it, was for
"sorry sisters," and the punishments were always more severe than the crime. To violate his routines or question his
authority was to get into trouble. We had to wait on him
without hesitation and follow his orders exactly. If he demanded a glass of water with cracked ice, we knew that
water with uncracked ice cubes would be thrown back in
our faces. When Dad told us to rub his back or draw his
bath, we did as he asked. We knew that the bath water must
be exactly the correct temperature or there would be a violent outburst. Once he threw a book and hit me in the eye.
His rages were frequent and frightening. Then they'd sub-
side and he'd be friendly again. We were kept off balance by
his unpredictable Jekyll and Hyde personality.

He seemed to enjoy being a father and even liked cooking
pots of spaghetti for our dinner night after night. We loved
it when he made his specialty, mashed potato ice cream

cones. At times, though, he'd be preoccupied, lying naked in his bed for hours with nothing but a sheet covering him, writing novels in longhand. He was writing a murder mystery and had certain books he referred to frequently. *How To Commit Murder And Get Away With It* was usually lying open at his side, and it had graphic pictures of mutilated bodies in it, which felt like an unspoken threat.

When I got frightened or angry, I'd try to remember how sweet he could be, like the time he got me my bike.

One Friday night I heard him calling my name before he even got into the house. He sounded very excited. I went running to the door, not sure what to expect.

"What is it, Dad?"

He was grinning. "See for yourself, Donnie."

He pointed to a bicycle propped against the wall of the house. It was a sleek racing bike with those thin tires.

"Daddy, oh, Daddy!" I squealed in disbelief. "Is this for me? My very own grown-up bike?"

"It's not yours yet, but it will be. Tomorrow I'm going to rig up the compressor and paint it so it will look brand new."

"What color, Dad?"

"Any color you like, Sweetheart. You've been talking about a big bike for a long time now and I want you to be happy with it. I'll paint it any color at all."

"Red! I want red!" I didn't have to think about it. This was the bike of my dreams.

"You got it." His smile came from deep in his heart as I threw my arms around his neck.

My shiny red bike was ready by Saturday noon and it was beautiful. I felt like a princess riding it up and down the street, and Dad enjoyed my riding it as much as I did.

Despite his many faults, he had that rare ability to play with children at their own level, and we had many good times. When he took us to Disneyland, he was nothing like those stodgy parents who browsed the shops. No, he went on every ride with us and had as much fun as we did. It got a little awkward as we got older and Sandy and I took our friends with us. We wanted to explore on our own and check out the boys, but I felt guilty if we did not include Dad. He seemed so lost if he could not go on the rides with us.

Summer 1956
Venice Beach

I had always taken day trips and weekend trips with Dad, but that summer after Mom left, we traveled even more. Maymie often came with us and helped pay the tab. I missed my grandfather a lot, but Maymie didn't seem to mind leaving him behind.

Even though I was too young to have a license, Dad insisted that I do a lot of the driving, and I enjoyed steering our new convertible down the highway, the breeze whipping through my hair. Sometimes he'd have Maymie drive and he'd pull me close to him under a blanket in the back seat, where he'd have his fly unzipped. I hated that! I was so embarrassed, I thought I'd die if my grandmother saw my hand working under that blanket. Part of me wished she would notice, stop the car and insist that Dad stop it right now. But she never did.

We'd had a good two-week trip to the Seattle World's Fair, and I was at the wheel, driving south toward home, happily inhaling the rich scent of the forest as we approached Olympia, Washington. Dad, who was napping alone in back, muttered something about stopping at the brewery. Maymie and I looked at each other and decided to keep going. We had a standing rule that the driver was the boss of stops and breaks. But fifteen minutes past the brewery, Dad looked up, realized I had disobeyed him and all hell broke loose.

"Pull over, you shithead," he yelled at me. "I said to stop at the brewery."

I eased the car to a stop at the shoulder.

"Get out. Get in the back seat," he commanded in a rage.

I did as he ordered and Maymie got in the back with me. Dad took the wheel and angrily headed back to the brewery, screaming and yelling all the way.

"I'm putting you on the next plane home. You are no good, you worthless piece of shit. You're not worth the time I spend on you. You disobedient little asshole, I'm not going to stand for this." There was no end to his fury.

"Now, Junior, you don't mean that," Maymie soothed, trying to rescue me from his verbal barrage. It did no good.

I cried quietly in Maymie's lap, my face buried in her soft cotton skirt.

As Dad pulled into the Olympia brewery, his mood shifted. We were going beer tasting.

"Cheer up!" he insisted brightly, the dark clouds of rage gone from his face.

I was furious but knew I must pretend to be over the humiliation he had piled on me, or I would be in deeper trouble. I stuffed my feelings, took a deep breath and pretended that I was okay. I often wondered how I managed to hide the hot coals of my anger, where it went to simmer quietly. Were there dark, smouldering recesses in my soul? It was a terrifying thought.

Dad used our tiny house trailer for our frequent automobile excursions. He would hitch the trailer to the back of the Ford and we would be off. Mostly it was the four of us, Maymie, Sandy, Dad and me. Sandy was a good driver, too, though she was even younger than I, and we could both maneuver the trailer around easily. I was in charge of cooking and could turn out a full meal in a matter of minutes. Maymie and Dad would rave about my breakfasts for miles, which made me feel proud.

These trips were Maymie's chance to teach us something about behaving like ladies, a cause that was very close to her heart. She helped Sandy and me dress up to attend high tea at the most beautiful hotel in Vancouver and took us to the legitimate theater where we saw Mary Martin swinging through the air as Peter Pan. Some of the greatest highlights of our youth were these motor trips and Maymie's treats.

Maymie was famous for her thrift, and Sandy and I laughed about her eccentricities. She was very well off but pinched every penny she could, even re-using Christmas cards by sticking labels over the signatures of last year's senders. Once she bought defective bargain gloves with no thumbs, and we giggled for months, whispering to each other that we must have a terrible birth defect because we were born with too many fingers. Maymie had given each of us one sterling silver antique spoon every Christmas, and when we elbowed each other and rolled our eyes about "another old spoon," she was quick to reassure us that some-day we would thank her.

On our trips she made sure we understood their value. She took us to visit the most exclusive shops where she taught us about sterling silver patterns and the difference between England's bone china and fine French Limoges porcelain. She mesmerized me with her knowledge of beau-tiful things.

"Girls," she would begin, "you know the European mon-archs were so desperate to own hard paste porcelain after Marco Polo brought it back from China in the late 1200s that they tried for 500 years to discover the secret Chinese formula. The English even used the ash from actual bones to create a type of fine china, which is why they call it bone china."

At other times she would tell us of elegant clothes.

"When I was about 14, your age, Donna, your grandfather bought me the most gorgeous white ermine coat you could ever imagine. I was the envy of my school chums in it. It held up wonderfully over the years."

Maymie had gumption. She was inspirational, educational, bold and fun. In our quiet times when it was just Maymie and me, she would talk about her childhood and describe lovely ladies in our family from another era, a time when gracious living was of paramount importance. Then she would mention the time she was sold, but I didn't understand what she meant.

Years later that kernel of information was to fall into place in a hideous puzzle that covered more than 100 years of history of the aristocratic Landis family.

Fall 1957
Venice High School

By the time high school started I was beginning to show characteristics of my future self. I had begun to blossom into womanhood. I'd had orthodontia and now had beautiful straight teeth. My blonde pony tail, smooth complexion and newly developing figure made boys turn their heads. My confidence soared. I enrolled in the college prep courses at my father's direction and settled down in my classes determined to earn an A average.

Kenny and I stayed in touch, and he was on my mind all the time. We were too shy to talk to each other on the telephone, and too far apart to see each other easily, so we had to settle for a letter-writing friendship.

Leanne and I were still best friends and we ate lunch together every day with our group of friends from junior high. I was the only one taking college prep courses.

When Leanne's mother saw my list of classes, she discouraged me from taking them. She had convinced Leanne to take shorthand and insisted that I have something practical, too. I stood up for myself. I was going to college. By now I was determined and was not going to waiver from my path.

When I turned fifteen-and-a-half, Dad gave me a one-year-old Ford Victoria. It was a dashing car, much more elaborate than many of my friends' parents' cars. It embarrassed me to drive it, especially with the fuss that my friends made to their own parents. Still, Dad insisted that I use it.

"Donnie, you need this car for your self-esteem. You've had some strange messages about who you are, living in beatnik Venice and coming from a divorce. You're the aristocracy and I don't want you to forget it. Yours is the nicest car in the whole family."

I soon found out, however, that this car, with its pay-ments, insurance and maintenance, was yet another way in which my father would control me. The car allowed me to pick up Sandy from junior high so that we could sell the remaining merchandise from our grandfather's pharmacy. The stock and fixtures were moved to a new location and we started a sundry store. My grandfather had finally re-tired to his checkers, and Sandy and I, at 14 and 15 years of age, were in charge.

Our new location in the heart of colorful, offbeat Venice attracted some strange characters. It was not unusual to look into the face of a long-haired, drugged-out man staring through the store windows at us. We learned quickly how to ignore these characters, but it was still scary. We had no gun or protection of any kind and hoped to stay safe by perfecting an "all business" demeanor.

Sandy and I opened the store each day after school for the next two years. We sold sodas, newspapers, candies and what was left of the stock of stationery, cologne and over-the-counter remedies. Most days we had few customers. We made cheese sandwiches in the back room for dinner, then closed the store at 9:00 p.m., drove home and organized our clothes for the next day of school. I would fall asleep ex-hausted, praying to be left alone.

The hard work was not as bad as the low income, personal danger and the demanding schedule. Behind the counter of that store on summer Sundays, I wished with all my heart that I could be one of the carefree, happy beach-goers I saw driving down the street in their colorful convertibles.

Dad would tell us in his professorial tone how much we were learning from running the store.

"Do you realize, girls, that you are learning to manage a real retail operation? Do this right and you'll make big bucks. Way more than someone in a stupid Junior Achieve-ment program."

Sandy and I thought we were living a nightmare. The summer before, he had made us clear sand from the back of his new lot at the beach for six hours a day. We were small girls — I was only 5 foot 3 inches tall and weighed in at 120 pounds, and Sandy was smaller — but my biceps grew so large that the boys made fun of me, and I was furious when I saw a backhoe on a nearby lot move as much sand in an afternoon as we had moved all summer.

Now this year Dad decided we would begin actual construction on the oceanfront house which was to become our permanent home. The three of us would build it ourselves. Sandy and I had to jackhammer out the thick round pilings on the lot and pour the cement foundation into Dad's home-made forms. Crudely constructed, they practically exploded under the pressure of tons of liquid grey cement pumped into them, and we ended up using hundreds of pounds of cement more than we needed. It was a mess!

"Daddy, we need to talk to you," I said hesitantly. Sandy stood next to me, quietly, letting me take the lead.

"Daddy, this is just too much!" I insisted. "I go to school all day and it's hard for me this year, especially chemistry. I go pick up Sandy. I work in the store. I can't do all of this. I don't want to build the house!"

Caught up in my own argument, I continued, my confidence and determination growing. "I really want to spend some time with Leanne, and Kenny keeps coming by the store on Sundays on his way to go surfing. He asked if I could go with him sometime."

My father just lay there, clenching his jaw as he often did when he was angry. Finally he spit out, "Are you defying me? We're going to damn well build this fucking house whether you like it or not. I've got too much money and time invested to let some chicken-livered kids stop me now. We're going to build this house and that's all there is to it."

His tone then changed from fury to sarcasm. "If you don't like it, you can leave right now. Do you have somewhere to go? How about moving in with your mother? All of you jammed into her one-bedroom apartment. She'd love that, wouldn't she? And you, young lady, could try walking again. What about college? Forget that! You'll have to work at J.C. Penney's."

I breathed deeply and tried to hold my ground. "It's too hard, Daddy. I can't do all of this. My throat is sore all the time. My tonsils always have white spots on them. I'm getting behind in chemistry."

He yelled and threatened some more, and in the end I had to give up. I could never win. In retribution he took away the Standard Oil credit card that I used to buy gas for all the errands he sent me on. He said that I would have to use my own money from now on. I never got the gas card back. Our punishment for challenging his authority was to have our labor tied into our pocketbooks. We were not allowed to work for anyone but the family. Our sporadic small allowances were now abolished, and extra cash for personal items disappeared. Now the only way to get money for clothes and necessities was to work for him.

We built that house, every square inch of it.

1958
Venice High School

I often came home from a study date in high school to find Dad waiting to rush me to the construction site to help him with something.

One night he'd found a plumbing leak and took me to the job site at 11:30 p.m. He needed two people to run the water. We did the plumbing tests, found several more leaks and spent the next few hours getting pipes ready for the inspector who was coming in the morning. There was no sleeping that night. I went home in the morning, cleaned up and went right to school.

My grandparents' beach house, which had no garage, did not have much storage for building materials. The tiny cottage was filled with a boxed toilet, sinks, a tub, pipes and pieces of metal. Dad's huge bed dominated the living room. Sandy and I had beds shoved into the corners. I knew that the house looked too weird to have anyone over.

It was during this time, while we were living at the beach house, that my father made me go into the bathroom with him. He locked the door behind us.

"No, Dad, no...," I protested.

"I just want to see you. To see if you have something," he responded.

"No!" I knew what this meant. I felt the fierce anger flood me.

This same conversation continued for several more minutes. Then he gave up. I couldn't believe he actually gave up. At first it seemed like a miracle. Then he handed me a paper bag containing a small bottle.

"Donnie, I'm so sorry, but you might have something called crabs. Here is the medicine to kill them if you do have them."

Horror filled me as it never had before. "Leave!" I yelled as I slammed the door to the bathroom shut again and locked myself in.

I sat on the floor, took off my Capri pants and my panties and examined my privates. They looked like little brown freckles, but they had legs. Legs! I thought I would die. I wanted to lock myself up in a closet or run away. I had always felt ugly and dirty and disgusting, but this was proof of it.

I hated my father at that moment, but I also depended on him for everything. I did not know what to do, so I turned the hate on myself. I prayed that I would magically disappear. I would just walk into the ocean and never come out. My chin began to quiver.

Then for the first time I felt a gentle voice coming from inside of me, silently saying, *You'll be okay. You'll be okay. Don't lose control.* I did not believe that voice. The quiver inside grew into a quake and a horrible cry escaped from me. I curled myself into a half-naked ball on the floor. My head was pushed between the toilet and the tub. The tears came then, the stored flood of a lifetime. I hurt so badly, way deep inside. I cried and it scared me to cry. I never cried.

After a long time I sensed the same loving voice inside of me again: *Donna, you'll be all right. I'll take care of you.* It was soothing and gentle. Finally my crying stopped.

Get up now, Donna. Get up. You'll be okay. I promise you...

As the weeks passed I applied the smelly purple medicine to the crabs. Eventually the infestation was dead, but pushing all of those powerful ugly feelings down was getting more difficult.

I wanted to get away from my father's house more than I wanted anything else in my life. Each lesson I learned, each paper I wrote, each exam I passed, brought me closer and closer to the day I would finally be free. That helped give me the determination to keep on working. I was not going to let my father ruin my life. Somehow it would become normal. The gentle voice inside kept telling me it would be all right, and I began to have faith in it. Perhaps it was actually faith in myself.

Our house on Ocean Front Walk was finished at last and we moved in. Dad still had his bed in the living room but Sandy and I each had our own bedroom now. That didn't stop Dad from bothering me, though. If anything, he was at me more often, forcing his way into my bedroom at night. I would always feign sleep, and if that didn't work, I would kick and bite and try to fight him off. I bought a lock but he removed it. I never won a battle, but still I kept fighting, hoping he would leave me alone.

While he was making me feel filthy and bad at night, Dad never lost an opportunity to tell me how important it was to be a good girl where the boys were concerned.

I was not allowed to date until my 16th birthday and then only boys Dad approved of. There was a boy named Don in one of my classes whom I liked very much. He was bright and athletic looking, and as the semester progressed our friendship accelerated to the point where he asked me out. I was ecstatic! He was funny and handsome, and he liked me.

I had turned 16 at last and was finally invited on a date. I went home on cloud nine.

"Daddy, that boy in my Spanish class, Don, the one I like, asked me to go to the movies with him next Saturday night. I want to go, but I told him I would tell him tomorrow."

"Donnie, I've told you I don't want you going to those Venice High dances or going out with those boys," he reprimanded me.

"Dad, he's a nice boy. I've known him all year. We're just going to a movie," I pleaded.

"What does his dad do?" sneered my father.

"He is a heavy equipment operator. He works for the state building freeways. Don has a nice car and nice clothes," I argued.

"Donna, I have told you hundreds of times. You are not going to go out with any boys who are going to be truck drivers. We are the gentry. You must only date boys who are going to college."

"Dad, he's a very nice boy. This is ridiculous!" My tone was angry. "I don't know any boys who are going to college. I like Don. I want to go out with him. It's only to the movies," I wailed.

"Absolutely not!"

"Why not?" I continued to argue. This was important to me. I could feel my temper rising to the surface. I knew his reasoning was not logical.

"Because he is not of your social class!" he countered.

"So what is so big about my social class? Is it this mansion we live in? Is it all the money you make? Is it the staff we have running that stupid store we slave away in? Is it your illegitimate child? Or Mom's job in the park? Or Bernie checking groceries at Safeway? Why do you think Don isn't good enough for me to go to the movies with?"

There was no reply. Dad stopped arguing and walked away. The discussion was over. Though I still was not permitted to go out with Don, I felt that I had somehow pushed Dad back, out of my life.

There were many instances when he would not allow me to have my own feelings or any control over my own life. I felt powerless, frustrated and furious. My feelings were so strong I was afraid of the anger I kept buried inside.

I had moments when I wished my father were dead. I shoved these intense feelings down, disgusting feelings I had about what Dad did to me and about those crabs, about all of it, since my memory began. My real thoughts and feelings were more than too horrible to deal with, so I pretended that I was okay.

Guilt overwhelmed me and I felt like a bad daughter when I let myself think that Dad was not the all-American good-guy he pretended to be, the Dad everyone else believed he was. My mind would banish these bad thoughts and replace them with memories of all the time Dad spent teaching me and helping me with my homework. I thought of how caring and sweet he could be sometimes.

Who was I to question my father? I put on a bright smile, a positive attitude and counted my blessings. After all, I was healthy, attractive, intelligent, strong, capable and adored by my whole family. I worked very hard to convince myself that this was all true.

To help compensate for my bad feelings, I demanded perfection from myself. I seldom missed a day of school, made sure that my papers were perfect, my grades were perfect, my behavior was perfect. Only when I was perfect did I feel acceptable.

Leanne's dad was part of my fantasy about having a normal family. He was the busy president of an aircraft factory and could spend far less time with his children than my dad, but I could tell that he was concerned about me. He seemed especially upset one day when I was leaving their house and the tire on my car went flat a few houses down the street. I went back and used her phone to call Dad for help. He berated me, "Jesus Christ, Donna. If you are going to have a goddam fucking car, you will damn well change the tire yourself."

"Yes, Daddy." I was so upset by his response that tears welled in my eyes. "Lee's dad is here and he'll help me change it. I'll be home in about 25 minutes."

"You will goddam well do it yourself. I will not have you inconveniencing Leanne's father because your tire is flat. You will change your own tire or you will walk, young lady. Don't you dare cross me on this!" He hung up.

The tears rolled down my face. Leanne and her parents had not seen me cry in the seven years they had known me. It was humiliating. What hurt just as much was the silent sympathy they showed me.

"C'mon troops!" Leanne's dad spoke up kindly, trying to change the mood. He steered the two of us out the front door.

"But, Frank, my dad told me to change it myself. I know how. It's okay. I really only called him because I knew that I would be late. I didn't want to get into trouble."

"You're my other daughter, remember?" He walked us to the car, one hand affectionately guiding each of us by our necks. "It'll just take a few minutes. You can help." His tone was reassuring.

Frank changed the tire while Lee and I looked on silently. I knew that Leanne's father respected me. He often praised me for being a "good Joe." It was strange and wonderful to have him defy my dad to help and protect me. Yet the entire incident embarrassed me. For the first time, I knew they had seen the reality of my life.

September 1959
Santa Monica High School
Santa Monica, California

I transferred to Santa Monica High School where I entered as a junior. Sandy had just graduated from junior high
and signed up at "Samohi," too.

Things were definitely looking up. I would finally be allowed to date and go to school parties. I joined a girls' service
club and was instantly involved in a new life of friends and
activities. The horrible recent burden of construction and
carpentry had been lifted from our young shoulders.

Sandy and I did well in school. At home we did what we
were told, ran the sundry store and always acted like young
ladies, just as our father demanded. We worked very hard at
being perfect, and in many ways we did very well indeed.

My grades allowed me to graduate a semester early and I
was honored as a California Gold Sealbearer at graduation.
I had earned an A average every semester of high school.
For some students this award might have been expected,
but for me it was a great achievement.

It was great, not only because I had so many other re-
sponsibilities, but because it showed me for the first time in
my life that I could accomplish whatever I set out to do. It
meant everything to me.

Fall 1960
Santa Monica City College
Santa Monica

After high school, my father decided I should attend Santa Monica City College, a junior college just a few miles from home. I had no idea that my grades qualified me for a scholarship to almost any university I could have chosen to attend. I worked hard at SMCC and became Associated Student Body Vice President, Miss Spindrift Princess, Woman of the Year and was an honor student, while I worked 20 hours per week at a park teaching charm classes to young girls.

I kept dating Ken on and off, though the long distance we had to travel to see each other kept our romance cool. Ken was still the only boy I had ever really been in love with, but our inconsistent relationship kept me from letting my guard down. We both dated other people, and I wasn't really sure how he felt about me.

In spring of the next year when school was out, Maymie invited me to accompany her on a six-week tour of the South Pacific aboard the *Mariposa*, a luxury cruise liner. It was the best trip I had ever taken.

Before we left, Maymie sat me down for our "ground rules of the trip" talk.

"Dear, you know how people always take you for my daughter because you favor me so? Well, I want you to pretend to be my daughter, not my granddaughter. I just don't want to give away my age."

"But, Maymie, what if people ask about me? What do I say if they ask if I have a sister? Are you going to tell them that you have a son? Is Dad to be my brother?" I felt overwhelmed by the deceit. What if Big Ray found out? How many secrets did my family have to have anyway?

"People don't ask that many questions. Just follow my lead. You will be my only child."

I knew that we would be dining with the same eight people for all of our meals during the six-week trip. I paused as the enormity of trying to keep this secret sank into my brain. What if I slipped up? Six weeks was a long time.

"It seems like they will still want to know about us. What if they ask about my family? What am I to say?"

"It won't be a problem. Just follow my lead and smile a lot," she concluded.

She was right. It was no problem at all. I had been so well-schooled in the art of pretending, I could carry off our little charade easily.

My grandmother loved to dance, so did I, and we became known as the "dancing Landises." The cruise ship was filled with older, retired travelers, so my young-looking grandmother and I especially enjoyed the attentions of the ship's officers and other passengers. As a young single woman, I was bombarded with attention. I won dance contests and costume parades, swam, studied, played and attended ship-style horse races. What a memorable trip!

During the cruise I saw the adult world from a new perspective. This was the first time I was included in adult activities as an equal, and it was shocking when one of the handsome middle-aged ship's officers told me in some detail about his vasectomy. It did not take much sophistication on my part to understand where the conversation was headed. Later that evening he asked if I would come see his exotic fish in his state room. I just smiled and said no. Later I saw him leave with an attractive middle-aged woman. I had talked to her on deck and knew she was married.

The adult world seemed to be fueled by a free flow of alcohol. By the fourth week at sea, I had become fairly friendly with the women at our table. For weeks they had made jokes about alcohol. In fact they started a chant which they repeated before dinner, while the champagne was poured: "Alcohol's the only way!" I frequently visited with them during the day in the library or around the swimming pool. On one particular evening, our table companions held a pre-dinner cocktail party that Maymie and I attended. We left early, but they all continued to drink. By the time they arrived at our round table in the formal dining room, they were all quite inebriated. Tom, the ship's first officer, and perhaps the most dashing and handsome older man I had ever seen, bobbed his head against his chest, barely able to mutter. Nan, my friend in her 60s, was seated next to me.

After the appetizer and cold soup, Nan's head slumped toward her plate. Her husband, unsteady himself, took her to their stateroom. An officer from an adjoining table came over and helped Tom to his cabin.

Perhaps this was just a typical moment in shipboard life, but it was quite significant to me. I had never seen people out of control like this. Drunk. The respect and admiration I held for Tom and Nan and the others diminished considerably after that night, and they seemed embarrassed to be around Maymie and me as well. Somehow, their jokes about "alcohol's the only way" seemed sadly pathetic and hollow to me. That incident caused me to examine my life and what I wanted out of it even more closely.

I did not want to be 60 and dependent on alcohol to have a good time. I never wanted my head to fall into my plate. I did not want to be married to a man like these men. They had a great deal of trouble relaxing, were impatient for the trip to be over and seemed somehow dissatisfied within themselves.

My ideas about the kind of life I wanted to carve out for myself were becoming even clearer to me, and I began to miss Ken. I'd had a big argument with him before I left on the cruise, and there had been no mail from him waiting at our ports of call. As the days went by, however, I began to look forward to seeing him when our ship returned to Los Angeles.

Summer 1961
Eagle Rock, California

Ken was glad when I got back, and we began to see more
of each other. By the end of summer we were becoming
serious. He was treating me like somebody special, and I
knew I was in love with him.

I remember one of our dates when I drove to Eagle Rock
where Ken was painting houses for the summer. I had bor-
rowed a colorful pants outfit from Mom. It was terrific with
my summer tan.

When I arrived at Ken's modest apartment, we greeted
each other with a companionable hug. I could tell right away
from his expression that he liked what he saw. I did, too. He
was freshly showered and smelled wonderfully of soap and
after-shave. Ken was always neat and clean about his person
and his surroundings, and I admired that.

"What smells so good?" I asked, poking around the stove.

"Ah ha! That eez for me to know and for you to find out!"
He teased in a pitiful imitation Italian accent.

"Nothing is too good for milady. I have prepared un spin-
eech soouffle and roasted cheeken for you," he concluded,
mixing his French and Italian accents. He smiled at me in his
curiously serious manner. Even when he joked, there was a
solemn flavor to it.

"Kenny, dare I look into the refrigerator?" I teased, remembering the dead cat that had resided there the entire
school year before. It had been his anatomy project, part of
a lab requirement for that particular course.

"Ah, my dear. Anything that you please. Tonight zee feline
eez not part of dee dinna menu. So sorry." He had now
mixed Chinese with his French and Italian accents.

I laughed. I was so in love with him. I thought he looked more handsome than ever. Tanned from his outdoor painting job, his heavily muscled arms were covered with sun-bleached hair. He worked diligently to prepare our meal as I set the table. We ate in relative quiet, each of us enjoying the companionship.

Later that evening Ken took me for a walk under the stars of the warm California night. It was fantastically romantic. We hiked the short distance to his college's amphitheater.

We sat on the cement steps, high at the top of the outdoor theater, talked about our future and resumed one of our favorite pastimes, imagining our future children. We dreamed about taking them on the merry-go-round at the Griffith Park Zoo. Ken cuddled me in his arms. I adored him and knew that he cared for me. It was wonderful to be together on this starry night.

After our return walk, we lay quietly on his sofa and held each other. We looked long into each other's eyes. I kissed Ken's face a thousand times with tiny kisses. I kissed his closed eye lids, his ears, his forehead. We held each other as if we could never let go.

We never said so, but we both knew that we wanted more. I held back, always, because I knew that I wanted this "nice" boy, and I wanted to be the kind of girl that he would marry. The hours flew by, and before we knew it, it was time to leave. As I drove the hour home to Venice, my thoughts were filled with Ken. I wanted him as a woman wants the man she hopes someday to marry.

I pulled my car into the driveway and looked carefully around before I got out of the car. This was Venice and it was dangerous. At the door of the house, I put the key into the lock quietly, ever so quietly, and opened the door. I did not want to awaken Dad. I silently tiptoed three steps.

"Donnie!"

Damn! I ignored him. I just wanted to go to bed with thoughts of my dearest, wonderful Kenny.

"Donnie!"

I continued to ignore Dad's calls from the dark living room.

"Donnie!" Finally he got up. He was nude as always. I grunted an unfriendly hello. He reached out to touch me. I pulled angrily away, my mood changing instantly.

"No! I have to go to bed!" My tone was fierce. "I have to get up in the morning. I have to be at work in six hours."

He reached for me again. I pulled away, defiantly on guard. He used his authoritative tone which I hated.

"I need you to take care of me!"

"No, no, no!" I whispered harshly, desperate to be left alone.

"Just help me!" He pleaded, trying a different tack. He went from begging to threatening to hissing.

This went on for a very long time. He would not leave me alone. I had to get some sleep. I had to be at work the next morning.

Oh, dear God, if you are there, please hear me. I prayed. Oh, dear God, please help me. I need your help.

My prayers and arguments did no good. He had been waiting for me, knowing that I had a date with Ken. It seemed to excite him knowing I had been out with my boyfriend. He kept after me, ordering, cajoling, begging and pleading with me.

"No, Daddy, no!" I argued back. I was crying now. "Oh, God, Dad, please leave me alone! I want to be normal. I want to be with Ken. I love Ken."

Still he would not stop. I usually tuned out when he grabbed me and recited to myself his familiar refrain — nice girls respect their dads, nice girls do what they are told. But tonight I was too angry to let him have his way.

Finally, he realized I was not responding to his demands, and he grabbed my right wrist and twisted, his special twist that left no marks. Pain shot through my body. I hated him that night more than I had ever hated him in my life! I was powerless to stop him and I despised him for that, but I would not let him touch my body the way he wanted to. A small victory.

I had to "help him" as he so euphemistically put it. I separated my mind from my left hand. I did the dirty work while I took myself far away where it was safe, to my dream place, where I was normal and everything was finally okay. I dreamed that I would be set free.

September 1962
"The Row" — 28th Street
University of Southern California
Los Angeles

I graduated from Santa Monica City College with honors
and an academic scholarship to the prestigious University of
Southern California. The combination of my scholarship
and money I earned at my recreation job gave me enough to
afford the luxury of belonging to a sorority, an opportunity
that changed my life. My new "sisters" were warm, helpful
and very funny.

Each day when I visited the beautiful colonial home that
was our sorority house, my dreams flourished. I often
dreamed of what it would be like to live there. About six
weeks into the semester, when I visited my new friend
Patty's room, I noticed that the cupboards on the side wall
were empty.

"Why is Laura's cupboard empty?" I asked Patty.

"Didn't you hear? Laura is sick again. She had to drop
out. Her mother came by this morning, took her out of her
classes, bundled up her stuff and they left."

"How long will Laura be out?" I tried to sound calm, but
the whirling sound in my ears and the sudden beating of my
heart were deafening me.

"They don't know for sure. At least for the rest of this
semester."

"So Patty," I tried to appear casual as I asked, "who's going
to take her place for now?"

"Probably no one. All of the girls have dorm contracts.
They can't break them this late in the semester."

"What if I could move in here?" I ventured in careful
tones, suppressing my increasing excitement.

"Donna! Could you? I would die to have you with us. We could be the Five Musketeers. It would be great! I saw our alum advisor this morning. She's downstairs reconciling the house books. Go ask her! Go right now!"

That night after getting the go-ahead from the advisor and finding out the exact amount that it would cost, I approached my father. Dad had made it clear that I was to live at home. I knew I would be in for a major battle.

When all of my high school honor society friends went "away to college" to Cornell, Purdue, Cal or Stanford, there was never a glimmer of hope for me. Never in all the years of talking about college did we discuss my living on campus. I knew I had to choose my words carefully, knew my speech to him must be the best that I had ever made because so much hinged on it. As a speech major, I had begun to learn the importance of audience analysis. I understood the art of persuasion.

I mulled over the problem all day. Never in my 19 years had I wanted anything as much as I wanted this. If I could live on campus, I would be free. It would be the equivalent of a golden emancipation. I decided to appeal to Dad's obsession with being a member of the aristocracy.

"Daddy, I had lunch at the house today." My tone was light. I adopted a casual air. This must not seem too important.

"It was real nice. Tasty goodies to fatten me up." I paused companionably. "When I was visiting Patty upstairs, I noticed that one of the girls had moved out. Laura, she's the pretty brunette you liked who lives in San Marino. Her mother took her home this morning."

I allowed a long silence to rest between my ideas. It was crucial that I handle this right. No rushes of excitement. Don't show too much feeling. I carried on about my new sisters. I mentioned the doctor's daughter, a sister's Hancock Park mansion and some details about another girl's dad who was a four-star general.

"I'm sure enjoying getting to know all of the girls. Dad, imagine if you had a daughter who lived in. A real sorority girl."

There was no response from Dad. He was in bed absently chewing ice. I was sitting on a chair nearby. I let more time pass.

"I bet Maymie would like it, too." I forced another pause. I looked at Dad. He seemed interested. Go on, but be careful, I thought to myself. His jaw isn't working. He's still listening.

"Dad, the advisor said the total cost is $50 a month. That includes food. It's as cheap as feeding me at home. And without that two-hour drive, I'd have more time to study. I'm making almost $50 a week at the park and with that scholarship..."

"I don't like that scholarship at all. They shouldn't give you a scholarship and then make you work for it. I could have easily sent you to USC myself if Maymie had not fucked up our money. Can you imagine some stupid broad charging around the world for a year in the middle of the worst depression this country has ever seen? I hope to Jesus that you'll never be a spendthrift like she is."

I sat quietly as he ranted on.

"I make good money. The aerospace industry is booming. There's a cry for good engineers across the country. Kennedy's gonna get an American on the moon. Mark my words, he'll do it. He may be a Mick bastard, and all those Kennedys are crooks, but he's right about the space program. They'll need the best minds. I could name my price."

"Dad, I know. That gyroscope you have orbiting the moon is super stuff. Important stuff!"

Taking an opportunity to give Dad the credit I knew he was looking for, I continued with what I hoped would sound like gratitude and sincerity. "Daddy, that job at school is nothing. I just spend two hours a week filling out book requests for the English professors. They are so funny to listen to. They argue about the weirdest stuff. One professor was all shook up last week because someone had corrected the way he pronounced the word spelled k-i-l-n."

"Kill," Dad said proudly. "Silent n."

"Right, Dad, I'm glad you taught me the proper pronunciation of such tricky words. Anyway, this professor was flustered to think he might be wrong. Since he couldn't get anyone else to agree with him, he finally came to me, a student, and asked me. I said, 'Kill.' He stormed into his office then and didn't come out again while I was there."

Dad chewed on the ice I had carefully cracked for his Coca-Cola as he thought for a moment. His mood changed back to friendly.

"You know that Big Ray's mother, Lydia, and his sister, Fay, both got their pharmacy licenses. Fay went to college at USC in...probably 1902. Pretty impressive women for you to live up to. All professionals. Your mother's side isn't too shoddy either. Her cousin Margie has her master's and is a college dean. You should be proud."

Minutes passed. I remained silent. I knew not to push too hard. I waited for what seemed an eternity. My trembling had almost subsided now. The conversation had calmed me some, but I could still feel the nervousness in my voice.

"So, Dad, what do you think?" I held my breath, then spoke slowly. "Could I move in until Christmas vacation? I'd really like to give it a try, 'til Laura comes back."

I breathed deeply, steadying myself for the verdict.

It was a yes! I was thrilled beyond belief.

I moved into the sorority the very next afternoon. My new roommates were ecstatic. Before the end of the fall semester, the girls had nominated me for their Sigma Chi sweetheart representative and their Helen of Troy candidate. They said they had to have a cute blue-eyed blond and I filled the bill exactly. I was so happy!

Trust in my gentle inner voice was beginning to grow. I began to really believe in those delicate whispers that had come to me in the most despairing moments, saying, *Donna, it will be okay.*

Life inside the sorority house was everything I had dreamed of and much more. The cook, Augustine, made me wonderful breakfasts and packed special surprises in my brown lunch bag for me to take to the park where I worked after school. The girls were funny to live with, sneaking cigarettes or swearing and telling off-color jokes. I did not understand at the time that it was only a slightly rebellious way for them to play; I was not about to join in their games. I had been taught that young ladies do not swear and I wanted to be a lady at all costs. I was reluctant to break any house rules, not wanting to jeopardize what I had become. More than that, I would not jeopardize my freedom.

With me out of the house, Dad abruptly married Bernie in the spring. At the same time, Sandy got into some kind of killer fight with Dad and mysteriously moved in with our mother. Sandy would not even discuss it with me. Wrapped up in my new life, I paid little attention. I was so thrilled to finally, joyfully, take charge of my own life.

It would be decades later before I learned the awful truth about why Sandy suddenly moved out of Dad's house in the middle of the night, never to return. I was to learn her story was much like my own.

September 1963
The Row
University of Southern California

I kept my engagement to Ken a secret from everyone, even Sandy, so that when school started again, I could participate in one of the oldest sorority rituals, "passing the candle."

It had been an incredible summer, a real rollercoaster of emotions. Big Ray died and there was tremendous grief to cope with. Then there was the excitement of learning that Bernie and Dad were expecting a new baby, plus the most unbelievable of all! Ken asked me to marry him!

Thursday night was House Night and all 60 sisters ate in our dining room. All day long on that special Thursday I had been excited, my mind whirling nonstop. I thought about the night a month before when Ken proposed. He'd been so wonderful and so nervous.

After a nice quiet dinner for just the two of us, he sat me down. He was very serious. I was smiling, knowing what was coming and appreciating all the romance. He carefully bent his knee before me and looked into my eyes. In his earnest way he began.

"Donna, you know that I love you. You've known that since we were 15. I want you to be my wife. Will you marry me?" At that moment he produced the shining solitaire diamond ring which we had carefully shopped for together.

Laughing at how wonderful he was, like someone in a romantic movie, I threw my arms around his neck and hugged and kissed him. How I had waited for those words! It was like dream come true.

"Yes, Kenny, I will marry you. And we'll have lots and lots of children! I love you. I always have, and I always will!"

Smiling, I brought myself back to the important matters at hand. Thrilling matters. I had ordered the traditional sorority engagement candle from the florist, a pink taper decorated with satin ribbons. I knew it would be beautiful. It would be delivered to the kitchen late that afternoon. I had been watching this ritual for a year now, every time one of the sisters became engaged or pinned. I knew what to expect and just how exciting it would be.

I had casually invited Sandy to dinner. She was living in Nichols Canyon now with Mom and Mom's new husband, Mac, and was always happy to come to the sorority house. During my classes that day I just couldn't settle down; I felt a magical electric charge course through my body every time I thought of the upcoming ceremony. It had been difficult keeping my engagement a secret, especially from Sandy.

At dinner, Sandy sat with me and Patty and my other roommates. Dinner went smoothly. Our conversation was animated, but I was waiting for dessert and what I knew would come next.

Suddenly the dining room lights went out. They blinked off and on three long times. My heart was pounding. I gulped for air. One flash of light was for a pinning and three meant an engagement. The room instantly became silent, deafeningly silent. My heart was really thudding now. The girls looked from one to another. Who was it? The whispers quickly swept around the room. Names were tossed about excitedly. Everyone's curiosity was aroused. Just who could be engaged?

My name came up. "Donna?"

I smiled and shook my head no. Then I tried to put an indifferent, curious expression on my face that said that I had no idea either. I had learned how to play the game.

A lean young waiter swept into the room carrying the most beautiful pink candle I had ever seen! It was burning and the satin ribbons flowed softly down around it. It looked like a fiery bouquet in the dim light of the dining room. The waiter carefully handed the burning candle and garland to the girl at the head of the table.

The candle circulated around the table, passing slowly from one expectant young woman to the next. With each pass, the intensity of the excitement grew. Sometimes a girl would bow her head as if to blow the candle out, but at the last instant would smile at her trick and pass it along.

Around and around the candle went. It came to me. I held my breath and kept my expression calm; I would not give myself away. I passed it on to Sandy. Her eyes sparkled in the light of the flame as she, too, passed the candle on. The candle went around to all 60 girls, still no one had claimed it. The intensity grew. This devious trick of not claiming it the first time was not new to the Alpha Gams. Every so often, a girl managed to hold on to her excitement and let suspense build.

The minutes ticked on. The candle found its way to me again. And again I did not betray the fact that it was mine. The tension in the room was literally breathtaking.

Finally, after one last round, the candle was heading toward me. I knew that I must claim it this time or it would burn down before it reached me again. It was now or never. My mouth went dry; my face shaded crimson. My heartbeat was so loud I could hardly concentrate. The candle was next to me now.

With a sharp intake of breath I received the candle in my trembling hands, and lifting it as if to pass it, satin ribbons swirling about, I quickly brought the flame toward my face and blew. The candle went out and the entire sorority house roared!

Sandy jumped out of her chair and shrieked as she threw her arms around my neck. "Sissy, you didn't tell me! When? When?"

I glowed back at her. The other girls were up and out of their chairs. Everyone was surrounding me. My sisters were giddy, thrilled with innocent delight.

It was a moment I would never forget. I felt like a character in the fairy tales that my grandmother told me when I was little, a beautiful princess who lived in a storybook house and was about to marry a wonderful prince. It was beyond my imagination.

I really was going to be able to live the life I had dreamed about. Now I felt safe, accepted, loved and beautiful. My heart was filled with hope, wonderful blossoming hope.

Only faintly could I still feel for that little girl with the green teeth, the dirty neck and the feelings she had on May Day when no one would hold her hand.

June 20, 1964
Wedding Day
Palos Verdes, California

I awoke in the smartly furnished bedroom that Mom kept for Sandy and me when we visited her West Side home.

I dressed hurriedly, thinking of the stacks and stacks of wedding gifts displayed in fancy boxes from elegant stores. I had never dreamed we would get so many gifts. They had been arriving for weeks. My beautiful wedding dress was hanging from the closet door, billowing down to the floor. I had made it myself and was very proud of it. It was simple and elegant, and I was so pleased that Mom had made the veil and train for me, after all those years of wanting her to make me a dress.

Daddy had given me only $300 for the entire wedding. He said any more would be a waste of money. My whole life he had told me about the days of wine, servants, free spending and about being the aristocracy. Then for my wedding he allotted me 10 percent of what my sorority sisters were paying for the same size wedding. He was making good money, had new cars and was always taking trips. I pushed my frustration down.

For several weeks Mom and I had made finger sandwiches for 250 people in our spare time, carefully trimming the crusts, wrapping and freezing them. Katy, Ken's younger sister, had taken full charge of the wedding flowers. She had been so much help and seemed to understand about my limited finances. We'd finally chosen daisies because they cost the least.

Together Ken and I had saved about $1,000 and we painstakingly budgeted how to live on it. We figured out exactly how we could go to school full-time to work toward our master's degrees. It would be tight, but Ken's mom, Helene, was letting us have her family's cottage at the beach on Balboa Island rent-free for one year. If we were careful, we'd make it. But today was no day to worry about that. Today were getting married!

Somehow we managed to get all the way to St Luke's Presbyterian Church in Rolling Hills on time. I was beyond excitement. Though my stomach was in anxious coils, I kept smiling. In fact my face just smiled on its own.

I was putting the finishing touches on my makeup when Sandy poked her head into the dressing room from behind the closed door. "Donnie, Cee Cee and Leanne are all set and they look beautiful in their bridesmaids' dresses. Five minutes and we're on!" Her voice, charged with 100 volts, was much higher than normal. She looked beautiful in the yellow floor-length taffeta dress we had selected.

Daddy came in to check on me one last time. He looked more handsome than ever, too young to be giving a grown woman away. He was tanned and slim in his white dinner jacket, bow tie and cummerbund with contrasting black trousers.

"Donnie, how's my girl?" he asked, smiling comfortingly. "You're the most beautiful bride I've ever seen. I'm so proud of you for making that dress all by yourself."

"Daddy, I'm fine, but I'm shaking like a leaf. This is worse than giving a speech!"

"You'll be great. You always are. You're perfect. I'll meet you at the sanctuary doors in five minutes and we'll head down that aisle. You look wonderful. You're the classiest beauty I've ever seen! I'm so proud of Daddy's girl for landing such a great guy as Ken."

The familiar strains of "Here Comes The Bride" floated into my dressing room. My stomach lurched. One last look in the mirror. Wow, I thought, I really do look like a bride. The reflection showed a slim young woman, golden and gleaming, energy and vitality flowing from her. I smiled at myself and winked at Little Donna who lived behind that jubilant smile. Little Donna who had so dreamed of one day marrying a nice boy and living happily ever after.

"You did it, girl, all those semesters of studying all night, the only one awake in the entire sorority house. Earned your bachelor's degree last Saturday and with honors yet, and now this Saturday, a husband. You did great!"

My grin remained as I continued talking into the mirror, "Nothing will stop you now!"

I believed that comforting voice within that kept encouraging me. She had been right all along. I smiled goodbye to the girl in the mirror, the girl I had been. I took in a long deep breath and exhaled slowly as I turned and walked through the door to become the woman of my future.

PART II
Family Life

Fueled by love and ambition, Ken and I wasted no time making our lives work. During our first year of marriage, we completed our master's degrees and found good teaching jobs. Ricky, our first child, was conceived during our honeymoon year on Balboa Island. Our daughter, Julie, was born three years after Ricky came into the world; then three years later, Danny was born and our family was complete. We had the three wonderful children we'd always wanted.

We moved to a brand new house in Huntington Beach and were enjoying the wholesome suburban lifestyle. Our teaching schedules allowed us to indulge our passion for boating, and we spent a lot of time moored in the harbor at Catalina Island.

In 1968, we bought a 43-foot Chris Craft with Maymie and Dad. Dad and Bernie's family grew as ours did. Before long there were too many playpens and cribs to make boating comfortable, so we sold the boat and Ken and I bought a mountain home at Big Bear. That added a new dimension to family life, and we were thrilled to be able to teach our children about the forest and the fun of skiing.

We invested in rental units and worked hard to build a substantial business. Between our teaching salaries and our investments, we were doing very well. But for us everything paled next to our family life. Some people are more cut out for parenting than others, and Ken and I always knew that it was our true calling. We knew we were lucky to feel that way.

For the most part, Dad was supportive and we spoke on the phone almost daily. He seemed to have our best interests at heart, as he gave advice and encouragement. Predictably, life wasn't always a picnic with him, but we felt his genuine concern for our family, and he and Ken got along well enough. The situation deteriorated when he moved in with his girlfriend, Crystal, and her daughter, Jamie, while he was still married to Bernie. Bernie filed for divorce and Dad quit his job to avoid paying child support. The family was in an uproar. Maymie said she had never been so upset in her life, and Ken was furious because the situation forced us to help bail Dad out when the bank refused him a loan.

Our cabin in the woods was our saving grace and we spent every weekend of 1972-1973 up there fishing for German brown trout in the river, hiking in the woods and riding our Honda 90 dirt bikes over the hills. We picked apples in the orchard and made pies on the old black woodburning stove. It felt like heaven, and it was. In fact, we enjoyed the country so much that we decided to move our main residence from Huntington Beach to a rural area, further away from Dad.

San Juan Capistrano, where the swallows return each year to the old mission, was the most beautiful community we could imagine.

August 5, 1973
New Beginnings
San Juan Capistrano, California

"Kenny, be careful with the passenger sideview mirror. It's tilted down and you may not be able to see everything behind you. I'll follow right behind in the station wagon with Danny and Julie." I stopped, looking at my husband. He seemed preoccupied.

I tried again, "Honey, are you sure you can really drive this thing? Have you ever operated such a big U-Haul?"

"I'll be fine, Donna. Just stay close behind me. It'll only take 40 minutes or so." He paused reflectively. "Just think, tonight we'll sleep in our dream house. Hard to believe, isn't it?" His voice was clear and deep and today there was excitement in it.

He walked over to the green 1972 Ford station wagon to check on our children. When he poked his head through the driver's window, our dogs, Ginger and Max, panting in the back seat, took it as a cue to wag their tails.

"Julie, Dan, are you all set? We're off to our new home; the place you'll always remember as the home where you grew up."

"Daddy, I'm kinda hungry. I didn't like the stuff at Aunt Katy's for breakfast this morning," confided Julie, our five year old.

"Juger, we'll take care of you. After we get the moving van to the new house, Mom'll get some burgers and drinks. Okay?"

Julie smiled her best smile, knowing that the next meal was not far away. Her big green eyes twinkled as she leaned back against the front seat. She was ready to go. Dan, our white-blond two year old, was secure in his blue vinyl car seat. He chewed his plastic GI Joe doll and smiled happily, sensing the excitement in the air.

I walked around the moving van and opened the passenger door. Rick was arranging some of the plants and more delicately packed boxes which were precariously jammed into the cab of the van.

"Rick, you all set?"

"Yeah, Mom. Let's go," replied our handsome eight-year-old son. "I can't wait to ride our new pony."

"I'm pretty excited, too, Ricky, thinking about having horses. Wasn't it great that those two Shetland ponies came with the house?" We held eye contact for a long minute.

"We'll go riding tomorrow." My heart pounded at the thought.

"Will you trust me with Weesha?" Rick asked, referring to our new Welsh pony.

When we'd bought Weesha, Ken had set me loose on her to try to learn how to ride. The only problem was she wasn't broken yet. "Your daddy is a nut, isn't he? An unbroken horse...an unbroken rider!"

"Mom, that just builds character!"

"Oh, so am I a character now, Ricker?"

"No, Mom you are the nut," he teased back. "You didn't have to try to break that horse. Dad could have done it first, then you."

"But that would have been too wimpy."

"But now you know how to ride. I'm impressed, but you can't have the Shetland because you won't fit."

Rick was chuckling. I guessed he was visualizing his mother standing up with the pony under her.

I reached up as he offered his cheek, "Time to go, son." I pecked his cheek gently. "Bye."

"We're off!" I yelled, slamming Rick's door and running back to the station wagon.

I started the ignition. The sweet strains of "She's So Beautiful" came from the radio as I slowly pulled away from the curb.

I couldn't help thinking about our new house. I had tried not to before the sale was final to protect myself from disappointment had the sellers backed out. But now I could allow myself to visualize my new life in vivid color. It was really our house now! I could get as excited as I pleased!

"And why shouldn't you feel that way, Donna?" asked my inner voice. *"You should be proud of what you have accomplished."*

I ran a mental checklist. It was a comforting rote for me. I had three beautiful children, a wonderful husband, a rewarding teaching career, lucrative investments, good health, a mountain cabin and now I could add "dream house" to the list.

No, I thought. This was not really my dream house. I had never dreamed of anything so elaborate. My dreams had always been grounded in practicality. Our new house had five bedrooms and sat atop two acres of land with a gorgeous view that stretched forever. This house was Ken's dream. We were making a huge reach financially, but we both believed that we could do it.

I looked over at Julie, mesmerized by the drive past open range land and strawberry fields. Her face was turned away from me, but I could imagine her green eyes dancing with amazement. I smiled as I thought of another beginning: Julie's birth.

It was the only birth of the three in which I was able to participate without medication. I remember gasping and pushing with every fiber of my being, sweat pouring from my brow. Suddenly the pain fell away as my beautiful baby slipped from my womb. It was miraculous. Overcome with emotion I heard her lusty baby cry.

"It's a girl!" The doctor announced triumphantly.

"My dearest baby!" I strangled out as the tears poured. This was more emotion than I had ever felt before. Truly it was the most profound moment of my life. It was beyond words, a spiritual experience.

I was not prepared for it at all. No one had ever expressed to me what motherhood could be about, or life for that matter. I had been reared from the cold perspective of factual science. There had never been room for the spiritual. Spirituality was just something quaint to keep the masses in line.

But now I saw that was a lie! Suddenly I knew differently.

There had been dark years in my past, but what I felt at Julie's birth was a beacon of light filled with understanding and hope. I had used sheer strength of will and determination my whole life. I had always known that I was a survivor. I had always held on knowing that somehow, someday...

But I had never heard the rest of the sentence from my gentle inner voice. It had always just told me that it would be okay. Now I understood. The past was safely in the past. The horrible ugly years were all behind me now. I was safe.

I grasped something higher in that moment, knowing it would stay with me always. I felt connected to the immensity of the universe. I had a place in it and was part of a greater plan. Being a mother was more about reverence, commitment, dedication and God to me than I could ever have imagined. I lost myself in those warm and alien thoughts. I also glimpsed something about God. Maybe God was in us?

I glanced briefly into the rearview mirror to check on Danny. He was still contentedly chewing on the GI Joe doll, a plump little toddler, sweet-natured and easy to care for. I remembered the day almost three years ago when Patty, my friend from college, had visited. We enjoyed trying to coordinate the births of our children.

That day I discovered that Patty had already started her third and I quickly decided that Kenny and I needed to add to our family, too. I called Ken at work and urged him to come home right away. We needed to get started so my teaching schedule would not get in the way.

Miraculously, two weeks later I knew that my mission had been accomplished. Dan was born in June, exactly nine months later, and two days before Patty's boy. I could enjoy a whole summer at home with my new baby.

I checked the road ahead cautiously, needing to keep a safe distance behind the formidable U-Haul truck as it sailed southward. The new I-405 freeway allowed workers to commute from homes in the fast-growing areas of Mission Viejo, Laguna Hills and El Toro to metropolitan areas. Sleepy San Juan Capistrano was still rural and quiet. Horseback riders on the main street of the little town were a common sight.

Our new home would be more than a new house, it would be a new way of life. Ricky, my sensitive child, would be starting third grade and was anxious to get moved in so that he could look for yellow racers, his favorite snakes, in the riverbed.

When he was little, I was the only mother whose child demanded that she stay at all the birthday parties. There was a shy cord in me that felt as he did. It had taken all I had to force my way past that, to make myself who I was. But we did things at Rick's pace. I understood that when his time was right, he would take on the world by himself.

I knew I was a lucky woman. Raising the children and having a family were the most exhilarating adventure of all. My eyes noted the freeway sign in front of me.

"San Juan Capistrano, Next Exit." Our friends thought we were crazy to accept a 70-mile commute just to live in the country. They also said we were lucky to afford such a home when we were so young.

Luck and grueling hard work were more accurate. We owned and managed 84 four-plex apartment units which formed our financial base, along with our two teaching jobs. We had made it the hard way. Our friends loved to hear our crazy landlord stories. They especially enjoyed the one about Ricky helping me paint an apartment. He caught his head in the rungs of a chair and I had to call the fire department to extricate him.

All those years of struggling were worth it now. It would be wonderful for our children to grow up in the open space of the 40-acre valley that lay at our feet. In the lush grove behind our house, Mexican braceros were picking fresh oranges. I could see their tall ladders leaning against the fruit-laden branches. The aroma of orange blossoms would fill the evenings.

I pulled into the driveway, set the parking brake and turned off the engine. We were home.

1975
Swallow's Day Parade
San Juan Capistrano

In San Juan Capistrano one of our community rituals is
the annual Swallow's Day Parade to celebrate the famous
return of the swallows, "Las Golondrinas." This year our
friends and neighbors decided that it would be fun to have
a cross-country horse race after the parade. I had never
really raced and only had three years of riding experience,
but with my usual enthusiasm, I agreed to join the group
and put up my entry money. There was to be a generous
purse for the winner.

During the weeks approaching the big day, I took our
horse, Windy, out for practice runs each afternoon when I
returned from work. We ran the course and got in shape.
On the day of the event, I was surprised to see dozens of
horse trailers parked throughout our rural valley. Word of
this race had really spread, and riders had trailered in their
horses from as far as 60 miles away.

The three-mile course was marked, and men were sta-
tioned with walkie-talkies along its rock-strewn course. It
was far more organized than I had imagined. Spectators
were gathering along the course and finish line. I felt nervous, and so did Windy.

What a mixed bag we riders were — middle-class busi-
nessmen turned weekend cowboys, construction workers
who fancied themselves "real men," working cowboys from
nearby ranches, local blacksmiths, stable owners, horse en-
thusiasts — and me, a schoolteacher who only rode bareback. I had not mastered the saddle yet and hadn't really
wanted to. I felt most comfortable bareback because I felt in
control with my thighs pressed against the horse.

I could tell that our blacksmith, Joe, thought my entry in the race was the funniest thing of all. That schoolteacher? What a hilarious joke! He delighted in teasing me about it. I could just hear him laughing good naturedly, "Donna?" he would say in an amazed tone, and break up laughing. I didn't care. It would be fun. Besides I had never raced before.

As race time approached, all of us lined up at the starting line, perhaps 40 or more riders. My heart was pounding. Windy was shivering beneath me. I heard the starting gun and we were off!

Pressing my thighs tightly against Windy, we glided smoothly around the pack of riders as we headed into the riverbed. I knew that this was not unusual for Windy. She did not like to lose a race, not to anyone. She hated being in another horse's dust. We were racing like the wind, through rock and sand, past bamboo and bushes, up onto the dike that ran along the creek. We passed every one of the riders and were comfortably out in front when we approached the first lookout with his walkie-talkie carefully in hand. It was Joe. Later he said that he screamed into his walkie-talkie, "Jesus Christ, it's Donna!!!" He was almost shocked speechless. He repeated that line many times that night at the post race party. He could not believe his eyes.

Windy, pacing herself now, kept the lead as we continued across the course. Along the top of the dike, I leaned low against her neck. Finally a sharp turn back into the riverbed, where the trail was uneven with rocks and stones. A horse could easily stumble and throw its rider off to be trampled by the pack of wild racers. The trail was much too narrow to avoid a catastrophe if someone fell. I was conscious of the danger, but I just kept crooning, "We can do it girl. Good girl. Bring us in, Windy."

As we came into the final turn, I gave Windy one last kick and leaned down on her neck. As she turned the final corner I slipped and fell halfway off.

"No! Not now!" I said aloud. "We're so close." And then to myself, "You're almost in, Donna, hang on!"

I pulled hard, grasping at Windy's mane and managed to right myself. My friends were applauding and yelling. I crossed the finish line and the crowd roared.

I had won the race! I was the champion! No one could believe it. The schoolteacher! I was elated, but in my heart I always thought I might have a chance to surprise everyone. I had practiced ahead and put my mind to what I was doing. And I knew that deep inside I had a streak of daring. I had experienced that before. I knew what my horse could do, and I knew my own determination.

My friends were thrilled, but some of the macho cowboys were not. One man, Hoss, was so disgusted with his horse for not winning that he tied her up without walking her down. Unable to cool off as she needed to, she died a few hours later.

I knew this was a tough crowd, but that dead horse showed a callousness I didn't understand. Some of the cowboys were missing teeth and most of them chewed chaws of tobacco and spit their smelly wads onto the dusty ground. Perhaps that was partly why it was so intriguing. I got to go up against real cowboys and win. This outstanding day with Windy came to be, in some ways, a symbol for my life. It gave me courage, later, to remember I could win against all odds.

March 1978
Sandy's Home
Mission Viejo, California

My sister, Sandy, and I remained close during the years and she even moved to Laguna Niguel, fairly close to our house. She had become a dentist and had two darling daughters, Joanne, 7, and Mindy, 3.

One Saturday morning, Julie, Danny and I were visiting with her and her girls.

"Well, shall we tackle that old box?" Sandy placed our coffee cups in the sink and steered me out of the kitchen door into the adjoining garage. I felt we were about to enter another world by opening up the box of our grandparents' memorabilia. I hoped it wasn't like Pandora's box.

"Boy, Sissy, I don't know about this. Do you think it's going to bother us, going through May and Ray's old pictures?"

"I hope not. 1977 was horrible enough. This year has got to be better."

We both nodded in understanding. The year before had been horrendous. Our grandmother, Maymie, died, our mother was diagnosed with malignant melanoma and our father got into terrible financial trouble.

"I think we'll be okay about all this. It's just old documents. Lots of pictures."

Sandy's head temporarily disappeared as she poked around the space above the rafters. Locating the box with her hand, she continued, "Dad doesn't seem quite as bothered now over Maymie's death as he was those first few months."

She lifted the huge brown carton down to me. "I couldn't believe how he stayed at Catalina on his boat all those weeks after she died. He has a little trouble with reality, doesn't

he? He didn't remove any of her things from the house for
six months. Weird."

I could visualize Maymie's silk slip as it had hung all those
months over a chair, as if waiting for her to claim it. I'd
often seen her put it on when she was dressing to go out.
In my mind's eye I could see Maymie in her dancing gown.

"Do you remember Maymie's 75th birthday party? Do
you remember what happened when she first arrived at my
house?" I laughed. "It was so funny. At first I couldn't figure
it out. Something was peculiar, but I couldn't put my finger
on it. She was all dressed up. Then suddenly I realized she
had her false eyelashes on upside-down. They fanned down,
forming a kind of bird cage over her eyes."

Sandy nodded her head. "I guess she figured that all of a
sudden the world grew lines!"

"The really hard part was peeling them off her eyelids
and gluing them on straight. I was laughing so hard inside
that my hands shook."

We both chuckled affectionately at the picture of our little
grandmother all dressed up with her upside-down eyelashes.
We missed her.

"Sissy," I reminisced. "She did do some pretty strange
things. Do you remember those gloves? The ones without
thumbs? And the way we giggled about that for months?"

Sandy took up the litany, "And how we would start to
imagine what odd-ball gifts she would find on sale for
Christmas."

I continued, "I'll never forget the silver spoons. You'd
watched me open mine, our eyes would meet knowingly,
and in a serious voice, I would exclaim, 'Oh look, Sandy a
new old spoon.' "

"Right!" Sandy's voice was filled with laughter. "We sup-
pressed our giggles, but later we'd burst."

I returned to the present moment and looked at the dusty
old box.

"How should we attack this project?" I asked, anxious to get it behind us.

"Well, we'll want an album for each of us, for sure. Cee Cee should have one and we should make one for Dad. The rest of the pictures can stay here until some of the kids are grown up enough to show interest."

"Yes, four albums will take long enough. But it does seem senseless to have more than 100 years of our family's life in a dusty box that no one can see."

For the next several hours we sorted through the box and studied ancient tintypes, report cards from the late 1800s, old documents, diplomas and pharmacy licenses. We pieced together our family's history using these artifacts. Near the bottom of the box we found several bundles of postcards. Sandy lifted one of the stacks and untied it.

"Sis, these look real old. Maybe 1890s."

"They must be Big Ray's," I guessed as I reached for the other stack and began to shuffle through them.

I continued nonchalantly through the cards for a few moments, remembering they always kept postcards from their travels. Usually they were marked with exotic stamps. I eyed these cards more closely. They weren't like the flowery old-fashioned cards I was used to seeing. I paused at one sepia-toned card: A beautiful little five-year-old girl smiled out at me. She tilted her face adorably against her index fingers. She was beautiful. And she was nude.

I felt a coldness spread across my chest. I rushed back through the cards, and stopped at a black and white photograph of a lovely two- or three-year-old child. Her little dress was carelessly falling off of one shoulder exposing her right nipple. I looked at the next one. This one was printed in German. It was a color picture of a little girl, maybe four years old, clad only in a garland of flowers around her bottom.

My heart was thumping and I was cold all over. The next card showed two girls lying in the forest. They were

completely nude! I looked quickly at the next and the next
and the next. Sirens began to go off in my mind. I hoped for
some other explanation. Trying to conceal my frightening
thoughts from my sister, I looked up at her. She seemed as
shaken as I. A silent look of understanding passed between
us, but we said nothing.

We efficiently rebound the cards and put them away.
These were things of which we had never spoken and would
never speak.

As I drove home from that visit, I was terrified of my
thoughts. What does this mean? Not Big Ray? Not my beloved grandfather. He had never been anything but sweet
and loving to Sandy and me. He had never touched me. He
was not like Daddy! Was he?

More sirens went off in my head. I tried to quiet my
mind, but it continued to grope for some understanding.
What could those cards mean? I was certain that they were
my grandfather's. They were a cherished collection, almost
100 years old, still bundled carefully, still in the family.
They were once important to him. And perhaps to someone
before him.

How much more stress would my marriage take without
falling apart? All of last year's problems crashed around in
my mind. Maymie's death, my mom's cancer, the $20,000
loan Ken and I had been forced to pay off for my father. We
had co-signed a note with him and he had defaulted on the
loan. Ken was still furious about it. My mind went chattering on, but I managed to keep my eyes on the road.

The last few times I had driven alone in the mountains the
thought of driving over the side had been painfully appealing.
I tried not to allow these thoughts to continue because of my
children, but they were real. I cut down on my speed as I
reached our valley. Big Ray. What about my beloved grandfather? My years of talks with Maymie all came back.

Maymie always did her best to keep our family history
alive and told me countless times of the successful Los An-

geles family she had been born into. The memories kept rushing in, and I could hear my grandmother's sweet voice in my head.

"We've lived in the city for so many generations, we qualify for membership in the exclusive First Century Families of the Los Angeles club, and don't you forget it, Donna," she'd say.

One night after dinner at her house, while Big Ray read his newspapers in the living room, Maymie told me about her grandparents who had come out to California from the South.

"Donna, your ancestors were among the first settlers to come to America. Among them were signers of the Declaration of Independence. My mother's mother had her plantation overtaken by Union soldiers and had to cook for them. Do you remember when I told you about my great-grandparents both being suckled by slaves? Kate and William, my grandparents, moved out here with 11 children. My mother was one of them. Cousin Emily's mother was another. I've enjoyed a lifetime of being close to Emily. Real chums, more like sisters..."

Emily. That was it! Now I remembered what she had told me about Big Ray and cousin Emily. She'd said she awakened in the night when they were all at Big Bear. She heard Big Ray with Emily. Emily was a teenager and Big Ray was in his forties. I did not understand what she meant at the time, but now I did.

Big Ray and Emily. Now it all made sense. My hands tightened on the steering wheel and I kept the car steady as random memories continued to fall into place. Shocking memories, tales my grandmother told in the nicest possible way. Did she know that one day I would piece them together and understand?

She loved to tell stories about the old days and she was good at it, too. She had even majored in speech and drama at USC where, she never ceased to emphasize, John Wayne had been one of her classmates. But today I could not have cared less about that old cowboy. Today I saw Maymie again in my mind's eye, resting in her bed, on a day when I was young enough to be cleaning her house to earn extra money.

"Today, Donna, I want to tell you all about my mother. Cordelia was a wonderful woman, and I want you to know her in your heart."

I settled down at the foot of her big bed, comfortable in the folds of her blue down comforter.

"Everyone called my mother Delia for short," Maymie went on. "Delia married my father, Jonathan, a tile mason from Ventura. He looked a lot like your father, Donna. Perhaps it was Jon's remarkable blue eyes and handsome build that prompted Delia to marry him or perhaps Delia was pregnant. Whatever it was, it certainly wasn't his character. Delia definitely married beneath her. I always suspected a shot-gun wedding because he deserted us when I was four or five. Such topics were not discussed in polite society in those Victorian times.

"Anyway, abandoned by Jon, Delia struggled to raise my brother Phillip and me, and survived on donations and gifts from her wealthy sisters. She scrimped and managed to feed the three of us, but still we were poor, Donna. I remember my mother preparing a dinner for us three on one small can of Campbell's soup!

"Delia was still husbandless in 1910 when she was friendly with the popular socialite, Fay Landis, whom she knew from high school. Fay was eagerly looking for a wife for her younger brother, Ray. She sort of courted Delia to encourage a match with Ray."

I had been a curious listener, sitting attentively as the tale went on.

"In private, Fay was having serious conversations with her father, Chadwick Landis, who later became the state senator from Los Angeles. Chadwick was concerned because his son was almost 30 years old and still had not found a wife. Ray was content with his studies of Latin, his checkers, chess, pharmacy business and the wonderful walnut ranch which he had recently purchased in Orange County. He had not got over the death of his mother, Lydia. She was only 43 when she died of cancer." Maymie's voice trailed off.

"Eventually Fay was successful at arranging a meeting between Ray and Delia. As a divorcee, Delia's marriage qualifications were not overly attractive for a man such as your grandfather, a man of wealth, education and social position."

The storytelling stopped while we enjoyed dinner with my grandfather. Later during the dishes, Maymie continued. I noticed a certain pride in her tone.

"As I grew older Ray confessed to me that he never noticed Delia at all. He only had eyes for me. My name then was Gladys May and I was nine years old, hiding behind my mother's skirts. He described me as a little girl with long blonde ringlets flowing down my back. He said that he was struck by my blue eyes which he found fascinating because they slanted so. Anyway, he was not the tiniest bit interested in my mother. He wanted to marry me!"

I grew intent. Fay wanted Ray to marry Maymie's mother, not little Maymie...I was silent, uncertain what to say.

"Apparently there were some negotiations and he agreed to wait until I was seventeen before we'd marry. He also agreed to support my mother, brother and me. I was to go on little outings with him."

There was a long pause then. Maybe she was looking back over the years. Perhaps she was imagining her life with her mother and brother in some long-forgotten kitchen. Finally, in a far-off tone she concluded, "No one ever did ask me how I felt, but I didn't want us to keep getting by on that Campbell's soup."

I decided that customs must have been much different back then. Her girlhood seemed centuries in the past to me.

I had seen a sepia photo of her in a starched white dress at age ten. My grandfather stood close, a tall man in a dark fedora, vest, and business suit with the gold chain of his pocket watch proudly displayed.

Maymie sighed. The far-away look was back in her eyes as she continued. "As Gladys May, I began going on outings with Mr. Landis. He seemed awfully old, but he was very nice to me. He encouraged me to change my name to the more stylish Vera-May, and bought me expensive clothes and jewelry. By the time I was 17, I had a huge diamond wedding ring, a large home, hired servants and the title of Mrs. Landis."

As I approached home, I realized what terrible evidence pointed to my grandfather. Big Ray *must* have been like Daddy. What an overwhelming revelation.

When I saw Ken's truck in the driveway, I knew I had to pull myself together fast so that he wouldn't know how upset I was. I tried to calm my mind and my emotions as the kids came running to greet me.

"Mommy, Mommy! Daddy's home early! Now we can go biking."

"Yes, guys. That's a nice idea." My cheerfulness was forced. I got out of the car and went in search of my husband.

With hose in hand, he was watering the vegetable garden and enjoying the beauty of the late spring afternoon. He was still dressed in slacks with the sleeves of his dress shirt rolled up. He looked so good to me. The children ran ahead, calling to him.

"Daddy! We want to go biking! You said we could!"

"Just let me change my clothes." He smiled, lifting Julie up and swinging her around.

Dan wrapped himself around his father's legs in his typical energetic greeting. Looking across the grass at me as I walked slowly toward him, Ken greeted me.

"Sweet Patootee, you look about done in. Was that picture sorting rough?"

"Yeah, it was pretty bad. Made me miss May and Ray. It was kind of nasty." I offered, keeping the postcards and their horrible implications to myself.

"It wasn't just the pictures, was it? It's been a difficult year on all fronts," he consoled, giving me a hug with his free arm. The children ran to look at our new garden.

"I guess having your dad dump Bernie and the kids for that young gal, Crystal, and quitting his job to avoid paying child support has not helped matters. Borrowing money from us and messing up our credit got me all bent out of shape. I know that hasn't made it any easier for you."

I tilted my head back and focused on his face. He looked me in the eye, and when he spoke again his voice was softer.

"Donna, I'll back off. I shouldn't have ordered him to stay out of our house. I've been selfish. He shouldn't have defaulted on the loan, but after all he is your father. And I know I'm gone entirely too much, but you never complain." He paused, and after a long silence said, "Your dad can come around. I've been a jerk. I've been furious at him and you've been stuck in the middle."

Of course I haven't complained, I thought, but this was no time to talk about it. I had other things on my mind. I remained silent for a long moment, trying to focus on Ken. My marriage was very important to me.

"Maybe we should talk about our ski trip," I said from my fold in his comforting arm. "It'll do us good to get away for a while. There's been so much happening." As we started toward the house to get ready for our bike ride, my mind still whirled with unspoken thoughts.

How could it be true? My darling grandfather with naked little girls; Maymie being sold to him. It didn't line up with my experience of Big Ray. But it made sense in a cold, logical way.

More pieces of the family puzzle were falling into place, and it wasn't a pretty picture. I stored it away in the back of my mind. I wasn't ready to deal with it then.

June 1978
San Juan Capistrano

"Mommy, it's such a warm day, let's get Barbie a lemonade." Julie tugged at my arm, thrilled with her new Barbie Doll soda fountain.

"You pour, I'll be a customer, too." I was as happy as Julie was, home from school for the summer with plenty of time for the children. Julie was a wonderful playmate. Dressed in her white shorts and pink polka dot top, she still looked like a baby to me, although she was ten years old.

The afternoon wore on and soon it was time to put the toys away and start dinner. As we folded up the soda fountain, Julie tugged at my arm with an odd kind of urgency. I looked down and wondered what was wrong. She stood there with a pained expression on her face, her blond ballerina Barbie clutched in one hand.

"What is it, Julie? Does something hurt?" I sat on the floor beside her.

She had trouble speaking, but finally managed to whisper, "Grandpa..."

Our eyes met. Inside I went on red alert but managed to stay calm for her. "Go ahead, Honey. You can tell me."

She hesitated for another moment, then blurted out, "He touched me."

Hot fury grabbed me and my temperature seemed to shoot through the roof. Then cold fear engulfed me. What more could I have done to keep her safe? I only left her with Dad in broad daylight. All the other kids were there, too, playing on the beach. I had just left for a few hours while I visited Mom and went to the mall. Just a few hours. I'd never left her when she was smaller.

I drew Julie to me and struggled to keep the alarm out of my voice.

"What do you mean?" I asked. Maybe it was nothing.

"I fell asleep," she said in a small voice, "and he touched me down there."

My head spun in a dizzying spiral. I felt like Alice falling down the rabbit hole.

"What happened?"

"I woke up. He's always so nice to me, I had cuddled up with him and fell asleep in his arms while he was reading a book. When I woke up, he was touching me under my panties." Her words were stronger now.

"Then what happened?"

"I woke up and jumped out of bed. I was scared." Her words were tumbling out now. "I yelled at him, 'What are you doing, Grandpa?' I ran across the room. I was real scared, Mommy!"

She paused for a minute to catch her breath and then went on, "He looked at me, but his eyes were different. He looked like a monster. He said, 'This is our secret, don't you dare tell your mother. Don't tell anyone!' Then his eyes got real mean."

In the silence I could hear the hammering of my heart.

Julie continued, "But, Mommy, I had to tell. You always said to tell. You said that no one is supposed to touch my privates until I'm grown up."

I drew my daughter close against me. "You poor baby. I'm never going to let him near you again. What he did was bad." I could hear the rage in my voice. "I promise I won't ever let him do that again. You were right to tell me."

I had many sleepless nights after that. I would keep my daughter safe from him no matter what. Somewhere deep in my heart I knew this was not the best answer, but what could I do? I could challenge him, but I knew that he would call Julie a liar. And then how would he behave?

"Sorry sisters end up six feet under. Betrayers are executed. People who talk have accidents. I will allow myself anything dogs do..." I could hear his threats in my ear. What would he do to Julie?

Still, I dared not tell anyone. If I told Ken that Julie had been molested, what then? Ken might do something drastic and end up in jail. I was tormented, but did nothing. Fear held me locked in its grasp, paralyzed. But my inner voice would not stop.

Donna, face what you are dealing with...take a good look and face it.

PART III
Turning Points

Though I sometimes had to make a concerted effort to push unpleasantness out of my mind, there were extraordinarily good things happening in life all the time.

We were such respected, public-spirited people that Ken was elected mayor of San Juan Capistrano and re-elected to a second and even a third term, a feat unequaled in the history of the community. I had framed his campaign posters and hung them in the family gallery in the hall, and it never ceased to warm my heart to see his picture there, earnest, honest and handsome.

I had been Ken's campaign manager and busied myself running precincts, directing volunteers and making up flyers. Ken was a very popular politician, truly a man of the people who fought for seniors' rights to continue to live in affordable housing, for the poor to keep their social services office, for the preservation of open space and the development of parks and baseball fields for the generations of children to come. He'd never shrunk from a battle on behalf of those who sought his aid, and I was very proud of him, of our whole family.

Some people in the community referred to me as the "first lady of San Juan," and that was fun. I thoroughly enjoyed attending openings of shows, cutting ribbons and sitting at the head table for so many lovely functions. Mayor and wife. The local newspapers constantly carried stories about us — our trips, our awards, our childrens' school activities.

We had succeeded in building something better than we had dared to hope for. Laughter filled our home and our hearts, and we marveled at how far we had come from the broken homes of both our childhoods.

If a shadow fell occasionally, I had only to look at the happy faces in our family gallery in the upstairs halls and the balance would tilt back. Back to the status quo. I didn't want anything ever to disturb the life we had forged for ourselves and our children.

Dad called me on an almost daily basis to catch up and check up, and for the most part his interest in our lives made me feel warm and loved. Since we had put more miles between us, the relationship seemed more friendly than before, and I wasn't afraid that he would harm Julie. All of that was behind us now. I had managed to put it out of my mind.

But I was to learn that the past has a way of impinging on the present, whether we want it to or not.

June 26, 1985
San Juan Capistrano, California

Danny's 13th birthday party was that night and he'd asked for Chicken Tortilla Ole! He always asked for it, and I was especially pleased to make it for him. School was out for the summer and with great enjoyment, I was throwing myself full-throttle into the joys of motherhood.

I was deboning the chicken with the help of my housekeeper, Rosa, when I saw a new Camaro pulling into the driveway.

Who could that be? Between the telephone calls and the interruptions, I was having a difficult time getting my casserole layered. My irritation gave way to surprise when I recognized Cee Cee behind the wheel. Her baby daughter, Keely, was with her.

"Cee Cee!" I yelled enthusiastically as I rushed out to the driveway. I hugged her and glanced down at her beautiful dark-haired baby. "I haven't seen you in ages. How do you happen to be here?"

"Oh, Donna, I should have called. Rand had a toothache. Sandy took him on an emergency appointment." We were all very proud of Sandy and grateful to have a dentist in the family. She took care of all the family's teeth.

"I have to go and get him in an hour. I just wanted to see you, wanted you to see how big Keely's getting." Cee Cee spoke sincerely, huge blue eyes looking to mine for approval. A kind of sadness emanated from her pretty face.

"Well goodness, I am so glad you did! My heavens, Keely is getting huge and soooo cute! Is she eight months now?"

A short time later, lemonade in one hand and adorable Keely poised on the opposite hip, Cee Cee leaned against the tiled counter in my kitchen. I went back to my deboning, while Cee Cee caught me up on all the latest family news from Los Angeles.

Her husband Rand's musical career was taking off and he was frequently on European or Japanese tours with his heavy metal group. His latest album was a big hit in Japan and he was soon to open at Madison Square Garden. She had every reason to be happy, but it soon became clear that she was not doing very well emotionally. She had been feeling suicidal more and more often, but she knew better with a new baby and four others to care for.

Listening to her I realized that Cee Cee had always had trouble with depression. Even before she got pregnant at 17 with her oldest daughter, Anne, she was either incredibly happy or miserably sad. As I aligned my corn tortillas and filled them with chicken, I knew that today was all about sad.

"Donna," her voice filled with misery. "I really am at the end of my rope. Daddy won't leave me alone. He drives me crazy. When Rand and I are on tour he follows us. Last month in Nashville, Dad showed up at our hotel right when we were making love. We were 2,000 miles away and there he was at our door, unannounced and uninvited!" Her passion flamed. "He actually came into our room, lay on the bed and asked me to fetch him a soft drink over cracked ice.

"Rand has about had it with me. He's furious and wants Dad away from us. When Dad comes around every day, Rand leaves the house."

Her voice was stronger now, charged with anger. "You know that's why Henri left me, because of Dad. He said he was always in our faces."

"Cee Cee, as long as he's supporting you, he's going to think he has a right to barge in any time he wants. We don't live all the way down here by accident. Ken was not about to spend a lifetime with Dad.

"Don't just hint, Cee Cee," I added firmly. "Dad doesn't hear hints. He'll even call down here at weird times like after 11 o'clock at night. He knows that I go to sleep early. Ken's short with him and never wakes me up. That's how you have to handle Dad. He's like a big lonesome baby. Mostly, he likes to read his novels to me," I concluded with a shrug.

"It's worse than that." Cee Cee's voice dropped an octave or two. There was a long pause. Her lids covered her eyes. I was adding green chilies to my casserole layers.

"Anne told me he has bothered her."

My heart stopped at the mention of my 17-year-old niece. Suddenly I was at attention. I could feel my face turning red. What I had dreaded all these years, what I had never allowed myself to think...

"What do you mean, bothered her?" I asked cautiously in as controlled a voice as I could muster.

A long pause followed. "He forces himself on her."

"What do you mean?" I couldn't keep the urgency from my voice.

"He forces himself on her!"

"What are you telling me?" I had to know exactly what she meant.

"He makes her have sex! She hates him. Wants to kill him. He hurts her. She's so tiny. God, Donna I don't know what to do. I can't get him to stop. He bothers me, too." She sounded like she was choking.

I cleaned my hands and shakily led Cee Cee and Keely, still in her arms, to the sofa. "Tell me about it, sweetheart." I forced myself to calm down. I had never solved a problem by panicking. I would not panic now, though adrenaline-fueled pounding was loud in my ears.

Forty-five excruciating minutes later, Cee Cee and Keely left to collect Rand and return to Los Angeles. I was stunned.

All those warm birthday thoughts I had been filled with an hour before had vanished. I was dazed from the ghastly tale Cee Cee had so haltingly revealed. Not only had our father molested her when she was very young, but by the time she was eight years old he had forced intercourse on her. It was horrible.

She had gone on to tell me that he had done the same to her daughter, Anne. Anne had finally told Cee Cee what had been going on all these years. Cee Cee kept Anne safe from him now by sacrificing herself.

This had been very difficult to hear. I could not imagine that Cee Cee at 35 years of age was still under Dad's control. The bile lodged in my throat.

I learned that Daddy had given Cee Cee over to our grandfather, Big Ray, who also had molested her. I was devastated. Those whispers in my mind the day we poured through old boxes turned into shouts. Big Ray, too! But I had loved my grandfather. I wanted desperately to hold his memory sacred.

Cee Cee also suspected that our youngest sister, 15-year-old Diedre, might have been molested by Dad, too. Diedre had lived with Bernie, her mother, since Dad divorced her back in the early 70s. Dad saw little of Diedre these days. Cee Cee thought she was probably safe now.

I quickly calculated the present risk. Everyone was away from Dad except Cee Cee. All the younger girls — Diedre, Connie, Anne and Julie — were away from him, and Keely was just an eight-month-old baby. Cee Cee was clearly the only one in danger now. I admonished her to find a new job like the one she had held for years as a Hollywood booking agent. She needed to be independent from Dad. She had to get away from him.

Cee Cee was frightened and told me that she had considered telling her husband. After a long while she concluded, "No, he'd leave me if he knew!" She started crying again after that.

Cee Cee was forced to drop out of high school when she had become pregnant with Anne. She had then attended a special school for unwed pregnant girls. While there Cee Cee performed with such superiority that she was chosen the class valedictorian. Dad must have been the most surprised. He'd always told us she was stupid.

I remembered watching her from my seat in the auditorium during her graduation ceremony. She was very pregnant and very young, but her valedictory speech was eloquent and well delivered. I was very proud of my sister that day.

Today's news from her had raised the tiny hairs on my arms and sucked my breath away. This was beyond my wildest nightmares. I had used the word crazy to describe Dad's bizarre actions, but I knew that he was not crazy. Crazy was not knowing right from wrong.

Dad certainly knew right from wrong. He had a sophisticated high-tech job, was educated, wrote novels, studied. He'd even been president of his Yacht Club. Knowing that Dad didn't qualify as really crazy was perhaps the most frightening thought of all.

Cee Cee also told me about Connie. She was part of my father's second family that he and Bernie had, after he divorced my mother. Cee Cee reported that Connie recently had come to her for help when she ran away from Dad because he continued to molest her.

What about Sandy? I remembered her agony when she revealed to me a few years earlier that Dad had sexually abused her. When Sandy reported him to Child Protective Services, the agency had simply done a cursory investigation. Because no child was living with him, there was no case. As always, our dad remained unaffected.

After that Dad took every opportunity to complain that Sandy was treacherous. "One who is treacherous might be eliminated," he intoned solemnly, sending chills down my spine.

I sat back and tried to think. The pain burned into my soul. I had promised myself that my nightmare was behind me, that everything was okay. Nothing bad could happen like it had when I was little. And here it was, spilled out all over my beautiful home where I had felt safe from that agony. Until now.

June 27, 1985
At Home
San Juan Capistrano

I awoke with Cee Cee's words whirling in my head and felt compelled to go on examining my memories. Something else was trying to force its way into my consciousness. I leafed through my imaginary Rolodex and came to "T" for my brother Trey. He was just a bit older than my own son Rick. Trey had just turned 21, loved school and college life. He was a dependable, sincere young man.

I recalled Dad's voice, syrupy on the surface, contradicting the sly underhanded messages they held.

"Trey's a bonehead. He'll never amount to anything."

"Cee Cee was dropped on her head as a baby. She'll never be intelligent."

I realized that Dad consistently said terrible things to me about each of my siblings: my brothers, Trey and Chad, and my sisters, Sandy, Cee Cee, Diedre and Connie. He was playing us one against the other. I'd often heard him refer to Cee Cee as a "savage." Our father was apparently a cold calculating liar. He had manipulated us by dividing us with lies.

To our faces he was love and kisses. Lots of smiles, extolling our virtues. His favorite line to us all was, "I love you more than anything." Behind our backs he invented the most fiendish of lies. Because of our father, we really did not trust each other. Divide and conquer was the basic warfare strategy. I recalled that my long-widowed grandmother Maymie once began dating a man Dad didn't approve of. My father put detectives on him and forced Maymie to stop their friendship. Dad ran the whole show, the whole family. He always had.

"The most bonded to the abusing parent." Yes. I'd once read that in a self-help book. How interesting that it did not make much of an impression on me at the time, but when I thought about it, I realized it was true. Who did I want to be the most perfect for? Daddy, of course. The abusing parent.

How often I hid my real feelings behind a mask of Super Happy. How about Super Agreeable? That too. Miss Cooperative, afraid to speak up. Afraid to look at the truth. Afraid to admit that Daddy hurt me, too.

I had never told Cee Cee my own secrets about Dad, about what he had done to me, not even yesterday when she was pouring her heart out. What if she told Dad that she had told me? I did not want to know what might happen...

June 28, 1985
San Juan Capistrano

My nights were sleepless. What should I do? I concluded
that everyone was safe for now, and Cee Cee had promised
to get away from Dad. Did I really want to get involved in
what was happening between Dad and his second family?
There was an impatient part of me that was not altogether
sympathetic about Cee Cee's dependent status, but I was
desperately sorry for all that had happened to her.

For years I had encouraged her to go to college or work,
anything to stand on her own.

I had studied Eric Berne's work on the psychological
games people play and understood that Dad and Cee Cee
were playing "victim-rescuer." I had showed her how Dad
liked to be Big Daddy, doling out money and favors as he
chose. Dad always kept Cee Cee down by repeating the
story of her being dropped on her head. She was "damaged
goods," he'd say.

I knew the only way to stop these games was for her to
become independent, to get away from Dad. Cee Cee had
remained dependent, however, always needing grocery
money, advice and even one of Dad's houses to live in.

Perhaps he talked about me behind my back, too, but he
always told me to my face that I was beautiful and competent. And he had never turned me over to Big Ray or anyone
else. I wondered how he had decided to do that with Cee
Cee, but not me. I was grateful that Big Ray had been a
wonderful grandfather to me but reflected for a long time
on how Dad and Big Ray perceived the difference between
us. I didn't like the answer I came up with.

Cee Cee, our father's illegitimate child, was thought to be
expendable. Dad must have always viewed her as worthless.

Perhaps he actually believed it possible that some humans were superior to others. Yes...I strained my mind. He clearly believed that men were superior to women, hated that women had the right to vote and resented having them on the road behind the wheel of a car. His vocabulary had always been filled with words straight out of a Victorian novel, like "mistress," "class," "bastard," "cuckold."

My mind was reaching back to things long forgotten that I must have always heard. Finally, I could hear my father's dogmatic voice: "Hitler had the right idea. Those Hebes are unfit to do business with. They deserved everything they got." "Blonds are higher class than brunettes." "Jigaboos are mentally inferior."

It was incredible. He must actually believe this nonsense! What seemed like relatively banal red-neck talk, which I had spent a lifetime tuning out, took on new proportions. I knew that soldiers depersonalized the enemy by stereotyping and labeling. It made the horrors of war bearable. "Gooks, Chinks, Japs, slants, slopes, sons of bitches, bastards."

Nonhumans. I saw it then. Cee Cee, a bastard, worthless, her feelings could not matter. Anne, like Cee Cee, was born out of wedlock. For Dad, her feelings would not matter either. He had dehumanized them.

I could hardly believe what I had been told. Big Ray. My wonderful grandfather must have viewed Cee Cee as inferior, expendable... Beautiful, talented, clever, loving Cee Cee. Funny Cee Cee, always ready with a joke.

And what about our grandmother, who said that she had been sold? This was too horrible. I wanted to switch the channel in my head, but it wouldn't switch.

Big Ray and Maymie? I had known it once, for a while, years ago. Suddenly it all became clear again. Poor Maymie. I understood.

I paused for a moment and thought of my always youthful, energetic grandmother. She was educated, cultivated, a lady. With her hard work she had pulled the family back from the devastation of the depression. She had found happiness in her life dancing, enjoying all of us, reading, visiting with her many friends. She, who had made so much of her life, had gone through the humiliation of being sold. It must have felt like a life sentence.

Why had Big Ray never bothered me? Perhaps he attributed some special quality to me. I had always felt something like that. I was born within wedlock, which seemed a rather select status in our family. Was that it? They abused little Cee Cee because she was born out of wedlock? I could not fathom what her life must have been like, was like now. It all seemed more depraved than the horror stories by V.C. Andrews my children read. *Flowers in the Attic*. That had been revolting. Freddie terrorizing Elm Street. But all those stories had been fiction. What does one do when faced with the undeniable fact that she is living in the middle of something worse than fiction?

Not having an answer to that question, I switched back to Cee Cee's childhood. Mine certainly had not been ideal, but still I had my father's last name, my father slept at our house. I did not feel like Cinderella to two legitimate sisters. How must it have been for her always to call her father, "Ray-Ray" and to lie about Sandy and me? Clearly the implication had to have been that she was not "good enough" to be a real sister or daughter.

June 29, 1985
San Juan Capistrano

Still anxious after several days, I called Cee Cee to see how she was. Her mood had greatly improved. She was much better since our talk. She said that sharing it had taken some of the shame and fear out of it.

Cee Cee believed that everyone was safe. She would just make Dad stop, make him leave her alone. It would be okay. She reassured me again that Anne was clear of Dad now. She decided to quit answering the phone every time he called, and to stop going to his house all the time to clean for him.

I felt relief. By the end of the second week after Cee Cee's visit, I was able to push my fears back behind their special safety-locked door, behind the tumblers and steel. Pushing my fears away seemed to be getting more and more difficult, but the pain and the fury had to be buried.

If Dad knew that anyone had told on him, it could be deadly. I kept placating myself by remembering that everyone was safe now. There was nothing more I could do.

I knew I would not consider telling Ken. He might do something drastic. I also had three children to consider, and our respect in the community. Ken was now in his third term as mayor. I forced my attentions back to my family and our summer plans. I had to put this to rest.

And Dad, had he changed? I didn't know what to think. This was all so difficult for me. After everything, I still loved my dad...

August 5, 1985
Avalon Bay
Catalina Island

I cleared away the breakfast utensils and went out on the deck of our boat. The bright sun danced off the water. It promised to be a golden day.

Hoping to cool off, I drove into the crystal water and swam into the fairway in front of our boat. As I hung from one hand, grasping the mooring line, I could see that someone was aboard my father's similar boat moored a short distance away. I had not seen him since Cee Cee's explosive news five weeks before. I was now finally sleeping again at night. Things also seemed to be going okay for Cee Cee.

I took a deep breath, let go of the mooring line and swam toward Dad's boat. He was sitting reading in the aft area.

"Hi, Dad."

"Hi, Bugger. How are you, Honey?" His voice was filled with joy at discovering me in the water below.

"Super. It's a real challenge cooking on the boat's alcohol stove."

"Come aboard. I'm just working on this new mystery novel that takes place here in Avalon. Can I read to you for a while?" he asked.

"Sure, let me climb up and dry out for a bit."

I dried my hair with a towel I found on the deck, then pulled a white plastic chair around and sat down. "Okay, Dad. Read on." The warm sun soaked into my wet skin. I closed my eyes as Dad read.

This story was an action murder mystery with some Hollywood bad guys behind a Catalina death plot. He called it *Escape From Evil*. As he read on for several minutes, I became interested. It was about a high-roller type who owned a 70-

foot yacht moored in Avalon Harbor. As the story continued the murderer nonchalantly ordered one of his burly employees to find an eight-year-old girl and bring her back to the yacht for sexual acts.

My eyes snapped open. Dad was reading this horrible story to me with a straight face and a calm voice. I was seeing the perverted story come alive in my mind's eye. I was that little girl.

"I can't hear anymore..." Tears sprang to my eyes as I turned away from him.

"What's wrong?" Dad asked in his most innocent, puzzled voice.

"I can't do this." My voice cracked as I muttered, "I'm not okay about what you did to me when I was little."

He looked at me blankly, making a note with his pencil in the margin of his notebook.

I rushed on. "Last semester a girl in my speech class gave a speech on incest and I got panicky and started to hyperventilate. I'm not okay about what you did to me when I was little. Ever."

I turned my face away, my chin quivering. I was struggling for control. I had not confronted my father in years. We had always pretended that it had never happened. A long silence followed.

"I'm sorry," I heard him mumble.

"I'd better not hear any more of these novels," I warned. "This upsets me too much." I spoke in strangled words, careful not to reveal any more, certainly nothing of what Cee Cee had so recently told me. I might jeopardize both of our lives.

At that moment my half-sister, Connie, who had been below in the cabin came out. "Hi, Donna, nice day!" She greeted me warmly.

"Yes...I've got to go!"

My father's attention had turned back to his writing. He didn't have anything to say to me as I left. He seemed totally unaffected by what I had said. I climbed down the swim step, eased myself into the cold water and swam back to our boat. My father was still writing notes in his book.

A nugget of truth nudged me as I kicked through the chilly waters: "No conscience." I had read that someone without a conscience couldn't really ever get one. Sociopaths didn't have a conscience. They felt no remorse or guilt. They could only veil their disorder to blend in with society. It was only upon close inspection that they could be detected.

The quiet inner voice spoke to me, *Donna, your father is not the good guy you've always pretended him to be.* That gentle inner voice would not go away. It kept haunting me.

I remembered other interactions when his response to me had been peculiar. The year before he had found a 21-year-old waitress in a restaurant he frequented for breakfast. He had given her a 2½ carat diamond ring, trying to get her to marry him.

That morning I was showing paintings at a local outdoor exhibit and he made a date to visit me there. He would bring his new lady to meet me. I was proud of a painting I had just completed of myself at age one. It was the centerpiece of my exhibit. I knew Daddy would adore it.

I waited for him all day, but he never showed up. I was about to drive out of the parking lot when I saw Dad waving and honking. I stopped and got out of the car.

"Hi Donnie!" He sounded youthful and happy. "Wow, I'm glad I caught you. I want you to meet Kitty!"

Introductions were made, the diamond was shown. I tried to force the ice from my voice. "Nice to meet you Kitty. Nice ring!"

"Donnie, she wants to have a whole bunch of kids the same as I do!" He was breathless with excitement. I felt like his mother. He had his new fiancee and dazzling plans. I stood feeling dull with my little handpainted plates packed into my car. I swallowed my hurt, trying to ignore the fact that Kitty was younger than my son, Dad's grandson!

Caught up in their own music, they did not notice my weak performance.

I went with them for a quick dinner. Afterward, at the car, I tried again to get the attention I had hoped for with my new painting. I handed it to Dad, holding my breath, anxious for the praise I knew would be forthcoming. I felt proud. My heart gave an extra little thump. I knew this self-portrait would really thrill him.

He glanced down briefly at the plate. "That's nice, Honey. So what do you think of Kitty? Isn't she something?" He beamed as he pulled her into another hug.

I stood alone. That had not been the time to examine this idea closely, but now, as I swam away to the safety of my boat, that small thought gnawed at me.

November 1988
At School

Sitting at my large desk in my corner office at the college
where I had been teaching for twenty-two years, I paused
and looked up at the wall in front of my desk. It danced with
pictures of my family. My three children smiled at me from
dozens of photos taken over the years. They were precious
to me. My office was also my sanctuary.

My students were eager to catch a glimpse into my private
life. They often brought their friends and other students to
see my picture wall.

Since Cee Cee's ugly revelations a few years earlier, I
devoted my energies even more to my family, my portrait
painting and my students. They all comforted me. I knew
how to keep busy, how to keep control.

Today something special had happened in my classroom.
Something that reflected why teaching was so important to
me. As my students were filing out after class, I had an
opportunity to say something to a young man whom I'd also
had in another class. I'd been noting a tremendous change in
him lately.

He was lagging behind zipping up his back pack. It hung
heavily under its great weight of textbooks. As Tran ambled
past my podium, I spoke to him.

"So, Tran," I used my most casual voice, "it seems I'm
noticing a change in you lately. Am I?" I smiled warmly. He
had been a tough one to get through to.

He looked directly at me, his dark almond-shaped eyes as
deeply serious as always. "I found out from you that I was
not a freak."

I laughed. "Who would ever say that about you?"

"I always knew I was a freak," his tone was matter-of-fact. "I've never had many friends. I haven't really fit in. Sports were out. I'm too small."

"Tran, I never thought of you as different."

"Well, I thought so until you taught us about those personality types. I have always hated everything about myself." He paused and looked self-consciously at me. "I'm okay with me now."

"Well, I'm glad." I smiled at him.

He nodded his delicately featured head and moved toward the door. I knew that our conversation was over. Not many words were exchanged but what had transpired was remarkable.

I had met Tran, a skinny 16-year-old, the year before when he had been an advanced placement high school student taking my college public speaking class. He never mixed in with the other students. He was aloof and unfriendly, seeming to be disdainful of me and the subject, superior to us all. He was going to be a scientist. His attitude was not an asset. He earned a B in my class, probably the first in his life.

Then at the first of the next semester, there he was coming in to register late for another one of my classes. I was shocked to see him. For weeks he seldom spoke to anyone. Then suddenly after a lesson on Sheldon's personality types, he began to change. I think he discovered that he was not alone. He was not only normal, but he had been described in a scientific textbook.

I felt Tran's pain for a moment. How sad to feel so set apart. Our culture stresses the active, outdoorsy type, so that those who are less athletic often feel inadequate. It made me angry. Why wasn't it okay to be who you are? Why can't we be all colors, all sizes, all cultures, all religions? Why can't we just be people who are happy and sad, who feel pain and joy?

Students like Tran who acknowledged that I made a difference in their lives came along every so often in my teaching career and made it all worthwhile for me. I knew that my gift was an ability to connect with my students, helping them to see just how important they were. School was such a wonderfully safe place for me.

July 15, 1989
San Juan Capistrano

Having the summer off from teaching had its positive and
negative sides. I enjoyed the freedom to do as I chose, but
when I had too much spare time, I found myself worrying.
Sometimes I worried about the uncontrollable flashes of the
past, other times I brooded about Keely. I needed to distract
myself, so I planned a big picnic celebration for Julie's 21st
birthday.

While I was working at my desk, making a list of supplies
for the party, the telephone rang. I reached for the phone.

"Donnie?" asked the youthful voice I immediately recognized as my father's.

"Hi, Dad! How's your fancy new hip today?" I asked with
a smile, successfully stuffing my anxieties for the moment.

"Hey, a few more of these operations and I'll be the bionic
man! It's amazing. I can actually walk now. No more crippled
old fogy."

"That's great, Dad. The physical therapist has been a big
help, hasn't she?"

"Yeah, but my speed isn't 20 steps and a pat on the back.
Fogy baloney. I'm ready to think body surfing."

"Dad, is it better being back at the beach? I can't believe
you ever moved away from the water."

"So much better. It's too hot in Hollywood. Hey, I called to
tell you that I received the invitation to Julie's party today.
Twenty-one. Where does the time go?"

"I don't know."

"Donna, that invitation is just too much. It's so clever I
can't believe it."

"Do you really think so?"

"Really! How many girls have a painting of themselves at

age one printed in color on an engraved invitation? Especially one painted by their own mother! It's beyond clever. Your talent is bursting at the seams!"

His words made me feel special and loved. I still liked Dad's praise.

"I know I'm biting off an awful lot to try to barbecue for 130 guests."

"Ah, people pitch in. And, Honey, we don't all have to eat at once. Some will still be swimming, some playing volleyball. Besides it's going to be the best party this family has ever had."

"Oh, Dad, do you think so?"

"Angel, it can't miss. It'll have everything. You're the hostess. Oh, Donnie, someone's at the door. Gotta go. I wanted to tell you all about taking Keely to the baby store. I got her three new dresses. She modeled each one like Miss America. So cute. I want to tell you all about it. Gotta get off now. I'll call back later."

"Okay. I want to hear about those dresses. Miss America, huh? Keely is something else."

"The party will be perfect. No more worrying. Kisses."

"Bye, Dad."

As I hung up the telephone, I turned my attention immediately back to the table decorations and center pieces. Balloons. We would need balloons...

August 10, 1989
San Juan Capistrano

This morning while I fed Cory and Cassie, my two dogs, one of those horrible pictures came over me. I fought it as hard as I could, but lately feeding the dogs was becoming an increasingly powerful trigger to my memory. For some reason the same image came into my mind almost every day.

I would see Daddy climbing off of me in the dark, when I was little, in the trailer on a trip to Chicago. I was pretending to be asleep in my sleeping bag on the floor. I could make out Dad's shape in the shadows of that trailer. He was going over to my small sleeping sister. Maymie was asleep in the front bed. My sweet little Sandy was in the double bed in the back.

Oh no...stop. Ugly, sick pictures. Images that I had never permitted myself to see. I wondered just how much more of this I could take.

They were coming all the time now. Sometimes different ones. They always left me trembling, nauseous and frightened. The most alarming part was that I could not control them. Donna, the master of personal control, now could not stop the foul images reeling across her mind.

I realized that these episodes had been occurring for several years. They had become more and more frequent since 1985 when Cee Cee visited me. I knew that I was deliberately trying to hide from their meaning, from the truth. But my mind would no longer allow it.

That gentle voice, the loving spirit who comforted me from within, was no longer reassuring me. I thought of my afternoon rests and the moments before I fell asleep at night. I could hear the gentle voice pushing me, urging me.

Donna, what about Keely? She is four years old now. She is almost school age. The age you were when you can remember him touching you. What about Keely? You must protect the children...

My concern had intensified since January when a big group of us had met at our boat. That was the first occasion I had really spent time with Keely.

We had immediately hit it off. She spent the entire day in my lap as we toured San Pedro Harbor in the January chill. We had cuddled and laughed. I photographed our hands together, my strong tanned one with her tiny, pale one lying inside my palm.

An idea for an interesting painting came to me and I took many pictures. I had painted her amazing face when she was two, and the portrait had been published in an artist's magazine. Keely was precious. Her lips were a bright natural red like her father's and her eyes were iridescent blue, fringed with a thick row of dark lashes. She was a very pretty child.

By the end of the day, straddling my lap and looking directly at me, playing absently with the rings on my finger, she said, "Aunt Donna, I'm so glad you fell in love with me!"

I had fallen in love with her. Her observation knocked me for a loop; she was so bright and direct. I laughed at her child's honesty and hugged her to me. We both wrapped up in my jacket against the wind of the brisk day. My heart spilled over with love for this four year old.

That day was the start of a heavy correspondence. My refrigerator was now covered with her drawings. I was getting more and more involved in Keely's life. She even had her mother call me once a week. We had wonderful talks about her pets, her nursery school and her baby brother, Kyle.

A few months later I dropped in unexpectedly to visit Cee Cee and her family. Cee Cee and Rand were going out for the evening. Cee Cee was on the telephone trying to arrange for Connie to baby-sit. Connie couldn't, but she said that Dad would. He said he wanted to take Keely to see a new movie.

Overhearing the conversation, panic seized me. I butted in, almost hissing at Cee Cee.

"No! Don't let Keely go with him, anywhere, alone, *ever!*"

My vehemence startled her. It startled me. I didn't know where it came from, but I was alarmed. After a long moment, understanding splashed across Cee Cee's face. She turned back to the telephone.

"Ah, Connie, that's okay. I'll make other arrangements for Keely. Thanks. I'll talk to you soon."

When she hung up the phone I admonished her *never* to let him baby-sit. Finally she had shaken her head in mute agreement. We both knew that Dad had been very ill. He had almost died from his recent prostate problems. I tried to tell myself that he was an invalid. He was too old to be a threat. Cee Cee probably told herself the same things, but I was not really reassured. I lived so far away I knew that I was powerless to protect Keely. Or was I?

When I got home I took the dogs for a long walk. As they bounded along, I thought of Ken. He was the one who insisted that we seek this rural life, introduced this beach girl to horses, orange groves, cowboys and swallows. He was such a steadying influence on my life. What would I ever do without him? It was a chilling thought.

It took me a minute to realize why I was contemplating the consequences of losing Ken, and when I did, it made me even more afraid.

August 18, 1989
San Juan Capistrano

"Donnie?"

"Oh hi, Dad." I answered distractedly, hearing the familiar voice of my father across the telephone line. My flashbacks were getting worse and it was becoming more and more difficult to make small talk with him as the mechanism that used to guard my memories gradually broke down.

"Honey, I called to say hi. I'm still thinking about Julie's party. It was fantastic."

"I'm glad you enjoyed it," I responded quietly.

"You should see the tent city that Keely and Russ are making across the chairs in my living room. They're having great fun."

We talked on for a short while. As I hung up the phone, the lump in my stomach reminded me how anxious I was feeling about Keely, and about the pictures from my memory that flashed so frequently now. I could visualize precious little Keely in my father's living room. How could Cee Cee let him baby-sit with her children? The worry was eating away at me.

Safely alone in the late afternoon seclusion of my silent home, desperate for some shred of reassurance about Keely, I went into Julie's empty bedroom. It was just the way she'd left it three years ago when she went away to college. I opened her double closet doors and sat on the floor in front of the bookcase. I was searching for her textbook on abnormal psychology.

I located it quickly and turned to the index where I immediately found an entry for sexual deviates. I turned to the page and began reading, hoping to discover some information to calm my fears about Keely's safety. I knew so little, truly almost nothing about this subject. I had always been afraid to read even the bare essential information about child molestation, incest or father-daughter rape. Just the mention of the topic sent me into a panic attack.

I knew this book would be helpful. I scanned the chapters: Incest, Pedophiles, Rape. "Pedophiles start with their eldest child and continue. They continue to abuse into their seventies. They never stop." Those words loomed out of the textbook at me: "They never stop."

Just last night Dad had called me and put Keely on the telephone. Her baby voice said, "Aunt Donna, I am so lucky you love me."

And then my father had come back on. Wistfully he had said, "Keely told me yesterday that I am the nicest man she knows and that she wants to marry me. I told her that they won't let us. Donnie, she is the only woman who loves me."

His remark shook me to my foundations. The hidden recesses of my soul began to open, releasing more pictures from my memory. What I saw did not reassure me about Keely's safety.

August 23, 1989
San Juan Capistrano

I spent an hour in the mall looking for a birthday gift for Ken's mother. I wanted another little gift to add to the chalk drawing I had done of her cat. We were having a dinner party for her tonight.

I was browsing at B. Dalton Bookseller when a display of the book *Toxic Parents* by Dr. Susan Forward caught my eye. Interesting title. I purchased a copy. A few days later I began reading it.

> There are many types of physical abusers. Many of these people look, talk and act just like human beings, but they are monsters totally devoid of the feelings and characteristics that give most of us our humanity...these people defy comprehension. There is no logic to their behavior.

As I read on, a tight feeling filled me. It was as if I were reading about my own life:

> Many physically abusive parents enter adulthood with tremendous emotional deficits and unmet needs. Emotionally they are children. They often look upon their own children as surrogate parents to fulfill the emotional needs that their real parents never fulfilled. The abuser becomes enraged when his child can't [won't] meet his needs.

I could hardly believe what I was reading. Daddy had turned me into his little mother by the time I was two. My childhood was filled with preparing his baths, his meals, massaging his back and keeping his house. To deny his demands, any of his demands, was to meet a violent rage. I thought about my wrist being bent backwards. I thought about the late night violence.

> He [the abuser] lashes out, and at that moment, the child is more of a surrogate parent than ever because it is the abuser's parent at whom the abuser is truly enraged.

It did not take much speculation to conjure up an image of Dad as a little boy, furiously staying on the back fence when his mother arrived home after a trip she took around the world. Dad had told us of that trip many times, and even when he was in his 50s and 60s he sounded petulant.

"She was gone for more than a year," he'd complained. "I'd never call her mother after that."

He never forgave Maymie for leaving him.

I read about the role reversal of the abused child with the passive other parent. The child assumes responsibility for the protection of that parent as if she were the child.

> By allowing herself [himself] to be overwhelmed by helplessness, the inactive parent can more easily deny her silent complicity in the abuse. And by becoming protective, or by rationalizing the silent partner's inactivity, the abused child can more easily deny the fact that both parents have failed her (him).

I thought about my mother's role in my life. She had always excused our hardships by saying, "We were just surviving." She clearly saw herself as a victim, not an adult protector of her own children. In the past ten years, my mother had questioned me about Dad on several occasions.

"Your father never touched you girls, did he?"

Her head would be shaking no when she asked the question. It was easy to answer her. I gave her the answer she wanted.

"No, Mom."

I felt obligated to protect her. I did not want to believe that my mother had failed me too. I wanted to believe that she loved me.

I was dazed by the section of the book entitled "The Keeper of the Family Secret." It could have been written about me. I knew that I would never have bought this book if I had known what it was really about.

> Moments of tenderness, love and support keep [a victim] yearning for a normal relationship with him [her father]. As a part of that bonding she believes she has to keep secret the truth of her father's behavior. A "good girl" would never betray her family.

What was I going to do about this? What was I going to do about Keely and Daddy? I knew that the anxious feeling I had been experiencing on and off all summer was about my fear for Keely's safety. She was fast approaching a dangerous age. She was now four. Five and six loomed perilously close.

Cee Cee guaranteed me that Keely was never alone with him, that her older brothers Russ, 9, and Jess, 14, were always present. I knew Dad's modus operandi. The boys were no protection at all from Grandpa, the baby-sitter. The more I read, the more convinced I became that Keely was in danger of being abused.

My logical mind returned to his hip replacement surgery in May. He used a walker. Dad also had severe kidney damage, and ketones in his blood from his prostate problem the year before. He had been very sick. Was I just over-reacting? I read on in the book:

> If one were a victim of childhood sexual abuse, he or she could not cure themselves. Such victims require professional help.

I thought of my frequent flashbacks. I knew that I had to do something. I knew that my mind was not going to let me evade the issue this time. I decided to make an appointment with a therapist. I told Ken and my family that I was considering getting counseling certification, and I wanted to get the therapy requirement out of the way first.

Ken knew that I was planning to get another degree and agreed that I should do whatever would work best for me. My gentle inner voice kept prodding me. *Is Keely safe? Is she?*

August 30, 1989
Rose's Office
Newport Beach, California

One week later Sandy accompanied me on my first visit with the therapist, Rose, a nice plump woman in her mid-fifties. Sandy stayed a short while, then left us alone in the pale pinkness of Rose's silent office. Rose looked at me and quietly said, "So tell me, what has brought you here?"

A long moment passed. Finally, chin quivering, I blurted out the words which I had so long held back: "When I was a little girl, my father molested me."

Tears came. They overwhelmed me. I was terrified, for I had violated every rule I had been taught. I had betrayed Daddy to a stranger. I had told the secret! Somehow I forged ahead and began to tell her everything. I knew I had to gain control over the flashbacks, the turmoil in my mind.

This was my first step.

September 10, 1989
San Juan Capistrano

I hung up the telephone. I'd been chatting with Dad. Dread
tore at me, terrifying me.

Dad was going to baby-sit with Keely overnight.

Armed with my new knowledge, I had become hypervig-
ilant. Dad's every word in every conversation took on new
meaning. I'd made some pathetic inquiries about Keely and
the logistics of the baby-sitting. I was still desperately hoping
to extinguish my growing suspicions.

"Donnie," Dad had begun, "Cee Cee and Rand wore their
black leather rocker clothes today. Rand was in stage makeup. They told me that a pedestrian was frightened by their
appearance and crossed the street to avoid walking near
them."

"Dad," I said, "I'm worried about Keely." He thought that
I was reacting to his story. I meant that I was worried about
Keely's spending the night with him.

Dad always played the innocent. I knew there was nothing
to be gained by confronting him about Keely's spending the
night at his house. But my mind just would not let go of the
thought of Keely. She was so tiny and so trusting. She was
just a little girl who loved her Grandpa.

Donna, do something before it's too late! You have to protect Keely.

I could not pretend to be okay when I was frantic and it
became harder for me to make telephone small talk with
Dad. A week or so later, I could not deal with him at all. Ken
made excuses for me for a few weeks, but I knew that I
could only be "showing apartments" so many times.

I told my husband that I was dealing with some childhood
issues in therapy and was too upset just now to talk to my
father. Ken accepted this, but it was awkward for him to

keep making excuses for me. He didn't really understand
why I wouldn't speak with Dad.

By September 15 I knew I could not keep dodging Dad's
calls. I wrote a letter to explain my sudden change in behavior, hoping that it would forestall the daily calls and buy
some time. I claimed grief over Danny's moving away to
college and the recent death of my horse, Windy. I was too
afraid to rock the boat by telling the truth.

I dreaded opening the envelope that promptly came back
in my father's exact engineer's lettering. Ken was sitting
next to me in my dressing room while I read the eight-page
letter. When I finished it, I passed it wordlessly to him.

"My word, look at his condescending tone," Ken laughed.

"Kenny, this is not about what you think. This is about
something else I cannot tell you," I thought. I knew that I
had not succeeded in slipping past Dad's watchful eye. He
was not accepting the written explanation I had sent. By not
taking his calls, I had started something frightening.

The entire tone of his letter was sarcastic. He started by
calling me his "Little Pen Pal." He gave chatty information
about all the family members, subtly reminding me what I
was cutting myself off from. He patronized me with advice
about how to live my life, suggesting that I had my values
and priorities all wrong and that I was a workaholic. His
tone of superiority and his threats told me without a doubt
that I was embarking on war.

He included a strange poem he had written with the letter:

> The troops, nearly always innocent of the nature of war,
> march boldly forth to the beat of the drum.
>
> Other innocents, at home, sit on volcanic soil
> never aware of its true nature.
>
> The leaders of both rarely apprise them of the facts.
> All go merrily to their various fates.

I was deeply frightened by the letter and not quite clear about the poem. I knew it was some kind of threat for the tremendous act of defiance I was committing by not talking to him on the phone. I considered calling and smoothing things over before the war got out of hand.

I thought of Keely's little hand in mine, secure, trusting. I heard, "Aunt Donna, I am so lucky to have you love me." My inner voice kept nagging me about her safety. I felt that my reputation as a human being was on the line. I was a mother, a schoolteacher, a decent citizen. I must keep Keely safe.

I knew that I had indeed started something I could not stop. An angry part of me goaded me on to respond to my father's letter. I would use his same sarcastic tone. Inwardly I composed the words I would never send:

Dear Dad,

I got a kick out of the closing of your letter as you described sitting back and watching "One Man's Family." I agree our family is fascinating. What a brilliant plot. One handsome, charming man molests babies, then rapes them, starting at about age 8 and continues the sexual abuse until they can escape. Then the father watches how they handle their own personal devastation.

The first child, Donna, the compliant one, tried to pretend it never happened. She tried to be perfect to cover up for her own overwhelming sense of shame.

Sandy, the second child, was so devastated that she ran away from you when she was 12. She also tried to be perfect but was so destroyed that she went through several failed relationships. You see she can trust no man.

Then there is the third child, Cee Cee. You broke her in with Big Ray and then finished her off yourself. She felt so helpless that she became the wild one, doing the Hollywood scene.

What about your other daughters, your granddaughters and their young friends?

Keely? I pray to God that she will remain safe.

As you mentioned, Dad, it does make for an interesting
story.

Donna

If I'd sent the letter to my father, he would have told me
that I was mistaken, and he was always right. I was never
to question or defy him. That's how the world worked
according to Dad, at least Dad's self-made world. It was his
way or no way.

Dad kept calling whenever he felt the urge, but if Ken
picked up the phone, it would go dead in his hand. I had not
answered it for weeks. If we let our answering machine get
it, there would be no message. Sometimes it would ring six
or seven times in an hour. Always hanging up. There were
even calls in the middle of the night.

The weeks of phone calls were wearing me down, and I
felt panicky and scared all the time at home. Ken was beginning to lose patience. He still did not understand what was
going on, and I was not ready yet to tell him. I didn't want
to place my marriage in jeopardy.

During therapy, Rose directed me to make signs and place
them next to the phones to help calm me. I printed them in
large letters and taped them around my home:

Poor dear. He is crazy and it's not my problem.

The signs were a good idea at first, but eventually they
exacerbated the whole problem. Even when the phone
wasn't ringing, the signs reminded me that it soon would. I
couldn't sleep for more than two or three hours at a time.
My nightmares had become more frequent.

In order to help regain my self-control, I read more books
on childhood sexual abuse, hoping to find something, anything, to allay my fears about Keely. During my therapy
sessions I kept dragging the discussion back to Keely. Rose
still believed that the real issue lay with me and my own

childhood abuse. She thought that all of this about Keely was a red herring. I insisted that I was frantic because of Keely. I had nothing concrete to verify my concerns, but I still worried.

I remembered once studying the great scientist Hermann von Helmholtz who examined the stages of human thinking. He described the first stage as "saturation," or filling oneself with the contradiction between the problem and the impossible solutions. I had poured over every detail of my childhood and of my father's childhood. I was indeed saturated with it.

I was afraid for Keely, but I was also afraid of betraying Daddy, of losing him. Surely he would hate me...or kill me. I was afraid of what Ken might do, of what my friends might think...of my children knowing, but my inner voice still would not be quiet.

Afraid because of what? Donna, you are developing a strategy.

Am I? The realization that I was indeed toying with a plan startled me. Yes, I felt an idea working its way forth. Helmholtz's second stage was "incubation." My subconscious was struggling to engender a plan. The nightmares and flashbacks were part of the process.

Donna, you know what you must do. You must ensure that your father never molests Keely...

The answer brought me great relief. I would not sit idly by while Keely was in jeopardy. No, I would do something. I wasn't sure what, but I fantasized an assortment of strategies. The best ones revolved around getting Keely completely safe, but it wasn't easy to do. I could trust neither Cee Cee nor our father. I knew he had guns and was perfectly capable of flying into an uncontrollable rage when crossed. If I got killed, I would not be any help to Keely. To do this right I needed to assemble an army to help me.

I would assemble the troops.

PART IV
Assembling The Troops

No, the past would not stay buried; the skeletons would not stay in the closet.

Over the span of a few short years, my beautiful life had been interrupted more and more often by external events, by revelations of my father's ongoing abuse of those who should have been able to trust him.

As pressure built, the truth took on a life of its own. Even in quiet times, the memories I had so carefully banished to the darkness would rise up, unbidden, to haunt my waking hours and infiltrate my dreams. Flashbacks. Scenes from memory that suddenly take over your consciousness, as if they were happening right now.

I was, more and more, feeling like a victim again, a victim of the past. It went against my grain. Once I had been that helpless child, but I had outgrown helplessness, earned my way out, and I had no desire to play the part of a victim.

My fervent desire was to keep my life on an even keel, but the situation with Keely wouldn't go away. Even keel or Keely? The conflict in my mind made it hard to think. What if Ken left me? What if my children couldn't look me in the eye? What if the neighbors never spoke to me again? What if my school district fired me? Yet something had to be done.

What could I do that wouldn't jeopardize everything I'd worked so hard to build? Wouldn't damage my husband and children? Our standing in the community, our choices for the future? I had so much to lose. How could I really carry out what I knew I must do?

As hard as it was to admit it, I knew I needed allies.

October 3, 1989
Rose's Office
Newport Beach

"I think you may be obsessing, Donna," Rose said at our afternoon therapy session. "You may be over-reacting to the possibility of danger to Keely. Besides, you're too fragile right now to call Cee Cee and open up this issue."

"But Rose," I countered, "Cee Cee is her mother and needs to protect her."

Rose was adamant: "Donna, please take care of yourself first. You are emotionally weakened and I don't think you're ready for this."

"Maybe I am over-reacting," I agreed, but when I got home, I felt so desperate to protect Keely that I dialed Cee Cee's number. She had to be warned. But I only reached a computerized operator saying her number was no longer in service. No new number was available.

I did not feel safe calling anyone else in the family. What if they told Dad what I was saying about him? And if I sent Cee Cee a warning in the mail, she might show it to him. No matter what she said, Cee Cee was still under his control.

I couldn't resolve anything now. I continued to go through the motions of day-to-day life, but my mind still churned. I hoped a solution would suggest itself.

October 19, 1989
San Juan Capistrano

My mom came down to my house for Saturday morning coffee. She knew I was in therapy and plagued with hang-up calls from my father. She was concerned, having spent so many years trying to figure him out. Mom's fury was still close to the surface about Dad's starting a second family with Bernie while he was still married to her, but I was used to her anger.

This morning we took our cups of hot coffee outside on the patio. It was unusually warm and lovely for October. As we resumed our conversation about Dad's incessant calls, Mom turned and looked directly into my eyes.

"Donnie, did your father ever touch you?" Her voice was level.

When she had asked me this before, I had never told her the truth. *Assemble the troops.* I knew that I needed an ally. I hesitated for only a moment, though my pulse was beating wildly.

"Yes, Mom. That's really what this therapy is about. I've been having a terrible time with flashbacks. My therapist says I have acute delayed stress syndrome. It's similar to what Viet Nam vets had after the war. When a person has suffered trauma, years later it can come back to haunt them. It's pretty bad, Mom. I'm having a lot of trouble."

I always suspected that if my mother knew, she would flip out, and now I watched her carefully, intent on each nonverbal clue. She went pale and the tears began to flow. Her hands began to shake, and she looked as if she'd stopped breathing.

"Mom, I never told you. I was always afraid it would make you crazy."

"Honey, I asked you before," she cried softly. "Why didn't you tell me a long time ago? Why didn't you tell me so that I could have done something?"

"What would you have done, Mom?" I asked. "You couldn't even get him to stop having Bernie around or stop having children with her." My words became emphatic. "I don't think you could have stopped him."

"Donnie, I won't go crazy. I want to help now." She sobbed, assuring me between broken sentences. "I always knew he was warped. What can I do? You poor baby. I am so sorry. I never dreamed...," her voice trailed off. "In the last ten years there's been so much more on television and in the papers. I began to worry after his third wife took him to court and had that warrant out for his arrest. I heard the rumors." Mother's voice was stronger now.

"I'd forgotten about Crystal."

"What about Sandy?"

"All of us girls, Mom."

"Oh, dear God!"

November 2, 1989
Driving Home
San Juan Capistrano

Ken and I were driving home from one of Julie's collegiate soccer games. We were haggard from ceaseless hang-up calls and began to discuss my father. Ken was still very puzzled by Dad's behavior. I knew that soon I must tell Ken. I needed him in my army.

Possibly reacting to intuition as long-married people often do, Ken asked in a tentative voice, "Donna, did your father ever molest you?"

"Yes," I was able to reply without hesitation. I felt I had waded into dangerous waters but I needed his stalwart support. I paused. "It started when I was a little girl."

Ken simply reached for my hand. For the time we each remained silent, letting what I had revealed sink in. His touch reassured me as we drove home, the darkness of the night intensifying our thoughts.

Once we were comfortably seated in our family room at home, Ken heard me out. I had been so afraid of his reaction, but he was immensely understanding, promising me that everything would be okay, that he would protect me.

Much later that night my husband turned to me. I could see the sadness in his face. "Donna, I've never said anything all these years, but tonight I have finally come to an understanding." His voice was comforting. "All these years I felt like we were two soldiers alone in the woods." He paused for a long moment. I could tell this was difficult for him. "Any time I came home late from a class or a meeting and tried to touch you in your sleep..." He stopped again.

I wasn't sure if I wanted to hear this. I looked at Ken in the semi-darkness of our family room. My eyes took in the numbers on the digital clock above the television. It was 1:30 a.m. Ken's eyes were large and serious in the dim shadows.

"What, Kenny?"

"Donna, if I ever tried to make love to you in the night..."

"Yes?"

"I could tell you didn't want me."

"Not want you? Kenny, I love you!"

"Donna, it always hurt my feelings so I quit trying. If I would caress your back or touch you, then you would start kicking. Hard. Sometimes you'd even try to bite me. I couldn't figure it out. Sometimes you'd even hiss out in a strange voice, 'No! No! No!' There was such pain in your voice. Then when I'd back off, you'd quiet down and go back to sleep. Donna, I think you were asleep when all this happened."

I was aghast. "Kenny, are you saying that I'd actually yell out 'No'? Oh, dear God..."

My chest constricted and I began to cry as I realized that all my life I had denied the deep, terrible pain that surfaced now. Kenny held me tight.

"Kenny, I'm so sorry."

"Donna, it's okay. Now we are one."

We both understood that my fears were a window into the anguish and fury stored in my unconscious. We did not need to say aloud what we understood. Kenny now had the whole lurid picture of my childhood.

There was still more for me to tell. Ken had to know about Julie, but that would be another day.

November 4, 1989
San Juan Capistrano

During the next few days, I took my children aside one by one and told them the story of my childhood abuse. They were each deeply hurt and angry. Danny and Rick wanted to kill my dad. My precious Julie cried for weeks. When I saw the pain in her face, I began to get glimmer of the suffering I had frozen inside me.

The day I told her, we were quietly sipping coffee in Nordstrom's empty dining room.

"Oh Mom, the safest place I've ever known in all my life was in my daddy's arms," she sobbed.

After that she was speechless for a long while. I reflected on Julie's words. Her father's arms had been a secure haven for her.

It was so different in my family. Few of my father's children ever hugged him hello or goodbye. We were always on guard.

Once I had talked with Julie, I knew I could no longer wait to tell Kenny that Dad had touched her when she was ten. My husband had been so good, so understanding when he learned about me. What would he do when he heard about Julie?

When I told Ken, he only asked me a few quiet questions to confirm that Julie was okay, to convince himself that it really was not more than I had told. Then he got into his truck and left, looking sad and hurt. I was afraid of what he might do, but I was powerless to stop him. He was gone for several hours. When he returned, he seemed very controlled and determined. He simply said he would take care of everything.

Later that night he told me that he had taken a large hammer from the toolshed and headed for Dad's house in Los Angeles. His plan was to use the hammer to see that Dad never hurt anyone again. On the way there he fought through his tears of pain and his anger enough to achieve some level of rationality.

Just before the off-ramp to Venice, he stopped on the freeway, realizing that attacking Dad physically would result in more problems for all of us. Ken would end up in jail and our lives would be ruined. He turned around and came home, determined to find a way to make the system deal with my father.

Ken knew there was more than one kind of hammer.

November 6, 1989
San Juan Capistrano

Months of sleepless nights and the stress of my full-time teaching activities were beginning to take their toll. This had to end. Then in the middle of the night, with thoughts colliding in my mind, I finally realized what I must do. Although I was physically tired, my emotional energy was waxing again, thanks to the support of Mom, Ken and my children. Getting the truth out into the open gave me strength.

I leaped from my bed and began typing a letter to Cee Cee. I had listened to her years ago, but I had never confided in her. Cee Cee had to know just how dangerous Dad really was. I had to tell her my story.

I wrote for two hours, pouring out everything I could remember about what Dad had done to me, from my first day of school until I moved into the sorority house. I told her how I had felt dirty and inadequate under my cheerful veneer, and how hard I'd always worked at pretending we were normal. I explained my need to be perfect, to be quiet to protect Ken and my children from scorn and ridicule.

By the end of this letter Cee Cee knew about my therapy and about the textbook definition of pedophiles, who abuse children well into their 70s. I pleaded with her to protect her precious daughter.

"Cee Cee," I wrote, "I want Keely to experience her innocence, to feel clean. I don't want her to have crabs when she is 13 or have nightmares about getting molested. I don't want her to die of shame because she is not a virgin."

As I wrote I felt so much love for my half-sister and her little girl. My mind and heart worked in unison to say the words that would finally bring truth and healing to our family.

"I know that in toxic families everyone has secrets that keep them isolated. Let us not stay so far apart in a lonely, distrustful world."

It was the kind of letter you might write to clear your mind, with no intention of sending. But the next morning I tucked it into an envelope and sent it off with the mailman. No matter what the consequences, Cee Cee needed that letter. I knew it beyond a shadow of a doubt.

November 14, 1989
San Juan Capistrano

Kenny answered the phone when Cee Cee called. She was almost incoherent.

"Kenny, I got Donna's letter," she cried. "I'm scared. Dad said you and Donna have been trying to get custody of my kids."

"Cee Cee," Ken's voice was warm but emphatic. "There is no way in the world we want to take your kids. Donna is just very concerned about Keely's safety."

"I know that now, Kenny." Tears choked off her words. "I really believed Dad though. I wanted to believe him. I did not want to think that he would hurt Keely, but I know now that it's true!

"Kenny, I tricked Dad today to test Donna's letter. I didn't want to believe her. She wrote that she thought Keely was in extreme danger. So I went to Dad's house. While I was cleaning, I told him in my best acting voice, 'Dad, I can live with it if you just touch Keely, but you musn't do anything else with her.' Kenny, I expected him to say that it was all lies." Cee Cee's voice broke for a moment and she paused.

"But, Kenny, he said, 'Coach her for me. Coach her.' He wanted her to not tell their secret. Then I knew that Donna was telling the truth. I grabbed Kyle and Keely and got out of there as fast as I could. I have tried all evening to call you. The phone was busy. I told myself that I would try one more time and you answered."

"Cee Cee, you have to come down here right away. Can you come tonight?" Ken was gentle but firm.

"Ken, I'm so afraid. I didn't want to believe it but Dad says he's going to destroy Donna. He also threatened Chad's life last week. His own son! Daddy kept squeezing the gun that he keeps under the front seat of his car and ranting about Chad. Do you think he would kill Chad?"

"Cee Cee, can you come down right now?" Ken's voice was urgent.

"I could come tomorrow with Rand and Anne."

"Do that, will you? We'll figure out what to do. We care very much about you, Cee Cee, and we've got to protect Keely." Ken paused to let that message sink in. "Be strong. You did the right thing to call us. You'll be okay." His words were powerful and directive. "Listen to me. Do not answer the telephone, leave the machine on. Keep Keely safely inside the house. You'll be okay. Have you told Rand?"

"He knew that I had been molested before we got married when I was a child, but he doesn't know anything of what's been going on."

"We'll get into it tomorrow. He has to be told." Ken was fierce.

"Now, do as I say. Lock the doors, lock the gate, put the answering machine on."

"Okay. Thank you, Kenny," Cee Cee was quieting down.

Ken hung up and turned to me.

"Donna, she's petrified. That bastard actually convinced her that you were after her kids!" My husband shook his head in disbelief.

I remembered the ominous words of Dad's poem: "The troops, nearly always innocent of the nature of war march boldly forth to the beat of the drum."

This was war.

November 15, 1989
San Juan Capistrano

Rand and Cee Cee arrived with their 21-year-old daughter, Anne, four-year-old daughter, Keely, and baby Kyle. Their sons, Jesse, Russ and Nick, were staying with friends. Cee Cee busied herself in my kitchen putting together the take-out hamburgers she had brought for all of them. Anne got me alone and told me about their trip down to our house.

"Donna, we barely got Mother here. At every off ramp she had an excuse as to why we should turn back. She was crying the whole time. Rand doesn't know what's going on. We'll have to tell him soon. Mom was afraid of what he might do if she told him without your help."

After the hamburger debris was cleared and the children were settled quietly with toys, we took our seats around my dinette table and waited for Ken to get home. Sandy came over for a few minutes to lend moral support.

Cee Cee began, "I told Donna in 1985. I wanted her to stop him then, but she was such a wimp. She didn't do anything."

"I told her in 1981. She didn't do anything then either," Sandy accused.

"Hey, wait a minute," I interrupted angrily. "I'm not the mother here. You two are both adults. I am not in charge of your lives."

I didn't like the blame being laid at my feet. The months in therapy had certainly taught me that all of these people were not my responsibility. My responsibility lay with myself and my own children. I was not about to accept this guilt trip. Sandy had called the authorities years ago but it had done no good. They said they didn't have a case. Also,

I had specifically told Cee Cee years before to get away from Dad and get a job. Instead, she had another child.

"Look, this isn't getting us anywhere," I added trying to stay calm. "We always seem to avoid placing the blame where it belongs...on Dad. Let's get a clear perspective on this thing and decide what we're going to do." I looked around the table at the three women.

"I'm not here to listen to all the gory details," Sandy inserted sternly. "I went through them years ago in therapy and I don't want to get into it again. I just want you to know that you can get well. I went to therapy for three years because of what dear old father did to me. After so many failed relationships with men, I had to learn to trust and learn how to be a girl. My big defense was to act like a tough boy. I'll be your inspiration, and I'm here for support always, but I can't get into it again. I have to leave."

Cee Cee, Anne and I looked at her. She was confident and straightforward. She seemed strong and sure of herself.

"I do have to go now. I have work tomorrow," Sandy added with a sad smile. "Cee Cee, I'm proud of you for coming down here. You've taken the first step toward getting better."

After Sandy left, Anne and Cee Cee began talking at once. Rand was busy with the baby in the other room, and we decided not to tell him about Dad and Keely yet. We knew we should wait until Ken got home from his meeting to help handle Rand's certain fury.

"Donna, it has been a nightmare," Anne confessed sadly. "I finally told Mom when I was 16. Since then he hasn't come near me, but she's been protecting me with herself."

Cee Cee interrupted. "Donna, he just won't leave me alone. I feel like I'm in prison. He comes by our house and honks every night at the dinner hour. We've tried ignoring him, but he just honks and honks the car horn until it drives us crazy! Last night it went on for two hours. We turned out all the lights and hid on the floor. The phone rang with hang-up calls all day long. He's driving us crazy."

"Cee Cee, I got those hang-up calls for weeks. Whenever someone would answer, he would hang up. I know he was waiting for me to answer but I never did. I tried to call you a few weeks ago. I would have written sooner but I thought you'd show the letter to Dad and I was afraid of what he might do." There was a long silence.

"Donna, I'm so ashamed. I did tell him you said that he molested you when you were little. He said that was 'a big load of crap,' that he worked hard then and did not have the time. Didn't have time! Pretty weird answer. I also told him some other things about your letter. I'm so sorry." Sobs wracked Cee Cee's slender body as she realized that she had put me in danger.

After several minutes she continued, "Dad convinced me that you really were after the children. He told me to run to Phoenix. Jesse told me two years ago that he saw Grandpa doing things...and I didn't do anything about it then. I thought Jesse would get killed. Dad had me so scared of him."

"Mom and I sat very quietly with Keely yesterday," Anne explained slowly. "After a long while we got her to tell us what Grandpa has been doing to her. It's really terrible. He has had her in the bathtub licking him. He has licked her. She told me about his lips. She said that when he would take her out to breakfast, he would sometimes put his tongue in her mouth while they were sitting in the car. When they went inside the restaurant, she said that Grandpa would put his fingers inside her panties."

"Honey, we must protect Keely. This has to to stop." I spoke firmly, my heart breaking inside because of what I was hearing. What I had worried about happening in the future was already true now. I felt sick.

People knew about the abuse and Keely still wasn't safe. Why wouldn't anyone stop him? Donna, you will stop him!

"Dad ordered me not to write to you. He saw me mailing that card to you and challenged me. I told him you were such a sicko that I would send you a get-well card. I even made a mean face about you. He liked my sarcasm and let me mail it. He didn't see the inside. He's after you, Donna. He said, 'If it takes my last two hundred thousand dollars, I'm going to destroy her.' He said he'd hire detectives and also plant someone at City Hall to say means things about Ken so that he will have to leave office. I don't know what he might do, Donna."

"I'm scared, too," Anne admitted. "The worst was when we were little. Diedre, Connie, the boys and I would all run for the car when it was time to go somewhere. The boys were bigger and would always beat us to the car, but we girls ran frantically. It didn't matter if you had to go to the bathroom or needed a drink of water, or couldn't find your new doll, you just ran. The one who was the slowest was the one who got molested that day while the others waited in the car."

Shivers of terror went through me. Those poor little girls. What kind of human being would do such a thing? My gentle inner voice responded:

Only a very evil one. A very evil one...

"Donna, Dad has been driving me crazy with that poem he wrote to you. He kept making all of us read it. It seemed like gibberish to me, but he insisted that we praise him for it. He was also going off about that letter Sandy read to him last month. He tore it into a thousand pieces and flushed it down the drain."

"That letter," I responded, "detailed the harmful effects of Sandy's abuse and told him to stop abusing everyone else. Sandy needed to confront him for her own healing."

"So what did Sandy do?" Cee Cee looked at me in wonder.

"It was on Halloween. She made a lunch date with him at Marie Callender's restaurant to confront him. She did it all herself. She was very brave. She read him a prepared four-page document, confronting him with it all. Dad's only denial was, 'I didn't love Diedre too much." Sandy listed all of us in the letter as well as Crystal's daughter, Jamie. She said that his eyes clouded up with tears a few times and at the end he said, 'I made a wrong decision.' That was all the apology Sandy got. Dad started sidetracking then and blaming everything on our mother. He was very eager to get away from Sandy."

We looked at each other for a long time. This was one of the only planned confrontations Dad had ever had to face for his acts. Was there hope of stopping him?

"When he told me about meeting Sandy," Cee Cee sighed, "he said Sandy just told him to take better care of himself."

"He left out the part about Sandy confronting him with sexually molesting everyone, didn't he?"

Cee Cee nodded her head. "Actually Dad has become pretty weird. One night when he was over, I left the living room for a moment. When I came back in, that vase you painted for me was shattered. He told me that Kyle had crawled over and knocked it down. 'You don't want her shit around here anyway,' he said. I didn't believe him for a second. Kyle never went near that table."

The sound of Ken's truck interrupted us, and I ran to the door to meet him. When he hugged me, I whispered that we had not told Rand yet. Ken understood that we needed him and hurried to join our tense little group. He gave Cee Cee his full support as she told Rand the painful facts.

Rand flew into a rage when he learned that Dad was molesting his wife and child and thundered at Cee Cee, "How could you leave our little girl with him, knowing he was a child molester? How could you?"

Cee Cee cried and begged Rand not to leave her. He was so furious he wanted to go kill Dad. Ken grabbed him by the arms to get him to sit down and finally calmed him enough so we could talk it through.

The night went on interminably, filled with tears and shouting. At last Rand and Anne convinced us to report

Dad to the authorities. Cee Cee and I were terrified at the thought, but knew that we must do it. I looked into her eyes and nodded yes.

My inner voice was strong: *Donna, you must protect the children.*

PART V
Launching The Battle

The Chinese tell us that the longest journey begins with a single step, but they fail to tell us how horrifying it can be when that step means certain warfare. Someone will be damaged. Perhaps everyone.

Between our decision to take action and our first real concerted step in that direction, our family members seemed to face a gulf as wide as forever. What we did next transported us into a new dimension, and as terrifying as it was, turned us from victims to warriors. We couldn't predict the outcome, or be certain we would win, but the tide really turned in our souls the day we took that step.

In many ways it seemed worse. I didn't lose my fear overnight; my flashbacks continued. Sometimes I'd even wake up dreaming that I was having one of those friendly phone calls with Dad when he asked about my children and how the dogs and horses were. It was hard to keep track of time.

But in the depths of my being, the part of me that believes all people should be treated fairly, scored a great victory when that first step was taken.

At the time, however, I wasn't so sure.

November 17, 1989
Early Morning
Santa Monica, California

In the gray overcast of early morning we met at Cee Cee's home in Santa Monica. All of my brothers and sisters were there except Connie. We hid our cars around her neighborhood in case Dad drove past the door. We held an emotional family conference led by Ken, and then traveled in small groups the few miles to Stuart House, a center for sexually abused children.

As I sat on the vinyl sofa in the waiting room, I could not help but reflect on the stories I had been hearing from my family all day. One of the girls had slept at Dad's one night. She was a flat-chested little child, ill with the flu, awakened and raped by my father. She described how sick she had been and that sex was dry and dreadfully painful. I was hearing examples of greater violence than I had ever known at his hand. I had never been beaten, locked out naked or whipped with a belt after being raped while Dad yelled, "Whore."

It was almost more than I could stand. For more than four decades I had protected myself by moving to my intellect, where I did not have to feel. I now switched to that more peaceful channel in my mind and tried to be analytical. What kind of a person was Dad really, I wondered? One book I had read stated bluntly that serious legal consequences are not generally imposed on incestuous abusers. Nothing much is done because our culture recognizes a man as the head of his family, the king of his domain. I remembered reading one story about a man arrested for incest. As they handcuffed him, he turned to the officer and said, "This is some country where you can't even raise your own fuck."

I had also learned that daughters and stepdaughters typically are the victims. The abuse usually begins early, preschool through about age 11, and average cases include all of the daughters. The books also told me that incest is the most common form of child abuse and that 85% of all crimes committed against children are sexual in nature.

Incest represents abuses of power and loss of control. An incestuous father wields absolute authority over a relatively powerless wife and children. Child molesters frequently feel justified in using their daughters. Occasionally a therapist could get an offender to acknowledge the harm done to his victim, but he would still feel no real remorse.

The interview procedure started with me as the oldest. I joined a detective and our social worker, Lila, in a small one-way-mirrored room. They told me that I would be observed from behind the mirrored wall. It took about 20 minutes to tell my story. I felt icy calm, the kind of calm people must feel as they face a firing squad. There was no more confusion. I was clear about what I had to do and I did it, simply and directly.

Dad pretended to everyone to be kind, loving, caring, honest and concerned. He was charming and clever, a steady earner and a voting citizen. He devoted a great deal of energy to helping all of us pretend he was a "nice daddy." I supposed that Dad was pretending for himself as well. Denial, I had learned, was a major weapon for the offender. He would never acknowledge that he had harmed us. He lived in his own little world.

At Stuart House we learned many things about sex offenders:

1. They seldom plead guilty.
2. Traditional therapy does not cure them, though they will pretend to be cured.
3. There are excessively high rates of recidivism.

4. Chemical sterilization and a type of brain surgery have been effective in curing offenders.
5. Most sex offenders have been molested.
6. About 30% of men molested as children go on to become molesters.
7. Molesters make a decision to molest.
8. Molesters come from all walks of life. They look like ordinary people.
9. Very frequently it is the natural father who molests his own daughter.

My lifelong friend, Leanne, came to lend her support and sat quietly at my side in the waiting room. Her beautiful brown eyes were filled with tears and grief over what she was hearing. Those eyes were a reminder to me that this was indeed real. It was not an awful nightmare I would awake from.

Before we left Stuart House, a case worker scheduled Keely for a physical examination. A doctor would need to check her to see if there had been any scarring or penetration.

After our long day we all went back to Cee Cee's and brought in Chinese food. It had been a harrowing week without many meals.

Ken and I played with Keely for a long time up in her room. We could feel that she needed our strength. Late in the afternoon she finally told me what Grandpa had been doing to her. She stuffed a handkerchief into her little rosebud mouth and tried to choke herself so that she could not tell. I still felt the sting of her words.

"Aunt Donna, I know what Grandpa is doing," she whispered to me.

"What is that?" I asked casually.

"He is using his finger to make my little pee pee bigger so that his big pee pee will fit in it."

Her tone was conspiratorial; it was a secret shared with a trusted aunt. I kept my cool, but the disgust floated up to the surface.

"I know, Keely, but it is not okay for Grandpa to do that with a little girl."

I was sitting on the floor playing with her dolls. Keely folded herself a bit unsteadily into my arms and leaned her head against my shoulder for a long time. I could feel her terror and understood that for now, I was her strength. I waited all evening, until she was ready for bed before we left.

"Honey, you were something today. You were so strong and so good with Keely. You are my miracle, Donna," Ken spoke softly, holding me against his chest, still damp from his shower. "I thought you were incredible all those years, but I really had no idea."

We turned out the lights. It had been a long day, and I had to teach the next morning. I lay in the dark and tried to recall what psychologist Alice Miller had said about trying to find witnesses who would not be afraid to stand up for children. She had come to the conclusion that their numbers were few. She maintained that society had betrayed its children and begged her readers to protect children from adults' abuse of power.

Alice, it is very scary...

Thanksgiving Day, 1989
Mammoth Lakes, California

We all left town for the holiday. Ken and I took our family
to our mountain condominium at Mammoth; Cee Cee and
Rand took their brood to Phoenix. The complicated and
lengthy police procedure had us hiding out.

Cee Cee called, sounding upset. Keely had stopped breathing the night before. "She was purple. It scared me to death!"

"How is she today?" I was trying to be calm.

"She seems fair, but I had to scream at her to breath. It
was so horrible. We got her back to sleep about half an hour
later. She cried for a while."

"How about you? How are you holding up?"

"I can't sleep much. Rand is still angry. Donna, if the police
don't do something, I'll never feel safe to leave my house
again! It was horrible keeping Keely out of school last week
and this week. I'm not sending her back until Dad's in jail.
When she freaked out last night, it was over a nightmare
that Dad would come into the school yard to get her and
steal her away. She panics every time she sees a car like his.
It could be a long winter."

"I know. I'm even careful where I park. I know Dad keeps
an arsenal."

"Donna, recently he bought a semi-automatic. I think he
keeps it in his car."

"Tell me how Keely's physical exam went." I was very
concerned about my niece.

"The doctor said there was no physical damage, but Keely
liked the doctor and told her everything. The doctor couldn't
tell me much because of the investigation, but she did volun-
teer to testify for us. She said she was sickened by what
Keely had told her.

"Stuart House made Rand and me and the kids all agree to come in for therapy. They had us sign an agreement. The therapy is free; it's part of their rape program. Rand isn't too eager to talk to strangers. Neither am I for that matter, but I've come this far. I will go through with it."

"We all need therapy. It has really helped me to have an objective person to talk to. Our crazy family rules have brainwashed us. Could I talk to Keely for a minute?"

Keely's sweet little voice came on the line. It warmed my heart. She sounded happy and rushed to tell me about her morning.

"Aunt Donna, Aunt Donna, thank you for loving me. I'm playing horsey now with my other Grandpa."

"It sounds like you are having loads of fun!" I encouraged her. It relieved me somewhat to hear her sound so carefree this morning.

"I am! I've gotta go now! Bye-bye!"

Rand's parents loved Keely dearly. She adored playing with this Grandpa. The thought that Keely's trusting little soul had not been safe with my own father filled me with rage.

December 3, 1989
Rose's Office
Newport Beach

When I met with Rose for therapy, she noticed I was in a
better mood. I had been granted my sabbatical leave request
for the next year. I'd have the entire year off from teaching
to study.

"I feel like my life is getting slightly back to normal," I
told her. "The misery you've heard from me recently is not
at all representative of my whole life." Our eyes met. "I
guess hanging out in denial for 40 years did allow me to
feel happy much of the time." I paused for a quick moment.
"I know that I have been involved on a deep level with
others. I have devoted my energies to my children, my
husband, my students. I had not really been concerned
about my *self*. I know you think my commitment to my
portraiture has helped me cope."

"I believe that you have purged much of your fury
through your artwork," Rose agreed. "You have been painting for 11 years. That's almost half of your adult lifetime.
Look at your paintings a little more closely. They aren't just
paintings, are they?" Rose paused, gathering her thoughts.

"Your paintings are almost always portraits of innocent
little girls. You have been trying to protect them by preserving their innocence through your brush. I have believed
all along that your artwork has saved your life, at least
your sanity. It has allowed you a break from the conflicts
you feel."

"I unconsciously put myself into art therapy, didn't I?" My
response had been a new awareness.

"Yes. You were able to find a way to take care of yourself.
Donna, you deserve credit for what you have done. You

could have discovered alcohol or food. Many do, you know." Rose continued, "You deserve credit for what you have done. You have had a loving 26-year marriage, and three very successful, happy children. That alone is a significant accomplishment. Your family system with your husband and children seems healthy. You owe yourself recognition for this. You didn't perpetuate the dysfunctions or the abuse. You've done all you could to stop the cycle. You need to be proud."

I stared at Rose silently, thinking about her analysis of me, of my life.

"And we haven't even got to you as a teacher or artist or businesswoman," Rose spoke with conviction.

I wondered briefly how many of my artist friends realized how much we mood alter when we take up our palette and brush? I knew that creativity was a safe harbor for me. I wanted to think about all of this.

What really brought human happiness? The doing, the creative process, involvement with others. I didn't have time for that idea right now, but something was there to examine. I knew I had made a conscious decision early to be happy. For me the glass had always been "half full."

"Rose," I began a moment later, "I think I have led a rather charmed life except for one little problem..." I smiled at her, trying to make a joke. I knew that sexual abuse was devastating. I'd been hurt, but I'd had a good life.

"Perhaps it is only denial," I added, not believing my own words, "and I have had a miserable life. But mostly I have always felt happy. I love being a mom and having a family."

Rose was not saying much. She was ill and I could tell she did not feel well.

Rose's lids were getting heavy. I wasn't sure if she heard me. I continued anyway, hoping that she would snap back.

"Over the 25 years that I've been a mother, I can hardly even think of unpleasant times. I loved it all: the trips to the orthodontist, the dancing lessons, the soccer games, the family wrestling matches on the living room floor, the birthday parties, the ski trips and the summers at Catalina. It has felt like a grand and marvelous party, and I was center stage helping to direct it. I made my life what I dreamed it would be. That cannot all be denial can it?"

"Take credit for doing a good job, Donna. And begin to be nicer to the little 'you' inside. She's been locked away for a very long time. When you told me last time that you couldn't stand to look at pictures of yourself from ages five through twelve, that means you've not been acknowledging that brave little girl. She needs credit for surviving what she survived and growing into the kind of person she has."

I replied, "I'm ashamed of her. She feels pain, she's all needy and screwed up. I like to keep her locked up. She bugs me." I meant it. "I can't stand to look at my childhood pictures."

"To get better you're going to have to let her out, feel her pain and then learn to love her and take care of her. You must learn to be as good to her as you have always been to your children. You wouldn't lock them up, would you?"

"Certainly not!" I answered too quickly. Rose gave me a look that said, "Well, then?" We sat without speaking for a long interval.

After a moment Rose asked, "Donna, your family means a lot to you, doesn't it?"

"They mean everything to me!" I thought of Keely, only a defenseless little girl. I would do anything to protect the children. I knew it wasn't over yet. I was in danger. Nothing was settled.

Rose continued, "I am very serious when I say that you deserve credit for what you have done."

My comfortable moment had passed. I heard Rose's words, but they were just noises scratching against my eardrum. I was still caught up in a war against my father. My family was in danger.

December 15, 1989
Cee Cee's Home
Santa Monica

Today the detectives wired Cee Cee to record her conversation with Dad. She was to make a breakfast date with him so that the police could get some more evidence for the trial.

Ken was trying to hold her together. He had gone to her house early in the morning to be there when the police arrived. Cee Cee was frantic with fear. She could not believe she had committed herself to having breakfast with Dad. Did he know we had all gone to the police? Was he planning to set her up? Would he shoot her, then turn the gun on himself?

Rand was trying to keep the kids from driving their mother crazy. They had been home for weeks, too frightened to go to school. Everyone was edgy and irritable.

Cee Cee started calling our father's house at eight o'clock to make the date. No answer. She tried every 20 minutes for three hours. The police stayed with Cee Cee while Ken disguised himself as a bum in an old overcoat and a baseball cap, and went to see whether Dad was home. He drove close to the house, parked and walked around the front of the property. The drapes were drawn shut. Dad's car was in the carport. He was there.

Ken called back to Cee Cee's from his cellular phone to report. Cee Cee dialed Dad's number again and again. No answer. Did he suspect something? Was he ill? Was the phone unplugged?

By one o'clock our brother, Trey, reported that Dad had called him. Dad was going to the bank with Diedre, our youngest sister, and was leaving town for Florida in the morning. The police left. They told Cee Cee and Ken that they would try another time. We knew this failure to get more evidence would put off the arrest for weeks.

The detective assured Ken and Cee Cee as he left her house that an arrest would be made after Dad's return from Florida. There were still some details he was concerned about. He had wanted something on tape. The warrant for Dad's arrest was drawn up and waiting to be implemented. We were asked to be patient.

Later in the day Trey was able to communicate again with Dad. Trey told Dad that Cee Cee was very sorry for ignoring him lately, that she had been upset about money. He got Dad to agree to call her at nine o'clock the next Friday morning.

December 28, 1989
Cee Cee's Home
Santa Monica

Keely sat quietly in the arms of her Uncle Trey, listening to the story he was reading her. After a while she turned her face up to him.

"I'm going away soon."

"Going away? What do you mean, you silly girl?" he teased.

"I'm leaving."

Trey tried to get more from her, but she wouldn't talk. He felt frustrated, but managed to read the story to her.

Later Trey reported the odd remark to Cee Cee and Anne.

Cee Cee spoke slowly, "Yesterday she told me that she was sorry she had caused all this trouble. She's been soiling her pants many times a day lately. I'm really worried about her."

Anne chimed in, "Mom, two days ago I had to break into the bathroom while she was having one of those privacy baths her therapist wants her to have. I knocked and knocked and called her name. She wouldn't answer. I was alarmed and finally used a hairpin to pick the lock. Keely had filled the tub almost to overflowing. I yelled, 'Keely, what are you doing? You didn't answer me!' She just gave me the weirdest, most detached look. All she said was, 'I was practicing.' Mom, I didn't know what she was talking about. It kinda spooks me."

"Yesterday she wanted to know exactly what day Grandpa would be back from his trip to Florida. I told her probably on Saturday. She was terrified." Cee Cee's eyes filled with tears. "You don't suppose she is thinking of..."

"Killing herself..." Anne said in a low monotone. "She is thinking of killing herself."

Cee Cee, Anne and Trey were stricken. Could it be possible that Keely was thinking of suicide? Was she going to drown herself?

December 29, 1989
The Stuart House
Santa Monica

Keely was given an emergency appointment at Stuart House. After talking at length with Trey and Anne, Cee Cee was convinced that Keely was suicidal.

That night Cee Cee telephoned me in the evening, certain that this day with Keely would go down in her life as the most tragic and bizarre she would ever experience.

Keely and Cee Cee had joined Nora, a therapist, in the children's private therapy room. Keely had immediately began to run around and around the room, hitting at toys and boxes, breaking everything as she ran.

"Donna, Nora and I sat in these little chairs while Keely slapped at the wall and knocked stuff around. Her eyes were glassy and she was breathing really fast. Nora said she was hyperactive, hyperkinetic. When Keely finally stopped breaking things, she ran over and started to beat on Nora's chest and face with her fists. She hit her so hard that she knocked Nora over in her chair. Nora didn't resist. She just took the beating." Cee Cee sounded exhausted.

"Then while Nora was struggling to get out of the tiny plastic chair and right herself, Keely climbed into the toy cabinet. We tried to coax her out, but there was no response. She stayed in there for more than an hour. It was awful. I've never seen Keely like that."

"Finally Nora got the idea to try to coax her out of the closet with walkie-talkies. Well, that did it. Keely slowly came out. It was absolutely surreal. After eight hours, Nora was finally able to get past Keely's anger and fear, by talking on the walkie-talkies. By late afternoon Keely came into Nora's arms and hit her again. Then she just fell into a helpless little ball and cried and cried. She said, 'I don't hate you, Nora, I love you.' It was such a nightmare. And that bastard father of ours doesn't think he has hurt any of us!

"Nora told me that suicide is common, even among very young children like Keely. It is statistically measurable for six year olds. Donna, Nora explained that Keely feels suicidal because she 'told' on Grandpa with the Barbie dolls last week. Nora feels that Keely is so fearful about what her grandfather will do to her for telling that she would rather die than deal with her fear of him."

"Last week Nora said that she and Keely played dolls nicely in the therapy room. When Nora introduced the grandpa doll, Keely took it, went into the closet and shut the door. Nora called through the door to her. 'Keely why are you in there?' Nora said she finally answered back. 'Nobody must know. It's a secret.' A while later when Keely came out of the closet, Nora tried to get her to explain. All she would say was, 'It's a secret.' The dolls were naked. Keely had taken off their clothes."

I was shaken. "Cee Cee, what are we going to do? Can I help?"

"Nora said not to leave her alone for more than a minute at a time. No more privacy baths. I'm moving Russ's bed into her room for now so she won't be alone at all. Donna, I just can't believe this is happening to my little Keely." Cee Cee was heartbroken.

After I hung up the phone, I made myself a cup of chamomile tea and took it into my blue living room. I needed quiet and peace just to think.

As I sipped the soothing brew, I tried to visualize Keely's alarming behavior. I had come to understand that I had frozen those feelings long ago because they were too painful to deal with. At five how could I have lived with mortal fear and love of my caretaking father? I could not have.

I had insight into mental illness, some understanding of the enormous burden of carrying around such tremendous emotions, such conflicting feelings and pain. "Going crazy" could be a way out of the pain for some people, but most of us freeze the feelings. We stuff them far away behind our protective wall of denial. Witnessing Keely's terror illustrated, in a way that books could not, exactly how intense the fears were that I had locked away.

My glance caressed the room. I loved this room. Country French, quiet and immaculate. It was always a haven for me, but it could not comfort me now. Dad would be back in town in a few days. I was still scared.

December 29, 1989
San Juan Capistrano

Sleep continued to elude me. I thought about many things
in the night, about little Keely, about how phobic I had
always been about incest.

I had been an incest victim, but until recently I could not
even use the word. Now I knew volumes about sexual
abuse. I knew that sexual abuse was generational. I knew
that my grandfather and grandmother were perpetrator
and victim. There were four affected generations that I
knew of in my family.

It was almost more than I could believe. I stared out of my
window into the night for a long time, my stomach knotted.
The darkness reminded me of a disturbing book by Dr. M.
Scott Peck, *People Of The Lie*. This psychology book, written
by a medical doctor, gave me much to ponder about my
family. Even his introduction alarmed me:

> THIS IS A DANGEROUS BOOK. I have written it
> because I believe it is needed. I believe that the overall
> effect will be healing...But I have also written it with
> trepidation. It has potential for harm. It will cause some
> readers pain.

Dr. Peck was correct with that point. It had given me
pain. It forced me to consider possibilities that I had never
dared to embrace. Ugly, monstrous possibilities. I allowed
my mind to consider some of what I had recently read:

> Psychiatrists call them psychopaths or sociopaths...
> people utterly lacking in conscience or superego. Psycho-
> paths appear to be bothered or worried by very little —
> including their own criminality. They are sometimes re-
> ferred to as "moral imbeciles."

This is hardly the case with those I call evil. Utterly dedicated to preserving their self-image of perfection, they are unceasingly engaged in the effort to maintain the appearance of moral purity... While they seem to lack any motivation to be good, they intensely desire to appear "good." Their "goodness" is at the level of pretense. It is, in effect, a lie. This is why they are the "people of the lie."

I was particularly disturbed when Dr. Peck came to a discussion about a patient of his, whom he had labeled evil. He said that he was overwhelmed to think of what it might be like to be the "child of evil." These thoughts turned my stomach. He also included intrusiveness in his definition of evil:

Intrusive parents do not allow their children personal boundaries. "Love is incomprehensible to evil." Evil people have a desire "to confuse." Their behavior is typified by scapegoating and lying.

I scanned quickly across my life and heard afresh in my memory the sound of my father's voice telling an eternity of lies: "Maymie lost the family money. Cee Cee was dropped on her head. Your mother doesn't want you. Donna is out to steal Cee Cee's children." A shudder passed through me as I continued to read:

First I have come to conclude that evil is real. It is not the figment of the imagination of a primitive religious mind feebly attempting to explain the unknown.

People who are evil...hate the light and instinctively will do anything to avoid it, including the attempt to extinguish it. They will destroy the light in their own children and in all other beings subject to their power.

Evil was real? I was so naive I had never really considered it before. Was my father evil? I considered that thought for a long time. More pictures and words churned to the surface of my memory. I had to face the truth. *He consistently said that he would destroy you...*

December 30, 1989
Mammoth Lakes

Dad was out of town so we felt it was safe to leave Cee Cee while we went to Mammoth for a few days. But she needed to stay in touch by phone.

"Donna," she wailed, "he called again tonight. I was so nervous I thought I would explode. I did my best acting. He seemed to buy it. He railed against you. Said that you're a Nazi and it's your Burwick German blood that would have you turn in your own family.

"He told me again," Cee Cee continued, "that you were after the kids. It was horrible. He said, 'Shut Keely up! It would be catastrophic if she talked!' I got lots of stuff like that on the tape. Just like the detectives taught me."

"What happened?" I asked, a million questions coming to mind.

"I started out all confused in the first call. I was Daddy's little nitwit. He bought that one. Then in the second call I still acted confused, but I laid some facts on him. He didn't like that much. I am so scared, Donna."

"Hey, this is your sister here. You think I don't know? You haven't seen me having any big talks with him lately. I'm scared of him, too. Don't apologize. I think you're incredible."

"Well, I hope I didn't sound phony. I kept my voice calm, but I kept hitting him with a few more facts each minute or so. He tried talking about the weather, how terrible you are, that you will get Keely, that I should toss Rand out. Dad kept contradicting himself. He would have been killed in debate class."

"What do you mean?" I was intrigued.

"I kept telling him that this can't keep going on with Keely. He said, 'Nothing happened.' Then pretty soon he

said, 'Nothing's going on now because I'm gone.' Can you
believe that he incriminated himself like this? Oh yes, there
was more of that stuff about conservatorship or guardianship or whatever. He kept going on about it."

"Ceece, do you remember when Daddy kept threatening
to put Maymie away?"

"Yeah, vaguely. It was a long time ago, wasn't it?"

"Probably 20 years ago, but that was one of my first
conscious awarenesses of how very scary Daddy really is. I
think I always knew that if I told, I would either have an
'accident' on one of our trips, like falling down the Grand
Canyon or end up locked away as a nut case. It was very
chilling when he was threatening her about that. Conservatorship. Who even thinks like that?" I stared ahead lost in
my own thoughts for a moment.

"Cee Cee, you used that genius brain in getting him to
admit so much."

"That damaged genius you mean?" Her voice was mis-
chievous for an instant. "I got so tired of being called 'some
kind of damaged genius.' Well, Dad, I hope you like these
tapes." Defiance spiced her words.

"Honey, I doubt that any Hollywood writers could have
come up with a better way of drawing him out."

"The police cleared their gear out of here a while ago.
They are going to listen to the tapes and see what we have
for court. I think it's pretty incriminating."

"Cee Cee, maybe you should be the actress in the family."

"I guess we all have been," she responded. "Just trying to
act normal. This episode tonight felt like the final reading
for a drama class."

Later we would study the three transcripts carefully. The
police used initials, describing Dad as RL and Cee Cee as
CK. Here are excerpts:

RL: Oh, Cee Cee, it is her word [Keely's] against her
grandpa's word and that doesn't count for much. Those

are absolutely horrible people [Stuart House authorities]. Keely has been very well treated, dear. But for God's sake, keep her away from everybody.

CK: Yeah. Okay.

RL: Don't let anyone near her.

CK: Okay.

RL: If they want to talk to her, tell them you want a lawyer present.

CK: All right. Yeah, well I haven't seen Anne in a few days because the last time I saw her she started talking about you and her.

RL: She had better be quiet. Explain that to her.

CK: Well, that really upsets me, too.

RL: Well, explain that to her. She needs to be quiet.

CK: Well, I will, I will.

RL: She is just making trouble and probably for herself.

CK: Well, the stuff she is telling me, I hope it isn't true.

RL: Of course it isn't true. You have people that would like to put me in a position where they can get custody of my money.

CK: Oh.

RL: That is what some of this is all about. If they could prove I am dumb enough to do these things they are claiming, they could get guardianship over me.

CK: Um hum.

RL: These are not nice people, dear. You shouldn't talk to them. Just keep away from them.

CK: Well, I am trying not to. You know I haven't.

RL: That's the idea, get a hold of Anne, tell her to put a muzzle on and behave herself.

CK: Well, I am just going to sit here and do the best I can, dodging the calls and stuff then. I don't know.

RL: Oh, dodge them. Coach Keely to say nada. Keely should absolutely say nothing. Donna and Sandy will make you more trouble than you ever believed possible. Donna is trying to get Keely. That is what this is all about.

CK: No, I don't...

RL: Does Rand want them to get Keely? Doesn't he realize that is what they are doing?

CK: No, he...

RL: He opens his big mouth, doesn't he know he will lose her?

CK: Well, he wants to make sure nothing, you know, nothing weird is going down with his little girl.

RL: Nothing weird is going down.

CK: That is all. He was just...

RL: She is absolutely fine. But if he manages to show that something weird is going down with his girl, enough to satisfy someone, he will lose her.

CK: Yeah, well...

RL: God, what an asshole he is. He must not have brains at all. Anyway the whole thing is dead. Just leave it that way.

CK: Well, I know, but it didn't sound too dead. It sounds like Ken Friess is in there doing something.

RL: Oh, sure, he wants to get a little girl for Donna. He couldn't make her one, so he's gonna take yours away from you.

CK: Oh, God.

RL: Explain to Rand that if he doesn't put a muzzle on Keely and so on, and a muzzle on Anne, that you guys are going to lose your little girl. Donnie will wind up with her.

CK: Yeah, well they are coming and asking me questions you know.

RL: Shut up and don't tell anybody anything!

CK: Rand said he was wanting to have Keely go up there.

RL: Well, explain that by having her go up there...if they find anything, he will lose his little girl.

CK: All right.

RL: You absolutely must say nothing. Anne must say nothing. Keely must say nothing and then there is nothing. Rand must not talk to Donna and Sandy. They are trouble makers. Why does he want to lose Keely?

CK: No, he is just trying to protect her.

RL: Protect her? He is trying to throw her to the wolves. Those are vicious wolves down there. Coach her not to say boo to anybody. You must not say anything to anybody. Let this thing go to sleep.

CK: Okay.

RL: Does Rand realize that he is screwing around with the house you are living in?

CK: I'll talk to him.

RL: I mean, my God, if they put me on the fryer, monster legal fees are going to come up, your house will just absolutely slide away from you, dear. I will be somewhere else. There is no way that you can sit in that house and have me fighting legal battles.

CK: Are you threatening me, Daddy?

RL: You are being threatened by Donna and Sandy. If they get me into some forty or fifty thousand dollar legal battle, it is going to eat your house up. That is what they are trying to do. Get a conservatorship over me and show that I am enough of a nut to do something like, along those lines, which I certainly am not. They would like to grab my whole estate and everything and you would be out on your ass.

CK: All right.

RL: So you have vicious people. Nothing has gone anywhere lately. Things are like they are. Keep quiet. Keep Rand quiet. Have Anne quiet. And everything quiet, and everything will be fine.

CK: Keely told me. She told me the same things that I did when I was little. She told me about taking baths and washing pee pees.

RL: Oh God, honey.

CK: And I did that, so I know she is not lying to me.

RL: No way, honey, no way.

CK: I can't have this happen to Keely.

RL: Oh, of course, nothing is going to happen to Keely. You know, I have obviously given Keely up. You know that. What else? People hadn't turned on me at that point.

CK: People aren't turning on you. People are finally telling the truth. And they are hurt.

RL: Yeah, I am so far out on my own, God.

CK: But you put yourself there. What you have done has divided all of us. You never wanted us to talk about that. It has been the big secret.

RL: It is an unspeakable subject.

CK: It is an unspeakable subject because it shouldn't happen. A man should find a woman, not his own daughters and granddaughters.

RL: It can't happen and I can't be in it. It is unspeakable.

CK: I really honestly feel that things could be all right if you could just maybe...you do need to have some help and therapy.

RL: Oh, honey, that would be nice if they could get me into that kind of a position where they give me some help and you know, I get to see the warden and I go into the prison library and so on. Then they rehabilitate me and of course by that time Donnie has all my money, and she has your little girl and everything else. Oh, my God.

CK: You just feel that everybody is out to get your money.

RL: I am weak and sick and, Jesus, I can't even be allowed to die in peace. You know what I mean?

CK: You are not dying.

RL: I am not in the best shape either.

CK: Everybody has put you, all of us, every girl, every daughter, everybody has gone beyond the limits of what a daughter should do to take care of you and love you. The issue is sexual stuff.

RL: There is no sexual stuff, period.

CK: You have done a lot of great things. There is no denying that. You could be a great grandfather and a great father. The only problem is the sexual stuff has got to stop.

RL: It has stopped. There isn't any. There never was and it has stopped because I am away. Don't you understand. I am not there.

CK: And what happens when you come home?
RL: Nothing...

January 17, 1990
Venice Beach

The black-and-white police car pulled up behind Dad's three-story stucco beach-front home early that morning. From the cellular phone inside the police car, the Los Angeles Police dialed my father's number.

"Hello?" I could imagine the youthful quality that would be in Dad's voice as he answered. He would still be sleepy from gambling at Gardena the night before.

"Mr. Landis?"

"Yes."

"It is the police. We have a warrant for your arrest. There are officers in the front of your house and in the back. We want you to come out slowly with your hands up."

The detective reported to me that Dad came out peacefully. He was dressed in slacks and a blue print shirt covered by his black leather jacket.

I felt sorry for my father, regret for what he could have been. He was brilliant, handsome, funny, gifted, charming and talented. But somewhere, somehow, Dad had chosen to follow a forbidden path. He might not have believed in God or sin or heaven or hell, but I knew that the loss of face, the loss of his family and the anticipation of a life of incarceration would be a living hell for him.

I felt a great sadness for all of us. We had all wanted a normal Daddy so much that we tried to turn him into one. It never did work very well. I thought of all the books I had read on psychological games and life scripts. I remember one explanation that stayed with me.

Claude Steiner said that one can easily determine a "life script" by its ending. Daddy's life would have a tragic ending, whether he was held in prison for the rest of his life or whether he got out. He had ruined all that was important to him. Maymie's long-ago prophecy was close to target:

"I'm so worried that he will end up a lonely old man in a rented room."

For the time being, his rent would be paid by the State of California.

And what of us? What would all of his children have been had he not raped our minds and bodies? The abandonment and abuse I experienced in my childhood had so colored the fabric of my being that I could not imagine another life, a life without terror or shame, a life anesthetized by accomplishment.

Maybe I would not have achieved all that I had. Maybe I would not have been so driven. I thought about that for a while. Perhaps I would have learned "to be" instead of "to do." Perhaps I would have known peace. Perhaps I will someday. I still have lots of time. The rest of my life.

January 18, 1990
Municipal Court
West Los Angeles

I sat in the spectator gallery of the West Los Angeles
Municipal Courtroom and diverted my eyes as the bailiff
brought in the prisoner, my father.

All but one of my father's seven children were here to beg
the court not to allow him bail. Many of his grandchildren,
his son-in-law and even a future daughter-in-law were here,
huddled in the back rows of the courtroom, clutching one
another's hands and praying that the system would not let
him out. Praying that Daddy would not get us.

I looked at my siblings, front-line warriors in our gruesome
battle. They were brave, wholesome, loving souls. My brothers had a clean-cut, all-American appearance. My sisters were
all so different, yet each attractive in her own way.

After a moment I looked across the small courtroom at
the handcuffed prisoner...Daddy, the aerospace engineer.
Daddy, the president of the yacht club. Daddy, the accused
felon. His gaze was fixed straight ahead, his face stretched
back into a demonic expression by overzealous plastic surgery. In his typical controlling manner he had ordered the
surgeon to pull his face even tighter than the doctor thought
appropriate.

With his athletic, muscular build, he looked younger than
his 66 years. He wore his favorite leather jacket and a print
jersey shirt. His sparse blonde hair was combed over to
cover his balding head.

The arraignment proceedings began as the young, slightly
rumpled district attorney rose to his feet, straightened his
tie and requested permission to show the judge a receipt for

a semi-automatic gun recently purchased by my father. It was a sophisticated weapon, twelve rounds.

My father's jaw worked back and forth as the legal proceedings began. He did not turn to look at us, but I could see his arrogance and anger as the judge examined the receipt for the weapon.

The judge, a serious-looking, middle-aged woman engulfed in black robes, studied the document placed before her carefully. Her head inclined slightly toward the district attorney as he spoke with her for several minutes.

Thinking about the gun that my father owned, I looked over at Diedre, my youngest sister. She had seen our father only three days before. I remembered what he had said to her.

"Diedre, do you know what they do to people who betray their family? It is the same as for people who betray their country. They execute them."

He had laughed hysterically as he floored his new white Chevrolet convertible and sped away, tires squealing.

How could he have hurt and betrayed us all so terribly? I knew the truth. He was malignantly evil and monstrously manipulative. I knew he had robbed us of our innocence, of our childhoods and of our very basic human dignity. I knew he was a dangerous pedophile, a child molester, guilty of sexually abusing helpless children. I knew he had lied and continued to lie about his actions. I knew he had tried to frighten his adult children with detectives, case workers and attorneys. I knew he swore he was being framed. I knew he would never admit the truth.

As the legal proceedings continued, I turned once again to my internal world, to the painful dialogue in my head. "Daddy's girl! Oh, how proud I had always been to be Daddy's girl. It was always Daddy who took care of you. How could you..?" I interrupted myself. "The 'lips' Donna, remember

what Keely told you? The 'lips' and all the rest. No. He is
where he must be."

The defense attorney stood to address the judge. My
father's counsel was immaculate in his expensive tailored
suit as he spoke. The motion he placed before the court was
quite brief.

"Your Honor, I request that a $2,500 bail be set," he ended
matter-of-factly, waiting for the judge to consider the matter.

I could see the district attorney flex his left fist, clenching
it open and closed as the defense spoke. After a moment he
stood, appearing incredulous at the low bail requested.
Looking slightly disheveled in his sport coat, the young prosecutor began:

"Your Honor, the people request that the accused be held
without bail due to the severity of his crimes and the duration of the abuse to his family. The State believes that he is
a clear danger to his family.

"Your Honor," he continued, his voice now louder and
stronger, "the people realize that this is an extraordinary
request. However," he paused, looking for a long moment at
the judge, "the severity of the defendant's sexual crimes
requires extraordinary measures. The State requests that
the prisoner be held without bail. Thank you, Your Honor."
He stressed the words "without bail," and a prolonged silence filled the air, all eyes locked on the judge.

The judge paused for a long moment. "Bail denied. The
defendant will be remanded to custody," she said gravely,
pounding the gavel three times.

Indeed the request was unusual. I only knew of one case
recently when the prisoner had been held without bail and
that was Richard Ramirez, "The Night Stalker." Even the
infamous McMartins, accused of molesting children in their
preschool, had been granted bail.

January 25, 1990
Bail Review Hearing
Municipal Court
West Los Angeles

My father's attorney had requested a bail review which the judge granted for one week after the arraignment hearing. Knowing that I could have to testify against my father, all three of my grown children, Rick, Julie and Dan, accompanied me to court.

My children had all been away at college. Rick flew down from law school in San Francisco. Julie and Dan drove up from San Diego. When I arrived, the three of them spotted me outside the courthouse simultaneously. They rushed to me, taking turns wrapping me in their strength.

As we walked inside the courthouse, Rick kept his arm protectively around my shoulders. It was a switch for my children to protect me. I had always been strong for them, but they knew that I needed them now. They were all subdued, though I sensed the ferocity of their anger toward their grandfather just below the surface.

Our group filled the small gallery of the courtroom we had occupied the week before. All of my brothers and sisters were there, except Connie who remained loyal to Dad. Our husbands, my mother, my aunt, my lifelong friend, Leanne, my husband's sister and my youngest brother's fiancee sat in the small gallery of the courtroom.

Ken, my sons, Rick and Dan, my sister Sandy and her husband filled the front row. I tried to hide behind them in my second row seat, clutching Leanne's hand tightly. Julie and Anne clung to each other nearby. I kept my eyes stubbornly toward the floor while Leanne whispered an urgent narration.

"They are bringing him in now. He doesn't look bad. He is walking around to his seat. The bailiff is unlocking his handcuffs." Her voice remained steady as she commented on the scene. My heart was racing furiously as it had the week before.

"The bailiff is cuffing his left hand to the chair." She held my hand tighter. "Don't look, Donna."

I tested myself, checking for strength. I glanced up where I knew the prosecutor would be. I was safe. I kept my gaze on him. He stood. The judge looked at him as the district attorney began.

"Your Honor, the prosecution is here at the request of the defense. The State's position has not changed. We believe that this man is a risk to the safety of his family. Certain family members are afraid of him, and he is at high risk of fleeing. The State requests that the 'no bail' status be continued until the preliminary hearing."

The judge, a calm, intelligent-looking woman, gazed expectantly at the defense attorney. "Present your case then, counselor," she demanded.

"Ah, Your Honor," he stumbled, seeming rattled and unprepared. "We do not have a case." A snicker stirred through our group of spectators.

Momentarily, the defender seemed to find more words. "Your Honor, it is the responsibility of the State to prove that this man is a threat to his family and that he has the potential to flee. I would like to remind the court that he has lived in Los Angeles his entire life, has owned property and has never been arrested before. He has no police record. Therefore, it is up to the prosecution to prove these allegations."

He paused for a moment, looking directly at the judge. "A 'no bail' status is highly unusual for the charges presented against my client."

The judge turned her glance toward the youthful prosecutor. "Sir, are you prepared to present your case?"

"Yes, Your Honor," he responded instantly.

The courtroom was cleared and we were ushered outside to wait in the hall. Within seconds the bailiff called my name. A quick rush of adrenaline charged through my body.

Head held high, I sucked in a breath of air and walked through the short swinging doors which separated the empty gallery from the trial space. I was escorted up to the witness stand and told to raise my right hand.

I knew that my father's eyes were on me. I knew that there would be no turning back. My father had recently called Trey and told him that I was after his money, that I was the ringleader. My father had also called the L.A. Times and tried to get a reporter to do a story about my framing him. I knew he was raging at me now.

"I do," I responded to the oath.

The bailiff led me to the witness stand. I sat down and she adjusted the microphone to my height. The district attorney had instructed me to simply tell the truth. He promised that I would be able to explain myself easily and that these proceedings were very informal. He was wrong.

I stated my name, age, occupation and residence. I tried to tell my story in response to the district attorney's questions. There were so many interruptive objections from the defense that we were getting nowhere. After a while he tried a different tactic.

"Were you ever molested by this man?"

"Yes." My face did not betray my feelings, but I knew that I had told the secret. I had told in front of a judge with my father as a witness. It felt right. In a peculiar way it felt good. It was something that needed to be told a very long time ago.

"At what age?"

"Since I was about six years old."

"Who is he?"

"My father."

"Do you believe that you are in any danger if he is allowed out on bail?"

"Yes."

"In what way?"

"He told my sister Cee Cee that he was going to destroy me if it took his last dollar."

"Objection."

"Sustained."

"Were you ever personally threatened?"

"He threatened me that if I told, I would be a 'sorry sister' and 'that people who told end up six feet under.' "

"Does your father own a gun?"

"Yes."

"Have you ever seen it?"

"Yes, on many occasions. He always carried it on our trips."

"No further questions."

The defense attorney stood to begin his questioning. I kept my gaze on the prosecutor as I kneaded the palm-sized fleece teddy bear which my therapist had forced me to take to the stand. Back and forth, I worked it in my left hand, unconsciously squeezing it. I could not look at my father. I knew that to see the fury in his eyes would scare me speechless. I heard the defense attorney's questions; I did not look at his face. He was a disembodied voice, cold and unfriendly, accusing and mean.

"Isn't it true that Venice is a high crime area?"

"No."

The attorney kept up a rapid-fire flow of questions. "Isn't it possible that your father is getting his car ready to sell to use the funds for his defense?"

"I suppose," I answered, thinking that it was much more likely he was getting ready to leave town. I didn't know if Dad really would come after me if he was released. I did think he would flee.

If found guilty, he faced up to 40 years in jail. It did not take a mental giant to figure that Dad would be more than 100 years old when his sentence was complete. Over the years he had frequently talked about living in the South Sea Islands or in Mexico. As the defense attorney continued his interrogation of me, I could feel a memory struggling to work its way up. It seemed jagged around the edges, sharp and ugly, trying to burst forth.

I remembered now. Daddy was holding me, crooning softly to me about how wonderful it would be for us to be together, married, in the South Pacific where no one would ever take me away from him.

It always scared me the way he said things like that. I could still easily remember his silky smooth words. My stomach flopped over. I could see that faraway dreamy look he would get. I had been afraid he might steal me and take me away where I wouldn't see my mom or Sandy or my grandparents ever again.

Yes, my father would flee if he were released. With his savings he would be rich in Mexico and could look for another young girl.

"That is all. You may step down. Thank you."

I sensed that the judge was speaking to me. I tuned back into the present and looked at the prosecutor. His face told me with a minuscule movement that I had done well. I made my way past the little swinging gate to the outside of the courtroom.

"Sandra Stevens." I heard the bailiff as she called my sister.

Two of my sisters, Sandy and Cee Cee, testified after me. The judge considered all of our testimony, and at the end of the day announced her decision.

"The defendant will be remanded to the Los Angeles County Jail without bail."

February 17, 1990
San Juan Capistrano

Waiting for the preliminary trial was agony. It could still be several months away. I was reeling from hour to hour in ambivalence. In the early months, I had so much indignation and anger that I was able to fend off the sadness. But these days it found its way into my heart like radioactive gases must have found their human targets, leaking silently out of Chernobyl, oozing forth their unmerciful poisons.

The ooze mostly attacked in the night, and I awakened dreaming of lying in a pool of blood or hearing Daddy's voice coaxing me, "Stop this, now stop this!" Or I woke up in a panic from a nightmare where I was running, being chased, a killer stalking me. Running. Once I was locked out.

It all left me feeling sad.

I flopped back and forth between knowing what must be done and wanting to run away. One self reminded me that it was not acceptable to molest little children, while the other self said, "Let it go. Let it be. He is your daddy, for God's sake!" Bernie had even been telling my sisters, "Donna and Ken are over-reacting. You shouldn't, any of you, be doing this. You turned out all right. What he did didn't really hurt you."

I worried all the time that the story would find its way to the news, and my family's entire sordid tale would be broadcast before the world. I could visualize myself covering my face as they led me to a long dark car outside of the Santa Monica Courthouse. I could see myself holding my purse in front of my face so no one would know that this was about me. But mostly a part of me missed my dad.

February 20, 1990
San Juan Capistrano

During a day of boating in San Pedro Harbor, I found myself painfully missing Dad. Returning home that evening, I replayed the telephone messages. Trey's voice, youthful and crisp on the recording, reported that he had spoken with Dad.

"Donna, Dad says this is all a frame-up, all lies, that you are after his money. He's hiring a detective. He says he's going to subpoena Cee Cee's therapist's records and prove that she is crazy. Call me. There's more." The machine beeped off. My heart throbbed against my rib cage. I felt nauseous, stupid. To think I had been missing my dad!

Donna, you are a stupid fool. You've been taken in your whole life. Dad wants to destroy you. Would probably kill you if he could and you want to take him for a little family boat ride! Stupid. Stupid. Stupid. My inner voice was screaming at me; it wouldn't let up.

*And while you're at it...*my blood was coursing, turbo-charged with fear and anger, as I digested Trey's call. My critical inner voice would not be ignored. *Remember back when Julie was about 10? You can't stuff that anymore. Remember* ...helping her put her Barbies away in her room, and she turned to you, huge eyes luminous in the dim light? They were filled with fear. Terror even. Do you remember her whisper to you?

Remember? You could hardly hear her? *What did she say?* My critical self mocked at me.

Yes, I remember. "Please, I don't want to remember!" begged my tender self. No, dear God. I don't want to re-member...

Remember and know what you are dealing with.

I stared out the window. The view was lovely. The sun was setting and the sky was a glaze of oranges and purples. It was so beautiful the way the colors touched the mountains. I thought of the thousand sunsets I had seen living at the ocean. A lifetime in living color. There had been so many good times. Wonderful sunny days filled with volleyball and swimming. Daddy had been in the center of it all, laughing and joking.

Donna, there you go again. You don't seem to focus on the problem here. Your father is evil. What do I have to do to remind you? E V I L Must I spell it out? He would have hurt your Julie. How easily you forget about Keely and the lips.

I know. I know. But this is so hard. I don't want to be brave.

You are brave. You always were. Have I ever let you down? Wasn't I there with you all those years when you felt hopeless? Didn't I promise you... Just because you have been feeling better doesn't mean anything has changed...

March 1990
Spring Break
Mammoth Lakes

Ken and I were enjoying a vacation at Mammoth. My mood swings between terror, guilt and sadness had leveled off. My nightmares were subsiding; my dreams frequent and clear.

I could hear my dad's voice in my sleep. One night he said, "Donnie, you should not be doing this." Then the voice was gone. Another night I dreamed that a young mother had come to a two-story house with a circular staircase. She was in a waiting room, waiting to have my father baby-sit with her little girl. I could hear myself interfering, felt my familiar knot of terror. I told her not to allow him to stay with the child.

She said, "Thank you." She did not know me, but she said, "I believe I remember that he molested me when I was little." With that she had gathered up her child and left. The other dreams had me waking up in pools of blood, my teeth falling out, being chased, locked out, running. They were horrible.

One night Ken answered a call from Cee Cee. I could tell from the way he was trying to calm her, the way he asked her to repeat herself, that she was hysterical, probably crying and choking. I felt panicky just hearing one side of the conversation. After 20 minutes Ken hung up.

"Cee Cee has discovered that your dad did hire detectives. Some woman visited your friends, the Moores, unannounced. She just surprised them at dinner time, got herself inside their house by posing as a representative of the court, an impartial investigator. She led them through some interesting verbal acrobatics before it became clear that she was investigating you." Ken paused.

I felt my face go pale. I was the innocent party. Why should I be investigated? The Moores had been family friends for 30 years. They were my parents' age, but I had kept up the contact between us with Christmas cards and letters. They knew me well.

"Well, two hours later, after ruining their dinner, the detective left. They told her that the frame-up charges against you were bogus. The Moores went on to explain that you had a many times greater net worth than your father. They told her that you were a woman of the highest character, a college professor who had been teaching at the same school for a quarter of a century, and that they trusted you beyond any doubt. They told her that they had even owned property with you for years. I don't think from what Cee Cee said that the detective got what she came for. At the end of their interview they had volunteered that your father's treatment of Connie was 'very peculiar and overly affectionate.' They also said that whatever Donna said had to be true."

"So why exactly is Cee Cee so upset, Kenny? It sounds like Dad is really just coming after me, like he always said he would." My heart was thumping. "She was frantic, wasn't she? She seemed to be from what I could hear."

"Oh, yes, she's upset all right! The detective next grilled Bernie for two hours. It was another surprise visit. Bernie won't take sides. Cee Cee is furious with her. She can't understand why her mother won't help her with this. And she's worried about your father's threats to obtain a court order to seize her therapy records. She thinks he will try to prove her to be a nut case."

"I think therapy records are confidential," I offered calmly, fighting to think clearly.

"Donna, it makes me so damned angry to see you girls frightened like this. You are being manipulated by these meaningless threats. No court in the land is going to sub-poena therapy records. If they did, big deal, they would show the depth of Cee Cee's abuse at your father's hand. I'd really like to kill the bastard."

Quivers of fear threatened to break loose. For Ken I tried to keep myself together. I had come this far. I didn't want to lose it now. I tied up those fears again with steel cables.

"Donna, let's get outside for a while. How about walking up to the ski lodge and back? You look like you could use some night air."

As we walked, I sorted out the pieces to my puzzle.

"Ken this is off the wall, but do you remember Crystal's paternity suit against Dad?"

"Oh, yeah!" His words were tinged with laughter. "You don't forget something like that. It was pretty strange when your dad married her. Didn't he say he married her because he was afraid she'd kill him?"

"Yes. That seemed silly until their bizarre divorce. You know I bought Dad's story that she trashed his house, flooded it, sprayed graffiti on the walls and all of that because she was nuts. But I think it was something else."

"What do you mean?" asked Ken.

"All these years I thought that her paternity suit against Dad was strange. It cost him $60,000 to beat it. I never really got why she did that. And then when the genetic testing results proved that her little boy could not have been Dad's, I thought she was just crazy as Dad said she was. He was always saying that she was very dangerous." I pondered their relationship for a moment. "You know, I always wondered what triggered such venom on her part."

As we walked on in the night, I considered it more fully. "Ken, she must have caught him with Jamie. Jamie was about five when Dad took them in. Wrecking his house, the paternity suit... Ken, it was her way of getting even. It was the only way she could get back at him." I paused and reflected. "I bet Dad's detectives were able to dig up enough dirt to discredit her."

"I bet you're right! Her actions don't sound crazy if she was getting even with him for molesting Jamie!"

We silently held hands as we strolled up the hill to the ski lodge, a three-story concrete colossus quietly bathed in moonlight. The skiers were gone for now. The mountain behind rose up majestically against the blackened sky. Orion and the Big Dipper were clear overhead. Ken and I climbed up an incline, snowless now as the ski season was almost over. He led me to a clearing under a pine's full skirt. Sheltered by the fragrant branches, he pulled me close. "Donna," he spoke softly, "this will all be okay. Look out there."

The mountains were serene under the stars. Ken and I embraced, and I remembered the years of good times with my family.

Once when Danny was six, he talked me into going up on the chairlift with him during a blizzard. My poles were askew and my skies crossed at the last second, and he worked so hard at getting me into my seat that he fell off his chair. The lift was stopped and the operator scolded me for not getting Danny on his chair right. When we got to the top of the hill, we were laughing so hard we practically collapsed into a snowbank.

"Mommy, he thought you knew how." Danny, the excellent skier, doubled over at the thought of his mom, "the klutz," being competent.

"Just wait, Danny. Someday I'll beat you down the hill." It was such a farfetched claim we both rolled our eyes skyward.

Yes, I reminded myself, there had been so many wonderful times. I don't know how I would have made it through this time of terror without my solid base of family love.

Slightly chilled from the cold night air, we hiked back home, hand in hand. I felt much better. Joy warmed me. Serenity calmed me. The fear had lifted for now.

I held my anxiety in check during the remainder of the week, but by the last morning of our vacation, as I cleaned up the kitchen counters in preparation for our journey home, the steel cables holding my icy block of fear in harness began to slip. I continued wiping. My breathing became shallow. I could feel another cable snap. My breathing was faster now. I was losing control. The demons of fear locked away in that steel chamber near my soul were climbing out. The last cable broke, and they tumbled forth.

Ken heard my choking cry and came to me at the kitchen counter. He surrounded me with his strong arms. I sobbed and sobbed.

When he thought I could talk, he asked solemnly, "Donna, what's wrong?" He was patient and understanding.

I tried to say something. It came out only a choked garble. I felt ashamed. I had always prided myself on my control. I could handle anything, but here I was, so pathetic that I could not even talk.

Kenny pressed a kiss into my palm. He tried again, "Donna, can you tell me yet what's wrong?" There was a very long silence. I suppose he thought I had not heard him, but I was trying to sort out what was so troubling.

Finally I answered, as we were headed down Interstate 395 on our way back home.

"I'm just so afraid he's going to get me." Kenny reached for my hand. There was no talking for a long time.

"Sweetheart," soothed my husband, "he won't get you. He cannot hurt you ever again. He is locked away in jail. Why are you still afraid?"

"Kenny," I took in a deep breath, "I broke my contract."

"Sweetheart, what contract?"

"I told." I began to cry again. "I promised that I never would."

"Donna." His right arm came behind the seat and he pulled me against his side. "You were only a little girl. No adult in the world has the right to involve a young child in such a contract. You didn't even know what you were promising."

"I promised never to tell." My words broke off again.

"Donna, you were a little kid. You didn't even know how bad it was going to get when you promised. You had to break your promise, Sweetheart." Ken raised his voice. "Sweetheart, you had to tell!"

"He always said he'd get me if I told. And I told." The sobs wracked my body as we headed toward home. It was a blessed release.

May 1, 1990
San Juan Capistrano

This morning as I drove the 37 miles to my college, I heard my favorite broadcaster on 104.3 FM wishing us a happy May Day. Of course I remembered that May Day long ago in second grade. I still remembered the looks on the other children's faces as they stared at the warts on my hands. I would probably always remember.

I slowly made my way north past the Irvine Ranch. Cows grazed on the dried spring grass close to the road. The 405 freeway was clogged with traffic. I had a lot of time to think.

I thought about our upcoming court date. Tomorrow we would have to take the stand after months of postponement. The prosecutor was hoping to get a plea bargain from Dad in order not to traumatize Keely by putting her on the stand, but all this waiting had produced nothing.

It would be the preliminary trial in front of a new court. Tightness choked my throat. I felt strangled. I swallowed and took one of those big breaths my therapist had harped on me to use.

"Breathe, Donna," I said aloud in the privacy of my car.

Seated in the comfort of my motionless vehicle, I thought back to a night when Cee Cee had called me, desperate for help. I had been asleep, but the ringing phone finally awakened me. I stumbled out to the kitchen and played the message. She sounded terrible.

I woke my sleeping husband. "Kenny, it was from Cee Cee!" The fear in my voice brought him fully awake. I punched in her number. It rang once.

"Oh, Donna, thank you for calling me back. I'm sorry it's so late. I didn't know what else to do."

"What's wrong?" I hoped that I sounded calm.

"It's Keely. She had another one of those nightmares. She woke up screaming and then stopped breathing like that time in Phoenix at Thanksgiving," Cee Cee's words raced out.

"When she stops breathing and turns all blue, her lips go purple, and I think what would I do if I didn't have my Keely anymore."

"Cee Cee, Keely's okay, isn't she?"

"Yes, when I couldn't get you, I yelled at her to breathe like you told me. That seemed to startle her and she coughed and took a breath. She's back asleep. I just don't know what to do anymore." Her voice sounded detached, past desperation.

"Cee Cee, we're all doing our best. You are doing well. Keeping everyone together right now takes everything you have. This will pass in time. We have to be patient." I hoped that I sounded reassuring. I was fighting my own demons. I tried to believe my own words.

A horn blasted, jolting me suddenly back to the present. The cars on the freeway had begun to inch forward again and a huge space loomed in front of me. I eased my foot off the brake, closing in the traffic gap.

As traffic let up, the line of cars accelerated to 25 miles per hour. "The Boss" was shouting out *Born In The USA* from the radio. I started to enjoy the beat of the music. Somehow this song connected with me and I felt strong as I continued on to work.

Deep inside I felt steel tumblers turn and fall into some unknown and precise sequence, and that familiar wall of strength slipped into place like a steel partition. I felt solid, secure. My gentle inner voice reminded me:

Donna, you are doing the right thing. You must protect the children.

May 2, 1990
Municipal Court Building
West Los Angeles

Ken and I walked up the wide cement steps in front of the
West Los Angeles Courthouse to await the preliminary hearing for my father. The court would decide today if there was
"just cause" to try him in Superior Court.

My father had now been in the Los Angeles County Jail
on a "no bail" status for more than three months. Using the
pay telephone, he had continued to run a successful reign of
terror from his cell. Cee Cee and I were ragged from his
jailhouse threats which came to us via Connie, Trey and the
hired caseworkers and private detectives who were probing
everywhere, asking questions about us.

Today was trial day. Ken opened the huge double glass
doors for me as we entered the foyer of the court building.
Far to the right, huddled on a wooden bench in front of
Division 91, sat Cee Cee, a tiny woman, looking fragile and
younger than her almost 40 years. She was dressed in an
attractive blue business suit trimmed with white lapels, her
long dark hair pulled back. There was no evidence now of
the hip, heavy metal seductress.

As I drew closer I could see her face. It was pale and her
body language read, "Near hysteria." Next to her sat Anne.
She was smaller than her mother at 4 foot 11 and maybe
100 pounds.

Anne greeted me with a sad silent look as she got up to
walk toward me for a hug. She was dressed perfectly in a
tailored navy blue dress. There was a bit more color in her
pale cheeks than in her mother's, but not much.

On the other side of Cee Cee sat Keely, precious in a blue
and white pinafore. Her black, silken hair was combed long

down her back. Evenly trimmed bangs framed her delicate features. She looked like a miniature Snow White. Immaculate. I always marveled at how clean and well-dressed Cee Cee kept her children. Keely and I enjoyed a bear hug for an extra long moment.

"Aunt Donna, say 'Hi' to my bunny."

"Hi, Mr. Bunny."

"I told you the bunny was going to talk," she stated in her high little voice.

"You sure did, Keely!" I smiled. I hoped my voice sounded okay.

Ken had learned that the district attorney would only call Cee Cee, Anne, Jesse and Keely to the stand. I felt relief that today would not be a repeat of January for me. I knew that my day would come again, however, if this case made it to trial. For now, though, we were all restricted from the courtroom.

We were very concerned about Keely. We could not predict how all of this would affect her or how she would react in the courtroom. Would she testify? She had not said one word on the stand during the "trial run" the week before. She had been afraid of the lady in the black coat.

Late in the afternoon Keely was finally called by the bailiff. I watched her through a small rectangular window in the door. She was dwarfed by the adult-sized courtroom. The floppy beige bunny, ears askew, was tucked under her left arm as she raised her right hand and spoke the oath which I had repeated months before from that exact spot. I had been scared then. Keely must be terrified now.

"Do you solemnly swear to tell the truth, the whole truth and nothing but the truth?"

I knew the words, and could see Keely saying yes. She then walked confidently to the stand. She looked so tiny standing there, next to the witness stand railing. She was only slightly taller than the partition which separated the gallery from the trial area.

Keely walked around to the witness stand, climbed up the step and pulled herself up onto the seat. I could see her head bobbing up and down. She was speaking with animation. The beige bunny was in her arms, but she was doing the talking. She had warned me again before she went into the courtroom:

"If I get really scared, the bunny's going to do the talking, but I'll be the bunny's voice!"

So far the bunny was mute. I could not see them from my vantage point at the door, but I knew that her feet in their lacy socks and black patent leather Mary Janes did not reach the floor. I wondered how there could be a culture in which little children are molested, abused and then forced to sit not ten feet from their abusers and tell the sordid details, so they can attempt to achieve safety through a complex legal system. I dreaded the scars this might embed in her memory.

Daddy could have stopped it. He could have pleaded guilty. He could have got six years, three on parole. That would have been a good deal for him. But Dad would not budge. He was a gambler. This time the stakes were his freedom.

After a long while Keely came out. She seemed pale, but okay. Later we learned that Dad kept waving cheerfully to her, trying for her attention, to the point that the bailiff had to come over and tell him to stop or have his right hand cuffed.

Still barred from the courtroom, I stood next to the crack in the door and looked at Dad through the tiny window while the judge rendered her decision. The case would be sent up to Superior Court.

I was frozen in fascination watching Dad. He was dressed in the blue cotton coveralls that he had worn previously. They were emblazoned with Los Angeles County Jail across the back in black letters. The flesh on his once huge biceps hung limp. I stared as the bailiff slowly unlocked his left hand which was handcuffed to the chair and brought his right arm around to join his wrists behind him. In that second, Dad flung out his arm in violent defiance, a mini-show of what hid beneath his friendly exterior.

In the next moment Dad stood and walked slowly away, escorted by the bailiff. He fell back into his pathetic prisoner role, displaying his arthritic limp. Why was he limping? His hip surgery and subsequent therapy last year had gone beautifully. Did he really think he could evoke sympathy?

May 16, 1990
Rose's Office
Newport Beach

I was tired of all this therapy, sick of not feeling happy.

"Rose, how much longer before I am well? As you know I'm very patient, but I don't have much time!" I looked down at my watch to emphasize the shortness of time. I liked my little joke. My mood lifted a little.

"I just don't know," Rose spoke seriously. "It takes people different lengths of time. Slowly the good days will string together and you will feel a bit better for a little while longer. You are experiencing grief. Grief is at the core of delayed stress syndrome. You are grieving over the death of your 'fantasy father,' the loss of the contact you have had with your real father and your lost childhood."

"Rose, it has almost been a year and I still only get a day or two off from feeling upset."

"I know. It will get better. You were never allowed to be a child, Donna. You've been a little adult since you were two years old and Sandy was born. You acted as a little parent to your baby sister and to your own parents. You were required to keep an adult secret and to understand adult issues. You were robbed of your childhood. You must grieve that loss before you will be better."

On my way home I thought of my father. Daddy always wanted me to perfect, to be good, to be honorable, to be his star child. Could some part of him have helped to shape me into someone who would stop him? I grappled with that ultimate irony. Perhaps Daddy built in his own nemesis.

May 22, 1990
San Juan Capistrano

"Donna?" inquired a low voice. It was the district attorney working on our case.

"Yes?" I pulled the telephone tighter against my ear.

"Is Ken there? I've been paging him for two days."

"No." I began to feel wary. "He's moving Rick home from law school. He'll be gone all week."

"Donna, I didn't want to call you before this," he stumbled hesitantly. "I...I didn't want to upset your weekend."

As he spoke the adrenaline began to speed through my veins. My stomach constricted. I knew bad news was on the way.

"Something went wrong last Friday at the Superior Court arraignment. I thought the new judge would rubber stamp the Municipal Court judge's decision, but..." He paused for a moment. "The judge set bail, a low bail." He paused again to let that news sink in. "But, Donna, you are safe."

Yeah, sure! I thought, gripping the phone.

"As of five o'clock this afternoon, your father had not yet been released from County Jail. Once the court directs a bail, there is no system in the district attorney's office or in the police department for monitoring when bail is made. Donna, you could know when he makes bail before we do!"

"What should I do?"

"If you have any problem, call 911 and a SWAT team will be there in minutes. We're not going to let anything happen to you. Tell the 911 operator that you are involved in a case with detective James Bowen of the Los Angeles Police Department. His name will signal the SWAT team status. The police are on standby. You'll be okay." He was trying to bolster me. It was not working.

The district attorney's voice grew more serious. I knew that he was genuinely worried about me, about us. He cared about this case. I strained to listen to his every word of direction.

"Donna, he might explode into violence. I don't know... Just don't forget. If there is a problem, dial 911. They are only a phone call away!" He was trying to sound reassuring as he ended the conversation.

"A phone call away!" I thought quietly. I was completely alone in my home except for my two dogs. My husband was going to be out of town all week.

I locked every possible access. I knew I had truly put my life on the line. I knew that if Dad were released, I was in big trouble. I recalled Dad's threats. Somehow they weren't enough to deter me. I had come to a new plateau in my personal development. The threat to my safety was less important than protecting Keely.

I felt like some mad fool loose on Maslow's last hierarchy. A professor friend once told me that if you get to Maslow's highest level, no one can have power over you because you have moved beyond their sphere of influence.

So much for philosophy. I didn't feel as if I had self-actualized or reached my potential as a human being. I just felt scared.

May 30, 1990
Emergency Bail Review
Superior Court Building
Santa Monica

Today was our fourth court appearance since Dad's arrest
in January. Dad had not made bail yet, and Ken had per-
suaded the prosecutor to appeal the low bail. We had another
chance.

The legal proceedings usually moved faster, but the law
took its time when children were involved. They were still
trying to spare Keely the agony of testifying. The defense
had requested two continuances during these past five
months and we had asked for one during the week of our
half-brother Chad's wedding and honeymoon.

The district attorney had gone in person to the jail to
offer a last plea bargain of only six years, three years of
actual time if Dad would plead guilty. Dad refused again. He
would not admit his guilt.

Tentatively I opened the door to courtroom number 208. It
was almost empty. The judge gestured for me to come inside.

"Is it all right?" I asked hesitantly. He smiled and assured
me that it was. I waved to my family and we filed into the
small wood-panelled courtroom. As we took our seats the
judge, a handsome man in his late forties, leaned back comfortably in his heavily upholstered chair and spoke to us. It
surprised me. The other judge had been unapproachable.

"Are you all here to observe?"

"No," I answered. "I wish we were. We have business
before you today." He looked at me with more interest; his
expression asked what business. I responded, "The Ray
Landis case." He checked his calendar and nodded his head
in agreement.

"We've had a circus here today," he said in an engaging voice, inviting conversation. He then proceeded to share some of the day's anecdotes with us. He was relaxed and charming, and I found myself breathing easier. I unclenched my fists.

Soon my father's defense attorney entered and took a seat near the jury box to wait for the hearing to begin. The district attorney entered the courtroom and joined him. The two men chatted quietly as we waited. They seemed friendly. The bailiff, a nice-looking black man, entered and both attorneys took places at the long walnut table facing the judge at the front of the room. We were told to leave. The proceedings were about to begin.

Through the two small panels of glass in the double doors of the courtroom, I could see the bailiff bringing in the prisoner. I was getting used to seeing Dad with grey hair now. A month before, at the preliminary hearing I had been shocked to see that his blonde hair had turned grey since he could no longer color it. It hung longish and unkempt over the collar of his blue coveralls. He had lost weight.

Nora, the case worker from Stuart House, came to the courtroom door and asked me to come in. My heart was pounding, but I took another deep breath and walked in.

I knew that I looked every bit of what I was: a college professor, a poised strong woman, a successful mother of three accomplished adult children. I was a woman up to fighting to protect the children, who finally had come to understand that she herself was worth standing up for. A woman who had somehow moved beyond her fears for her own safety, who could go into battle if she were forced to.

The court clerk asked me to raise my right hand and to swear to tell the truth. I did so. I walked the three steps and stepped up to the witness stand which was to the left of the judge. I adjusted the microphone and breathed slowly, deeply. I avoided looking to my right, to where my father was sitting next to his attorney at the mahogany table.

The questions began. The district attorney asked my name, age and relationship to the defendant. I answered confidently, slowly spelling out my last name, clearly articulating my age. My voice was disciplined.

"Have you ever been molested by this man?"

"Yes, since first grade when he took me to school. He accomplished rape when I was nine years old in our trailer at Sycamore Cove above Malibu."

"Do you feel in personal danger?"

"I was always told that 'people who talk end up six feet under.' Yes, I feel in personal danger." I couldn't keep the anger out of my voice.

"Have you ever personally been threatened?"

I lifted the single sheet of paper I held in my right hand. "I received this reply back from the last letter I sent my father. It's a poem. I'm not sure what it means. Perhaps it is a threat on my own children's lives. I'm not sure."

"Would you please read the poem?" The judge asked kindly.

I read it aloud in my best speech-teacher voice.

"The troops, nearly always innocent of the nature of war, march boldly forth...Other innocents, at home..." I stressed the phrase "innocents, at home." I let my voice make the nuance. I completed the poem and looked at the judge.

"Has the defense seen this?" he asked. I sat quietly.

"I believe so, Your Honor," replied the defense attorney. "May I see it again?"

With that the bailiff approached me and took the paper. As the moments passed, the judge spoke to me in a low voice.

"This is just routine. Don't let any of this bother you. You are doing fine." He was soothing. I felt better, not too scared. The questions continued.

"What effect would the prisoner's release on bail have on Keely?"

"She would be severely affected. I have had two past-midnight phone calls during the recent months from her mother. Both times Keely stopped breathing in the middle of the night. She was having a nightmare each time. In one of her nightmares Grandpa was coming to steal her. In the other Grandpa was under the bed and he was going to get her."

The courtroom was silent. Everyone waited for me to continue. I reached back in my memory to find what I had said to Keely. I began again.

"I said to her, 'Breathe, Keely. It's Aunt Donna. Breathe, Keely. It is okay. Grandpa isn't going to get you. You are okay now, Honey. Breathe, Keely.' There was no response. I didn't know what else to do. I was frightened. I shouted at her, 'Breathe, Keely!' After a bit she cried out and took a breath."

I paused for a moment, all eyes on me. "Your Honor, Keely also attempted suicide. She said, 'I'm going away soon.' She meant that she was going to drown herself during one of her privacy baths. We found her 'practicing' with a tub full of water."

"No more questions," the district attorney concluded.

The defense attorney rose to question me. He stood right next to my father. I would not risk looking in his direction. I did not have the strength to look at Dad.

The defense established that I frequently chatted with my father on the telephone. The sound of the defense attorney's voice seemed to imply that if I talked to my father, he could not be guilty of the charges.

"I talked to my father several times a week, four or five times, until I got so bad last summer that I couldn't talk to him anymore. I wrote him a letter and explained that I was very upset."

The defense attorney avoided following up that line of questioning. He seemed to avoid any discussion of my mental health. Trying a new line of interrogation he asked, "Isn't it true that your father sent you through college?"

Obviously the defensive position was to prove what a good guy Dad was. I could not believe what a platform they were giving me.

"No, it is not true."

I carefully recited my educational degrees and honors and described my scholarships. I even got to tell them I was currently enrolled in a Ph.D. program. Perhaps Dad had led his attorney to believe that he had paid for my education or he had even convinced himself. Who knows?

Dad was always saying that Bernice had sent Sandy through dental school. What a lie. Our mother and aunt had loaned her the money. It had taken years to repay.

"Have you ever known your father not to show up for a court appearance?"

"I find it difficult to equate tenant evictions with raping your own little child," I responded in a controlled, slightly sarcastic voice. No, Dad never missed his day in court if some tenant owed him money.

"Have you ever known your father to own a gun?"

"Yes, always."

"Were these guns ever anywhere other than at his home?"

"Yes, on the boat," I replied.

"Did you ever see him shoot anyone with it?"

"No."

"Did you ever see him threaten anyone with it?"

"No."

The judge turned to me. "You may step down."

Six of us testified. After our testimony the judge looked right at Dad and said, "Mr. Landis, you are a dangerous pedophile and a threat to society. Bail is set at $500,000."

After it was over, we all met on the steps of the Santa Monica Courthouse. We were relieved for the moment, but we still needed to be together for a little while. We sat in a circle on the grass and visited. We planned Cee Cee's birthday party the next month at our house. Afterward Ken took me out to dinner and a Goldie Hawn movie. I laughed all the way through it. He held me close.

As we drove the hour home to San Juan Capistrano, I leaned back against the upholstered seat of Ken's oversized truck. Resting my head on his shoulder I put the courtroom and the past out of my mind. I looked out of the window. We were coming onto the south end of Orange County where four new multi-storied glass buildings had recently arisen out of the strawberry fields. We had witnessed an incredible amount of development during our 25 years here. Our home had once been in the country. The original Juaneno Indian Tribe had lived on our land, and our children had found an Indian arrowhead in our yard after a heavy rain. I felt deeply rooted, connected to this land.

A new strength was asserting itself in my center. I felt okay now. Maybe even better than okay.

June 15, 1990
San Juan Capistrano

I made my way out to the kitchen. Warm air rushed into the room from the open windows. Summer was definitely here.

Rosa, our housekeeper, was busily collecting plastic cups and party remnants from Cee Cee's fortieth birthday party the day before. I poured myself a cup of coffee and admired my china cup. I had painted my dogs' faces on it.

The party had been special. We enjoyed the pool and had lots of good food, and Ken had taken the kids on horse rides. Cee Cee had even made a speech. Surrounded by a brightly colored stack of gifts, she had begun in a soft voice.

"I've had one of those grins all day that won't go away. Everyone knew that my sister was having a birthday party for me today. My first!" She smiled.

This was a new Cee Cee, a more confident happy woman. At least having Dad in jail all these months had helped her to find herself. And what a delightful self she had found. Her face glowed with love and excitement.

"When I was a little girl, I spent a lot of time thinking. When I was in the closet hiding, which was often, I would dream that a day would come when people would really know me. When I did not have to pretend anymore. Well, that day has come. Thanks to Donna for breaking me out. For stopping it."

With those words she smiled warmly at me and our eyes met. She told me more in her look than her words could ever express. She was thanking me for her life. Dear God, I did not mean to be responsible for anyone's life. I just knew that I had to stop him. I tried to tune back to Cee Cee's words, but my inner voice reminded me gently:

Donna, evil can only flourish where people do nothing to stop it.

Yes, I believed those words, but why me?

Why not you, indeed? Exactly you, Donna. Exactly you.

I heard Cee Cee as she continued, "And I want to thank Sandy, who had the courage to confront him and for helping me to find my courage." She then searched the room and her blue eyes stopped at Kenny.

"And I especially want to thank Ken who has held me together all these months. If it had not been for Ken, I never would have made it. He is the only man that I trusted for a very, very long time." She smiled warmly at Ken. "I want to thank you all. This is the most wonderful day of my life. I feel so loved by everyone."

We had a wonderful birthday celebration. Cee Cee's friend from childhood, Michelle, even joined us. Michelle was thrilled to be reunited with Cee Cee after almost 25 years. It was strange the way Michelle had suddenly come back into our lives.

Six weeks before, Michelle had been awakened from a dream about our family at exactly 2:30 in the morning. She thought it was odd because she had not had any contact with us for two decades. When the dream persisted, she had to get in touch with us. She found Sandy's phone number in the book, called and explained the odd awakenings.

Sandy had immediately replied, "Michelle, our dad is in jail. He has been molesting Cee Cee's little daughter."

"Oh no," she muttered. "He did that to me when I was little. I was so young I didn't know what a condom was. He taught me. It took me five years of psychotherapy and shock treatments to get better."

When Sandy relayed this to me, I plunged into terrible despair. I clearly remembered picking Michelle up from fifth grade when I picked up Cee Cee. She had been a skinny little girl with a long blond pony tail. To know that a child visiting our home had not been safe from Dad was almost more than I could bear.

July 2, 1990
San Juan Capistrano

Alone on my patio I lay in a lounge chair, eyes closed. I pulled my sun hat across my face. I tried to turn my mind off, hoping to rest. The Fourth of July would be quiet this year as it came on a Wednesday. There would not be the usual big weekend with our friend Patty and her family.

We had enjoyed 15 years of volleyball weekends with them, competing over a little trophy that moved from one mantel to the other. I smiled at that thought. The warm sun beat against my skin, still cool from working inside. My thoughts moved back to the last court appearance, the bail review on May 30, in Superior Court.

Ken and I had arrived early to wait for Cee Cee, and I'd remembered another time I had waited for her. It was such a clear memory, it might have been last week. Cee Cee was two years old and I was nine. I could still see her in minute detail. She had twin pony tails and bangs. Her dark hair was cut to just above her deep blue eyes. I was happy it was her birthday.

Two years old. I could still see her racing up the sidewalk in front of Big Ray's drug store, her chubby little legs carrying her as fast as they could toward my arms so that I could twirl her around. A shiny #2 button was pinned to her green dress. She was a big girl now.

I pulled her into the familiar swing she loved. As I lifted her, I could feel the soreness. Every muscle in my body ached. I could barely move fast enough to get the right momentum. It took everything I had. I moved my feet in their familiar circular pattern, and spun her around as best I could. My sister loved the twirling, but I had to stop. I just could not continue, the pain was too much. I still remember Cee Cee's puzzled look.

"Donna, Donna, more! More, Donna!" She had demanded.

I tried to divert her attention. I knew I could not continue to swing her. Just walking was painful. "I have something for your birthday." I smiled, putting on my cheeriest voice. "It's a big surprise!"

"What? What?" She was curious at once. She wanted her birthday present.

I set Cee Cee down very gently and straightened up slowly. We went inside the drug store then to get Cee Cee her present.

That was the morning after Daddy had taken me to Sycamore Cove to fish. I caught a shark. He told me I was a real woman.

Cee Cee's birthday always reminded me of that terrible trip. That memory was a difficult one to put to rest.

July 3, 1990
Rose's Office
Newport Beach

Seated in my favorite spot on the corner of Rose's soft leather couch, I began to talk. I felt miserable.

"So, Rose, why do you think my father did these things?" I stopped to think for a moment.

"I know this is funny, but discovering that he molested other little girls, little girls outside the family, somehow seems even more horrendous to me. I'm not sure why, but it really does bother me. Something deep inside me feels responsible for his hurting them. I just don't understand it."

"Donna," Rose responded thoughtfully, "studies show that most sex offenders were molested themselves as children. So, as adults, many re-enact that same abuse. Maybe it makes them feel superior to overpower a helpless child. Maybe it is about their own rage. Some researchers think that the offender identifies with the victim. We don't really know. These are just theories. It may be that they are most stimulated sexually by recreating their original abuse."

I shared a dream I had just had that morning. In it we all visited Dad in jail. He had gifts for us. He was at Terminal Island Federal Prison and his cell had an ocean view. He wasn't angry with any of us.

Rose just sat quietly and let me describe the dream. She listened intently as I continued.

"You know, the psychological literature is full of the term 'magical thinking.' That is what kids do to make things better. It occurs to me that perhaps this magical thinking actually takes place in the unconscious where there are no conscious controls, and then somehow spills over into our consciousness and becomes thoughts. My dream magically gave me Dad's forgiveness." I stopped to think for a moment.

"It is really an issue with me," I paused. "Though I try to push it down, it is really an issue that Dad is angry with me." The thought hung in the air for a long while.

"Let's get back to your question a little earlier. Why is your father a child molester?" Rose brought our focus back to my original question. "We know how homophobic your father is. I suspect that it was your grandfather..."

My grandfather? What had he done to Dad?

September 8, 1990
San Juan Capistrano

We were in and out of court many times. We lost the rape charges brought by Cee Cee and two of the girls.

The district attorney told us that too much time had passed for Anne and Diedre's charges to be valid. California has a six-year statute of limitations. I reacted with shock when told the reason that Cee Cee's rape charges would not hold.

"Let me get this straight," I asked the district attorney. "You mean that because Dad was not holding a knife to Cee Cee's jugular, it is not considered rape? She was afraid that he would kill her son, Jesse, because of what he'd witnessed. Are you telling me that's not menace and duress?" My tone was harsh. Where was the fairness in this law? What about the rights of victims?

"That's what I'm telling you. The law doesn't provide for this kind of rape."

The molestation charges on Keely would remain, and Cee Cee could at least charge Dad with incest. The trial was scheduled for the end of September. It was difficult to settle down and live life, with such desperately unfinished business. It had been almost a year since our battle had begun and still it was not settled.

I thought of a Bible quotation that my friend Sharon had sent me. The words from *Luke* comforted me greatly: *"To the one whom much is given, much is required."* I knew that there was truth to this quotation. I had been given so much good as well as bad. I always tried to choose the good.

Another quotation came to mind. Trey's fiancee, Shelby, had asked me to do a reading at their wedding. She had chosen something from *Corinthians: "Love takes no pleasure in other people's sins but delights in the truth. It is always ready to excuse, to trust, to hope and to endure whatever comes. Love does not come to an end."*

I had dedicated my life to that idea, been sorely tested by it, and yet continued to believe it with all my heart. I felt this love glowing in my heart, content, tender and hopeful. I thought of my beautiful grown children, my loving husband, my friends, my extended family and my students. So many to love. So much to look forward to.

October 22, 1990
San Juan Capistrano

"Hello," I answered the phone on the third ring. It was Monday evening.

"Aunt Donna?" asked a little girl's voice.

"Hi, Keely. How are you, big girl?"

"Aunt Donna, um, I, um...I'm working on my birthday list. My birthday is Thursday."

"I know, Keely! I sent you a box full of surprises. You'll get it soon!"

"Aunt Donna, Anne was here. First, I asked Mommy for a trip to Jamaica. Then I asked Anne. They both told me to call you. Aunt Donna, I want to go to Jamaica for my birthday."

"Jamaica?" I laughed. "You silly. What's this about? Wait, first tell me what else you might want."

"The ballerina doll. She dances and has pretty clothes and an outfit just like my Halloween outfit. She has a little ruffled pink dancing skirt. Anne said she was getting that for me."

My warmest laughter filled the distance between us. "Keely, I don't think the trip to Jamaica is going to work out, but I put some neat stuff in the birthday box I just sent you!"

"You did? What?" she wondered excitedly.

The diversion I hoped for had worked. "Well, just watch for the UPS man. He'll be there soon."

"Aunt Donna, would you and Uncle Kenny come to my birthday party on Saturday?"

"You bet. We'd love to. Why not put your mom on and I'll find out what I can bring. I love you, Keely."

"Okay. I love you."

"Donna," Cee Cee laughed, "I didn't know what to do with her trip-to-Jamaica plans. I thought you might. I have no idea where that came from!"

"Thanks a lot! Hey, I just let it go right on by. She is so funny. You and Anne get off with a doll and I'm stuck with the travel plans!" We were both laughing now.

It was so nice for us all to be laughing again. The defense attorney was still arranging for delays, and the prosecution cooperated in hopes of a plea bargain. We all knew it wouldn't happen. Dad would never admit anything. But for the time being he was safely locked away and we could relax.

November 3, 1990
The Beach
Dana Point Harbor

This morning I packed my textbooks in a bag with a bathing suit, suntan lotion and a yogurt lunch. Now on sabbatical leave from my teaching position, I was a full-time student with lots of homework to do.

Fifteen minutes later I settled myself into my beach chair on the warm sand. A school of porpoises greeted me from offshore, swimming in close. The peculiar southern current which had warmed our waters all summer was still with us. It had delighted us with exotic species of fish.

The days were shorter now and tinged with autumn coolness, but today was still a California beach day. Textbook open on my lap, I looked past the porpoises to the distant outline of Catalina Island resting peacefully on the horizon. Ken and I had spent whole summers there with our little ones. Julie, Rick and I had collected shells and made necklaces out of them.

We had enjoyed a lifetime of family pleasure. Many such happy memories included my father. Today was his 67th birthday. I hadn't forgotten. I envisioned him with his latest toy, an air buoy. It was an air compressor attached to hoses and masks, a kind of scuba system. He loved that crazy thing.

With his trial approaching in just ten days, my ocean-view cell dream was recurring. In one dream Dad even had presents for us when we visited. He wasn't angry. He said he was fine and he smiled at me. His look told me that it was okay. Then I woke up to realize that it was all just a dream. Ugly reality washed over me. Nothing was okay.

Last week Dad subpoenaed Keely's and Cee Cee's therapy records, trying to prove that Cee Cee is mentally disturbed. No, nothing is all right.

These thoughts of Dad brought me despair. I searched my consciousness for something more peaceful, and my mind turned to my marriage. There were some difficult years, financially and emotionally. No marriage of 26 years was all smooth sailing. The truth through it all was that Ken and I never lost our faith that two people, two bad risks for marriage, coming from troubled and broken homes, could make a marriage work.

Sometimes we white-knuckled it as we went along. I suspected that Ken had been doing this all year, holding me and my siblings together during this awful time. He'd also had to deal with the disillusionment of not having been allowed into my private world. Although he hadn't known me as he thought, Ken stuck by me when many men would have run away.

As the heat from the sun danced over me, my heart did a little race and my lips moved instinctively to a full smile. I probably looked like a dope, lying on the beach in late autumn, smiling like a moonstruck young girl. I knew that I had something precious with Ken. He was my friend, my lover, my soul mate. I would always be grateful for that.

December 20, 1990
Superior Court Building
Santa Monica

The trial finally started, five weeks late. It was 8:50 in the morning, on a California day that was crisp and chilly.

Ken and I were posted outside the courthouse searching the traffic for signs of Cee Cee. She was late and we were getting nervous. She was supposed to take the stand in half an hour and still needed to go over her testimony with the district attorney, Bill Peters. We'd all been wrecks for weeks. This made it worse.

"Cee Cee has been so punctual all week," said Ken peering down the street for any sign of her blue van.

"I know. They're starting with her at 9:30." I was worried, too.

By 9:30 Ken and I were really unnerved. Ken left me to go inside and tell the District Attorney that his witness wasn't here yet. Minutes later I spotted Cee Cee across the courthouse lawn. Rand had let her out of the van while he searched for a place to park. Rand had been wonderful through this ordeal, supportive and loving toward all of us.

"Cee Cee!" I called. "Over here!"

"Donna!" She yelled, hurrying over toward me. "I was so bummed this morning. Just getting all the kids up, dressed and organized to be here this early is bad enough but then there was an accident on the freeway. The traffic on 405 just stopped. I tried not to wig out. I just told myself that they could always slip another case in front of ours."

We hurried into the courthouse and took seats in the waiting room of the prosecutor's office. Ken came in and reported that the judge had given us a half-hour delay. Cee Cee began to dig around in her large handbag for the transcripts of her conversations with Dad. She had about 60 pages to work from and was to be questioned on the last two conversations this morning.

Dad had succeeded in removing the judge who had heard the bail review from the case. He claimed that the judge was prejudiced against him. It had added months to the trial process. We were all very frustrated, especially Bill, the district attorney. The new judge had imposed severe constraints on the case.

The district attorney complained to us that he was boxed in. During the first two weeks of the trial, the new judge ruled that a major portion of the evidence was inadmissible. No mention of the histories of the noncharge victims could be entered. None of Dad's photographs of partially nude children which had been used at the preliminary hearing could be entered. There could be no actual playing of the taped telephone conversations with Dad and possibly not even any testimony from Cee Cee's and Keely's therapist.

In fact, Bill reported, if any of us so much as uttered a sound about our own abuse in front of the jury, it would result in a mistrial. He admonished us time and time again to be very careful about what we said in the courtroom. It was absolutely clear that we should not tell much at all. For days we all had been very angry about the heavy prohibitions.

This judge had a reputation for being very tough on both defenders and prosecutors, consequently his cases were seldom reversed during an appeals process. I have since learned that 95 percent of all Superior Court cases go through the appeals process. I was getting a crash course in how concerned our system was about protecting the accused.

Until proven guilty, Dad was considered innocent and his rights were protected. Not only had he been allowed to change judges, but he now had a special van bringing him to and from jail to the courthouse. He claimed the regular prison bus got him back to jail too late and it interfered with his sleep. Ten of the initial 15 counts against Dad had also been dropped because of technicalities. He had definitely scored some serious victories.

We were all critically aware that the district attorney had promised us no easy victory and that juries can go either way. He said "beyond a reasonable doubt" actually means "absolutely without a doubt" to the jury when it comes to their verdicts.

I was coming to believe that the guilty have the advantage. Certainly in this case Dad did. The deck was clearly stacked against us. The burden of proof lay completely on us which meant, ultimately, that it rested on the words of a scared little six-year-old girl. When I thought of what Keely was being put through, what we were all being put through, my anger flamed to the surface.

The reality of going up against someone like my father, of actually trying to get him to stop molesting our family, was unimaginable. No wonder I had never seriously tried in the past. As far back as elementary school I had known that I needed power. I had always known that without power I would be dominated forever. As I grew older I realized that the key to my freedom and future lay in education.

I turned my head and observed our newly selected jury forming a line in front of the door to our courtroom. There were 16 of them, ordinary, nice-looking human beings. Four were alternates. Emotion went through my body like a 7.4 earthquake. It seemed deplorable to have these strangers help us stop our father from molesting us. It was all so pathetic.

No one before now had ever had the power to stop Dad. No one had ever been able to stop him from doing exactly as he pleased. What would these 16 people do?

Would we be able to stop him? I understood the possibility that Dad could be set free. A shiver shot through me as I tallied what had been involved all along. First you had to deal with your own abuse, figure out how to admit that it happened, come out of the comfortable cocoon of denial, confront the issue, the shame and the risk of Dad's wrath. Then you had to convince the social worker and the police that you had a problem. Then you had to put together a case, wait a year, have the judge rule that Cee Cee's charges under California law did not qualify as rape and that Diedre and Anne's counts exceeded the six-year statute of limitations. It all seemed so unfair.

The judge had also ruled that Keely's therapist could not testify regarding Keely's behavior or any conversations she'd had with Keely. It had been a terrible blow to the prosecution. The D.A. was furious. We were all furious.

"Good morning, Donna," Los Angeles Police Detective Jim Bowen greeted me as I entered the room. He had worked tirelessly on our case.

"Donna!" Cee Cee turned from her work at a long walnut table. "Bill wants me to find out where we left off in court yesterday afternoon and rewrite the lines that are left. Remember the judge won't admit any line that refers to any of the other girls. We can only use references to Keely." Cee Cee leafed through a stack of pages. "We got about halfway through yesterday."

I sat beside her. "Bill said that when he took his position as D.A., he took an oath in which he promised to find the 'truth' in his cases. This is such a monumental irony that should any of us slip up while we are on the stand and let a little of the real truth be shown to the jury, we'll end up with a mistrial."

Suddenly Cee Cee stood in her sailor-style suit, ridicule playing across her pretty face. She raised her right hand in a parody of an oath.

"I hereby promise to tell just the tiny weeny slice of the truth that you will allow, Your Honor, so help me, God. I understand that under no circumstances do we want to find out all of the truth. Amen." She chuckled, enjoying the moment of comic relief.

"Your Honor," I mimicked, feeling my anger dissolve as I raised my own right hand. "I hereby promise not to let the jury know what really happened, lest they think that Dad is really not a good guy. So help me, God."

We both smiled mischievously. Perhaps black humor was better than no humor at all. Our eyes met in merriment and lingered affectionately. I knew we were a study in what sisterhood was all about. Glancing at the clock, I noticed that we had only two more minutes. Bill Peters and Jim Bowen walked through the office area.

"Ready, ladies? We're on," said Bill, sounding relaxed. Since the afternoon before he had been mostly smiles, having finally convinced the judge to allow Keely's therapist to testify. He thought our case might still have a chance. Bill looked much more confident now. His youthful grin had returned.

As we headed toward the courtroom, I scanned the last pages of the telephone transcripts. Over and over again Cee Cee had brought the conversation back to sexual abuse. Over and over again Dad had dodged it. She had done a brilliant job of coming back to the point. Perhaps Cee Cee should have been an attorney.

We all gathered around Cee Cee, flanking her. Rand, Ken, my mother, Bill, Jim and I marched down the hall, past Bernie and Connie. Bernie had not spoken to Cee Cee all week. A family divided. Those two were on Dad's side.

December 26, 1990
Superior Court Building
Santa Monica

The presentation of evidence ended today. The defense
simply rested. They presented no case. The entire burden
had been on the State. The judge spent the morning admon-
ishing the jury regarding procedure and law. The jury then
left for the day. We had only to wait for the verdict which
we expected in the morning.

It had been a very hard few weeks. The final awful week
in which 13 of us testified against our dad had probably
been the worst. All those long weeks leading up to it were
plagued by never-ending continuances. Dad's demand for a
new judge took the longest time because it meant that our
case had to trail behind another case.

We had been in limbo for three weeks, with no certain
date for our case to begin. On the day it finally was to
begin, the prosecutor charged Dad with two more counts
against Keely. There were more continuances by the defense. It had dragged on for what seemed like an eternity.

At last our day in court came. Keely arrived upstairs to be
the first witness for the State. She was nervous. Her six-
year-old little hand was hot and sweaty in mine. She was
wiggly and easily upset.

Finally the bailiff gently called "Keely Kelly." She reluctantly left my embrace and walked through the double doors
of Department F. She was a very little girl in a very grown-
up battle. That thought tormented me. How can we have a
system that sends a tiny little person in all alone to testify
against a big strong adult sitting only a few feet away from
her? Why is our society so reluctant to believe that this goes

on? Why are there so many hurdles? I wanted to scream my indignation out.

Keely testified for the rest of that day and for most of the next. Those were long, difficult days, but we made it through them, all of them. The detective and the district attorney both said that Keely was the best child-victim witness they had ever seen. I hoped this would pass quickly into a blurry and foggy memory for her.

During my testimony, I was numb. It amazed me that I did not feel much. Somehow I had detached myself. I was even able to look at Dad.

He didn't look like my dad though. The father of my dreams was laughing, young and funny. This man was old and angry as he attentively listened to my answers, his jaw muscles working furiously.

The details of our testimony were devastating. It was enough to render anyone who loves children emotionally incapacitated. I hadn't let it do that to me, however. I remained semi-detached, mostly in control. My iron reserve protected me. Cee Cee's strength grew during the many days we spent in court. It was truly a test of our mettle. Now we just had to wait for the jury to make a decision.

"Donna? How are you holding up?" Ken asked as we walked from the courthouse to our hotel across the street.

"Average. Shifting gears from our happy Christmas yesterday back to this mess is pretty difficult."

"Do you want to take a nap this afternoon?"

"No," I shook my head. "What I really want to do is rent bikes and ride down the beach on the bike path. I want to see the place where I grew up. To see if I'm okay."

It all happened in such close proximity, the wonderful and painful events of my childhood, and our terrifying effort to bring my father to justice. We could almost see the beach where I grew up from the courthouse steps. I needed to close the circle. No matter what the jury decided about the fate of my father, I needed to connect with my childhood again, to try to lay the demons to rest.

We found a place to rent bikes, and Ken and I pedaled our way south along Santa Monica Bay toward Venice. My spirits began to lift as we followed the sand-strewn bike path past the scenes of my youth, and pleasant memories flooded in. There was the restored Hippodrome Carousel building at the entrance to Santa Monica Pier. Nearby I saw the place where Big Ray used to play checkers. All through my childhood in the late 40s and early 50s, Sandy and I would find him there.

I could remember paying my nickel to ride the tram north from the Ocean Park Pier to the Santa Monica Pier to look for Big Ray. Sandy and I would always find him at one of those tables, intent on his checker game. All the players on the beachfront called him Doc. They said he was one of the best in the state, a champion player.

Ken and I pedaled slowly, past a sign announcing, "Original Site of Muscle Beach." Forty years ago in the span between the Ocean Park and Santa Monica piers, private beach clubs attracted the affluent, while the amusement piers attracted families. Thousands and thousands of people thronged to this area yearly. It was the "in" place.

Now it was empty on this winter day. We rode along the cement strand and I pictured it as I had known it as a child. The benches along the sidewalk had been occupied by hundreds of short, thick-bodied European refugees, speaking their own native dialects. I had marveled at the many layers of clothing that they wore, even when it was hot. As a child I did not understand the terrible fates they had barely escaped in Hitler's Germany. Those refugees were gone now, their progeny, no doubt, well integrated into the life of southern California.

We rode past stands selling T-shirts declaring "Muscle Beach," "Venice" and "California" on their fronts. A Hyatt

Hotel was under construction next to the old Del Mar Club. The club had become Synanon in the early 60s, a drug rehab house before its time.

We rode on. I couldn't be sure just where the old Ocean Park Pier had been. The landmarks had all changed. I searched for any sign of it. I could almost hear the din of the crowd along the boardwalk, could almost feel the calliope music and the excitement of the carnival rides.

Riding the carousel, I had loved it when I actually got the brass ring. It was a cinch to reach my right hand up and grab at the rack holding the rings. I always tried to pick the white horse with the black tail and fierce jeweled eyes. He seemed to rise up higher than the others so that I never missed my ring. I rode and rode for hours while Big Ray played his "last" game of checkers.

My husband and I pedaled slowly, enjoying the sound of the gently breaking waves and the smell of the salt air. I could still remember the audacious cackling of those big fat ladies. They were only wooden dummies, laughing hysterically as they tried to lure us into the dark mysteries of their fun house. I could taste the vanilla custard. The stand was decorated like the North Pole with penguins and icebergs. Dad would buy me a custard, an early version of a frosty. It always had a cherry on top. It tasted so creamy and yummy. He would pay for it and hand it down to me smiling.

"Here's sweets for my sweetest girl."

"I love you, Daddy."

Ken and I were entering the Venice area now and pedestrian traffic picked up. There were still so many tourists. Affluent Asians, old people sitting in the sun, black youths trying to look tough. A melting pot. A colorful mosaic. I loved the diversity of Southern California.

I craned my neck to look down Windward Avenue. A few of the colonnades still remained from the early Venice days. I remembered the shoe store next to what used to be a Bank of America. Bernie took me to buy my first pair of school shoes there. Now it was just an empty lot. We were almost at the entrance of the old demolished Venice Pier.

"Ken, let's walk our bikes!" I yelled over the noise. "I want to see what's going on. Why do you think that crowd has gathered?"

"There's a limbo dancer in there somewhere." He paused, waiting for me to catch up to him.

"Kenny," I whispered, "see that man?" I nodded toward the tall turbaned man on rollerblades. "I've noticed him for years. I want to have him play a song for me. He has the most incredible green eyes." I felt excited, happy. "Want to come with me?" I urged.

"Ah...no, I'll just watch," he refused with a smile.

A few minutes later I bounced cheerfully back to my husband. "It was a dollar a song. Did you hear it?"

"Yes, I did. So what's his name?"

"Would you believe Karma Kosmic Krusader? He's probably really Wilfred Green from Detroit," I added. We both laughed. "He says that he has been skating and playing his guitar along here since 1974."

"Only in Venice," my husband responded with a little smile.

"Now I want to go into that little building over there." I pointed to the tiny cement office where my mom had supervised the playground 42 years before. I noted that the current play equipment was much fancier than it had been back then.

The girls' bathroom was the same but seemed much smaller to me now. Water pipes were still visible against the wood-sided walls. The red cement floor still had a fine layer of sand.

We remounted our bikes and continued slowly, visiting my first elementary school. The alley next to it, where I waited for Sandy to get out of kindergarten, was the same. We visited the remains of the canal bridge, near where I caught guppies. Now million-dollar homes graced the waters. We passed the Edgewater Market Building, which had become a realty company. I remembered reaching for Sandy's five-year-old hand as we stood in front of that big store ready to cross busy Washington Boulevard.

"Donna, maybe we should go another way. It's only a few more minutes to your dad's house. I'm not sure this is such a good idea."

"I need to do this. If I'm not okay, we'll turn and go on Pacific Avenue."

Pedaling at a comfortable pace, we soon came to my father's home, over 4,000 square feet of beach-front structure. It was three stories tall. We stopped our bikes in front. It looked the same except the new owners had changed the color. I looked across the sand to the sea and felt the rhythmic pulse of the waves breaking. The ocean was a constant in my life, comforting me.

"Are you sure you're okay with this?" Ken asked, worriedly examining my face.

"Yes," I answered, still very much preoccupied with the past.

I opened the gate and looked for names carved into the cement. Leanne, Donna, Sandy. We were always laying cement and carving our names in it. But now there weren't any names. The patio had been covered over with Mexican tile.

Not much of us was left. There was no hint that we had been there, struggling to build the foundation forms. No clue that two young girls moved yard upon yard of sand from the front of the lot to the back, no clue to reveal that a father and two young daughters had removed foundation pilings from this site with a hand-held jackhammer.

I realized suddenly that I was letting go. The pain that I had pushed back for so many years was being exorcized. I knew that I would be all right. There would be no more dark secrets, no more night terrors about Keely. There would be no more pretending to be okay. From now on, it would be true.

Exploring the scenes of my childhood was an impromptu ritual, moving me from a chrysalis to a butterfly. I could imagine butterfly wings, brightly colored in blue and white, spreading open, allowing me to fly into my future. A great weight was lifting from my shoulders. The days of anxiety would soon be over.

I knew I had come full circle. I had reclaimed my childhood and was free to move on.

January 3, 1991
Superior Court Building
Santa Monica

The jury was still out. We had been certain that the verdict would come in by late the Friday before. Surely the jurors did not want to interfere with their long New Year's weekend as they had with their Christmas holiday. Again we had been wrong. By 5:00 on Friday afternoon there was still no verdict.

We suffered through the long weekend, returning on the first business day of the new year, certain there would be a verdict. No such luck. Today we were again hopeful for an end to our long vigil.

The district attorney, Bill Peters, came in as he did frequently to speak to our family. "Wow, your ranks have grown!" He smiled noticing the increase in the size of our group. Bill turned to Cee Cee and spoke very seriously, "I wanted you to know that as of January 1, two days ago, menace and duress are grounds for rape charges in the state of California." He nodded, handing her a thick document. "Because of you, Cee Cee, we managed to get a law changed, and that is extremely difficult to do. Never again will a judge be able to discard rape charges because they were based only on threats to the victim. If it's any consolation, the injustice you suffered may not happen to anyone else."

Cee Cee leaned against the wall with a wide smile. Pride gleamed in her eyes. "That's pretty good, huh? At least something positive will come out of all of this." Her voice filled with emotion. A state law had been changed because of our case. We all felt that something significant had been accomplished. Our battle had been worth it.

At last at 3:30 in the afternoon we were ushered into the courtroom. The verdict was in. Ken and my sons determinedly took the front row of spectator seats, instinctively moving to protect me. Rick, now an attorney, wore a grim expression. Dan's strong young warrior face showed his determination. Tears stung my eyes. It occurred to me that I had borne and raised my own private militia led by Ken.

Julie took a seat next to me in the second row. She reached gently for my palm and held it reassuringly between her strong hands. Ken reached behind his seat and found my right hand. Chad, sitting next to me on the right, put his arm around me. Leanne sat close by, keeping a silent vigil should I need her. It hurt in a peculiar way to finally have a safe place. My husband, my sons, my daughter, my adult brothers, my family and friends would protect me.

There was a stirring in the courtroom as they brought Dad in through the prisoner's door. He looked strong and angry, dressed in a beige corduroy sports coat and handcuffs. He studied us carefully for a long two minutes before he took his seat. In a loud, tinny timbre, much higher than his usual voice he spoke to his attorney.

"Well, there are my little darlings!"

We were always in trouble when we were "little darlings." The sarcasm, however, was lost in the oddly elevated pitch. His words no longer instilled fear. How peculiar! My breathing became easier.

The jury was brought in and they took their seats quietly. The judge began immediately.

"Mr. Foreman, has the jury reached a verdict?"

"Yes, Your Honor," answered a heavy-set man in a dark suit.

A slip of paper was passed to the judge, then handed to the court clerk. The court clerk stood.

"Your Honor, the jury finds the defendant guilty of two counts of lewd and lascivious conduct with a child, guilty of one count of oral copulation with a child and guilty of the charge of incest. The jury could not reach a verdict on the fifth count."

At that point, the judge rasped in a fierce voice, "The court finds the defendant guilty on four counts. The defendant has broken the sacred trust of a grandfather caring for a small child. Sentencing will be February 1, 1991."

Oral copulation! Oh no, I thought. Emotion once again seized me. It was terrible enough to know what Daddy was, but to hear it out loud was even more terrible. Julie clutched me tighter. Ken gently stroked the top of my hand with his thumb.

The jury was excused. As the bailiff handcuffed Dad and took him away, he glared defiantly at us. I turned my head to look at Cee Cee. Tears streamed down her face. She, too, was in the throes of emotion, caught between what was left of her love for Daddy and what he had done to her little girl, to all of us little girls.

We filed quietly out of the courtroom. Cee Cee and I embraced, our tears mixed together on our already wet cheeks. We had come so far in our struggle. Neither of us dared to trust our voices. Sandy embraced us both. She was dry-eyed, tough and triumphant.

"I've been waiting 30 years for this! This is the best day of my life!" Her voice was exuberant.

My children came to me then, one by one. Rick silently held me to his strong chest. Dan stood by patiently and then when his brother released me, he enclosed me in his arms. Beautiful tenderhearted Julie stayed close by my side, watching me for any cues that I might falter. Leanne, too, a few feet away, kept a close watch over me.

Finally there was Ken, waiting for me, standing quietly by. Dear, sweet Ken. I shuffled into his arms. He wrapped me in his embrace. We stood there for a very long time in the late afternoon shadows of the courthouse hall. For all of our ups and downs over the years, he was always there for me. Ken had led the charge in a most ghastly war and we'd won. He had supported me and guided me in our battle.

My gentle inner voice reminded me.

To protect Keely.

To protect the children...

Epilogue

My father was sentenced to the maximum term allowable by California law on March 8, 1991, a term of 12 years and 8 months in state prison. During his sentencing the judge said that my father was worse than the mass murderer Charles Manson and wished that the laws allowed his sentence to be a thousand years.

As of January 1, 1991, California state law was changed to include menace and duress as grounds for rape charges. This was a direct result of the court case against my father. Never again will a judge be able to discard rape charges because they were based only on threats to the victim as happened to Cee Cee.

Suggested Reading

Bateson, Mary Catherine. **Composing A Life.** New York: Atlantic Monthly Press, 1989.

Berne, Eric. **What Do You Say After You Say Hello?** New York: Bantam, 1972.

Blume, E. Sue. **Secret Survivors: Uncovering Incest And Its After Effects In Women.** New York: Wiley and Sons, 1989.

Bradshaw, John. **Bradshaw On: The Family.** Deerfield Beach, Florida: Health Communications, 1988.

Bradshaw, John. **Healing The Shame That Binds You.** Deerfield Beach, Florida: Health Communications, 1989.

Csikszentmihalyi, Mihaly. **Flow: The Psychology Of Optimal Experience.** New York: Harper and Row, 1990.

Ennew, Judith. **The Sexual Exploitation Of Children.** Oxford: Polity Press, 1989.

Finkelhor, David. **Sexually Victimized Children.** New York: The Free Press, 1979.

Fortune, Marie M. **Sexual Violence: The Unmentionable Sin.** New York: The Pilgrim Press, 1983.

Forward, Susan. **Toxic Parents.** New York: Bantam Books, 1989.

Gil, Elianna. **Treatment Of Adult Survivors.** California: Launch Press, 1988.

Kaplan, Louise J. **Female Perversions: The Temptations Of Emma Bovary.** New York: Doubleday, 1991.

Lifton, Robert Jay. **The Life Of The Self: Toward A New Psychology.** New York: Basic Books, 1983.

Masson, Jeffery M. **The Assault On Truth: Freud's Suppression Of The Seduction Theory.** New York: Farrar, Straus and Giroux, 1984.

May, Rollo. **Love And Will.** New York: Norton, 1966.

Miller, Alice. **The Drama Of The Gifted Child.** New York: Harper and Row, 1981.

Miller, Alice. **Thou Shalt Not Be Aware: Society's Betrayal Of The Child.** New York: Farrar, Straus and Giroux, 1986.

Peck, M. Scott, M.D. **People Of The Lie: The Hope For Healing Human Evil.** New York: Simon & Schuster, 1983.

Rush, Florence. **The Best Kept Secret: Sexual Abuse Of Children.** New Jersey: Prentice-Hall, 1980.

Shengold, Leonard. **Soul Murder: The Effects Of Childhood Abuse And Deprivation.** New York: Fawcett Columbine, 1988.

Steiner, Claude. **Scripts People Live.** New York: Bantam, 1974.

Thomas, T. **Surviving With Serenity: Daily Meditations For Incest Survivors.** Deerfield Beach, Florida: Health Communications, 1990.

Tillich, Paul. **The Courage To Be.** New York: Yale University Press, 1980.

Williams, Mary Jane. **Healing Hidden Memories: Recovery For Adult Survivors Of Childhood Abuse.** Deerfield Beach, Florida: Health Communications, 1991.

Woolf, Virginia. **A Room Of One's Own.** New York: Harvest/ HBJ, 1929.